The Wide Wide Sea

Also by Hampton Sides

Ghost Soldiers
Blood and Thunder
Americana
Hellhound on His Trail
In the Kingdom of Ice
On Desperate Ground

The Wide Wide Sea

————◆————

THE FINAL, FATAL ADVENTURE OF
CAPTAIN JAMES COOK

Hampton Sides

PENGUIN MICHAEL JOSEPH

UK | USA | Canada | Ireland | Australia
India | New Zealand | South Africa

Penguin Michael Joseph is part of the Penguin Random House group of companies
whose addresses can be found at global.penguinrandomhouse.com

First published in the United States of America by Doubleday,
an imprint of Penguin Random House LLC 2024
First published in Great Britain by Penguin Michael Joseph 2024

008

Copyright © Hampton Sides, 2024
Title page engraving of Kealakekua Bay after a sketch by John Webber,
from *A Voyage to the Pacific Ocean*, 1784. Author's collection.

Book design by Maria Carella
Maps designed by Jeffrey L. Ward

Printed and bound in Great Britain by Clays Ltd, Elcograf S.p.A.

The authorized representative in the EEA is Penguin Random House Ireland,
Morrison Chambers, 32 Nassau Street, Dublin DO2 YH68

A CIP catalogue record for this book is available from the British Library

HARDBACK ISBN: 978–0–241–43733–9
TRADE PAPERBACK ISBN: 978–0–241–43737–7

www.greenpenguin.co.uk

for ANNE ALMIGHTY
with all my love

Alone, alone, all, all alone,
Alone on a wide wide sea!
And never a saint took pity on
My soul in agony.

—SAMUEL TAYLOR COLERIDGE,
The Rime of the Ancient Mariner

Contents

Book Three
Faraway Heaven

Book Four
New Albion

Book Five
Apotheosis

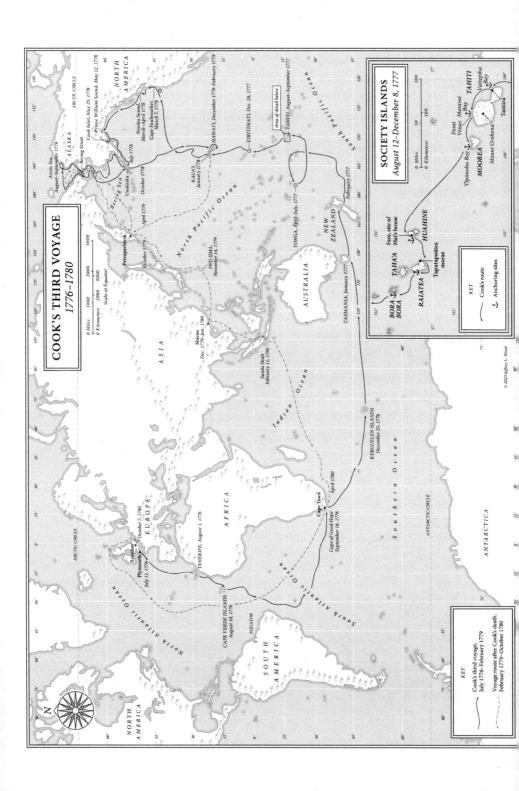

COOK'S THIRD VOYAGE
1776–1780

SOCIETY ISLANDS
August 12–December 8, 1777

KEY
Cook's route
⚓ Anchoring sites

KEY
Cook's third voyage,
July 1776–February 1779
Voyage route after Cook's death,
February 1779–October 1780

© 2023 Jeffrey L. Ward

NORTH AMERICA

ALASKA

Arctic Sea, August–September 1778
Cook Inlet, May 25, 1778
Prince William Sound, May 12, 1778
Nootka Sound, March–April 1778
Cape Foulweather, March 7, 1778
Bering Strait
Bering Sea
Unalaska, October 1778
April 1779
KAUAI, January 1778
July 1778
HAWAI'I, December 1778–February 1779
KIRITIMATI, Dec. 24, 1777

Area of detail below
TAHITI, August–September 1777

North Pacific Ocean
South Pacific Ocean

Petropavlovsk
October 1779

ASIA

IWO JIMA, November 14, 1779

Macao, Dec. 1779–Jan. 1780

Scale at Equator
0 Miles 1000 2000 3000
0 Kilometers 2000 3000

NEW ZEALAND
TONGA, April–July, 1777
February 1777

Sunda Strait, February 12, 1780

AUSTRALIA

TASMANIA, January 1777

Indian Ocean

KERGUELEN ISLANDS
December 25, 1776

Cape Town
Cape of Good Hope, September 18, 1776
April 1780

Southern Ocean

ARCTIC CIRCLE

EUROPE
London
October 7, 1780
Plymouth, July 12, 1776

AFRICA

TENERIFE, August 1, 1776

North Atlantic Ocean

CAPE VERDE ISLANDS, August 10, 1776

EQUATOR

SOUTH AMERICA

South Atlantic Ocean

ANTARCTIC CIRCLE

ANTARCTICA

N

NORTH AMERICA

ARCTIC CIRCLE

Society Islands detail:
SOCIETY ISLANDS
August 12–December 8, 1777
0 Miles 50 100
0 Kilometers 100

TAHITI
Vaitepiha Bay
Point Venus Matavai Bay
Tautira
MOOREA
Mount Orohena
'Opunohu Bay
Fare, site of Mai's house
HUAHINE
TAHAA
Taputapuatea marae
RAIATEA
BORA BORA
February 1777

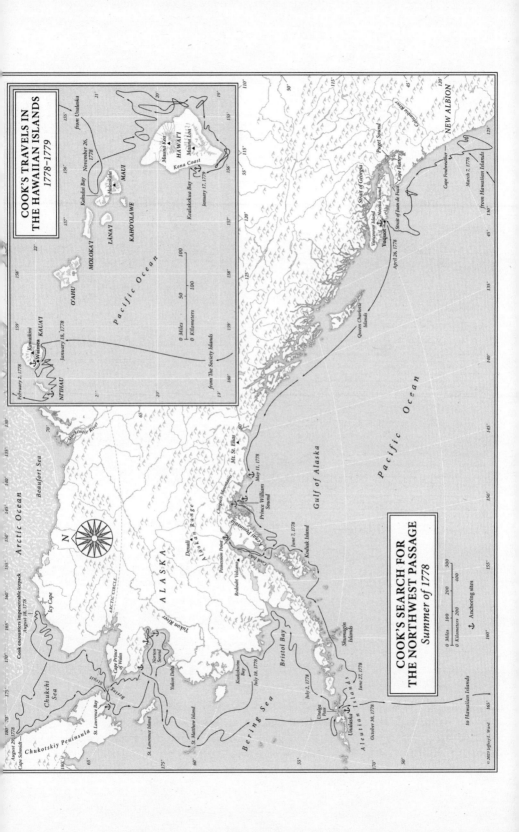

COOK'S TRAVELS IN
THE HAWAIIAN ISLANDS
1778-1779

from Unalaska

November 26, 1778

Mauna Kea   HAWAI'I   Mauna Loa

Kona Coast

Kealakekua Bay   January 17, 1779

Kahului Bay   Haleakalā   MAUI

MOLOKA'I   LANA'I   KAHOOLAWE

OAHU

Kawaikini   KAUA'I
Waimea   January 18, 1778

NI'IHAU   February 2, 1778

Pacific Ocean

0 Miles   50   100
0 Kilometers   100

from The Society Islands

Mackenzie River

Beaufort Sea

Arctic Ocean

Icy Cape

Cook encounters impenetrable icepack
August 18, 1778

ARCTIC CIRCLE

Chukchi Sea

Cape Prince of Wales

Bering Strait

ALASKA

Alaskan Range

Denali

Yukon River

Yukon Delta

Norton Sound

Koyukuk Bay

Cape Seddall
August 29, 1778

Chukotskiy Peninsula

St. Lawrence Island

St. Lawrence Bay

St. Matthew Island

Bering Sea

Bristol Bay

Unalga Pass   July 2, 1778

Aleutian Islands   June 27, 1778

Unalaska Island   October 30, 1778

Redoubt Volcano

Possession Point

Cook Inlet   June 2, 1778

Kenai Peninsula

July 18, 1778

Chugach Mountains

Mt. St. Elias

Prince William Sound   May 11, 1778

Kodiak Island

Shumagin Islands

Gulf of Alaska

Pacific Ocean

Queen Charlotte Islands

Strait of Georgia

Vancouver Island   Nootka Sound

Yaquot   Strait of Juan de Fuca

April 26, 1778

Puget Sound   Cape Flattery

Columbia River

NEW ALBION

Cape Foulweather

March 7, 1778

from Hawaiian Islands

COOK'S SEARCH FOR
THE NORTHWEST PASSAGE
Summer of 1778

0 Miles   100   200   300
0 Kilometers   200   400

⚓ Anchoring sites

to Hawaiian Islands

© 2023 Jeffrey L. Ward

Author's Note

In recent years, the voyages of Captain James Cook have come under increasing attack as part of a larger reassessment of the legacy of empire. Cook was an explorer and a mapmaker, not a conqueror or a colonizer. Yet throughout history, exploration and the making of maps have usually served as the first phase of conquest. In Cook's long wake came the occupiers, the guns, the pathogens, the alcohol, the problem of money, the whalers, the furriers, the seal hunters, the plantation owners, the missionaries.

And so for many Native people across the Pacific, from New Zealand to Alaska, Cook has become a symbol of colonialism and of the ravages that came with European arrival. In many corners of the world, his name has been vilified—not so much for what he did, but for all the trouble that came after him. And also because the Indigenous peoples he encountered were ignored for so long, their voices rarely heard, their perspectives and cultural significance scarcely considered.

Over the past few years, monuments to Cook's explorations have been splattered with paint. Artifacts and artworks stemming from his voyages, once considered priceless treasures, have been radically reinterpreted or removed altogether from museum and gallery collections (in some cases, rightly returning to the lands from which they originated). The people of the Cook Islands have been talking seriously of changing the archipelago's name. In 2021, in Victoria, British Columbia, protesters toppled a statue of Cook into the city harbor. Cook, in some respects, has become the Columbus of the Pacific.

There was a time when Cook's three epic expeditions were seen by many as swashbuckling adventures—worthwhile and perhaps even noble projects undertaken in the service of the Enlightenment and the expansion of global knowledge. Cook sailed in an age of wonder, when explorer-scientists were encouraged to roam the world, measuring and describing, collecting unfamiliar species of plants and animals, documenting landscapes and peoples unknown to Europe. In direct ways, Cook's voyages influenced the Romantic movement, benefited medical science, bolstered the fields of botany and anthropology, and inspired writers ranging from Coleridge to Melville. The journals from Cook's odysseys were turned into best-selling books and became the impetus behind popular plays, poems, operas, novels, comics, even one TV show set in outer space. (Captain James Kirk of the USS *Enterprise* is widely thought to have been inspired by Captain James Cook.)

Yet today, Cook's voyages are passionately contested, especially in Polynesia, viewed as the start of the systematic dismantling of traditional island cultures that historian Alan Moorehead famously called "the fatal impact." Moorehead said he was interested in "that fateful moment when a social capsule is broken into," and Cook's expeditions certainly provided an excellent case study of the phenomenon. Taken together, his voyages form a morally complicated tale that has left a lot for modern sensibilities to unravel and critique. Eurocentrism, patriarchy, entitlement, toxic masculinity, cultural appropriation, the role of invasive species in destroying island biodiversity: Cook's voyages contain the historical seeds of these and many other current debates.

It was in the midst of this gathering antipathy toward Cook that I began to research the story of his third voyage—the most dramatic of his journeys, as well as his longest, both in terms of duration and nautical miles. It seemed a good time to try to reckon with this man whose rovings have stirred so much acrimony and dissension. It was curious to me: Other early European mariners who had crisscrossed the Pacific—Magellan, Tasman, Cabrillo, and Bougainville, to name a few—don't seem to generate so much heat or attention. What is it about Cook that has singled him out?

I don't have an easy answer for that—more likely there are many not-so-easy ones—but I hope this book will lead readers toward some broader understanding. Perhaps part of the current resentment toward Cook has to do with the fact that on his final voyage something wasn't quite right with the formidable captain. Historians and forensic medical researchers have speculated about what was ailing him, whether it was a physical or mental malady, perhaps even a spiritual one. Whatever the root cause, his personality had definitely changed. Something was affecting his behavior and his judgment that marred the conduct of his last voyage. It may have even led to his death.

Whenever it has seemed relevant and interesting, I've let present-day controversies infuse and inform this book. I've tried to present the captain, and the goals and assumptions behind his third voyage, in all their flawed complexity. I neither lionize, demonize, nor defend him. I've simply tried to describe what happened during his consequential, ambitious, and ultimately tragic final voyage.

A CAVEAT HERE about the word *discovery:* I hope I've made it clear throughout the narrative that James Cook did not "discover" many of the places he's often mistakenly credited with having discovered—New Zealand, Hawai'i, and Australia, for example. It's obvious and yet no less important to stress that these and other lands that figure into this story had already been found and settled far earlier by intrepid explorers like the ancient Polynesian wayfarers. Most of the geographical features and life forms that Cook and his fellow expedition members named and described already had Indigenous names and contexts. Locations described in the voyage accounts as "uncharted" or "untouched" had been inhabited for centuries, if not millennia.

In some places, it's fair to say Cook was the first European discoverer, or one of the first European discoverers. In others, it might be more accurate to say that Cook and his sailors were merely visitors—albeit significant early ones.

What made Cook different from most explorers was that he was also a preternaturally accurate mapmaker, a skill aided by his use of the latest navigational technology and his deep understanding of astronomy. When he came home, the places he visited were forever fixed on maps, some of them widely published, showing exact coordinates. His reports told where the best anchorages were, which peoples were friendly, where good food and water might be found. It was as though Cook had revealed the secret addresses of many remote islands whose inhabitants had lived in splendid isolation for ages. Now these places could never hide from the eyes of the world again.

AN ISSUE THAT frequently crops up in accounts of Cook's voyages has to do with the concept of private property. At many of his anchorages, but especially in Polynesia, he complained constantly about objects—almost always *metal* objects—going missing from his ships. His journals are rife with accounts of what he refers to as stealing, and of the punishments he visited upon Indigenous people he viewed, essentially, as criminals. This very issue, in fact, is central in the story of his death.

Polynesians and other Indigenous groups Cook encountered during the voyage held ideas about property and ownership that differed greatly from European ideas. To Polynesians, for whom most possessions were considered communal, swiping objects from Cook's ships was hardly a crime—especially since Cook and his sailors were already taking (*stealing*, one might say) so much from their island communities in the way of food, water, fodder, timber, and other finite resources. In many islanders' view, Cook was being stingy with a substance—metal—that came from the earth and should be communally shared; his ships had an abundance of iron, while their islands had none. Although there are only so many descriptors to characterize what Cook and his officers unequivocally viewed as theft, in portraying these incidents I've generally tried to use neutral terms, while taking note of the deeper context behind what was often a tricky clash between cultures concerning the nature, meaning, and purpose of physical possessions.

———

ONE MORE DELICATE matter that repeatedly arises in the story of the voyage is the question of sexual mores. Most of Cook's crewmen were in their late teens and twenties, and naturally they were fixated on the subject of sex—as were many of the officers and scientists. While Cook himself is said to have abstained from encounters with local women, his sailors assuredly did not. Their often one-dimensional view of women as erotic playthings can make for difficult reading here in the twenty-first century. Still, their prurient yet often joyful descriptions loom so large in their journals that the theme is impossible to ignore. In Tahiti, Hawai'i, and other locations, Cook's men found the women to be quite willing and enthusiastic participants; in many cases, deeper romantic bonds began to form. But because few written records exist to tell us what the women themselves thought and felt about the subject, our knowledge of what happened (and why) must rely on the existing accounts—which unfortunately are almost all from the English, and male, perspective.

As I sifted through these accounts, I couldn't help wondering: How could these young Polynesian women have possibly found Cook's men attractive—these aliens with rancid teeth and shabby clothes rank with the stench of long months at sea? Were the overtures of the women really as passionate and as genuine as the British sailors described them in their journals? Were powerful Native men—priests or chiefs—orchestrating events behind the scenes, instructing daughters, sisters, and nieces to beguile these strange new visitors? What hidden strategy could have been afoot—a belief, perhaps, that sexual union might be a way to absorb, or neutralize, whatever powers Cook's men might possess?

These are questions that have been debated by historians of Polynesia, as well as by anthropologists and even modern-day sexologists. Some anthropologists have speculated that sex was a way for young women to defy, at least for a moment, a stratified, male-ruled society that had boxed them in with draconian taboos. Others have suggested that the true answer might be simpler: Maybe it was about pleasure and little else—an adventure, a diversion, a sporting fling with strangers. In expressing their sexuality, young Polynesian women were remarkably free. They had no Judeo-Christian stab of shame about nudity, no gnaw of guilt, no code of celibacy. They had a measure of latitude they'd learned to use and enjoy—and in this arena their power, their sense of agency and autonomy, was quite real.

SUBSTANTIAL PORTIONS OF this book are based on the journals, logs, and other writings of Cook and many other voyage participants. Some of these were "official" accounts, while others were written in secrecy and published without the authorization of the British government. In quoting from these antique documents, I've made occasional edits for clarity, concision, and readability, striking some confusing archaic expressions and streamlining erratic capitalization, spelling, and punctuation styles that might trip up the modern eye or ear (turning "ye" into "the," for example, or "&" into "and"). And because I'm an American writer with an American publisher, I've generally Americanized British spellings and copy styles. Otherwise, the words I've quoted are exactly as they flowed from those eighteenth-century quills. It's been consistently amazing to me how clear and strong their voices come across on the page, even after two and a half centuries.

Inevitably, readers will find an imbalance between the voluminous record conveying the English perspective and the limited written sources that shed light on the Native perspective. Still, wherever possible, I've tried to bring in Indigenous points of view by employing oral history passed down through the generations and collected by Native speakers. In places, I've integrated the oral history with insights from archaeology, anthropology, and natural history, as well as from my own travels to many of the places Cook's third voyage visited. Time and finances, as well as the obstacle of a global pandemic, prevented me from visiting all the spots where Cook anchored, but over the years I was able to make some unforgettable trips to places important to the narrative—including New Zealand, Tasmania, the Society Islands, the Oregon and Washington coasts, Vancouver Island, Alaska, the Russian Far East, Hawai'i, and England.

A FINAL DISTINCTION: This is not a biography but a narrative history with a large, diverse cast of characters moving over many thousands of miles of oceanic expanse. It's about a journey undertaken by more than 180 people in two wooden ships that embarked from England in July of 1776, a turning point in history. It's the story not only of James Cook but of the men who accompanied him on his swan-song voyage to the Pacific. They took part in a monumental enterprise that left lasting impacts, good and bad, on the world.

Cook and his men sailed at a fascinating moment when there were still a few extremely large geographical mysteries left to solve, when there were few remaining swaths of our planet human eyes had never seen, and when it was still possible for radically different cultures from distant parts of the world to encounter one another for the very first time.

The Wide Wide Sea

Your bodies, O Lono, are in the heavens,
A long cloud, a short cloud,
A watchful cloud,
An overlooking cloud...
Lono, the rolling thunder,
The heaven that rumbles,
The disturbed sea.

—ANCIENT HAWAIIAN CHANT

Prologue: And Louder Grew the Shouting

KAUA'I, THE HAWAIIAN ISLANDS, JANUARY 1778

On the night the ships appeared, some fishermen were out on the ocean, working by torchlight. One of them, a man named Mapua, was bewildered by what he saw: An enormous silhouette approached, rising high above the surf, fire burning at its top. It had holes on its side, Mapua noticed, and a long spear in front like the sharp nose of a swordfish. Then a second creature appeared, much like the first. Mapua had no idea what they were, but he was sure they were something malevolent.

Mapua and his fellow fishermen paddled hurriedly to shore. According to oral accounts assembled by the Hawaiian historian Samuel Mānaiakalani Kamakau, they were "trembling and frightened by this wonderful apparition." When they reached the village, Mapua immediately informed the high chief, Kaeo, about this strange and disturbing sight.

By the next morning the two leviathans had drawn closer to shore. What were they? Where had they come from? What did they *want?* An onlooker, thoroughly astonished by them, is said to have wondered, "What are those branching things?" (Probably the ships' masts, sprits, and spars.) Another replied, "They are trees moving about on the sea."

No, the local priest countered, they were the floating heiaus, or temples, of the gods. "This is not an ordinary thing," the kāhuna insisted. He said the branches must be steps reaching toward heaven.

As the vessels moved still closer, wrote Kamakau, the villagers were captivated by this "marvelous monster," and "great wonder came to the people." A large crowd began to assemble on shore, "shouting with fear and confused thought." Judging by the way the ships had appeared, silent and ghostly, the edges of their sails furling and fluttering, backing and filling, they seemed to some like giant stingrays that had emerged from the sea.

A few canoes were dispatched to investigate, and the brave paddlers crept just close enough to catch glimpses of humanlike creatures walking upon the decks of the ships. Never having seen tricorne hats before, they thought these strangers' heads must be deformed. They mistook the odd, close-fitting uniforms for an epidermis. "Their skin is loose and folding," one said. Unacquainted with pockets, the paddlers imagined they were little doors that opened into the men's bodies. "Into these openings they thrust their hands, and take many valuable things—their bodies are full of treasure!"

As the ships edged closer to shore, the watching crowds on the beach grew larger and larger, the anticipation building to a frenzy. The people were full of fear and dread, but also a kind of rapture. They sensed something ominous was happening, that their island world was about to change forever.

"The harbor resounded with noise," wrote Kamakau. "And louder grew the shouting."

BOOK ONE

The First Navigator of Europe

———◆———

Cook was a captain of the Admiralty
When sea-captains...
Were more like warlocks
... [and] drove their ships
By their own blood, no laws of schoolbook steam,
Till yards were sprung, and masts went overboard—
Daemons in periwigs, doling magic out,
Who read fair alphabets in stars
Where humbler men found but a mess of sparks

—Kenneth Slessor, "Five Visions of Captain Cook"

1 *Negative Discoverer*

It was the start of a very important year—1776—and James Cook had become a very important figure, a celebrity, a champion, a hero. Leading scientists wanted his opinions. The best portrait painters invited him to pose in their studios. Cook had met King George III and had received a promotion to the rank of "post-captain," a position that could put him on a fast track to becoming an admiral.

This modest son of the Yorkshire moors, who had risen from virtually nothing, was moving in higher circles, mingling with London's best and brightest at coffeehouses, in private salons, in gentlemen's clubs. During a speech before the House of Lords, he was declared "the first navigator" of Europe. Some people in authority were beginning to tout him as the greatest voyager England had ever produced, even greater than Anson, Hudson, and Drake. He had been nominated to the prestigious Royal Society and would soon win its highest award, the Copley Medal. Some speculated he would be knighted.

Only six months earlier, Cook had returned home from his second circumnavigation of the globe. He had ventured into the frozen basement of the world and come back with important findings and magnificent maps of unfamiliar realms. He had been at sea for some 1,100 days and had probably sailed more than 100,000 nautical miles.

The main goal of his voyage had been to prowl the southern oceans and determine the existence, or nonexistence, of a hypothetical continent known as Terra Australis Incognita. Many scientists at the time posited that there must exist an immense southern landmass, far larger than Australia, to counterbalance the weighty preponderance of terrain in the northern hemisphere. Without a southern supercontinent, the earth would be so top-heavy, it would tumble into space. As the Flemish mapmaker Gerardus Mercator ominously phrased it, such a wobbly planet would "fall to destruction among the stars."

The imaginary continent had many champions, although none more ardent or vocal than a Scottish geographer named Alexander Dalrymple, who insisted not only that the mythic land existed but that it almost certainly was inhabited by millions of people. Cook had doubts, but he saw the merits of exploring the high southern latitudes, a part of the world that was virtually unknown.

Cook's ship, HMS *Resolution*, along with a consort ship, HMS *Adventure*, left England in July of 1772. The *Adventure* lost contact with the *Resolution* off the coast of New Zealand and eventually headed back to England, but Cook continued onward, becoming the first captain known to have crossed the Antarctic Circle (though there are theories that Māori voyagers may have ventured that far south in ancient times). Cook made multiple dagger thrusts deep into the southern seas—at one point reaching latitude 71°10' South. He did not encounter anything that could be deemed a continental landmass, although he drew within a hundred miles of Antarctica, with towering icebergs floating around him, the ship's rigging rimed in ice.

By November 1774 Cook had turned the *Resolution* north and threaded through the ice fields toward home. He pronounced the unknown continent a fiction, and the thoroughness and probity with which he had made his sweeps through the southern seas convinced the Admiralty that he was right. Cook had made an important contribution to "negative discovery"—that is, finding nothing where something was widely presumed to be. As one biographer put it, he had become an "executioner of misbegotten hypotheses."

"If I have failed in discovering a continent," Cook wrote, "it is because it does not exist...and not for want of looking." Yet Cook seemed almost to have gotten the scent of Antarctica. Any large landmass that did exist, he concluded, was locked in ice farther to the south, unreachable by ship, and uninhabited—"a country," as he put it, "doomed by nature never once to feel the warmth of the sun's rays, but to lie forever buried under the everlasting snow." It would be more than a century before explorers reached the frozen shores of the continent of Antarctica—which, while substantial, was still nowhere near the size of the mythic Terra Australis.

During his long search in those icy latitudes, Cook had proclaimed, with breathtaking frankness, his larger aspiration: He wanted to go not only "farther than any man has been before me," he wrote, "but as far as I think it possible for man to go."

JAMES COOK WAS a taciturn man with a craggy forehead, a thicket of reddish-brown hair turning steel gray, and an austere face cured by weather. His large-boned frame—as a young man, he stood six feet three—was slightly stooped from years of crawling through holds and other confined spaces on His Majesty's ships. He had a hawk's nose, a strong chin with a slight cleft in it, and intense, deep-set eyes that seemed to bore through whatever met his gaze. His fingers were as rough as any seaman's, yet they were also nimble, accustomed as they were to handling sextants, quadrants, and other fine instruments of astronomy and navigation. Running across the palm of his right hand, between his thumb and index finger, was an ugly scar from an accident he'd had in Canada as a young man, when a gunpowder horn he was holding exploded. The incident could have killed him, and for the rest of his life he sometimes wore a glove on his right hand.

Cook drank sparingly and, though he had a thunderous temper when aggravated, he never cursed. He was not particularly religious, but as an apprentice in the merchant marine, he had trained under Quakers. He had by all accounts absorbed their values— temperance, frugality, modesty, truthfulness, a ferocious work ethic, and a disdain for arrogance and ostentation. Like many Quakers, he was a master of directness. He spoke mostly in brusque, declarative sentences, packed with monosyllables, delivered with a slight lilt in his native Yorkshire brogue. Dourness, too, was said to be a Quaker trait, and Cook could seem dour at times, but a grin sometimes crept across his face, and when one least expected it, a wry joke or turn of phrase might escape from his pen or his lips.

He strove for simplicity—in his dress, in his speech, in his surroundings, even in his food. He favored drab fare like sauerkraut and peas, but he would also go along with unfamiliar Polynesian dishes like baked dog, or pre-chewed kava spat into a bowl, with copious saliva, from the mouth of some chief's lowly servant. Cook wasn't particular—a midshipman who traveled with him thought Cook's taste buds were "the coarsest that ever a mortal was endowed with." He had a gastrointestinal tract made of iron and viewed it almost as his duty to sample what was set before him. "His stomach," wrote a young officer from one of his voyages, "bore without difficulty the... most ungrateful food."

Cook's lodgings were simple, too. He lived with his wife, Elizabeth, the daughter of a respected tavern keeper, in a snug brick row house on a road called Mile End. It was in a throbbing middle-class neighborhood just east of London, not far from the Thames— although during the past seven years he had hardly been there. He had been at sea during the births of most of their five children, and absent as well for the tragic early deaths of three of them. Their eldest son, James, twelve, was already in the navy, hard at work at his academy studies down in Portsmouth, and their son Nathaniel, eleven, had similar ambitions. Elizabeth was with child again. She was expecting in a few months.

Yet Cook was never exactly at home when he was at home. He surely enjoyed his intermittent visits with Elizabeth, a strong, no-nonsense woman thirteen years his junior. There was a formality, a respectful distance, to their relationship, which was not uncommon in those times, especially in marriages whose partners differed so greatly in age. She called him "Mr. Cook."

But the master mariner soon grew restless on dry land. He lived for the sure rhythms and protocols of a naval existence. He needed to be immersed in a project, an enterprise, a puzzle. "Action was life to him," wrote a navy officer who sailed with him, "and repose a sort of death." Cook seemed happiest when in command of a ship. "On land, he was at the mercy of other people's chaos," one English biographer has written, but "within the confines of the ship his world was orderly, disciplined and emotionally safe—his word was law, and his men obeyed."

One of the extraordinary things about Cook is how little we know of his interior life—what he really thought and felt, his fears, his whims, his sorrows. Between his journals and his logs, he wrote more than a million words about his voyages, but in all those pages we rarely get a glimpse of Cook's emotional world. Most of his entries have to do with mundane minutiae like barometric pressure, wind direction, the amount of seaweed in the water, or the viscosity and color of the mud on the bottom of the bay where he might be anchoring.

Unfortunately, late in her life, for inexplicable reasons, Elizabeth destroyed nearly all her personal papers, including Cook's letters to her, thus obliterating the best chance historians might have had to glean deeper insights into his psyche—or, for that matter, into hers. "His inner thoughts and private life were a closed book, one of those old-fashioned books with a brass hasp," wrote a biographer. "Even in his private correspondence—what little of it has survived—this same iron reticence manifests itself."

Some of that reticence was the style of the times, and of his profession. Eighteenth-century navy captains operated in a close, mean, and competitive world and were seldom known to emote, whether on the page or in person. If the cliché had any merit, reticence was also the style of a Yorkshireman. People from Cook's part of northern England were said to be tough, practical-minded, and very much to the point. Cook was a hard person—hard to please, hard to fool, hard to reach, hard to know. One writer described his laconic persona this way: "There were depths, but the soundings were few."

As for his voyaging, Cook has been called a technician, a cyborg, a navigational machine. It could be said that he lived during a romantic age of exploration, but he was decidedly *not* a romantic. He traveled to some of the world's most gorgeous and pristine islands, but, as a professional mapmaker with little regard for sentiment, he rarely remarked upon their beauty. As one biographer noted, Cook had "no natural gift for rhapsody."

If sailing was a rough and ragged art, Cook had tried to make it a science. He had a systematic approach. He hated sloppiness or any lapse of schedule, just as he hated the exaggerations, superstitions, and tall tales in which sailors often reveled. Most of all, he valued exactitude. The writer James Boswell, who had become acquainted with Cook, called him a "plain and sensible man with an uncommon attention to veracity." Cook, Boswell said, had "a balance in his mind for truth as nice as scales for weighing a guinea." Now that Cook was ascending into higher circles, people at various gatherings were sometimes disappointed in his lack of social skills. He was, said one prominent London doyenne who met him several times, "studiously wrapped up in his own purposes and pursuits, and apparently under a pressure of mental fatigue when called upon to speak."

In most things, Cook was understated and self-deprecating, and he had an aversion to drama. His instinct was to cast attention away from himself and to give others credit. It was remarkable that through all his travels, he'd never named a landmark or feature after himself or any members of his family. (True, Cook's name would eventually become attached to scores of places—such as Cook Strait, Cook Inlet, Mount Cook, Cook Glacier, the Cook Islands, even a Cook Crater on the moon—but these were all appellations suggested by others, not the result of his own cartographic hand.) It was also true that Cook had an admirable habit of affixing an Indigenous name, when he definitively learned of one, to his charts. This was rarely true of European explorers, but Cook was respectful of local people and kept his ear attuned to what had come before.

JAMES COOK WAS a farm manager's son with scant formal education. Born in 1728, he'd grown up in the village of Great Ayton in a cottage made of mud and thatch. But as a teenager he had moved to Whitby, a tight hamlet of shipbuilders, whalers, and fishermen hunkered by the cold North Sea. There, starting as an apprentice, he worked his way up through the merchant marine, serving on sturdy vessels, known as "cats," that were designed to haul coal and timber. He learned how to manage the collier ships, how to read the mercurial storms of the North Sea, how to use dead reckoning and trigonometry to plot his location along complicated shorelines. In those early years he traveled as far as the Baltic coast, and even visited St. Petersburg.

But at the not-so-young age of twenty-seven, on the verge of promotion to become a commander of a merchant vessel, he quit the coal ships and volunteered for the Royal Navy. He started all the way back down the ladder as an ordinary seaman, but quickly climbed the ranks.

Cook displayed a genius as a surveyor, hydrographer, and mapmaker while serving in Canada. These were skills that played an important role in England's decisive victory over the French at Quebec City in 1759, during the Seven Years' War (which Americans know as the French and Indian War). Cook was assigned the herculean task of charting the St. Lawrence River, from its mouth to Quebec City, and during the siege of Quebec, he was responsible for re-marking the navigable channel after the French had removed their marker buoys to impede the British fleet. Cook's cartographic prowess, aided by his growing talent as an astronomer and mathematician, caught the attention of high officials within the Admiralty, especially after he earned the title of king's surveyor and produced, during several summer seasons, an elegant and painstaking map of Newfoundland, a glacier-carved island with one of the most intricate shorelines in the world. Comparing it against modern satellite images of Newfoundland, one can see that his chart was a cartographic masterpiece of almost chilling precision.

By the late 1760s the Admiralty had recognized Cook's value, and its lords rewarded him. His first round-the-world voyage of exploration, as commander of the HMS *Endeavour,* left England in 1768, bound for Tahiti. There, Lieutenant Cook (for that was his rank then) was instructed to witness and document the transit of Venus, a rare astronomical event that was of keen interest to the European scientific community. After leaving Tahiti, the *Endeavour* explored broad expanses of the South Pacific, charting the east coast of Australia and both islands of New Zealand, among other lands virtually unknown to Europe. Along the way, Cook added more than five thousand miles of shoreline to the map of the Pacific. Through all these travels, he kept an eye out for the mythic Southern Continent but decided that a more thorough expedition would have to be mounted to give the search the time and dedication it required.

Upon his return to England in 1771, Cook's first voyage was hailed as a triumph, but it was the gentleman-scientist aboard the *Endeavour*, a young botanist and bon vivant named Joseph Banks, who captured most of the attention and garnered most of the praise for the expedition's successes. Cook earned the Admiralty's plaudits as well, but it was his second voyage, to search more definitively for the undiscovered continent, that sealed his reputation and catapulted him into the pantheon of English explorers.

2   *Proto-Anthropologist*

Although he had failed to find a supercontinent in the southern seas, Cook had found that those vast stretches of ocean were peppered with islands, some inhabited and some not, and he visited many of them. His ships, said one biographer, "seemed to be drawn to land as if by magnetic navigational attraction." He stopped at Easter Island, the Marquesas, the Society Islands, Tonga, the New Hebrides, New Caledonia, South Georgia, and New Zealand, as well as other islands and archipelagoes, many of which had never been seen by a European before.

As he wended his way across the latitudes of Oceania, Cook had proven to be a surprisingly open-minded observer of the cultures he met. He had no training in this regard, yet he became a kind of proto-anthropologist and ethnographer. By the standards of his time, his descriptions of Indigenous peoples were tolerant and often quite sympathetic. Cook never attempted to convert Native people to Christianity and rarely moralized on the supposed shortcomings of their customs and beliefs. In his writings, he was neutral, objective, agnostic.

Like most English officers of his era, Cook doubtless believed in the technological superiority of European civilization, but he seldom spoke in that vein. He tried to have meaningful exchanges with the islanders, to gather without judgment some sense of their rituals and ceremonies, their style of warfare, religion, agriculture, and economy. Approaching a new island, he was often the first man ashore, and was usually unarmed. There had been misunderstandings aplenty, and violent conflicts, some of them lethal. In heated moments, his men had spilled Native blood, had taken Native life, but Natives had killed Cook's men as well. For the most part, though, Cook's encounters with Polynesians and Aboriginal Australians had been peaceful—rare in his trigger-happy age, when commanders of European ships preferred to shoot first and ask questions later.

Cook wasn't naive; he knew very well that he was doing the work of empire, that his voyaging advanced the brazen and sometimes ruthless strategic goals of a nation jealously competing against other European nations to claim new lands and exploit resources in faraway places. But in reading his journals, one senses he was not deeply engaged, on a personal level, with the gambits of the larger colonial chess game; his interest was more inquisitive than acquisitive, more empirical than imperial. He was an English patriot, to be sure, and a loyal subject of the Crown, but he was also a citizen of the world—a world that, through his own peregrinations, he had done much to thread together.

Cook saw himself as an explorer-scientist, and he tried to follow an ethic of impartial observation born of the Enlightenment and the Scientific Revolution. What seemed to animate him most were the moments of pure discovery, moments when he felt called upon to study, measure, and document something entirely new.

DURING HIS TWO voyages, Cook had shown himself to be a benevolent though strict leader of his own men—sparing with the lash and solicitous of his crew's happiness, comfort, and health. These should be attributes for any good naval officer, but so many ship captains of the era could be unimaginably brutal in their punishments, tyrannical in their command style, and indifferent to conditions belowdecks. The Royal Navy, it was famously said, was "manned by violence and maintained by cruelty."

Cook, however, was a different sort of captain. He constantly experimented with schemes for shipboard hygiene and diet. He knew that prolonged dampness and darkness were eternal enemies that worked in concert and must be mercilessly fought. Many diseases killed sailors on long voyages, but most of them, Cook found, could be prevented by maintaining strict cleanliness, especially in the galley.

Germ theory was only a nascent and controversial concept among medical scientists at the time, but Cook intuitively seemed to grasp its essence. Ever at war against grime, he kept his men scrubbing the decks with soap and vinegar, and often ordered smoking fires, set in pots, to be lit deep within the ship. His perpetual campaign against cockroaches, rats, weevils, and other vermin was resourceful, almost scientific, in its approach. "To cleanliness, as well in the ship as amongst the people, enough attention cannot be paid," Cook insisted. "The least neglect occasions a putrid and disagreeable smell below."

Then there was the most dreaded maritime disease of all: scurvy, a ghastly disorder that was considered an almost inevitable occupational hazard of long ocean voyages. During the Age of Sail, it was generally assumed that scurvy would kill off half the crew members on any lengthy expedition. The malady's progression was all too well known: spongy gums, fetid breath, protuberant eyes, scaly skin, a breakdown in the tissues and cells of the body, convulsions, and, eventually, death.

But amazingly, during his two odysseys, it seemed that Cook had beaten scurvy. On his second voyage, the *Resolution* was at sea for three years, but not a single one of his men died of the disease—or even, it seems, developed advanced symptoms. This was a historic breakthrough. He didn't understand scurvy's true cause, its etiology; that it resulted from a deficiency of vitamin C would not be determined until the 1930s, when scientists deduced the compound's chemical structure.

But Cook, following his own hunches while building on a host of older theories, had put in place an astoundingly efficacious system of prevention. A Scottish surgeon named James Lind had demonstrated as far back as the 1750s that scurvy could be treated by consuming citrus fruit, but it took decades before his ideas were aggressively adopted. Building on Lind's findings, Cook insisted that whenever possible, his sailors—accustomed to a diet of salted meat and stale biscuits—consume fresh fruits, vegetables, and greens. On the *Resolution* he kept some strange-sounding supplementary items on the menu as well, such as carrot marmalade, wort of malt, rob of orange, inspissated lemon juice, and a concoction known as saloop, which was steeped from the root of a common meadow plant, *Orchis mascula*.

Cook didn't know precisely which of these foodstuffs did the trick (some of them, we now know, were useless in fighting scurvy), but something in his regimen, when scrupulously and consistently applied, had worked wonders. Another factor in Cook's success was his decision not to serve his men salt fat skimmed from copper stockpots, a common practice in the galleys of navy ships at the time. Intuitively, he seemed to understand that this was not healthy, though he didn't know why: Copper residues could cause a reaction during the boiling process, generating compounds that interfered with the small intestine's absorption of vitamins.

Cook hadn't really conquered scurvy, though—the particular lessons he'd learned through hard and patient experimentation would be unlearned and then learned again, dismissed and revived in piecemeal fashion, over the next several decades. But for now, the Admiralty viewed Cook's apparent mastery over the disease as possibly an even more consequential achievement than proving the Southern Continent's nonexistence. So many sons of England, so many sons of so many countries, had died of this horrible malady. It has been estimated that nearly two million European sailors perished from scurvy between 1600 and 1800. The notion that a thousand-day voyage could be undertaken without the disease's appearance represented a radical shifting of the possibilities; it meant that His Majesty's ships could range wider and longer, extending the reach of the Crown to the world's most distant nooks and corners, to complete the maps of the globe.

COOK'S SECOND VOYAGE had performed at least one other feat of historic significance: It had served as a proving ground for a new

device, known as the marine chronometer, that went far in solving
an ancient perplexity of navigation. For centuries, sea captains had
tried to devise a way to determine exactly where they were on the
planet. Latitude—how far north or south one was—was easy enough
to ascertain, especially while sailing in the northern hemisphere, by
using standard tools that measured, among other things, the precise
angle of the sun as it made its arc across the sky. Longitude—how
far west or east one was—was significantly harder to measure, especially while tossing about at sea. Geographers, thinkers, and inventors had been trying for centuries to come up with a method, or
an instrument, that could reliably fix this elusive but all-important
piece of data.

Over the preceding decades, a theoretical solution had been proposed: If a clock could be built that told the correct time at a pre-
determined reference location—say, Greenwich—a voyager could
compare the reference time (as shown on an ever-ticking "sea clock"
kept on board) with the current time at his ship's location. (Anywhere one traveled, the sun directly overhead meant it was noon.)
By counting the degrees and minutes separating Greenwich from
where the ship was, he could figure out longitude.

It was a brilliant idea. The problem was, it was hard to make a
timepiece that could endure the unusual shocks and stresses a long
ocean voyage entailed—the punishing waves, the constant fluctua-
tions in humidity and barometric pressure, the buildup of corrosion
from steady accumulations of salt. It was difficult enough to design a
clock that kept good time on dry land; for a clock meant to function
at sea, the challenges were exponentially harder. By trial and error,
an inventor had to build a mechanism with just the right configuration of gears, pins, wheels, screws, coils, and tiny buffering parts,
some made of wood, some made of metal.

By 1759, a self-taught carpenter and clockmaker named John
Harrison seemed to have succeeded in the task. After refining his
designs for decades, he had finally produced a chronometer that
worked well during an extended sea trial across the Atlantic Ocean.
Harrison's creation was truly ingenious, but his best prototype, the

H4, had proven prohibitively time-consuming and expensive to manufacture, and so was considered impractical for common use.

However, by 1770, a London clockmaker named Larcum Kendall had built a less expensive copy of Harrison's H4. Kendall's device, the K1, was a magical thing a little smaller than an abalone shell, with a white clockface and svelte hands that swept across elegant Roman numerals. It weighed just over three pounds.

The K1 was brought aboard Cook's *Resolution* for his second voyage, and the contraption performed magnificently. Joseph Gilbert, master of the *Resolution,* called it "the greatest piece of mechanism the world has ever seen." Cook himself very much agreed, reporting to the Admiralty, "Mr. Kendall's watch... did not deceive us... [It] has exceeded the expectations of its most zealous advocate, and has been our faithful guide through all the vicissitudes of climates." In his log he called it "never-failing" and "our trusty friend."

Harrison and Kendall deserved full credit for K1's design and construction, of course, but it was Cook's disciplined regimen during all those many months at sea that had proven it could actually work. He'd seen to it that his officers kept it high and dry even in the most ferocious storms, and that they protected it from the innumerable thunks and shocks of the sea. Most importantly, his officers had made sure, without fail, that it was kept wound; just one lapse, just one forgetful day, would have wrecked the entire experiment. At stops when the voyage astronomer was able to set up an observatory on shore to closely consult the heavens and do a lengthy, exacting lunar distance calculation, he was able to check the chronometer's accuracy. Again and again, the K1 was found to keep nearly perfect Greenwich time. Years into the voyage, the instrument was off by only a few minutes.

For something so small and compact, the implications of this practical seagoing clock were immense. The device allowed Cook, or any future voyager, to know exactly where he was on the globe. More importantly, it enabled him to pinpoint the locations of all the new lands and features he had encountered, so that the next navigator could quickly and reliably relocate them. Those lands and features could now be placed on maps with a facility and precision unknown before. For many Indigenous people, this profound advancement in the art of navigation spelled the beginning of the end for their traditional cultures. Forever after, Europeans knew exactly where to find them.

But in the Admiralty's view, the K1's success was yet another triumph that could be credited to Cook's second expedition. What was it about this man? Good fortune and impressive results seemed to follow him most everywhere he went. Not only had he smashed a colossally wrong theory about a supercontinent; not only had he gone far in conquering a disease that had killed millions; he had also helped to solve one of navigation's longest-standing problems.

In a way, the K1 was an apt metaphor for Cook himself. Like him, it was dependable and exact, a seamless blend of toughness and refinement, driven by mathematics, sound rules, and meticulous design. And wherever it went in the world, it showed the proud face of England.

3   A Human Pet

Captain Cook wasn't the only celebrity who had emerged in the aftermath of his second voyage around the world. In 1774, a young Polynesian man had arrived in Britain aboard HMS *Adventure,* the consort vessel that had been separated from Cook's *Resolution.* He had since become a sensation in the press, the darling of the intelligentsia, a star of the London social set. This Native islander's life story offered a poignant allegory of first contact between England and the people of Oceania. His name was Mai.

Mai was a young man in his early twenties, with copper skin and a winsome smile. He had large slits in his earlobes, and his small hands were tattooed in ornate patterns that had been pecked by needles of bone and shell with ink made of charred nut oil. His hair, lustrous and black, grazed his shoulders.

Mai was a native of Raiatea, a volcanic island about 130 miles northwest of Tahiti that was considered the Ur of Polynesia, the cradle of this extraordinary seafaring culture. Raiatea, which means "faraway heaven," is believed to be one of the first places where ancient navigators, coming from the west, landed several millennia ago and developed a rich civilization. Their culture had reached its apogee at Taputapuatea, a complex of marae temples that more or less served as the spiritual center of the South Seas. Taputapuatea was a pilgrimage spot, the birthplace of Oro, the god of war and fertility. There, upon sprawling courts of black volcanic rock, priests from all across Polynesia held elaborate ceremonies, sometimes performing human sacrifices. It was also a gathering place where navigators would compare notes on their distant discoveries.

Mai's kin owned property and enjoyed some prestige on the island, and his early boyhood seems to have been happy. But then, one day in about 1763, when Mai was ten or so, invaders from the nearby island of Bora Bora, under the command of the great chief Puni, came in their long canoes. They were fierce warriors with an expertise in amphibious attack, known for the "silent stroke," a stealth technique for paddling their fleets of canoes without making noise.

Puni succeeded in conquering Raiatea. His soldiers killed Mai's father and seized his family's land. The Bora Borans ransacked much of the island and demolished the god houses of Taputapuatea. The impressionable young Mai likely witnessed many horrors. In Polynesian warfare, battles were often fought just offshore. Warriors would lash two canoes together and fight with clubs, rocks, and spears crafted from stingray barbs, until every last person in the losing vessel had been killed. If the battle occurred on land, the fighting was just as fierce. Warriors would fight to the death, and it was not uncommon for the victors to mutilate enemy corpses. They would sometimes rip away the chin of a dead foe, pulling out the jawbone as a trophy. Or they would flatten the eviscerated corpse with clubs, then cut a hole through the abdomen, through which the triumphant warrior would insert his head to "wear" his victim as a sort of macabre serape.

The Bora Borans enslaved much of the Raiatea population. Mai escaped with some of his family and fled to Tahiti, where he lived in poverty as a refugee, festering with grievance but vowing to return to Raiatea someday to restore his family's honor.

In 1767, when the English navigator Samuel Wallis became the first European to anchor at Tahiti, aboard HMS *Dolphin,* the teen-aged Mai was there to witness the British arrival. Wallis was too ill to leave his cabin, but one of his officers, Tobias Furneaux, came ashore to declare the tropical paradise King George III Island, claiming it for Great Britain. But the Tahitians had no interest in being appropriated by these pale foreigners. Theirs was a complex civilization, and a populous one, too—with as many as seventy thousand people living on Tahiti itself and perhaps another quarter million dwelling on nearby islands. They had been here for centuries, having migrated across the Pacific in various voyaging surges from a prehistoric maritime culture that scholars believe originated on the island of Taiwan.

Hostilities soon erupted between the English and the Tahitians. Wallis fired his guns at a promontory overlooking Matavai Bay, scattering shrapnel and grapeshot through a crowd of angry onlookers. Scores, possibly hundreds, of Tahitians were killed.

Mai was one of the many injured that day. A piece of shrapnel or a musket ball sliced through his side, causing a wound that left a jagged scar; for the rest of his life, his body offered literal proof of the first encounter between the British and Tahitians. But the awesome power of the cannons had made an impression on Mai's imagination. He began to fantasize that English guns, if he could obtain them, would provide the means to vanquish the Bora Borans and reclaim his land. It was a belief he would cling to for the rest of his life.

Sometime in 1772, Mai—now a headstrong man of about nineteen or twenty—took part in a vicious sea battle against a contingent of Bora Boran warriors. The enemy killed four of his relatives and speared Mai in the arm, causing a serious wound. They seized the young man along with six of his comrades, imprisoning them on Bora Bora. Mai and his fellows probably would have spent the rest of their lives as slaves had an influential woman on the island not intervened on their behalf.

A year later, when HMS *Adventure* was cruising the Society

Islands along with HMS *Resolution* as part of Cook's second Pacific voyage, Mai presented himself to the captain of the *Adventure*, who was none other than Tobias Furneaux. The meeting occurred on the island of Huahine, about thirty miles from Mai's native Raiatea. Mai begged Furneaux to take him to England. Furneaux reluctantly consented, and Mai climbed aboard the *Adventure*. It was a courageous leap of faith on his part to join ranks with such utterly strange people, bound for an unfamiliar place so far away.

As Furneaux's ship sailed away from Mai's beloved islands and continued on the voyage, the officers and crew began to warm up to the Polynesian. Mai served as an able crewman on the official muster roll, earning regular pay, and he acquitted himself well. Lieutenant James Burney, who understood some Tahitian, took him under his wing and taught him a little English. Mai made many friends during the voyage. Some of his mates called him Omai, or Omiah. (The *O* was a redundancy, for in the Tahitian language, *O* was a throwaway article, meaning "it is.") Others just called him Jack.

During a storm off New Zealand, Furneaux's *Adventure* became separated from Cook's *Resolution*, and Furneaux returned home to England a year earlier than Cook. At Portsmouth, on a hot July day in 1774, Mai became the first Polynesian to set foot on English soil.

FURNEAUX AND MAI went straightaway to London by horse-drawn coach and reported to Admiralty House, in Whitehall. After conferring with navy officials there, Furneaux placed Mai in the care of Joseph Banks, the noted botanist who had accompanied Cook on his first voyage and who had underwritten the lion's share of the expedition's scientific efforts. It was decided that Banks would be Mai's principal patron and chaperone during his time in England.

Joseph Banks was a busy man, with a busy mind. An affable bachelor, thirty-one years old, he had a doughy face, impish eyes, and an incipient Falstaffian paunch. A product of Harrow and Eton, and also Oxford, where he attended but did not graduate, he was a person of wealth and renown. When he wasn't traveling the world collecting plant specimens, he spent much of his time immersed in the arcane politics of gentlemen's clubs and intellectual fraternities.

Banks managed to be profane and elegant, eminent and approachable, jovial and pompous, all at the same time. A biographer called him "one of the spoilt children of fortune."

It was fitting that Banks should become Mai's sponsor. Not only did he have the financial wherewithal to properly host Mai; he had a love and fascination for Polynesia. Upon his return from Cook's first voyage, Banks had done more than anyone else in England to popularize the joys and charms of beautiful, sensual Tahiti. His journal entries from the island were racy and raw, full of enthusiasm and insights. His reports recounted his amorous adventures, described his participation in dances and feasts, and included what is believed to be the first description of the process of tattooing.

Banks was eager to be Mai's patron for another reason. There had long been a tradition in England of bringing home "human pets" from wild places—for entertainment and for study. For more than a century, explorers had hosted Indigenous people from North and South America, the Caribbean, Africa, and Asia, to see how they would fare in a European city. Perhaps the most widely celebrated of all the arrivals from the New World was Pocahontas, the Native American woman from present-day Virginia who came to England in 1616 and was widely feted.

Banks had been hoping to have his own human pet for some time. He asked his friend Daniel Solander to come meet the newly arrived Polynesian. An accomplished naturalist from Sweden, and a protégé of Carl Linnaeus, Solander had voyaged with Banks and Cook aboard the *Endeavour*. At first Solander seemed unimpressed with Mai. "He is very brown, almost as brown as a mulatto," Solander wrote in notes that read with the analytical style of an autopsy. "Not at all handsome, but well made. His nose is a little broadish." But as Solander got to know Mai better and watched him interact with others, the naturalist revised his opinion, deciding instead that Mai was a "valuable acquisition." Mai, he noted, "is a sensible communicative man. He is well-behaved, easy in his manners, and remarkably complaisant to the ladies." Solander, on the basis of scant evidence, decided that Mai was something like the Polynesian equivalent of a country squire—"a private gentleman," as he put it, "of a small fortune."

Still, in Solander's estimation, Mai paled in comparison to a certain Polynesian man Banks had befriended during the first Cook voyage. In 1769, Banks had taken aboard the *Endeavour* a respected priest and navigator named Tupaia. He was a proud, severe man steeped in the intricacies of Polynesian politics, religious ritual, and voyaging lore.

Banks decided he would bring Tupaia to Britain, teach him English, and parade him around London as a living souvenir from his travels. "I do not know why I may not keep [Tupaia] as a curiosity, as well as some of my neighbors do lions and tigers," Banks had mused in his journal—an offhand remark that speaks volumes about the sensibilities of the patrician world in which he moved. "The amusement I shall have in his future conversations," he added, "will I think fully repay me."

Journeying with Cook and Banks on the *Endeavour*, the Polynesian savant proved enormously helpful as a translator and a navigator. At one point, Tupaia produced a map that appeared to show all the major islands of the South Pacific; at first glance, it seemed a crude document—he had merely scribbled it, off the cuff, on a piece of paper, without reference to scale or geographical coordinates. Yet scholars who subsequently studied Tupaia's map have found it, in its own way, to be astonishingly accurate.

Banks couldn't wait to show Tupaia around London. But while the *Endeavour* was en route to England, Tupaia died in the Dutch East Indies enclave of Batavia—now Jakarta. Some accounts say the cause of Tupaia's death was scurvy; others suggest dysentery or malaria.

With Mai's arrival in England, Banks had a second chance to host a human trophy from the South Pacific. The botanist had retained a number of Tahitian words, so he could carry on a rudimentary conversation with Mai from the start. In a remarkable bit of serendipity, Banks learned that Mai had known Tupaia well. Mai said that as a boy he had served as a religious assistant to Tupaia and other learned priests. In Banks's view, it was a most agreeable coincidence: In place of Tupaia, he was getting Tupaia's apprentice.

BANKS BRIEFLY ENSCONCED Mai at his town house at the edge of Mayfair. The first order of business, the naturalist decided, was to secure for Mai an audience with King George III. The royal representatives promptly accepted Banks's request. Now Mai had to prepare himself. A tailor would take his measurements to fashion some proper clothes. Mai would have to memorize a short speech and perfect his bow. Banks helped Mai compose a few words, but because the English he'd learned aboard ship was fairly basic, and because the Tahitian language lacked many of the consonants found in English, Mai struggled to form some of the sounds.

Soon the day came. Mai was dressed in a new suit made of maroon Manchester velvet. He wore a white silk waistcoat and gray satin knee breeches. Banks and Mai made their way to the royal country estate at Kew, where King George liked to reside during the summer, a verdant preserve on the south side of the Thames. The king's representatives ushered Banks and Mai into the royal residence, a Palladian structure of pale limestone known as the White House, and presented them to the sovereign.

George III, thirty-six years old, had bulging blue eyes, a long slender nose, and pouty lips. A tall, pious man, he refrained from spirits, went riding nearly every day, and was an energetic dancer.

The White House was surrounded by gardens of exotic plants, many of which Joseph Banks had collected during his travels or had solicited from armies of plant "fossickers" he personally knew. Banks was an adviser to the king himself, and his collections formed the nucleus for what would become the world's most extensive botanical park. The king loved the time he spent at Kew—it was his country home on the outskirts of London, a place where he could escape from the suffocating strictures of royal life.

Mai greeted His Majesty with a convincing bow, but he was so flustered that he forgot the salutations he and Banks had practiced. He went down on one knee and grabbed the king's arm with his tattooed hand, blurting, "How do, King Tosh!" "Tosh" was as close as he could get to pronouncing the name George.

If the king was offended, he didn't let on. He presented Mai with a sword. The Polynesian, fixing it to his waist and regaining his composure, thanked him, then launched into a speech, in broken and heavily accented English, that attempted to communicate his desire for revenge back home. With Banks translating here and there, he is said to have uttered something like "Sir, you are king of England, king of Tahiti. I am your subject, come here for gunpowder to destroy the people of Bora Bora, our enemy."

King George probably had no idea what Mai was talking about. He was interested in solidifying England's hold over Tahiti and its surrounding islands, for he knew that the French and probably also the Spanish had designs on the lovely archipelago. But he had no appetite for entangling the British Empire in inter-island rivalries in the way Mai was advocating, and so the king moved the conversation on to other topics.

His Majesty tendered a formal promise that England would return Mai to the South Pacific as soon as another expedition could be organized and a captain chosen to lead it. The Crown had every intention of ferrying Tahiti's special envoy safely home.

But George III had bigger plans for Mai's return voyage. The king wanted to send Mai back with a large assortment of animals—horses, cows, sheep, goats—culled from the royal farmlands. His Majesty would provide flocks of domestic birds, too, and a profusion of bulbs and seeds. The king, who had made a study of animal husbandry, was widely known as "Farmer George." He believed the greatest gift England could bestow upon Tahiti and her surrounding islands would be a starter stock of animals and plants so the Polynesian people could create British-style farms. He seemed troubled by what he'd heard about the cuisine of the South Seas, even though the islanders, who enjoyed a nearly limitless supply of fish and fresh fruit, had a much healthier diet than most Englishmen.

But King George was also worried about something more immediate and pressing. He had given some thought to Mai's health and fretted that the Polynesian was in serious danger of contracting smallpox. While bidding his guests adieu, the king suggested to Banks that Mai should be inoculated, at the Crown's expense. Banks, who had himself been vaccinated when he was seventeen years old, vigorously agreed. A proper vaccination would be scheduled.

4   A Fine Retreat

Despite his soaring fame, James Cook, at the age of forty-six, had decided he was finished with exploration. "I was in hopes that I had put an end to all voyages to the Pacific Ocean," he wrote. Some accounts said that he seemed like a spent force. Forty-six certainly wasn't dotage, but nautical life, especially on prolonged circumnavigational odysseys, had a way of accelerating the aging process. For all but one of the previous seven years, Cook had been at sea, dealing with the physical stresses and onerous worries of command.

The Admiralty had offered an honorary position that paid him handsomely but required little of his energy or talents: He had been made a captain at the Greenwich Hospital, on the banks of the Thames, a grand old dormitory for elderly and infirm sailors who had fought their country's wars. This cozy sinecure would give him the financial freedom to write an official account of his most recent travels while also allowing him to spend time with Elizabeth and their growing family. The post offered living quarters, food, drink, firewood for warmth, and a host of other amenities.

If he wanted to, he could live right on the grounds at Greenwich, surrounded by magnificent domed buildings of baroque architecture designed by Sir Christopher Wren, with manicured parklands that swept up the steep hillside from the river to the Royal Observatory, with its esoteric collections of clocks and pendulums, its camera obscura, its long telescopes and other scientific paraphernalia. Here, astronomers studied the mysteries of the heavens and compiled star catalogs and planetary tables for the improvement of navigation. It would seem to be exactly Cook's kind of place, a campus where mathematicians ruled the greenswards and astronomers, on morning constitutionals, clasped their hands in thought.

Greenwich was just downriver from London, built along a pronounced bend of the Thames, across from a wild preserve known as the Isle of Dogs. The air in Greenwich was pure, the grass a brilliant green, and herds of tame deer flitted through the woods, as they had since the time of Henry VIII.

All of this could be a playground for Cook and his family. He would have no responsibilities other than to keep a paternal eye on the thousand or so navy pensioners who lived in the Greenwich Hospital and its corridors of apartments. These battle-scarred veterans were bawdy spinners of tall sea tales, grog-loving old tars, many of them sporting a peg leg or an eye patch. The American writer Nathaniel Hawthorne, who visited the hospital nearly a century later, observed that the Greenwich pensioners were the "petted children of the nation, and the government is their dry-nurse."

The adjacent town of Greenwich seemed a carefree and comfortable place, with its taverns and inns built along the narrow, winding lanes and its twice-annual fair that drew tens of thousands of merrymakers for games and dances, markets and freak shows, and menageries of exotic animals.

Greenwich was, all in all, a lively spot for Cook to rest and recollect, and to bask in the praise of his country. This precise location, which the Admiralty had fixed on their maps as the prime meridian, zero degrees longitude, offered a felicitous refuge for an emeritus explorer; it was a place by the river where heaven and earth seemed to merge, where the ticks of time and the invisible lines of the geographers intersected.

The question was when Cook's terrestrial boredom would take hold. "It is a fine retreat and a pretty income," he conceded in a letter to a friend, "but whether I can bring myself to like ease and retirement, time will show." Already, he was starting to sound constrained. "My fate drives me from one extreme to another," he said. "A few months ago the whole Southern Hemisphere was hardly big enough for me, and now I am going to be confined within the limits of

Greenwich Hospital, which are far too small for an active mind like mine."

PREDICTABLY, ONLY A few months into his tenure, James Cook found himself missing the open ocean and seemed generally bored. His restlessness was compounded by the fact that the Admiralty was planning a new expedition that would once again take the *Resolution* to distant reaches of the Pacific—but without him at the helm.

One goal of the proposed voyage was to transport Mai, the young Polynesian, back to his native Tahiti, along with an assortment of royal farm animals, just as King George had promised. But the primary objective of the project was far more risky and extensive. It was to explore the so-called backside of North America, to chart the continent's icy northwest extremities, probe its scalloped coastlines, and hunt for a passage leading all the way across Canada, eastward, toward the Atlantic Ocean.

The search for the Northwest Passage—a navigable waterway connecting England to the coveted markets of Asia—had long been one of the great, if quixotic, quests of English exploration. What made the proposed voyage different was that this time the search for the passage would be reversed: It would be attempted from the faraway Pacific side of the continent, an approach that had not been seriously tried before. As Cook was well aware, that swath of the world—present-day Alaska, more or less—was terra incognita. Among the European powers, only the Russians were known to have visited it, but the accounts of where they had been and what they had learned were vague at best.

As Cook was also aware, whoever discovered the passage stood to win a substantial monetary reward. Parliament had offered a prize of £20,000 to the captain who found the long-rumored shortcut across Canada. This bounty was to be parceled among officers and crew, but the captain would retain the lion's share. The prospect of such a handsome sum must have taunted a man like Cook, who enjoyed no inherited wealth—as did the prospect of monies that would derive from a published account written by whoever captained the voyage.

As though to taunt Cook further, the Admiralty had chosen to moor the *Resolution* at the Deptford Dockyard, a maze of wharves built along the Thames, right beside Greenwich Hospital. Worse, navy superiors had periodically called upon Cook to advise the shipwrights and other contractors who were outfitting his old vessel for the coming voyage. Understandably, Cook was proprietary and maybe a bit nostalgic about the ship that had been his home for the past three years, and as plans for the new expedition progressed, he seemed to grow sullen, and not a little envious.

"The *Resolution* will soon be sent out again," Cook moped to a friend in a letter. "But I shall not command her." Cook understood that another officer had already been suggested to lead the voyage— and as it happened, he was a man Cook knew and loved like a brother.

CHARLES CLERKE (pronounced "Clark") was a celebrated officer, with a temperament calibrated very differently from Cook's. He was a lenient man with a sharp wit and a taste for Rabelaisian humor. Tall and fair-haired, Clerke had ruddy skin and large, sensitive eyes. He was described as a "wag" and a "lusty extrovert." Clerke could be a colorful raconteur and loved a good hoax: He was famous for having sent the Royal Society a sensational account of discovering a race of giants in Patagonia—"there was hardly a man there less than eight feet," he insisted. Clerke's paper was read aloud during the society's proceedings, and many members seemed to believe his incredible claims, not realizing it was all a good-natured spoof.

Clerke was born in the Essex countryside, the son of a justice of the peace. He descended from a landed family with wealth, but as the fourth-born son, with little chance of enjoying an inheritance, Charles had decided at an early age to pursue a career on the high seas. He began his studies at the Royal Naval Academy, in Portsmouth, at the precocious age of thirteen. Like Cook, he served in the Seven Years' War.

Then, in 1764, Clerke signed on to sail around the world with Captain John Byron aboard the HMS *Dolphin*. Clerke found that he took to these extended odysseys—he was a gifted sailor and an amateur naturalist of some talent, and he got along well with all sorts of people. He loved animals, too, and was especially fond of the cats that lived in his cabin and took care of rat problems. He had served ably on Cook's first voyage as a master's mate and on Cook's second voyage as a lieutenant, and these extraordinary experiences seemed only to quicken his appetite for more.

It was a curious but not uncommon thing for people who had been on one long voyage around the world to sign up for another and, close upon its heels, another one still. These journeys were dangerous and punishing, but they were also addictive. Having once traveled around the globe, these hard-bitten mariners often found it difficult to settle back into the staid ways of lubberly society.

Still, one had to wonder, what sort of masochists were they? How much punishment could a veteran circumnavigator tolerate? How much could one man take of rotten food, malodorous quarters, aches to the back and joints, and indignities to the vanity and spirit? If you were James Cook or Charles Clerke, apparently a whole lot. It was a rough profession—in an era when, as the saying went, ships were made of wood, and men were made of iron.

Cook and Clerke: While they were old friends who'd traveled the oceans together, the two men differed in fundamental ways. Clerke, who was sixteen years younger than Cook, was sometimes criticized for his willingness to fraternize with his men. He liked to have a good time and saw no point in hiding it. On his previous trips around the world, Clerke had shown a fondness for liquor and for the Native women in the South Pacific. Some thought he was a little too soft. As a surgeon who sailed with him put it, he "did not possess that degree of firmness and resolution necessary to constitute the character of a great commander." Still, Clerke was cool and competent under pressure, and when urgent situations presented themselves, he was decisive. "When a certain line of action is chalked out to him," one of Clerke's contemporaries said, "then no man is readier to pursue it than himself."

In the descriptions passed around by men who had served under both Cook and Clerke, Clerke was usually the favorite. If Cook came across as an omniscient father figure, admired and respected but also a bit feared, Clerke was the beloved uncle.

Now it seemed that the beloved uncle would assume command of an expedition of his very own—and one every bit as ambitious as Cook's first two voyages. He had lived in Cook's shadow long enough.

IN EARLY FEBRUARY of 1776, Cook received an invitation to have dinner at the London home of one of the most powerful men in England: John Montagu, the Fourth Earl of Sandwich and First Lord of the Admiralty. It must have been clear by the nature and timing of the invitation that something very important was to be discussed. Cook promptly accepted and a date was set.

Lord Sandwich was a shrewd, cynical, and sometimes ruthless politician, adroit in the power games of London. He and his fellow lords presided over an institution that was the largest organization in Britain and indeed in all of Europe. But Sandwich was much more than a Machiavellian bureaucrat; he was an intellectual of sorts, interested in the science of the day, and an advocate for exploration—probably the staunchest advocate, in fact, behind Cook's second voyage of discovery.

Sandwich was lanky and tall, with such an odd, shambling, lopsided gait that people liked to say he could walk down both sides of the street at the same time. When at the Admiralty, he was known to be a workaholic. He was, one critic said, a man of "limitless ambition to which he has sacrificed everything," and he kept such fiendish hours that he would often forsake his meals, opting instead to place a piece of beef between slices of toasted bread, which is how he came to be known as the "inventor" of the sandwich. He was a competitive card player and gambler, and the handy snack he had devised is said to have sustained him through many a long night at the gaming table. Lord Sandwich was a man in a hurry, in other words, and so perhaps it's fitting that he should be known for a food architecture that can be gobbled quickly—for, through his relentless advocacy of exploration and global cross-pollination, he had accelerated many a timeline.

To find relief from the general toil of his job, Lord Sandwich had cultivated a deep affection for the voyages of exploration that the Admiralty periodically supported. He was perhaps the country's greatest admirer of James Cook, and everything that had emanated from Cook's two expeditions to date. Sandwich had been a catalyst, a patron, a sponsor. As far as he was concerned, Cook could do no wrong.

Politically, Sandwich was the gray eminence behind the proposed expedition to North America's "backside." In advocating for the voyage, he had confronted considerable resistance within government circles. Mounting tensions in the American colonies had caused the Royal Navy to shift its already strained resources. In a time of imminent war, yet another expedition to the far side of the world seemed a luxury England could not afford. Yet the ever crafty Sandwich had managed to circumvent the naysayers to win official approval.

THE NIGHT OF the dinner party came, and Cook's carriage pulled up along the cobblestones of the Admiralty building. As he entered Admiralty House and greeted Lord Sandwich, it must have been obvious to Cook that something significant was afoot. The additional guests included other consequential men within the bureaucracy, such as Hugh Palliser, a rear admiral then serving as the comptroller of the navy. Palliser had been an early friend and supporter of Cook, going back to their days together fighting against the French in Canada. Another of the dinner guests was Philip Stephens, secretary of the Admiralty, a power broker of the first order and a master of parliamentary back channels.

During the dinner, the conversation inevitably turned to the matter of the upcoming expedition. Cook's friend Charles Clerke was still the presumptive candidate to lead the voyage, but doubts were raised. Was he serious enough? the Admiralty officials wanted to know. Had he a too keen affinity for the bottle?

Cook's replies to these questions aren't known. But his first biographer, Andrew Kippis, who was a contemporary, noted that Cook reacted in unexpected ways as Sandwich and his guests drew the explorer into a lengthy discussion of the coming project—possible routes, possible anchorages, and the profound strategic importance of the endeavor. They discussed the voyage's "grandeur and dignity,"

Kippis wrote, its "consequences to navigation and science, and the completion it would give to the whole system of discoveries."

At some pregnant moment during the dinner, Kippis noted, Cook became so dazzled by the lofty discussion that he suddenly rose from his seat and proclaimed that he would lead the mission himself. "Captain Cook was so fired," as Kippis described the scene, "that he started up, and declared that he himself would undertake the direction of the enterprise."

Although Sandwich, Palliser, and Stephens reacted with surprise and delight, this was the answer they had secretly hoped to elicit from Cook all along. After the hardships Cook had already endured on the high seas, they couldn't in good conscience overtly ask him to lead another arduous odyssey. So they had inveigled Cook, over good food and wine, cunningly setting the hook. It had worked brilliantly.

Within days, Cook, having received his official commission, reported to the *Resolution,* where he began to interview prospective officers and crew members for the voyage. According to Admiralty orders, the ship was to be "sheathed and filled and fitted for voyage to remote parts."

It made sense that Cook would feel comfortable about a voyage that would return him to North America. He had fond memories of his youthful days spent on that continent during and after the Seven Years' War. In many ways, he had built his career in America. He'd had good luck there, and he'd honed his skills as an astronomer, surveyor, and mapmaker on American shores. To be offered an opportunity to explore the far coast of the same continent would be the crowning achievement of his work—but also a circling back to his professional roots. To others, including later historians and biographers, it seemed more like hubris. Was he pushing his luck? Third time's a charm, perhaps, but just as often throughout history, the third venture had brought trouble. Christopher Columbus's third voyage, to name a prominent example, had ended with the Italian explorer being arrested, put in chains, and sent back to Spain in disgrace.

Surely a measure of pure audacity fueled Cook's decision to go out again. Based on the success of his previous adventures, he seemed to think that providence would see him through. It would be his final achievement, his valediction. He could scarcely imagine failure. By now, wrote one nautical historian, Cook was "that blessed creature, a man to whom good luck had become a habit."

HISTORY DOESN'T RECORD what Charles Clerke thought of it all—to have been so close to commanding his own voyage, only to have the assignment abruptly snatched away. His only consolation was that Cook, with the Admiralty's approval, had decided that Clerke would command the *Resolution*'s sister vessel, which Cook had personally selected and which would be christened HMS *Discovery*. Once again, in what was becoming a groove-worn theme, Clerke would serve as Cook's number two.

As for Cook, so much for Greenwich Hospital. So much for a placid early retirement spent in the company of his family. He had an expedition to mount, with its thousand worries and nagging details, while he simultaneously completed the account of his second voyage—and with Elizabeth expecting a child in just a few months.

Though outwardly confident, he seemed to entertain trepidations about the abrupt decision he had made. As he wrote John Walker, the Quaker shipping entrepreneur who had been his mentor in Whitby, "I know not what your opinion may be on this step I have taken. It is certain I have quit an easy retirement for an active, and perhaps dangerous voyage. If I am fortunate enough to get safely home, there's no doubt but it will be greatly to my advantage." He struck a similar tone in a note to another friend. "If I am not so fortunate as to make my passage home by the North Pole, I hope at least to determine whether it is practicable or not. From what we yet know, the attempt must be hazardous, and must be made with great caution."

5 A Natural Politeness

After their visit with King George, Joseph Banks arranged for Mai to be inoculated for smallpox. The naturalist made an appointment for Mai to see a prominent physician named Thomas Dimsdale, who had refined a method of inoculating patients for smallpox, using material taken from active pustules on the skin of individuals suffering from a relatively mild case of the disease. Among Dr. Dimsdale's many famous patients was Catherine the Great of Russia, whom he had successfully vaccinated in 1768 in St. Petersburg.

Dr. Dimsdale's "Inoculation Institute" was located in Hertford, about twenty miles north of London. When Mai and Banks arrived, the doctor took pains to explain the procedure—that in order to protect oneself from smallpox, one first had to catch a weakened form of it. Mai still didn't understand. Nearby stood a church whose cemetery was snaggled with headstones, and Mai asked if these were the graves of Dr. Dimsdale's many patients.

A few days after Dimsdale performed the procedure, Mai began to develop the expected sores on his skin, as well as inside his mouth and throat. He fell into despair. Banks did his best to comfort the suddenly morose Polynesian, but in a few days, when the sores began to recede, Mai was relieved and elated. As Banks wrote in a letter, "Omai has now got through all danger from inoculation [and] he fears nothing."

A few weeks later, Dimsdale declared the vaccination a success. The doctor discharged his patient, and Banks took Mai on a tour of the English countryside, visiting the estates of squires and noblemen and the salons of his intellectual friends. "I do this," Banks assured an acquaintance, "to make him known agreeably, without becoming a show."

Everywhere Mai went in the green, green country, people were taken by his good humor, impeccable manners, and ready laugh. The country life agreed with Mai. He learned how to fire a fowling piece, how to catch fish in the local streams, and how to ride a horse (although apparently not very well). He loved to roam the heaths and moors. He learned to play backgammon and became more and more sure-footed on the dance floor. He sailed on Whittlesey Mere—a large, shallow lake in the fen country that has since been drained. There were horse races, fox hunts, picnics, concerts, dinner parties, tea parties. It was a happy time.

His English was slowly improving. He was far better at understanding the strange new language than he was at speaking it—his ear, it seemed, was quicker than his tongue. He mastered the inflections and intonations, the body language and facial expressions, of those around him. Banks worked with Mai to improve his deportment. Mai learned quickly. A lady of prominence thought he "seemed to shame education, for his manners are so extremely graceful, and [he] is so polite, attentive, and easy that you would have thought he came from some foreign court."

Many Englishwomen were attracted to Mai, and he reciprocated their affections. Rumors of Mai's liaisons grew over the summer of 1774, raising eyebrows among gossips and puritanical newspaper writers. "The novelty of his figure drew much attention upon him, more particularly from the women of quality, for with many of them he was intimate and familiar," wrote a journalist in an unsigned article. "I have a higher opinion of my fair countrywomen than to think they would be so condescending; and yet, philosophy cannot reconcile the depravity of female inclinations."

PEOPLE WHO ENCOUNTERED Mai grew to love his playful and curious manner of speech. He freely invented his own words and expressions. A bull was a "man-cow." Snow was "white rain." At a country estate where he stayed, he referred to the butler as "king of the bottles." He called ice "stone water."

One morning he was stung by a wasp. When asked what had bitten him and caused his hand to swell, he replied that it was a "soldier bird." Later, a member of the local gentry pinched him a bit of snuff to snort. "No thank you," he replied. "The nose not hungry."

His hosts were pleased to learn that he was an excellent cook. Banks asked Mai to roast an assortment of fowl in a traditional Polynesian style. Mai constructed an *umu,* an earth oven. He dug a hole, built a fire there, then partially filled it with stones. He laid the birds in the pit, wrapping them in butter-smeared paper, for want of his usual plantain leaves. He covered it all with dirt and let the mess of fowl smolder for hours. The result was scrumptious. "Nothing could be better dressed, or more savory," gushed a critic. "The smoldering pebble-stones and embers... had given a certain flavor to the fowls, a soupçon of smokiness, which made them taste as if a ham accompanied them."

And so it could be said that barbecue—or at least a South Seas strain of it—had arrived in Great Britain.

At the estates he visited, Mai liked to practice his marksmanship and became a devoted hunter, especially during grouse season. Much to the chagrin of the local groundskeepers, the trigger-happy Mai "popped at all the feathered creation which came in his way"—not only grouse but chickens, geese, even ducks haplessly playing in a pond. "His slaughter of domestic birds," the observer lamented, "was by no means inconsiderable."

Guns lay at the heart of why Mai had volunteered to travel to England in the first place. He knew he had to master firearms, to collect them, to understand their inner workings and the ammunition that made them lethal. "He had a sense of mission," wrote historian Michael Alexander in his book *Omai: Noble Savage,* and he knew that "these people he had come amongst held the key to his intrinsic purpose, the avenging of his father."

Other times, Mai would set aside his fowling piece and revert to the hunting techniques he'd learned as a boy. A friend later recalled how Mai crouched in a stubble field and crept up on his prey. "His eye sparkled," the friend reminisced, when "on a sudden, he darted forward like a cat, and sprang upon a covey of partridges, one of which he caught and took home alive, in great triumph."

Though he could be a steel-nerved hunter, Mai was acutely sensitive about other things. He became disturbed when he saw a live worm wriggling on a fisherman's hook. As a friend put it, Mai "turned away from a sight so disagreeable, declaring his antipathy to eat any fish taken by so cruel a method." (In his home islands, a religious stricture forbade the harming of worms.)

Mai had a maudlin streak. At concerts and dramatic performances, he was quick to tear up. Funerals were so distressing to him that he found he couldn't get through them—at one service, halfway in, he put a handkerchief over his face and fled the chapel. He took pity on beggars and gave them whatever he could spare. The poverty and hunger he encountered while on brief visits to English cities upset him; he'd seen nothing like it in the land of tropical plenty that was Tahiti.

All in all, though, Joseph Banks was enormously pleased with how well Mai was assimilating into English society. The botanist was surprised by what he called Mai's "gentility." The experiment seemed to be working beautifully. "He succeeds most prodigiously," Banks wrote to his sister. "So much natural politeness I never saw in any man: wherever he goes he makes friends and has not I believe as yet one foe."

THE ESTATE WHERE Mai remained the longest and seemed to get on most famously was Hinchingbrooke, Lord Sandwich's country place in Cambridgeshire, about sixty miles north of London. The old Elizabethan house was a rambling, book-lined edifice that harbored trapdoors, mystery staircases, and secret passageways. Accounts from the time describe Hinchingbrooke as an "irregular old house" surrounded by "venerable elms"—a "good house for the robust and the jolly."

The First Lord of the Admiralty had become an important sponsor of Mai's tour of England, a patron and protector, as engaged in the details as Joseph Banks himself. Perhaps more than any government official, Lord Sandwich appreciated the larger implications of Mai's sojourn in Britain. But more than that, Sandwich grew genuinely fond of Mai, introducing him to his neighbors, who, according to one account, "vied with each other in varying his diversions, in order to raise his idea of the splendor and gaiety of this country."

Mai made himself at home at Hinchingbrooke. He called Sandwich "king of all the ships," and seemed to view him as an uncle. Sandwich made sure the staff indulged and pampered his favorite guest, and little by little Mai became quite spoiled. He developed a taste for rich sauces and fatty foods—and was especially fond of port. He liked to dress up in finery, with capes and scarves, lace ruffles and fancy boots, and he often wore a sword—the one King George had given him—cinched to his waist.

Still, Mai had such a gleeful smile and such a game spirit that even the snobbiest of callers at Hinchingbrooke overlooked his growing affectations. Many visitors to the estate had been led to believe that Mai was not a commoner from Tahiti but rather a prince, or perhaps a high priest. Mai didn't fabricate or broadcast this fiction, but neither did he do anything to correct it. He could tell that Britain was itself a place with a rigid social hierarchy, so he did nothing to dispel the notion that he was a person of wealth and consequence back home. As one historian put it, Mai's sponsors had set in motion "a deception, a masquerade in which [he] was positively acquiescent."

WHILE AT HINCHINGBROOKE, Mai sometimes left the house in search of companionship. The stories of his escapades were numerous and no doubt exaggerated but, on some level, probably true. According to one account, "He liked to wander around the landscaped park and would call in at the cottages to flirt with, and possibly hope to seduce, the country wenches dependent on the estate."

At Hinchingbrooke, Sandwich's mistress, Martha Ray, was often present during Mai's stay there, hosting the festivities, essentially functioning as the First Lord's wife. Ray, who was well known as a talented singer, liked Mai, but in a patronizing way. She called him a "child of Nature," and found that his "simplicity is certainly very diverting." Ray suspected that Mai was having relations with one of the farm girls, and a letter she wrote about it went far in articulating the thinking of the times, even among relatively "enlightened" people, on the subject of mixed-race sexual unions. "What kind of animal should a naturalist expect from a native of Tahiti and a Huntingdonshire dairymaid?" she mused. "If my eyes do not deceive me, Mr. Omiah will give us a specimen."

After one dinner at Hinchingbrooke, guests asked Mai to sing a tune from his native islands. He seemed bashful, but when they insisted, he couldn't refuse. Lord Sandwich was interested in the question of whether Polynesian music embraced the concepts of harmony and counterpoint, and here was his chance to study the matter.

Mai started to sing, but what emerged from his throat was punishment to all ears. "Nothing can be more curious or less pleasing than his singing voice," wrote one witness to Mai's singing. "Tune or air hardly seem to be aimed at; so queer, wild, and strange a rumbling of sounds never did I before hear; and very contentedly can I go to the grave, if I never do again."

People were not above teasing Mai. On a trip to the Duke of Manchester's palace, he encountered a "shocking machine." A novelty item based on Benjamin Franklin's experiments with electricity, it had a crank that could generate a low-voltage current, giving a person who happened to be touching the electrodes attached to the top of the mechanism a surprisingly strong jolt. One day, while guests were gathered around, some joker pulled it out from the estate's cabinet of curiosities and gave the Polynesian a shock. But Mai, who was unacquainted with electricity, didn't think it was funny at all. He fled the room, flush with alarm and outrage. He was so cross that he said he wouldn't return until he could elicit a guarantee that the pranksters would put the offending machine away.

As winter came on, Banks decided it was time to acquaint Mai with London, which he had seen only briefly before his inoculation. Sandwich hated to see Mai leave Hinchingbrooke but knew he would catch up with him soon enough. As he wrote Banks upon their departure from the countryside, "I am grown so used to him, and have so sincere a friendship with him, that I am quite depressed at his leaving me." Sandwich pleaded with Banks to look after Mai in the big city. "His safety," vowed the Admiralty lord, "must depend upon you and me; and I should think we were highly blameable if we did not do everything we can to prove ourselves his real friends."

6   The Problem of the Ice

The Northwest Passage: For nearly three hundred years it had been the grail, the phantom, the will-o'-the-wisp. Many European nations had yearned to find it, but for the British it had become an obsession. Over the centuries, the search for it had led to an unfortunate expenditure of blood and treasure, with many gothic narratives of frostbite, scurvy, mutiny, and starvation. Each new expedition would start out with optimism, but, often as not, within months the poor explorers would be lost in the wilderness, eating boot leather. It had become one of the grim motifs of the empire, full of lurid dispatches from what amounted to a low-grade war on weather, geography, and frozen water.

A circular argument was at play: The more British citizens who suffered and died in their search for the mystical passageway, the more vital it became to find the damn thing, for otherwise all that suffering and death had only been a terrible waste.

And then there were the memories of those explorers themselves. So many stalwart names had passed down through the ages—Frobisher, Davis, Baffin, and Hudson, among others, supremely confident men who had tried so hard to find the way through. The English had to honor them. Painfully, determinedly, these argonauts had wormed their way into North America's high latitudes, only to find dead ends, tangled landscapes, fantasies and false leads.

COMMERCE, OF COURSE, was the main impetus behind the quest—the benefits for English trade were potentially enormous. A northwest passage, advocates claimed, would render obsolete the dangerous and time-consuming journey around the bottom of Africa or South America, cutting the long trip in half, they said, reducing a one-year voyage to China down to six months.

There were broader geopolitical reasons as well. A northwest passage would allow the British to avoid the Spanish, who controlled the waters and ports of South America and absurdly claimed, with a decree of Vatican support, that the entire Pacific Ocean was their exclusive property. A northwest passage would be a shortcut, a bypass—a way of triumphing over the Spanish without having to fight them, or even encounter them at all.

Then, too, it would be a way of outmaneuvering the French, something that always appealed to the English. Throughout the seventeenth century, French explorers such as Champlain, Marquette, Jolliet, and La Salle had pieced together the enormous puzzle of the Great Lakes and many of the continent's interior rivers, while also trying to find their own version of a passage to the Pacific. In these bold and desperate feats of exploration, they pushed ever westward, ever southward, only to reach the inevitable cul-de-sacs. But they had enjoyed other successes. By the end of the 1600s the French had established an enormous empire in North America that had tapped the continent's riches—principally, its hides, furs, and fish.

The Seven Years' War changed everything, however. The 1763 treaty ending the war forced France to cede much of Canada, leaving the English as the dominant European power in North America. But the French were still interested in the interior of the continent, and they had not given up on exploration. In 1775, English spies in Paris heard rumors that the French were planning their own search for the Northwest Passage over Canada, an expedition to be led by Louis Antoine de Bougainville, the country's greatest explorer-scientist and, in a sense, Cook's direct rival. This intelligence, though it proved false, was an additional goad that may have helped solidify Cook's third voyage. England and France, although under more or less amicable terms by treaty, were still locked in mortal competition. Like wounded animals not quite done with the fight, they watched over each other's every move.

But a British discovery of a convenient passage over the top of Canada would positively unnerve the French. How would they respond? It would be, for the English, an achievement of such prestige and glory that it would serve as a parting insult, the final spit in the eye, to punctuate the end of the Seven Years' War.

THE BRITISH OBSESSION with finding the Northwest Passage seemed to rise and fall on a thirty-year cycle, as though every generation of Englishmen had to discover for themselves the magnificent puzzle and its irresistible allure. It was a quest pursued by "geographical romantics," wrote Cook biographer J. C. Beaglehole, "an illusion just as sedulously nurtured as that of the great southern continent." Each generation had to apply its own inventions and resources and ideas, throwing everything they had at the same old transcontinental problem. *Maybe this time, with what we know now, with all that we've learned, it won't be so hard.*

Luckily, the country's brightest minds had been hard at work on

theoretical aspects of the problem of the ice. Foremost among them
was a gentleman thinker named Daines Barrington, a lawyer, antiquarian, and naturalist and a council member of the Royal Society
who was also close to Lord Sandwich. It was Barrington who had
first proposed a voyage to hunt for the passage from the Pacific side
of North America. In a direct sense, he was the conceptual architect
of Cook's third expedition. If Sandwich was its hard-nosed, practical
sponsor, Barrington was its intellectual progenitor.

The eccentric Daines Barrington was a lifelong bachelor with
a mousy countenance and a small, knobbed chin. He had studied
at Oxford and loved to burrow into odd nooks of natural science
and history. Among other pet projects, Barrington had authored an
exhaustive history of early English law going back to the Magna
Carta, studied the life cycles of trout in Wales, investigated the
card-playing customs of ancient societies, and written about child
geniuses (an interest that was sparked by his having interviewed
Wolfgang Amadeus Mozart when the musician visited London as a
nine-year-old prodigy).

But the topic that most intensely interested Daines Barrington
was the Arctic. He had written numerous tracts on the subject,
some of which he read before the Royal Society and others of which
he compiled into a curious little volume entitled *The Possibility of
Approaching the North Pole Asserted*.

Among his many dubious theories, Barrington maintained that
there was no ice at the North Pole, because seawater cannot freeze.
Ice in the high north, Barrington contended, was solely the product
of frigid rivers and streams emptying into the sea. Collars of freshwater ice thus might form and adhere close to Arctic coastlines, but
farther out from shore the deep ocean was reliably ice-free. "In the
seas near the Pole," Barrington wrote, "it is very probable there is
little or no ice, for that is commonly formed in bays and rivers during winter."

TO BUTTRESS HIS odd hypotheses, Barrington had interviewed
Arctic whaling ship captains, some English but many of them Dutch,
who shared beguiling anecdotes that were also probably apocryphal.

In reading the accounts Barrington so earnestly assembled, one gets the distinct impression that many of his interviewees had a good time pulling his leg.

There was, for example, a Dutch captain named Goulden who made the incredible claim that a few years earlier he had sailed within one degree of the North Pole. Goulden and his crew "did not meet with any ice," Barrington reported, and they had enjoyed shirtsleeve weather the whole way. It was as warm, said Barrington, "as in the summer at Amsterdam."

The story had to be true, he noted as an aside, for people from Holland "are not commonly jokers."

What all of these anecdotes meant, in Barrington's mind, was that prior attempts to find a northwest passage had failed principally because the captains had looked for routes too close to land. If they had ventured much farther to the north, out into open seas, they would have sailed unhindered by ice.

In the early 1770s, fired by his optimistic theories about ice formation, Barrington successfully lobbied for a new expedition to hunt for a northwest passage. Command of the voyage was assigned to a friend of his named Constantine Phipps. In the summer of 1773, Captain Phipps ventured to Norway's Svalbard Islands in hopes of sailing up and over the pole and all the way to China. But just beyond the eightieth parallel, Phipps was thwarted by a solid wall of ice. After a dicey retreat through treacherous floes, the explorer returned home, lucky to be alive.

Barrington was in no way dismayed by the expedition's alarming experience. He offered the facile explanation that perhaps Phipps had visited the Arctic pack at a bad time, during a bad year. The ice, he admitted, sometimes had a habit of piling up in one random place or another—but that was merely a temporary "assemblage," he asserted, and in no way a "perpetual barrier."

In spite of the nearly disastrous expedition led by Phipps, Barrington managed to convince his friend Lord Sandwich that another voyage to find the passage must be mounted, with one of Britain's best commanders running the operation. Someone of James Cook's capabilities, he believed, someone as reliable and methodical and persistent as Cook, could make a success of it.

It was Barrington, also, who proposed the Pacific as the best angle of attack. He was aware of several Russian-backed explorations to Alaska—one of them led by the Danish explorer Vitus Bering and another by Russian fur interests. These voyages had produced maps that had recently been published in London, and one chart in particular, known as Stählin's map, showed a very wide strait separating Alaska from the North American continent, a substantial waterway that would seem to allow a navigator to pursue an unobstructed northeastward course, up and over Canada, directly toward the Atlantic Ocean.

Barrington seemed to have no inkling that these maps were fantastically inaccurate. The large, enticing strait shown on Stählin's map *had* to be ice-free. He was so confident of this that he did not think the hull of the *Resolution* needed any reinforcement. Why would the ship need strengthening, when Cook wasn't going to encounter serious ice pack at all?

There was another crucial matter that curiously never arose in Barrington's considerations: Even if Stählin's map was correct and there was a wide strait that could lead Cook from Alaska over Canada toward the Atlantic, what would happen when his ship reached the other side of the continent? Generations of English explorers had become hopelessly lost in those eastern labyrinths, and often their ships had been squeezed and throttled by the ice. Why was Barrington so optimistic that the same calamities wouldn't befall Cook's *Resolution* as it approached the same pinched puzzles of geography from the opposite side? In Barrington's writings, the question didn't come up.

Ultimately, though, Barrington appealed to Lord Sandwich on patriotic grounds. Whatever dangers the voyage might entail, it must be pursued for the greater glory of England. "There is unquestionably no country in Europe," he wrote, "so well situated for such an enterprise as this." Barrington hoped his arguments would serve as "cogent reasons for wishing that a project which has dwelt in the

mouths and memories of some from the time of Henry the Eighth
should be revived, and at length, for the benefit of his subjects, carried into effect under the auspices of George the Third."

7   No Tutor but Nature

After his arrival in London, Mai became a favorite of the social
scene, meeting nearly everyone of importance and distinction. He
attended sessions of Parliament, learned to ice-skate on the Serpen-
tine in Hyde Park, and toured the catacombs and hideaways of St.
Paul's Cathedral. Poets and songwriters, journalists and playwrights
had penned or would soon be penning works about him. He was
present for the opening of the House of Lords, where he heard
George III, from his throne, rail against "a most daring spirit of resistance" in Boston. He made an excursion to Cambridge, where he met
learned doctors and professors in their sumptuous robes. He visited
a second time with King George, also meeting Queen Charlotte and
kissing her hand. With Lord Sandwich he toured the royal dock-
yards and inspected the navy fleets.

Meanwhile, he sat for several portrait painters, including England's most celebrated artist of the day, Joshua Reynolds, founding
president of the Royal Academy of Art. Reynolds had become the
go-to painter for English aristocrats, royals, and other well-heeled
clients who paid high commissions for the honor of sitting before
him. A contemporary described the perpetual bustle inside Reynolds's studio: "What a rustling of silks! What a fluttering of flounces
and brocades! What a cloud of powder and perfumes!"

In the finished painting, *Portrait of Omai,* an oil-on-canvas nearly
eight feet in height, Reynolds captured a barefoot Mai standing
against a backdrop of palm trees and volcanic mountains. His hair
is wrapped in a white turban. Reynolds, who was infatuated with
Greek and Roman statuary and liked to work in what he called the
Grand Manner, depicted Mai in a classical *adlocutio* pose—as though
he were in the middle of an oration. He appears to be a member of
the South Seas aristocracy, extravagantly gesturing as he addresses

a crowd of his island subjects. (The painting, widely considered Reynolds's greatest masterpiece, was recently co-purchased for $62 million by Britain's National Portrait Gallery and the J. Paul Getty Museum.)

In much the same tones as Reynolds's painting, another notable London portraitist, Nathaniel Dance-Holland, captured Mai in a princely light, showing him holding a traditional stool or headrest carved from a single piece of wood, known as an *iri*. This was an overt symbol of aristocracy in Tahiti, where chiefs were at no time allowed to tread, sit, or lie directly upon the ground. The *iri* was an artifact that Furneaux (or possibly Banks) had brought back from Tahiti. In the caste-based society of Tahiti, for a commoner like Mai to carry such an object reserved for royals would have been considered *tapu*, a subversive act, for which he could be severely punished, perhaps even killed.

WHEN HE WASN'T sitting for some of the finest artists in England, Mai frequented the city's taverns and gaming parlors and became something of a card sharp—he was supposed to be particularly cunning at whist. He had become a formidable chess player, too; when he checkmated Giuseppe Baretti, an eminent man of letters, the proud Italian refused to admit the loss, although many had witnessed the match in question. Said Baretti indignantly: "Do you think I should be conquered at chess *by a savage?*"

In due course, Mai met the most famous writer and public intellectual in Great Britain, Samuel Johnson, the inexhaustible author and compiler of *A Dictionary of the English Language*. Friends of Mai worried that the cantankerous critic, who had odd mannerisms and facial tics and probably suffered from Tourette's syndrome, would dismiss or ridicule his Polynesian visitor.

On the contrary, Johnson seemed impressed by Mai's innate sense of etiquette. "There is so little of the savage in Omai," Dr. Johnson asserted, although he added that this was no surprise, since Mai had "passed his time, while in England, only in the best company; so that all that he had acquired of our manners was genteel."

Mai had lived for a time with Joseph Banks, at his tall, narrow town house at 14 New Burlington Street, but then was furnished with his own place on Warwick Street, with the Crown giving him an allowance of five guineas a month. During the bleak winter months, he was often melancholy and homesick and could sometimes be heard crying out, lost and alone, as he wandered the cobblestone streets at night.

He didn't like the big city much, with its crime and noise, its fetid cesspools, and its residue of coal dusting everything. Yet the city very much liked him. Throughout much of 1775, Mai was considered "the lion of lions," noted Frances "Fanny" Burney, a prominent socialite and writer who would later enjoy acclaim for *Evelina* and other satirical novels. (She was the sister of Lieutenant James Burney, who had sailed with Cook on his second voyage and would also sign on for Cook's third.) At lunches, dinners, and other functions, Fanny Burney studied Mai and came to regard him as a living exhibit in support of the proposition, popularly advanced by Jean-Jacques Rousseau, that *natural man* could be every bit as decorous and cultivated as *civilized man*. Mai had "no tutor but nature," she wrote, but he "appears in a new world like a man who had all his life studied the Graces."

Burney was captivated by everything Mai said and did. She noted that he "committed not the slightest blunder at table, neither did he do anything awkwardly. He appears to be a perfectly rational and intelligent man, with an understanding far superior to the common race of us cultivated gentry."

EVERYONE IN LONDON, it seemed, had ideas about how Mai should be educated, and how he should spend his time. Those of a religious bent worried that Mai's soul had been neglected. European explorers had brought back accounts from Tahiti of human sacrifices, infanticide, and other heathen depravities, not to mention stories of debauched sexuality. Pious Christians throughout England thought that if he were returned to Tahiti with a solid religious training, Mai might spread the gospel to the islands and help end these appalling practices.

Others in London thought more emphasis should be placed on

Mai's basic education in letters and arithmetic, rather than on sports, games, and gentlemen's pursuits. It was widely said that Banks had turned Mai into a show pony for the entertainment of his posh friends.

These criticisms seem to have reached Banks, who decided that Mai should keep regular appointments with a well-known pedagogue named Granville Sharp, "to pour the light of divine truth into his ignorant and untutored mind," as one account put it. Sharp, a biblical scholar and a noted abolitionist, was supposed to teach the Polynesian how to write, while also imparting the rudiments of the Christian faith. Neither lesson plan was progressing very well—although Mai had shown himself to be solemn when exposed to the rituals and ceremonies of the Anglican Church. People found that, while he didn't understand the Christian religion, he was a deeply spiritual person and projected an abiding respect for the ways in which people all across England practiced their faith.

One day, Sharp was reviewing the Ten Commandments with Mai. Upon reaching the seventh stricture, "Thou shalt not commit adultery," Mai seemed confused.

"Adultery," he said. "What is that?"

Sharp endeavored to explain that it was contrary to God's wishes for a man to have two wives, or one wife and also a lover who is not his wife. The scholar probably knew from his readings that in Tahiti polygamy was not uncommon, and that the sin of adultery was a dim concept at best.

Mai interjected: "Two wives, very good. Three wives—very, *very* good!" Sharp tried to convince him otherwise, but it was no use. The best he could do was give Mai a big, elegant Bible with elaborate colored plates to bring home to the South Seas.

THE INSTITUTION THAT tried, perhaps more than any other, to roll out the red carpet for Mai while he was in the city was the Royal Society for Improving Natural Knowledge, which held weekly dinners at a famous place called the Mitre Tavern, on Fleet Street. Members of the esteemed conclave invited Mai to dinner at least ten times. The Royal Society, founded in 1660, included the cream of

England's cognoscenti—doctors, scientists, mathematicians, explorers, inventors, natural philosophers. The club's functions were regularly attended by Joseph Banks and Daines Barrington. Cook, too, was often a guest, and his formal nomination to the society was moving quickly toward full approval.

The Royal Society dinners were lavish events, and the bottles of claret and brandy flowed freely. But its members tended to be very sober-minded men. One fellow in particular, Sir John Cullum, a noted classicist, clergyman, and antiquarian, made an ongoing analytical study of Mai, as though the islander were some dancing bear unknown to science.

Mai, Cullum wrote, "is rather tall and slender, with a genteel make. He walks erect, and has acquired a tolerably genteel bow. He appears to have good natural parts." The Polynesian, he noted, often became distracted with "trifling amusements." At a Royal Society dinner, one of the fellows showed Mai a magnifying glass, a contrivance he'd never seen before. For much of the dinner, Mai toyed and fumbled with the glass, ogling various objects in the room. "He was perpetually pulling it out of his pocket, and looking at the candles etc. with excessive delight and admiration," wrote Cullum. "We all laughed at his simplicity, and yet probably the wisest person present would have wondered as much, if that knick-knack had then for the first time been presented to him."

AS THE DEPARTURE date for Cook's third expedition became further delayed, it was plain to all that Mai had grown deeply impatient to return home. The Polynesian wondered when Sandwich would arrange a ship. He kept asking Banks, "How many moons? How many moons?" and wore on his face a look of longing.

Banks, deciding he had to get Mai out of London to cheer him up, organized a carriage trip up the east coast of England. He and Mai and a party of several others—including a twelve-year-old boy named George Colman—climbed into Banks's enormous carriage. Eventually they reached the North Sea, stopping at the beach near Scarborough.

Mai peeled off most of his clothes and waded into the cold gray surf. In body-conscious England, public swimming was an exotic enterprise with an elaborate etiquette that involved special "bathing machines"—enclosed, horse-drawn wagons parked along the beach in which people changed into proper swimming attire and then were discreetly released into the breakers. Colman found it glorious how Mai ignored all this rigmarole and jumped in.

But Mai could see that the scrawny young boy was frightened—Colman didn't know how to swim. Tentatively, he hopped on Mai's back and they slipped into deeper water. Mai was "as much at home upon the waves as a rope-dancer upon a cord," Colman later wrote. The Polynesian was so steady and strong in the water that the lad's fears subsided—he rode on Mai's shoulders "as smoothly as Arion upon his dolphin." After more than a half hour in the brisk North Sea, Mai brought Colman safely to shore. The boy was laughing and grinning in the salt air, and so was Mai.

8   Fresh Discoveries

On June 8, seventeen blasts from the *Resolution*'s cannons boomed over the murk of the river. The Admiralty was holding a farewell dinner aboard the ship, which was docked east of London at a place called Long Reach, not far from where the Thames widens into its estuary. Lord Sandwich arrived by carriage, as did Hugh Palliser, other top brass from the Admiralty, and assorted noblemen. The crew, manning the yards, saluted the honored guests with three cheers.

On board, Lord Sandwich greeted Captains Cook and Clerke effusively. *How are you satisfied with your ship?* he asked.

Cook was pleasant but characteristically terse, reporting that all was well. Clerke agreed, telling Lord Sandwich, "Our equipment is in every way adequate to the voyage."

At first glance, the *Resolution* did appear to have been scrubbed and restored from her long, hard odyssey to the high southern latitudes. For the better part of a year, the engineers at the Deptford Dockyard had overhauled the ship and covered her hull with fresh copper sheathing attached with closely fitted nails to protect her against the bane of all wooden ships, the teredo worm (which was not a worm at all, but a species of boring mollusk).

Built in 1771, she was a three-masted collier ship of 462 tons, 110 feet long, 30 feet in the beam, squat, flat-bottomed, and square-sterned. One account described the *Resolution* as "stout as a publican's wife." The ship had little in the way of adornment, other than a figurehead of a prancing horse. Cook, who said he "had not one fault to allege against her," called the *Resolution* "the ship of my choice, and the fittest for service of any I have seen...remarkably stiff and dry and very easy in the sea." These Whitby-built "cats," the same kind of ships Cook had sailed while working in the merchant marine, were neither sleek nor pretty nor fast. They were said to be a "very dull sailing vessel." They dipped and wallowed and yawed, but they seldom capsized. And because they had such a shallow draft, they rarely scraped bottom or banged into rocks should they draw close to shore. Cats like the *Resolution* were sometimes also called barks, but the Admiralty lords seemed to think neither term possessed quite the romance or panache they were looking for in launching a grand voyage, and so they chose to formally redesignate them as "sloops."

Cook thought he knew his ship, but his optimism about its condition was misplaced. Over the past several months, he had been so immersed in writing his account of his second voyage that he found little time to inspect the work. He did not realize that the *Resolution* had been shoddily caulked and that other important repairs had been neglected altogether. The Deptford contractors had a reputation for being corrupt even in good times, but over the spring and early summer they had been unusually busy overhauling and outfitting transport ships headed for America to put down the revolt. The Admiralty, preoccupied with the deepening troubles in the colonies, had made the *Resolution* a low priority.

But Sandwich seemed pleased with Cook's positive assessment of the ship, and he expressed satisfaction. The feast began, the mingled aromas of fine food competing with the brackish stench of the river. The platters kept coming—according to one account, the menu included pigeon pie, Westmoreland ham, lobster, turbot, trout, and strawberries. The *Resolution* squatted in the Thames, creaking slightly in the wind, holding her secrets as the guests raised their glasses high. They offered toasts to Cook and his men, wished them Godspeed, and expressed the nation's hopes for their safe return.

IT WAS A festive celebration taking place at a benchmark moment in the curious ebb and flow of the British Empire. For even as England was struggling to keep its North American colonies, it was sending its preeminent explorer to the far side of the same continent, to scout and probe—and stake a claim. The news from New England had been grim all summer. British troops had been forced to abandon the town of Boston, and nearly every day the London papers carried reports of some new outrage committed by the rebels.

Throughout the colonies that summer, it had become fashionable to hold mock executions, trials, and funerals of George III. Insurgents in Philadelphia took to hanging public portraits of the monarch upside down. In Manhattan, a crowd toppled and beheaded an equestrian statue of George III; the statue ended up in Connecticut, where it was melted into bullets.

More and more, the Admiralty was gearing up for war, and its most experienced commanders were headed for American waters. In the midst of all the commotion and urgency, the launch of yet another exploratory expedition to the Pacific seemed an extraneous luxury, a quaint mission from another age.

The troubles in America created an undertow of doubt within London society. Was Great Britain expanding, or was she in decline? Or, more likely, were both things happening at the same time? That year saw the publication of the first volume of a colossal work, *The History of the Decline and Fall of the Roman Empire*, by a corpulent, gout-ridden Londoner named Edward Gibbon. The observations running through Gibbon's masterpiece echoed clangorously—and were acutely topical—among English readers.

"There is nothing perhaps more adverse to nature and reason,"

Gibbon wrote of imperial Rome's difficulties in maintaining her distant conquests, "than to hold in obedience remote countries... in opposition to their inclination and interest." To do so required a "refined system of policy and oppression," he noted, "to check the first effort of rebellion; and a well-disciplined army to inspire fear."

Such was the dynamic atmosphere out of which Cook's present expedition grew. His voyage was the exploratory offshoot of an empire that looked restlessly outward in quest of new lands, markets, resources, and trade routes. The possibility of losing the lucrative colonies in America seemed to presage the loss of other British possessions around the world. Adam Smith, the author of *The Wealth of Nations* (which was also published in 1776), noted how alarmed Great Britain had become by the escalating tensions across the Atlantic. "The expectation of a rupture with the colonies," he wrote, "has struck the people of Great Britain with more terror than they have ever felt for a Spanish armada, or a French invasion."

Cook was not inattentive to the historical ironies surrounding his voyage. England's energies, it seemed to him, were about evenly divided between growing the empire and maintaining it. With this expedition, England was beginning an endeavor "the object of which," as he put it, "was to benefit Europe by making fresh discoveries in North America." Yet at the same time, His Majesty's warships were being deployed "to secure the obedience of those parts of that continent which had been discovered and settled by our countrymen in the last century."

AS THE DATE for the *Resolution*'s departure neared, Cook found himself overwhelmed with the work of finishing his account of his second voyage. The task would have been difficult for anyone, but it was especially so for a man who considered himself uneducated and, though literate, certainly not literary. In Cook's own estimation, he had "neither natural, nor acquired abilities, for writing." Still, he believed it was important that he pen the work himself and not pass it off to a professional scribe, as had happened with the published account of his first voyage.

Although Cook's style was by no means polished, Sandwich and others within the Admiralty, after reading early samples of Cook's work, decided that he was a capable writer, refreshingly direct and down-to-earth. "The public," Cook wrote, "must not expect from me the elegance of a fine writer, or the plausibility of a professed book-maker, but will, I hope, consider me as a plain man, zealously exerting himself in the service of his country."

As it happened, Cook came close to having a "professed book-maker" join him for his third expedition. The Scottish lawyer and diarist James Boswell, future biographer of Dr. Samuel Johnson, had become friendly with Cook and was seized with a desire to sail aboard the *Resolution* to write his own account of the voyage.

One day Boswell dropped by Cook's house on Mile End Road and had a pleasant visit, sipping tea in the garden, while a blackbird trilled a song. Boswell would recall, "It was curious to see Cook, a grave, steady man, and his wife, a decent plump Englishwoman, and think that he was preparing to sail round the world." (Elizabeth was plump, Boswell failed to note, because she was quite advanced in her pregnancy.)

Now burning with the idea of joining Cook, the writer consulted his mentor, Samuel Johnson. But the ornery intellectual dissuaded his protégé from undertaking the journey. Johnson, a notorious homebody, could not imagine a more dreadful experience than voyaging on the high seas. "Being in a ship," he contended, "is being in a jail, with the chance of being drowned." Johnson thought all adventure narratives about primitive places were intrinsically unedifying. "Who will read them through?" he pressed Boswell. "There is little entertainment in such books."

In the end, to the detriment of the literature of exploration, a deflated Boswell decided to stay home.

9   The Secret Instructions

On June 23, the time had finally come for Cook to say goodbye to Elizabeth, their sons James and Nathaniel, and their swaddled, red-faced infant, Hugh, who was only six weeks old. The Cooks savored one last day and night together at their snug brick home in London's East End. It was a family he hardly knew—and a family he would never see again.

Amid the uncertainties of his departure, Cook could at least be assured that Elizabeth and their children would be provided for: Lord Sandwich had arranged for the Admiralty to send her a handsome stipend. "I cannot leave England without tak[ing] some method to thank your Lordship," Cook would write to Sandwich, "for the very liberal allowance made to Mrs. Cook during my absence. This, by enabling my family to live at ease and removing from them every fear of Indigence, has set my heart at rest."

The next morning, June 24, Lord Sandwich sent a carriage to collect Cook and Mai. The captain and the Polynesian departed Cook's house at six o'clock, just as London was stirring for another muggy summer day. They left the slop and coal dust of the city behind and sped overland through the rolling pastures of Kent. Cook and Mai rode thirty-eight miles from London to the Chatham Dockyard. The ride took more than five hours, and inside the jouncing carriage, gazing out over the English countryside for the last time, Mai seemed in a chipper mood. Cook thought Mai was "fully sensible of the good treatment he had met with in England and entertained the highest ideas of the country and people." The London *General Evening Post* reported that Mai had had a farewell card printed and circulated among his English friends. "Omiah to take leave of good friend[s]," the card reportedly said. "He never forget England. God bless King George."

At Chatham, a navy official threw Cook and Mai a dinner and took them by private yacht to the royal dockyard at Sheerness, where the *Resolution* was moored. Cook and Mai boarded, joining a skeleton crew already on the ship. On the morning of the twenty-fifth, Cook weighed anchor, steered past the Nore, a sandbank at the mouth of the Thames estuary, and eased into the cold gray swells of the North Sea. He turned south and entered the English Channel. On the twenty-sixth, when the *Resolution* briefly stopped off the port of Deal to take delivery of two boats, Mai found that he, not Cook, was the man of the hour—well-wishers had assembled on shore to give the

Polynesian a final farewell. Cook steered the ship past Portsmouth, arriving in Plymouth on June 30. Along the complex of wharves and piers there, the tedious process of gathering the final stores and filling the holds of both the *Resolution* and the *Discovery* could begin in earnest.

Throughout the week, laborers hoisted hundreds of casks of water aboard and countless puncheons of beer, wine, and rum, as well as supplies of salted meats, molasses, sauerkraut, and hardtack biscuits. Crates filled with books and charts and various meteorological and navigational instruments—including the prized K1 chronometer—arrived on the docks, compliments of the Board of Longitude. More than a hundred men would take up residence on the *Resolution:* carpenters, coopers, sailmakers, cooks, blacksmiths, gunner's mates, quartermasters, midshipmen, and dozens of able seamen. A contingent of twenty red-coated Royal Marines, under the command of Lieutenant Molesworth Phillips, sauntered aboard with their muskets. Phillips was a stout, hotheaded man who, according to one account, "came from Ireland and suffered all the advantages and disadvantages of that fact."

Then came the animals, blatting, squawking, shrieking: sheep, geese, goats, cattle, hogs, rabbits, turkeys, chickens, peacocks. The creatures, nearly fifty in all, were herded onto both ships, with enough feed and fodder to sustain them for several months. Cook was none too happy to see them; he did not particularly want to play the role of Noah, and he realized what a nuisance the noisy beasts would create and what a stench they would give off as the ship sailed through roiling seas. He had brought modest assortments of farm animals along on his previous voyages, but this time around, thanks to King George's zoological passions, animals were to assume a major role in the whole operation.

As the dockhands continued loading the *Resolution,* numerous intrigues, real or imagined, swirled in the shadows: It was assumed that the French and the Spanish had spies watching the wharves at Plymouth. Few European diplomats believed for a moment that the object of Cook's mission was merely to return a young Polynesian man to his home island. The French agent in London suspected that

Cook's voyage involved a plan to conspire with the Russians in Kamchatka to conquer Japan. The court of Madrid, on the other hand, hypothesized that Cook's expedition aimed to seize Spanish possessions along the coast of Alta California. The Spaniards would order the viceroy of Mexico to arrest and imprison Cook should he be encountered anywhere in California's waters.

Daines Barrington, the theoretician behind the voyage, was outraged by Madrid's distrust. The Spanish, he wrote, should be "convinced that the English Nation is actuated merely by desiring to know as much as possible with regard to the planet which we inhabit." Still, the Admiralty, aware of Spain's aroused suspicions, ordered Cook to play it safe. He was "not to touch upon any part of the Spanish dominions on the western continent of America" and should be "very careful not to give any umbrage or offense to any inhabitants or subjects of His Catholic Majesty."

On July 6, Plymouth bustled with activity of a more forthrightly military nature. That day, as press gangs worked the docks, a squadron of ships packed with hundreds of conscripted soldiers, as well as a division of mercenary troops from Germany, left Plymouth for the colonies. Cook noted their departure in his journal: "His Majesty's ships *Diamond, Ambuscade,* and *Unicorn,* with a fleet of transports consisting of 62 sail bound to America, with the last division of Hessian troops and some horses, were forced into the Sound by a strong northwest wind."

Two days earlier, across the Atlantic, representatives of the thirteen American colonies, meeting in Philadelphia, had signed their Declaration of Independence. The document, drafted by Thomas Jefferson, accused King George of numerous "injuries and usurpations" and insisted that he had "plundered our seas, ravaged our coasts, burnt our towns," and "excited domestic insurrections amongst us." The document went on to assert that the monarch's character was "marked by every act which may define a tyrant" and declared that George III was "unfit to be a ruler of a free people."

Six American men were recorded in the *Resolution*'s muster book, hailing from such diverse birthplaces as Pennsylvania, Connecticut, and Charleston, South Carolina. One of the Americans who would serve on board Cook's ship claimed to have fought the British in Boston's Battle of Bunker Hill. The feisty young man—whose name is uncertain—said he'd been injured twice during the fighting, and he had the scars to prove it.

The most interesting of the Americans was a footloose young marine from Connecticut named John Ledyard. As a teenager, Ledyard had spent time at Dartmouth College, but, finding the curriculum stifling, he fashioned his own dugout canoe and solo-paddled much of the Connecticut River. After several nautical journeys, one to Gibraltar and the Barbary Coast, Ledyard had been pressed into the Royal Navy and somehow found his way to the *Resolution*.

COOK'S OFFICERS WERE taking their places aboard ship. Foremost among them, in rank, was John Gore, another American, Virginia-born, and a seasoned navy veteran. Gore would serve as the *Resolution*'s first lieutenant. He had a fair complexion and thin strands of red hair. Gore, forty-six, had thrice circumnavigated the world and had helped lead a notable Royal Society research expedition, led by Joseph Banks, to Iceland. He had served aboard the *Endeavour* on Cook's first voyage and was in tune with the captain's temperament. Among his more dubious exploits, Gore, while in Australia, had become the first person to shoot and kill a kangaroo with a firearm.

Other notable officers and specialists included the *Resolution*'s surgeon, William Anderson, a Scot who would turn out to be an excellent naturalist and ethnologist; William Bayly, who would serve as the expedition's astronomer; David Nelson, an accomplished green thumb from Kew Gardens, who would collect and describe plants for the expedition; and John Webber, a young artist from Switzerland, who would brilliantly document the expedition on sketchpads and later on canvas. There was also surgeon's assistant David Samwell, a Welshman, lyrical and lewd, who would prove to be the most gifted writer on the voyage. The *Resolution*'s second lieutenant was James King, variously described as gentle, kind, fastidious, and a polished intellectual. King had joined the navy at the age of twelve but had also studied at Oxford and had traveled to France. Although he was only twenty-six years old, about half Cook's age, he would become one of the captain's closest friends, and a confidant, throughout the voyage.

Finally, there was a remarkable young officer, only twenty-three at the time, who would serve as master of the *Resolution*: William Bligh. He was a severe man with a wan face set with penetrating eyes. He had a sharp chin and a thin, tight mouth that rarely formed into a smile. Much like Cook, he was known for his extraordinary skills as a mariner and a surveyor of coastlines. Bligh was fiercely competent, but at times he could be a martinet and something of a prude. He had an acid tongue, a thin skin, and a tendency to make dogmatic pronouncements that others found deeply annoying, although he was usually right. Eleven years later, Bligh would serve as captain of the HMS *Bounty*, which was dispatched to Tahiti on a botanical expedition, and would become the victim of perhaps the most storied mutiny in history—though Bligh and those still loyal to him would survive after he piloted an extraordinary four-thousand-mile journey across the Pacific in an open boat.

It was a testament to Cook's reputation that so many talented officers had signed on for the voyage during a time of war, when there was much prestige and a high potential for career advancement to be won in America. Lower-ranking men who'd sailed with Cook before also signed on in large numbers. More than twenty men on the voyage had served on either Cook's first or second voyage—or both. Cook engendered that sort of loyalty. Crewmen who'd journeyed with him knew what was in store; he fostered a safe, steady, and predictable atmosphere. One of his loyalists, oddly enough, was someone who could have harbored a lifelong grudge: Sergeant Samuel Gibson of the marines. On Cook's first visit to Tahiti, Gibson had quit the ship and disappeared with a Native lady into the island's interior jungles. The crime of desertion was considered egregious. Cook had Gibson tracked down and flogged. Yet here he was, signing on for another voyage with Cook.

As with all of Cook's expeditions, the dangers and risks would be significant. Cook's men could expect stifling conditions, weevily slops of food, and exposure to many lethal diseases. Given the mission's audacious plan to sweep through distant uncharted waters, it was highly plausible that the ship would not return home. Still, the best naval officers and some of the brighter young minds of English society had lined up once again to be part of it. The captain was forced to turn away many accomplished applicants.

Cook had grown tired of gentleman scientists and had decided to have mostly military professionals on board, with as few civilian "supernumeraries" as possible. This third voyage would be slightly different from the first two, less about natural science, botany, and biology and more about the straightforward navigational quest to find a waterway through North America. On the first two voyages, Cook had learned much from the natural scientists, members of the "botanical gentry," as they were sometimes called. He had soaked up their modes of inquiry and, to some extent, their style. Men like Joseph Banks could be entertaining, but they also caused a lot of bothersome drama. On this voyage, Cook didn't want such distractions. When he was asked why so few scientists would take part in his third expedition, Cook is said to have retorted, in obvious overstatement, "Curse the scientists, and all science into the bargain."

IN A NEARBY berth, the *Discovery* was also being prepared for departure. The *Resolution*'s sister ship was another Whitby-built cat, squat and boxy. At ninety-one feet in length and 298 tons, she was the smallest ship used by Cook in all his voyages, and also the newest, having been purchased only eighteen months after she was built. *Discovery* would take on sixty-seven officers and men, and abundant stores.

But the ship faced a glaring problem: Her captain, Charles Clerke, was nowhere to be seen. Some months earlier, Clerke had learned that his older brother, Sir John Clerke, a captain in the Royal Navy, had defaulted on loans totaling £4,000, then sailed from England to India. John Clerke was a respected figure in the navy, but he had lost great sums of money on a flawed wine importation enterprise, among other schemes. Charles Clerke loved his improvident brother dearly, and had agreed to serve as his guarantor. Because his brother had absconded, with no intention of repaying his creditors, Charles had been arrested and obliged to report to a notorious debtors' jail known as King's Bench Prison, in south London.

It was a depressing and overcrowded place—a census taken in the summer of 1776 reported that nearly fourteen hundred people were living within the facility's high walls; there were no infirmaries or baths, and diseases like typhus and tuberculosis were rampant. The prison offered little in the way of recreation, only some cheerless courts where detainees could while away the days playing marbles or racket sports.

Clerke, like many inmates, was allowed to leave during daylight hours to attend to his affairs but was required to report back to the foul bastille by dusk and lodge there each night. So far, despite the Admiralty's assiduous efforts, the authorities had refused to let him go. It wasn't clear whether he would ever be released. Clerke considered shirking his responsibilities and making a run for it—"to decamp without beat of drum," as he put it—but then he thought better of it. Though he was a cheerful man, a deepening pessimism had crept into his thoughts. As he wrote despairingly to Joseph Banks, "There's a fatality attends my every undertaking."

Cook, growing more impatient with the delays, was beginning to wonder if he would have to depart England without his consort ship. Clerke, if released, would have to assume a hasty command of the *Discovery* and race down the Atlantic in the hope of catching up with Cook at some agreed-upon stop in the southern hemisphere.

While the two ships lingered in the harbor, Cook gave Mai spending money of three guineas and sent him into town, where he enjoyed one last fling of his celebrity—it was gossiped, too, that he consorted with one of Plymouth's prostitutes. It seemed everybody wanted to meet the famous Polynesian before he left England for good. Mai was "in high spirits," Cook thought, "indeed he could hardly be otherwise for he is very much caressed here by every person of note."

But Cook sensed that Mai was leaving England with some regrets. "When he talked about England and about those who during his stay had honored him with their protection or friendship,"

Cook wrote, "I could observe that his spirits were sensibly affected and that it was with difficulty he could refrain from tears."

On the *Resolution*, laborers had completed the task of loading Mai's belongings—a burdensome cargo that included an arsenal of muskets, much crockery and kitchenware, an "electrical machine," a jack-in-the-box, and a globe of the earth. King George and Lord Sandwich very much wanted Mai to have all this stuff—they were not only presents but talismanic artifacts meant to broadcast among the Tahitians a sense of the awesome strength and ingenuity of English society.

The king had also assembled a pile of presents that Mai was supposed to distribute among the Tahitian royalty. These included broadswords, telescopes, cut-glass bowls, laced hats, and handkerchiefs stitched with the words GREAT BRITAIN. Cook thought that every method had been employed to make Mai "the instrument of carrying to the islands of the Pacific Ocean the most exalted opinion of the greatness and generosity of the British nation."

ON JULY 8, Captain Cook received his "secret instructions" for the voyage, which the Admiralty had sent by express mail from London. These orders bore no surprises, as Cook had been actively involved in planning and advising the entire voyage—he "virtually drew up his own instructions," said one historian. Some accounts say Cook opened the sealed packet then and there and studied the long, ornate document.

The first goal of the expedition, after sailing around the Cape of Good Hope and proceeding to the Pacific, was to transport Mai back to Tahiti, along with his belongings and the stock of animals provided by King George. "Upon your arrival in Tahiti or the Society of Isles," the instructions read, "you are to land Omai at such of them as he may choose, and to leave him there."

Cook was then to steer north and east, aiming for the Pacific coast of North America, which was vaguely known as New Albion. Along the way, should he find any new lands, he was to claim them for England. "With the consent of the natives," the Admiralty ordered him, "you are to take possession in the name of the King of Great

Britain . . . and to distribute among the inhabitants such things as will remain as traces and testimonies of your having been there."

But then the real purpose of the expedition would click into place: "Upon your arrival on the coast of North America," the instructions read, "you are very carefully to search for and to explore such rivers and inlets as may appear to be of considerable extent, and pointing toward Hudson's or Baffin's bays." Should Cook find any promising inlets, he was to use his "utmost endeavors to pass through with one or both of the sloops."

This search was envisioned to take two years, perhaps longer. "Having discovered such passage or failed in the attempt," Cook was ordered to make his way back to England with both sloops, "by such route as you may think best for the improvement of geography and navigation."

ON JULY 12, Cook, frustrated over Clerke's delays, decided he could wait no longer. He left orders for Clerke to meet him in Cape Town, more than five thousand miles away. Now the officers and men of the *Resolution*, 112 in all, would bid England adieu.

It was four years earlier, to the very day, that the *Resolution* had left this same port to embark upon Cook's second trip around the world. His men fancied this coincidence as an auspicious sign that they would safely return home, just as the *Resolution*'s previous crew had. "The singularity of the circumstance," wrote Lieutenant James King, "made us look upon it as an omen of a like prosperous voyage." Shortly after noon, Cook hauled up his anchor and nosed down the sound, in desultory winds. The ship, her sails slowly beginning to fill, passed Drake's Island and the cragged coastline of the Rame Peninsula. That evening, in the glow cast by the chandelier of twenty-four large tallow candles hung within the Eddystone Lighthouse, the *Resolution* stood out to sea.

BOOK TWO

The Weight of My Resentment

Seek out distant horizons, and cherish those you attain.

—Māori proverb

10 *Isla del Infierno*

After three weeks at sea, the men of the *Resolution* spied a massive peak far out in the green vapor of the Atlantic. It was Mount Teide, a snow-sugared volcano, which at just over twelve thousand feet was the highest point on Tenerife, the largest of the Spanish Canary Islands. The men could see it for days as they approached the island.

Although he had been underway only a very short while, Cook was impatient to land. So far it had been a miserable, slow sail. Only hours after leaving Plymouth, squalls had begun to punish the *Resolution*. Surly seas and slanting rains revealed the poor workmanship that had been performed at Deptford. Rain and seawater gushed through gaps in the caulking. The sailrooms and storerooms became saturated. After a few more days at sea, everything belowdecks was turning clammy and sour with mildew. The men, swinging tightly in their hammocks, couldn't get dry. Cook was thoroughly disgusted. The *Resolution*, he wrote, was "exceedingly leaky in all her upper works... There was hardly a man who could lie dry in his bed."

Cook did his best to combat the moisture by "smoking" the ship between decks. This was a common technique widely believed to improve hygiene on long voyages. Small fires, sometimes fueled by gunpowder sprinkled with vinegar, were lit throughout the interiors of the ship. The stinging black smoke was thought to disinfect the timbers, purify the air, arrest the progress of mildew and mold, and, in secured holds, kill rats and other vermin. The smoking procedure may have helped some, but it likely did as much harm as good—clogging the sailors' lungs as it did with tar and acrid soot. Of probably greater efficacy was Cook's insistence that the men haul up their bedding, clothes, and other articles on clear days to aerate in the sunshine and the strong salt breeze.

Cook understood that disease sprang from the filth that was so prevalent, and often tolerated, on so many ships of the day. "He was particularly cleanly," wrote a young German seaman, Heinrich Zimmermann, "and the whole crew had to follow his example. On Sundays, every man had to don fresh clothing." Woe to the man who didn't obey his protocols. "He was very strict and hot tempered," thought Zimmermann, and "unyielding where the ships' rules were concerned."

On the afternoon of July 24, the *Resolution* had passed the northwesternmost cape of the Iberian Peninsula, a rocky land the Romans had named Finisterre—the "end of the earth." From Cape Finisterre, in close, gloomy weather, Cook steered south for the Canary Islands and the volcano at Tenerife. He and his drenched men were thrilled to arrive in the sunny port of Santa Cruz, the largest town on Tenerife. A French frigate rode at anchor in the azure harbor, as did a miscellany of Spanish vessels and an English brigantine bound for Senegal. A stone pier ran out to sea, and a crescent beach glimmered nearby. Behind the town, a wooden aqueduct carried a steady rivulet of fresh water down from the foothills.

The Spanish had colonized Tenerife in 1496, and over the centuries its Indigenous population, the Guanches, who originally hailed from North Africa, had intermarried with the Spanish to create a vibrant creole culture of fishermen and merchants. Tenerife had long been a stopping station for extended voyages, and the crew were eager to see its sights. After dropping anchor, Cook was rowed ashore and met with the island's officials. The governor was friendly enough, but Cook didn't seem to think much of the place. The oxen there were "small and bony," he thought, and compared with the celebrated wines of nearby Madeira, Tenerife's offerings, though cheap, were subpar. In his estimation, the island looked barren and bleached, its alkaline soils incapable of growing much of anything.

Yet to his surprise, he was able to purchase large quantities of fresh produce: pumpkins, onions, potatoes, grapes, figs, pears, mulberries, plantains, and muskmelons, as well as hay for the many animals on board his ship. He also managed to buy a large supply of American-grown corn.

Most of the men were relieved to disembark from the water-logged ship and seemed to enjoy themselves in the port of Santa Cruz—though an anti-Spanish, anti-Catholic bias, typical of the times, seeped through the diaries. William Anderson, the ship's surgeon, made a slightly more open-minded study of the island. He became intrigued by some of the fruits that grew on Tenerife, including something he called an "impregnated lemon," which he described as "a perfect and distinct lemon enclosed within another." The countryside thrummed with wildlife—parrots, dragonflies, partridges, geckos and other lizards. Anderson, with a few col-leagues, hired mules and rode up to La Laguna, a quaint town with winding cobblestone streets, its outskirts scented with aloe plants in brilliant bloom.

"The road was very bad and the mules most indifferent," Ander-son groused, but he was enchanted with the local guides, who con-stantly laughed and sang songs. He was impressed with Tenerife's pure air and dry climate, which he thought would be beneficial for anyone suffering from tuberculosis. He met a well-informed local gentleman who "expressed his surprise that English physicians should never have thought of sending their consumptive patients to Tenerife instead of Lisbon or Nice."

In the distance to the south, seemingly inescapable from any angle, the Teide volcano loomed, tendrils of smoke issuing from its summit. Old maps referred to Tenerife as the Isla del Infierno—the Island of Hell. High above its pine forests was a world of sulfur and steam. Its lava fields were known to shudder with seismic activity, and fumaroles spewed noxious gases. The volcano's considerable elevation made Tenerife the tenth-highest island on earth.

Mai appeared to enjoy himself on Tenerife. The men of the *Resolution* were curious what the Polynesian thought of the tawny-skinned Spaniards, their mores and mannerisms. Mai observed, to the dismay of some of his fellow voyagers, that the Spanish differed little from the English. He only noted that, with their darker skin, the people of Tenerife reminded him of Tahitians.

THAT SAME WEEK, as the *Resolution* replenished her stores at Tenerife, her sister ship, HMS *Discovery*, departed England, with seventy souls on board. Its captain, Charles Clerke, had finally been released from debtors' prison. He made haste for Plymouth and paused only one day before setting sail, in high hopes of catching up with Cook. "I shall get hold of him I fear not," he wrote. "Huzza my boys and heave away."

Through the month of August 1776, the *Discovery* made good headway. Clerke's ship was better caulked than the *Resolution,* and his men stayed drier than Cook's men had as they yawed and pounded south through high seas and repeated squalls. A few instances of smallpox were reported, as were numerous cases of what Clerke called the "French pox"—another name for syphilis—but for the most part his men stayed healthy. Clerke seemed to be in good health, too, and in high spirits. What he didn't know was that in the squalid prison where he had just spent several weeks, some sickly inmate's cough or sneeze had infected him and he had contracted a disease, the same malady that Dr. Anderson had discussed while on Tenerife: tuberculosis.

By all appearances, Clerke was still a vigorous man, only thirty-five years old. He was full of hope and excitement to begin the journey—finally in command of his own ship, even if he wasn't in command of the entire voyage. But in the tubules and sacs of his lungs, the bacilli were multiplying, and as Clerke would soon learn, one of the world's deadliest pathogens was taking hold of him.

AFTER THREE DAYS at Tenerife, Captain Cook weighed anchor and turned the *Resolution* south, in the direction of the Cape Verdes, a cluster of rugged volcanic islands off the coast of Senegal that had been colonized by the Portuguese. The days were uneventful, marked by the occasional appearance of porpoises breaching the water or flying fish hurling themselves across the ship—and sometimes thudding right onto the deck.

On the evening of August 10, the lookout spotted Boa Vista, the easternmost island of the Cape Verde archipelago. Boa Vista was a hot, dry place, much of it desert and dunes, that was known for its large turtle populations and its long, golden beaches.

It was also known for its shipwrecks. Cook was aware that submerged rocks were scattered about the island, and his charts indicated the locations of the worst hazards. But later that evening, as the *Resolution* approached the southeast shores of Boa Vista, Cook failed to see the froth in the waters ahead: The ship was making straight for a reef that could easily smash the hull to pieces.

Part of the problem was Cook's risky decision to approach Boa Vista at night—if he had held off and waited until morning, he probably would have had plenty of time to react. Belatedly spotting the hazard and recognizing the severity of his predicament, Cook gave out a cry of *"Hard-a-starboard!"* The ship made a mad correction and assumed a position parallel to the breakers, but she was still not out of danger. A powerful swell continued to drive the *Resolution* toward the sunken boulders. Anderson, who had no experience as a sailor, fretted for his life. "For the space of ten minutes," he wrote, "I thought it utterly impossible we should avoid striking on the rocks."

Cook, in his own terse account, conceded that for a few minutes "our situation...was very alarming." But after a series of desperate maneuvers, he managed to escape the reef and sail the *Resolution* clear of danger. Cook shrugged off the incident and said nothing more about it in his journal.

Still, it was a sobering close call so early in the voyage. A near collision in well-charted waters seemed a glaring mistake out of character for the competent and risk-averse captain. In one catastrophic instant, the expedition would have ended and the lives of all 112 men on the *Resolution* would have been in peril. Anderson wondered whether the apparent lapse in seamanship was a onetime aberration or an indication of something deeper—revealing, perhaps, a change in Cook's state of mind. Had he become cavalier? Had he lost track of the ship's location? Was he distracted by something else?

Anderson was scathing in his journal: "To bring a ship into so alarming a situation as we were in at this time without being able to give a satisfactory reason for it certainly deserves the severest reprehension." In the end, Anderson decided the incident had been caused by a certain complacency born of overconfidence: The captain's wealth of experience had led the crewmen, in turn, to let their guard down. The near collision, the surgeon wrote, "proceeded from too accurate a knowledge which often renders us too secure."

CLERKE'S *DISCOVERY* WORKED her way past Spain and Portugal, then hastened down the coast of North Africa in pursuit of Cook. The ship was doing well and catching up, but on September 1, heavy weather bore down on her. Lieutenant John Rickman, though he tended toward hyperbole, penned the most eloquent passages during this stretch of the *Discovery*'s journey. Rickman described the approaching storm as a "dreadful tempest" and said that at any moment "we expected to be swallowed up." The waves were gargantuan, larger than any Captain Clerke had ever seen, and at certain moments the *Discovery* seemed in peril. The gale carried off her topgallant yard and tore away the jib and middle staysails. Other sails were "frittered in a thousand pieces," as Rickman put it. All hands were sent to the pump. Much of the next day was devoted to redressing the damage and, said Rickman, "discharging the water which had been shipped as well from the heavens, as from the sea."

Passably repaired, the *Discovery* continued on toward the south. The men noticed a distinct increase in the number of dorsal fins swirling about the ship. The vessel had created its own ecosystem: Garbage and human waste, strewn overboard, had attracted small fish, which had lured larger fish, which, in turn, had brought sharks. Clerke's crew, having grown sick of dried biscuits and tinned meats, put out fishing lines, and they caught a monster. Wrote Rickman: "When he was cut up, there were six young ones found in his belly, about two feet long each. These were divided among the officers and one was dressed for the great cabin. The old one was eaten by the ship's crew, to whom fresh food of any kind was now become a dainty."

Later, Rickman became fascinated by the spectacle of flying fish. He loved watching "their numberless windings and shiftings to elude the attacks of the dolphins and bonitos, their declared ene-mies." Rickman decided that, despite their gift for leaping, flying fish were a marked species. "Whatever may be the design of providence in the formation of these fishes," he wrote, "one cannot help consid-ering their existence as a state of perpetual punishment."

While nature has "given them the power to quit [one] element, and to fly for refuge to the open air, yet other prosecutors are there in wait for them who are no less cruel than those they have escaped. Boobies, man-of-war birds, and other sea fowl are continually watch-ing to make flying fish their prey, while the ravenous sharks are no less vigilant in making reprisals on the dolphins and bonitos."

Rickman decided he hated the doldrums of the low latitudes—"nothing could be more tedious and disagreeable than this calm," he said. And underneath its seeming placidity, one encountered a good deal of carnage. As they drew closer to the equator, Rickman's firm opinion was that, even in its most languorous patches, the Atlantic Ocean was a cruel place. "A passage through the tropical latitudes, in this sea," he mused, "exhibits one continued scene of warfare."

A graphic illustration of Rickman's proposition played out around dusk one evening a few weeks later. A young marine corporal named George Harrison was idly perched on the bowsprit, passing the time by watching the darting fish. Harrison lost his foothold and tumbled overboard. Others saw him splash into the sea, and the ship instantly hove to. Clerke ordered a small boat to be launched, with five men. The boat traced a wide circuit around the area, in hopes of rescuing him, but Harrison had vanished. As Rickman put it, "He was never again seen to rise." All they found was his Dutch cap, floating on the surface.

Harrison was said to be a solid marine—"young, sober, and of good character." He was also known to be a strong swimmer. This led the men of the *Discovery* to one inescapable conclusion. As Rick-man put it: "It is more than probable that [he was] swallowed up by the sharks that constantly attend the ship."

In accordance with naval protocol, Harrison's personal effects were auctioned off six days later.

———

AFTER CAPTAIN COOK'S near disaster off Boa Vista, the *Resolution* passed by the island of Maio and touched at Porto da Praia, on Santiago Island, the largest of the Cape Verdes, where he made a cursory search for the *Discovery*. Before leaving England, he had reported to Clerke that he would stop at Porto da Praia, and he thought it remotely possible that his consort ship had leapfrogged him on the way south and might be waiting for him there. But, finding no signs of the *Discovery* in the Cape Verdes, Cook continued on. In search of more favorable winds, he swung far out into the open Atlantic, in the direction of Brazil.

Out on the heavy seas, the rain came down in torrents. This was good and bad—Cook was able to fill his empty water casks, but he also had to fight anew the vexing problem of leaks. The ship was a sieve—the men could see daylight peeking through some of the seams. First Lieutenant John Gore quipped that he'd just as soon venture out "in a ship built of ginger bread."

At least the winds had begun to cooperate. Cook caught the easterly trades north of the equator, and sturdy breezes filled the *Resolution*'s sails. Tracking southwest across the Atlantic, the ship finally made good progress. There were wonders to behold—in the sea and in the sky. At night, the men watched meteors arcing across the bowl of the stars above and marveled at mysterious patches of glittering water, probably caused by chains of bioluminescent salps, tiny gelatinous invertebrates often mistaken for jellyfish. As the ship approached the equator, sunsets became curiously abrupt, as though a lamp had been snuffed out; when the sun dropped into the sea, darkness would descend with scarcely any twilight. This was because at extremely low latitudes the sun sets not at an oblique angle, but perpendicular to the horizon.

Sometimes, on calm days, stultified by the creak of the ship's wood and the sigh of the cordage, the crew plunked fishing lines into the water, hoping to catch something to supplement their diet. Here Mai turned out to have the magic touch. Wrote Cook: "Omai first showed us the way and caught twice the number of anybody besides." No one could figure out what Mai's secret was—he simply used a rod and a white fly—but he just seemed to have a sense for the water, for the play of the wind and the currents, and was particularly adept at landing sharks.

Most of the men of the *Resolution* had begun to warm up to Mai. He could be vain and fanciful, and his bumptious energy could be annoyingly childlike at times, but he was brave and he laughed loudly and often. The men were taken by his constant good.

Some members of the expedition, like surgeon's assistant David Samwell, initially had doubts about Mai. Though willing to admit that he was a "droll animal" who "causes a good deal of merriment on board," Samwell felt that Mai had learned almost nothing during his two years in England except how to play cards—"at which," the Welshman conceded, "he is very expert."

Samwell also found Mai naive, overly attuned to portents and omens. When a shooting star blazed across the night sky, headed toward the north, Mai pointed to it, exclaiming that it was "God going to England." The crew ridiculed him for talking gibberish, but Mai, growing resentful, insisted he was right. "Like all ignorant people," Samwell declared, he was "very superstitious."

On September 1, the *Resolution* passed over the equator, and for Cook this illustrious occasion called for a ceremony that was itself steeped in a bit of superstition. The Royal Navy had an old and rather silly initiation rite called "ducking," and Cook intended to carry it out. The captain gathered all hands who had never crossed the equator before—there were thirty-five in all—and offered them a choice: They must either surrender their ration of rum for some number of days or submit to an ocean immersion—a ducking. Alcohol being a cherished substance among sailors, most of the initiates opted for the latter. (Cook, of course, was exempt from the ritual—by then he had already crossed the equator five times.)

Each of the greenhorns was tied to the yardarm of the mainmast and dropped into the ocean three times. It may have seemed like harmless horseplay, but this mariner's hazing could be dangerous: Men were sometimes injured, and accidental drownings were not uncommon, for few of the mariners knew how to swim. One would think it a prerequisite of navy enrollment, but throughout the ranks a popular notion held that knowing how to keep oneself afloat only prolonged the agony; once thrown overboard, the thinking went, it was better to submit to the inevitable and drown quickly than to struggle and writhe in vain.

Master Bligh, who at the tender age of twenty-two was already playing the role of a curmudgeonly killjoy, took a dim view of this line-crossing foolishness. "We had the vile practice of ducking put in execution to afford some fun," he wrote, "and to my great surprise most chose to be ducked rather than pay a bottle of rum." Dr. Anderson was similarly disdainful of the practice—he called it an "old ridiculous ceremony ... which every sensible person who has it in his power ought to suppress instead of encouraging."

Luckily, the hazing went off without any accidents, and thirty-five neophytes to the southern hemisphere were baptized.

Cook seemed to delight in the ritual, and that day he was very much his old self. But the veterans from Cook's earlier voyages were gradually beginning to think this was a different man from the storied captain who had so ably led two celebrated voyages of discovery. It wasn't just the near catastrophe off Boa Vista that caused people to wonder; there was something else. Cook had changed. He seemed restless and preoccupied. There was a peremptory tone, a raw edge in some of his dealings. Perhaps he had started to believe his own celebrity. Or perhaps, showing his age and the long toll of so many rough miles at sea, he had become less tolerant of the hardships and drudgeries of transoceanic sailing.

He seemed tired. That, at least, was the opinion of the venerable New Zealand scholar J. C. Beaglehole, who wrote a definitive Cook biography and is considered one of the man's most admiring defenders. Of the third voyage, Beaglehole wrote, "We have a man tired, not physically in any observable way, but with that almost imperceptible blunting of the brain that makes him, under a light searching enough, a perceptibly rather different man." It was as though the strains and stresses of the previous voyage were finally catching up with Cook. This was certainly true of his vessel, for the *Resolution* was revealing her many cracks and flaws. She was, wrote one Cook scholar, a "tired ship, commanded by a tired man."

At times Cook appeared to be in a good deal of pain, plagued by several ailments including some undiagnosed neurological condition (possibly sciatica). To deal with it, it has been suggested that he may have taken opiates, to which he conceivably could have become addicted—but that is nothing more than speculation. Others have conjectured that he was afflicted by a diseased gall bladder and had serious problems with his bowels—caused, perhaps, by a colonization of coliform bacteria or a parasitic infection tracing back to spoiled fish he may have eaten while on his second voyage. Still others have surmised that he suffered from a vitamin B deficiency.

Whatever the case, his officers were noticing subtle shifts in his mood and command style. He had become erratic, and at times tyrannical. Cook was known as humane and reasonable. But increasingly, he, too, began to dole out the lashes, the bread-and-water treatment, and other punishments. As he headed into the southern hemisphere once again, it appeared to some that Cook's judgment—and his legendary equanimity—had begun to falter.

THE *RESOLUTION*, PUSHING deeper into the torpid air well south of the equator, drew within a hundred miles of the coast of Brazil, then altered course abruptly and, catching fresh westerly winds, swooped back across the Atlantic toward the southeast. It was as though she'd been flung by a slingshot. August turned to September and, as Cook approached the African continent, birds began to clutter the sky: pintados, noddies, then an albatross. For days and nights, the feathered opportunists stalked the ship—sometimes taking up residence in the rigging and dropping down onto the decks to scrounge for scraps.

The ocean seemed different, as did the atmosphere, the sea life, and the weather. In the evening, the constellations were different, too. Cook and his men were on the southern tilt of the planet, with night skies that Cook, a meticulous astronomer, knew almost as well as the ones he had grown up with. Drawing closer to the southern African coast, the ocean grew chill and became choked with sea wrack, and the men spotted penguins bobbing on the swells.

11   Tavern of the Seas

CAPE TOWN, OCTOBER 1776

Table Mountain loomed over the bay, a blunt slab of sandstone roiled in mist. At the foot of the mountain, a village shone in the African sunshine. Stately pollarded myrtles and oaks lined its roads. Along the ridges, troops of baboons scrabbled through the brush, and the occasional lion could be heard roaring from a distant ravine. The Castle of Good Hope, a granite bastion built in the shape of a star, squatted at the blue water's edge, protecting the wares and secrets of the Dutch United East India Company.

Kaapstad, or Cape Town, was known as the "tavern of the seas." It was a well-established meeting place and replenishing station at the bottom of the continent, a midway point for ships plying the spice route between Holland and the East Indies. Nearly every vessel that rounded the African landmass stopped here—for wood, water, and fresh produce, for relaxation and entertainment, for gossip and news of the world.

In the 127 years since they first settled at the Cape, the Dutch had managed to carve out an orderly, efficient, and in many ways lovely preserve here, not far from the shores where the barbarous Atlantic currents met and warred with those of the Indian Ocean. The seas and the weather were wicked here, so much so that Portuguese explorers had originally named it Cabo das Tormentas—the Cape of Storms.

The Cape Colony wasn't a Dutch possession, per se, but rather the exclusive domain of a global corporation that happened to be Dutch in origin, the Verenigde Oost-Indische Compagnie, arguably the world's first transnational conglomerate. The Dutch United East India Company's directors were smart designers and canny businessmen, and the base they had constructed, this port of refuge and refreshment five thousand miles from Amsterdam, was well known to navigators around the world.

The *Resolution* had entered Table Bay on October 18, pulling alongside two French ships and a Dutch vessel that happened to be riding in the harbor that clear, hot, calm day. Cook had made good time here—despite the trip's miseries, he'd shaved twelve days off the time of his last voyage from Britain to the Cape. Among all his expeditions, this was the fourth time Cook had stopped at Cape Town; he knew the place well and could rest assured that he would find the provisions his ship needed after ninety-eight hard days at sea. Here were bazaars run by Arab and Chinese merchants. Here were bakeries, breweries, and butcher shops, forges and mills, sail-making concerns and lumberyards and warehouses crammed with goods, the whole operation set beside a splendid harbor.

The town's inhabitants seemed surprised to learn that the explorer was back so soon, and they extended him every courtesy, starting with an eleven-gun salute. There were toasts, parties, and state dinners. The rotund governor, Joachim van Plettenberg, greeted Cook effusively and pledged his support. At the Castle of Good Hope, Plettenberg put on a review of the local militia—some five hundred soldiers in all—composed mostly of Boer farmers from the interior of the colony who, "though not very dexterous at their maneuvers," Anderson allowed, "are a set of strong healthy men." Through it all, members of Cook's entourage were surprised by their captain's celebrity in this far-off place at the bottom of Africa. Cook, wrote David Samwell, "is as famous here and more noted perhaps than in England."

In groups of ten, Cook's men had begun to stagger ashore, testing their wobbly legs on terra firma. They erected tents by the bay, and the caulkers, coopers, smiths, and carpenters got to work. Many of the animals were led off the *Resolution* and turned loose to graze. It was the austral summer, and the climate seemed capricious—dry and hot on some mornings, foggy on others, but by the afternoon the colony baked in the smiting glare of the season.

Cook's astronomer, William Bayly, set up the observatory on shore. By taking close readings of the moon, sun, stars, and other bodies in the firmament, Bayly was able to determine that the ship's chronometer, the beloved K1, was still keeping good time. Cook bragged about his staunch chronometer: "We have reason to conclude that she had gone well all the way from England."

CAPE TOWN WAS a cornucopia. Cook's men could get good wine here, crisp greens, succulent fruit, and fresh meat—especially beef from the hardy Nguni cattle herds that thrived across southern Africa. It was impossible to exaggerate how fabulous such commodities seemed to sea-weary sailors, their stomachs shriveled and their taste buds dimmed by months of lemon, vinegar, and salt. (The monotonous diet of salt pork served on ships was why sailors were sometimes referred to as "old salts.") Here the men had their pick of fresh foodstuffs. Wrote Samwell: "The Cape is a very plentiful country & we live upon the fat of the land." Midshipman George Gilbert rhapsodized in his journal of the "delightful gardens, which provide vegetables and fruits of every kind in the greatest plenty and perfection."

But as in his previous visits, the captain was shocked and irritated by the exorbitant prices the company's administrators charged; this colony, after all, was run by a corporate monopoly that combined Calvinist punctiliousness with a razor-sharp instinct for profit. Free of competition, and expert in the dark arts of manipulating a captive market, the East India Company bureaucrats could name their price for most any item—and they did. "The Dutch," carped Cook, "strictly adhered to the maxim they have laid down at this place which is to get as much by strangers as they possibly can."

The Dutch administrators may have been extortionists, but actual thieves lurked on the fringes of the colony. Late one night, some miscreants placed a savage dog inside the stockade where Cook had penned sixteen sheep. Driving the animals out of the enclosure, the dog attacked and killed four of the sheep while the rest scattered into the hills.

Cook, receiving little assistance from the Dutch authorities, decided to pursue unorthodox methods to find his lost (and presumably stolen) flock. He hired what he described as "some of the meanest and lowest scoundrels in the place," the sort of men who for a farthing would "cut their master's throat, burn the house over his head, and bury him and the whole family in the ashes." It was entirely possible that the rogues Cook engaged were the very same ones who had set the dog loose among the sheep in the first place— but so be it. With their paid help, Cook was able to locate all of the remaining stock except for two ewes.

As if that weren't enough, Cook had to confront an act of larceny within his own ranks. One day an armorer from the ship obtained leave to go ashore and became intoxicated. To pay for his grog, he offered some coins that seemed suspect to the Dutch tavern owners. The Cape police arrested the armorer and hauled him before an officer aboard the *Resolution,* who discovered several more pieces of this strange-looking specie on his person. When the officer examined the contents of the suspect's sea chest, he found a contraption that had been used to stamp the fraudulent coins, a device ingeniously hidden in a false bottom. The counterfeiter immediately received "the discipline of the ship."

So far, Captain Cook seemed to be encountering far more disciplinary problems than he had during his two previous expeditions. While in Cape Town, Cook would apply the lash on nine occasions, for a variety of infractions, many of them minor. Since leaving Britain, he'd already ordered a third as many floggings as were recorded during his entire second voyage—and the *Resolution* hadn't yet passed out of the Atlantic.

MAI SEEMED AT home here in Cape Town, this being his second visit to the colony. The locals were fond of the returning Polynesian and gave him special attention. Mai loved gawking at the exotic creatures in the zoo and the botanical garden the burghers kept here— there were zebras, giraffes, ostriches, and other curiosities—and he mingled effortlessly with his Dutch hosts. "The people here are surprised at his genteel behavior and deportment," wrote Cook. "He continues to enjoy a good state of health and great flow of spirits."

Whether he knew it or not, Cook's assertion about Mai's state of health wasn't entirely accurate. In a letter to Joseph Banks while in Cape Town, Anderson mentioned that Mai had "brought a pox with him." By this he meant venereal disease of some form—probably gonorrhea—and it has been speculated that Mai may have contracted it in the brothel he visited while the *Resolution* was docked at Plymouth during his last days in England. Cook had given Mai three guineas to spend on shore, and had noted that Mai was "very much caressed" by the people of Plymouth—which may have been true in more ways than one. Anderson noted that, after some weeks in South Africa under his medical care, Mai had been cured of his ailment.

While in Cape Town, Cook bought more animals for Mai, adding to the Tahiti-bound menagerie the king had provided. Among the purchases were four horses, which Mai admired, and which he thought would command much prestige in Tahiti. Mai, wrote Cook, "consented with raptures" to give up his own cabin to make room for the four African-born horses.

Cape Town was a special place—Mai loved it, as did so many men in Cook's expedition. The accounts were glowing. One lieutenant called it "exceedingly picturesque...Nothing can be more romantic, nor any prospect more pleasing to the eye." John Ledyard, the American-born marine serving on the *Resolution,* found the surrounding landscape "somehow majestically great by nature; the mountains that form the promontory are as rugged as lofty, they impel the imagination to wonder."

Corporal Ledyard also had to admire the work ethic and vision of the Dutch, who, in a few generations, had turned the prickly karoo and the parched veld into a garden. "The land near the town," he wrote, "was entirely barren until improved by the industry of the inhabitants, which has rendered it very fertile."

One day, a small party of men, including Anderson, Gore, and Mai, took a wagon trip inland to Stellenbosch, a small village east of Cape Town. Anderson wanted to do some botanizing and see the countryside. Along the way, he caught several species of snakes and insects, and he had Gore and Mai venture into the bush to shoot birds for later study. But on this glorious day of gun blasts and butterfly nets, what most caught Anderson's notice was the little community of Stellenbosch.

It was a fetching spot, graced with orchards and vineyards, with the Jonkershoek range hanging over the scene, its weird notches and crags gnawing at the skyline. Anderson thought there was something magical about the place. "The air here," he wrote, "has an uncommon serenity." In the highlands, leopards, caracal cats, honey badgers, and other wild animals roamed, but down in the alluvial valleys, the Dutch had fashioned networks of dikes and canals to bring a steady flow of river water to irrigate this thirsty soil.

It was not only the Dutch who had left their mark on the colony, however: A community of French Huguenot refugees, escaping religious persecution, had immigrated to the Cape in 1687, bringing with them, among other things, an ardent love for grapes. The Dutch East India Company had already been encouraging viticulture here, erroneously believing wine to be a good deterrent against scurvy. But the French immigrants had brought something special to the mix. With this unexpected mingling of French passion and Dutch rectitude, the Cape had become renowned for its wine—especially a particular variety of sweet wine known as Constantia, which is celebrated to this day. Captain Cook would acquire a number of the Cape vines for Mai to plant in his gardens when he resettled in the Society Islands.

Here and there, through the rustling grape leaves, the white farmhouses would shine like bleached bones. They had a certain look: simple and square but ornately gabled, their steep roofs woven from thatch, their walls slathered in a blinding whitewash of lime and crushed shells—"Cape Dutch," the style would later be called. In one of these stout and elegant farmhouses lived a jocular man named Mr. Cloeder, who feted Anderson, Gore, and Mai with dancers and a multipiece band. "This gentleman," Anderson raved, "entertained us with the greatest hospitality and in a manner very different from what we expected. He showed us his wine cellars, his orchards and vineyards, all which I must own inspired me with a wish to know in what manner these industrious people could raise such plenty in a spot where I believe no other European nation would have attempted to settle."

In back of the cultivated beauty Anderson saw around Cape Town and Stellenbosch lay an odious truth that seems to have escaped his notice: These gracious farms and tidy villages had been built largely by chattel labor. The Dutch, having tried with mixed success to exploit the local Khoikhoi pastoral nomads of southern Africa, had resorted to importing enslaved people from as far away as Madagascar, Mozambique, and Indonesia to work the fields and vineyards and to accomplish a thousand other tasks required to keep the company's operations functioning and profitable. The Cape Colony, so rich and fecund and trim, was the product of more than a century of human bondage and toil.

This stark fact, so omnipresent yet also hidden from Anderson's view, wasn't lost on Cook. The captain noted how the local burghers prided themselves on their prowess at hunting down anyone who might try to break free from his shackles. "They tell us," Cook wrote, "that the policing is so carefully executed here that it is hardly possible for a slave, with all his cunning and knowledge of the country, to escape."

COOK WAS EAGER to make his own escape from Cape Town. It was a week into November and the *Resolution* had been lying at anchor for nearly a month. Cook had completed necessary repairs and had procured "every article we could think of" for the next phase of the journey. He wrote his last letters home. He stuffed the ship with more livestock, including cattle, sheep, goats, hogs, dogs, cats, rabbits, ducks, geese, turkeys, peacocks, and even a monkey. "Thus did we resemble the ark," wrote Ledyard, "and appeared as though we were going to stock, as well as discover, a new world."

Cook was eager to leave, yet he couldn't. For where was the *Discovery*? Had something dire happened to his consort ship? Had Captain Clerke never secured his release from debtors' prison? Cook was beginning to think he would have to travel on without the *Discovery*. Day after day, he cast a worried gaze out over Table Bay.

Then, on Sunday, November 10, a little ship, wind-battered and sea-tossed, glided into the harbor and anchored in six fathoms of water. Moments later, it saluted the garrison with a salvo of thirteen guns: The *Discovery* had arrived. Soon the two old friends, Cook and Clerke, were warmly embracing each other. Clerke could scarcely contain his excitement. "Here I am," he wrote to Joseph Banks, "hard and fast moored alongside my old friend Captain Cook."

Clerke told Cook how he had met mighty seas in the southern Atlantic, with waves so large and menacing "as to make our bark plunge exceedingly." The *Discovery* had taken 102 days to reach Cape Town and, except for the one marine who had fallen overboard and been eaten by sharks, had encountered few mishaps. The little collier had proven sounder than the *Resolution,* and overall, Clerke's men had arrived in Cape Town drier and in better health than Cook's men.

The crews hastily repaired the *Discovery.* In short order, they stripped the main mast, caulked the decks, and mended the rigging. The process of refurbishing the consort ship took only twenty days. By late November they were prepared to embark and, as Clerke put it with his characteristic panache, to begin "our intended attack upon the North Pole."

Clerke was beginning to show early signs of tuberculosis—chills, night sweats, anemia, a persistent cough—but it's not clear whether he knew yet what was ailing him, or whether he told Cook *that* he was ailing. Few things could be worse for a consumptive than to head into the blustery, cold, gray weather they were about to experience south of the Cape, but Clerke seemed cheery as ever. What he didn't know was that two months earlier, his brother John had died while in command of a small squadron near Madras, on the southeast coast of India. Charles loved John more than anyone in the world, even though his prodigal older sibling had caused him so much trouble and had created the circumstances that likely led to his contracting a lethal disease. Because the news from India would not reach Cape Town for several more weeks, Charles would never learn that his brother had died.

On November 30, Cook ordered their departure from Cape Town. He wrote in a final letter to Banks, "We are now ready to proceed on our voyage, and nothing is wanting but a few females of our own species to make the *Resolution* a complete ark."

Finally the two ships headed out to sea. England would receive no further word from them for more than three years.

12   *The Isle of Desolation*

KERGUELEN ISLANDS, DECEMBER 1776

The cold swells rose like a succession of mountains, and the winds lashed the dull sea, releasing tails of spume. As the *Resolution* pitched and plunged, her mizzen topmast ripped away. Cook seemed mildly alarmed by the "very high sea which made the ship roll and tumble exceedingly and gave us a great deal of trouble." The animals, shivering in their holds, were knocked about with such force that many, including Mai's prized horses, became seriously injured. A number of billy goats, their constitutions unsuited for the shock, simply expired. The men were miserable, too. They had grown sick of the fusty gloom and the all-suffusing dampness. They couldn't coax the chill from their bones. On the way from Cape Town they had changed into warmer gear—heavy fur-lined "fearnought" trousers and coats—but the winter garments did little to ward off the cutting cold, which, Cook wrote, "we began now most sensibly to feel."

It was mid-December, and Cook was venturing into the "Roaring Forties," that terrifying zone of the southern oceans where merciless Antarctic winds whip their way around the planet without landmasses to impede or divert their force. Winds of more than a hundred miles an hour are routine. Here in the so-called South Atlantic convergence zone, where the balmier waters of the Indian Ocean swirl into the cold currents welling up from the Antarctic, one finds some of the most tempestuous seas on earth, with sixty-foot waves not uncommon.

The *Resolution* and the *Discovery* were lonely specks inching across this howling vacuity. The two ships held themselves together, bucking through the spray, confronting waves that at times seemed impossible to surmount. "The sea frequently broke over the ship with great violence," the astronomer William Bayly wrote, "running down the hatches so that the water between the decks was ankle deep."

Charles Clerke, who rarely complained about anything, had to admit it was "nasty, raw, wet, disagreeable weather... [and] very indifferent." It seemed strange, for this was the austral summer, and their present latitude was no farther south than England was north; yet the rasping cold reminded Clerke of the very depths of a bad English winter. The sun only occasionally winked through the clouds, like a tarnished coin.

For days and days, the men saw nothing living on or in these forbidding seas—no birds, no seals, no whales, and few fish—though at one point the lookout spotted curious streaks of crimson red suspended in the water. Crewmen hauled up a sample from one of these bloodlike splotches and, when Anderson examined it under a microscope, the mystery was solved: Numerous red-hued crustaceans could be seen squirming under the glass slide. They were tiny crayfish, Cook noted, no bigger than "a large louse." Clerke, from his vantage point aboard the *Discovery,* noted the same phenomenon. He believed the creatures were "a kind of prawn or shrimp." (They were actually a species of pelagic krill.)

The two ships, nosing deeper into the southern ocean, were forced to slow down, for they had encountered something far more frightening than strenuous seas: fog. For more than a week, they crept through banks of mist so thick that at times the men of the *Resolution* and the *Discovery* couldn't see beyond their bowsprits. Lieutenant King fretted about the "great hazard in sailing in so thick a fog." Clerke declared it "most importunate" and lamented the way it "intrudes itself upon us at present very inconveniently... [and] renders exploring a miserable business."

Groping through this ghostly soup tried Cook's nerves. He called the passage "tedious and dangerous" and was continually haunted by twin fears: that the ships would vanish from each other's sight or, worse, that they would collide. Nearly every day, the two crews lost track of each other. "In these situations," wrote Lieutenant James Burney, "we kept company by sound, firing great guns every hour, sometimes oftener, and guessing from the report the place of the other ship."

Cook lost patience with their slow pace and ordered the vessels once again to raise all sails and forge ahead through the fog. Some of his officers considered this a reckless decision and, again, so different from the Cook of prior voyages. The captain was operating on wild hunches no one else could apprehend. No charts existed for these waters, so racing through them, with scant visibility, seemed the height of hubris. It appeared to some that Cook had developed a blind faith in himself. Yet no one had forgotten how close he had come to wrecking the ship in the Cape Verde Islands only a few months before.

What made this terrible progress through the fog more distressing was that scarcely anyone on board either ship had a clue where they were headed, or what lands they were supposed to be searching for. Cook held "secret instructions" for this segment of the voyage and, always a stickler to the letter of his assignments, he refused to divulge details to anyone, not even his officers. Out here on these empty seas, Cook's attention to secrecy seemed misplaced. What was the point of keeping his people in the dark now? It was a question his officers, growing more baffled and frustrated, kept asking. Some of them found Cook's reticence insulting and seemed offended by the lack of trust it implied. "We who are not acquainted with the plan of the voyage," sulked King, "nevertheless indulge conjectures."

Cook was looking for a remote island that the French had reportedly discovered a few years earlier. In the early 1770s, an explorer named Yves-Joseph de Kerguelen-Trémarec had embarked on an expedition to search for the mythical southern continent, the same fabled Terra Australis that Cook had searched for. During that expedition, Kerguelen was said to have found a landmass deep in the southern Indian Ocean. Supposedly he touched there in 1772, and again in 1773. Details were sketchy, but Kerguelen seemed to suggest that the landmass might be an extending arm of Terra Australis. Cook scoffed at this notion—after all, he had already demolished the idea of a southern continent. (And, as would later be learned, Captain Kerguelen had a reputation for grossly exaggerating the importance of his discoveries—one account called him "an adventurer whom on close scrutiny it is not possible to admire.") Still, the Admiralty wanted Cook to find the mysterious Kerguelen Land to learn its true extent and its possible value as a victualing station for future voyages. Whatever the French had found, the English must of course investigate. This foggy reconnaissance was but a side errand for Cook. Yet it was one the Admiralty had insisted he must perform.

A WEEK LATER, portents of land began to appear, visible through rips in the fog: a penguin floating on the swells, thick clumps of kelp rolling by, the dim shapes of seabirds streaking through the mist. Then, promising but also ominous, the sound of waves, smashing onto distant rocks. Cook described it as "a prodigious sea" that "broke on all the shores in a frightful surf."

Could this be Kerguelen Land? Cook could hardly see a thing— tantalizing vistas of emerald real estate would peek through the shifting fog, then abruptly vanish. Cook wanted to proceed but thought the better of it. Worrying that he might get "entangled amongst the islands in a thick fog," as he put it, he pulled back to wait for clearer weather.

The following day Cook was able to draw closer and get better views of the land, and the day after that—Christmas Day—the *Resolution* moored in a protected bay that was ringed by a sandy beach. Clerke's *Discovery* pulled up beside Cook a few hours later. Boats were hoisted into the water, and soon men were fanning out across the beach. A long receiving line of penguins greeted them; the blubbery denizens stared at these strange arrivals but did not show the slightest fear. Seals and sea lions brayed along the shore, and seabirds wheeled in the sky. The land seemed otherwise uninhabited—nor could Cook see any indications that humans had ever been here.

After Cook was rowed ashore, he marched past the beach, and climbed the hillside to a natural amphitheater of basaltic rocks. When he got a good look at the countryside through the fog, his heart sank. He could see nothing for his animals to eat. What had appeared from

a distance to be rich green grass was only a thin veneer of moss—
and the underlying soil was a pulverized black scree. The island,
Cook declared, was "without the least sign of fertility." Higher up,
Anderson noted that the ground was spongy underfoot—"a rotten
kind of turf," as he described it, "into which one sinks a foot or two
at every step."

Cook couldn't see a single tree anywhere. His carpenters needed
timber to repair the wind-thrashed ships, and his men, drenched and
chilled to the bone, had hoped to build bonfires to dry themselves.
But this land was a barren tundra. "Not a stick of wood," Cook wrote
in disgust, not so much as a shrub.

At least the island had an abundance of fresh water. "Every gully
afforded a large stream," Cook wrote. "The rain swelled all the rivu-
lets to such a degree that the sides of the hills seemed to be covered
with a sheet of water that precipitated down their sides in prodigious
torrents." Cook's men hauled out the water casks and had easy work
filling them.

For all its moisture, Anderson found the island botanically bleak;
it lacked not only trees but virtually any plant life at all. "Perhaps no
place hitherto discovered in either hemisphere under the same parallel of latitude affords so scanty a field for the naturalist as this barren spot," Anderson wrote. Besides lichen and moss, only one other
plant grew in abundance: a small cabbage prolifically scattered along
what he called the "boggy declivities."

If the plant kingdom was conspicuously meager here, the island
abounded in marine mammals, especially seals and sea lions, which
the men wasted no time clubbing and butchering for food and blubber to render oil for their lamps. The seals were "so insensible of
fear," Cook noted, "that we killed as many as we chose." It was savage, bloody work, the *Discovery*'s Lieutenant John Rickman conceded, resulting in "not the most delicate" fare, but to "stomachs
cloyed almost to loathing with salt provisions, even seals were not
unsavory meat."

Though this lonesome land may have been a refuge for sea mammals, it seemed to be meant primarily for winged creatures. The

beach was crowded with birds, including ducks, geese, terns, giant petrels, albatrosses, cormorants, gulls, skuas, sheathbills, and several species of penguins. Thousands of nests could be seen in the rocky alcoves, and copious streaks of guano slimed the cliffs. The frigid air was filled with their constant mewing and cawing. Thomas Edgar, master of the *Discovery,* became annoyed by the incessant "melancholy croaking" of so many birds.

WHEREVER THIS PLACE was, Cook couldn't understand why the French explorer had celebrated its discovery, or why he had cloaked his finding in such mystery. It was a most dismal spot to spend Christmas. Cook had his men occupied doing chores and maintenance all day, and the day after that, but on the twenty-seventh he called a holiday. Serving out a double ration of grog to each member of the crew and an equally generous portion of wine and spirits to each petty officer, he gave his men a full day's leave to go ashore. Egalitarianism was one of Cook's best qualities: As someone who'd come up from nothing, he was opposed to the custom, common on many ships at the time, that allowed officers during celebrations to indulge while average crew members carried on as usual. "In all enjoyments," wrote Heinrich Zimmermann, "he loved equality, and on special occasions food and drink were served out to officers and men in equal portions."

Various parties broke off and went exploring in the hills, while others, savoring their allotment of liquor on the beach, lounged away the afternoon in revelry. "Past dangers were forgotten," John Rickman mused, "and the day was spent by the common sailors with as much mirth and unconcern as if safely moored in Portsmouth harbor."

That evening, one of the crewmen brought back to the ship an intriguing relic he had discovered across the harbor, fastened with some wire to a prominent rock. He gave it to Cook, and it turned out to be a quart bottle that contained a piece of parchment inscribed in Latin. Translated into English, the message read: LOUIS XV, KING OF GAUL AND LORD DE BOYNES, HIS MAJESTY'S SECRETARY OF THE MARINE, YEARS 1772 AND 1773.

Here was proof that this was Kerguelen Land. The French had been here twice, and had left their mark in the hope that if an explorer like Cook happened upon it, he would know the French had arrived first. Cook's response was to turn over the parchment and, with some brisk translation work back into Latin, write: NAVES RESO-LUTION ET DISCOVERY DE REGE MAGNAE BRITAINNIAE DECEMBRES 1776. Cook slipped the parchment back into the bottle, along with a piece of twopenny silver dated 1772, and closed the mouth with a lead cap. The next morning, in a formal ceremony, he tucked it inside a cairn erected on the harbor's north shore. He raised the Union Jack and named the place Christmas Harbor.

Some found this pro forma solemnity in the service of the distant motherland's real estate aggrandizement a bit ridiculous. Anderson thought it was "perhaps fitter to excite laughter than indignation." Even here, the jealous intrigues of the British and the French remained intense. No European nation could possibly be in a rush to take possession of this forlorn land that, as one midshipman described it, was "too barren for any human being to exist upon." Yet the two age-old adversaries had to at least give the appearance of vying for it. Cook decided to rename the place. As far as he was concerned, it was no longer Kerguelen Land. He called it the Isle of Desolation, and marked his charts as such.

THE SPOT WHERE Cook had landed, now known as Grande Terre Island, is the largest and highest landmass in the Kerguelen archipelago, a French possession consisting of more than three hundred volcanic islands and islets, most of them still uninhabited. Geologically, it is part of a vast underwater plateau that extends all the way from Africa; in a sense, the Kerguelen group is the bitter southern end of the African continent. Gouged by glaciers, swept by perpetual winds, seething with fog and the steam of numerous fumaroles, Grande Terre is one of the most remote places on earth. Its coastline is notched with fjords, and its mountains rise to majestic heights—the island's loftiest peak is slightly more than six thousand feet above sea level.

But on that blustery December day, Captain Cook seemed unimpressed by it all—not only by the dreariness of the land but by the act and ritual of exploration itself. The French had been here, but only superficially; a new world of thousands of square miles could be discovered on Kerguelen Land, mapped and measured and gawked at, terrain no human being had ever trod upon. Cook had seen only a minuscule fraction of it. Where was the old excitement, the explorer's sense of wonder?

It was true that Cook had a much larger timeline and strategy to consider, but still, this seemed to be a new Cook, jaded, rolling his eyes in the face of the unknown. On previous expeditions, he had rarely shied from opportunities for pure discovery. But after four days, he was impatient to leave.

And the island seemed to *want* him to leave. The seals and the penguins were already showing signs of wariness. They weren't stupid; in a few short days, they had learned to fear these murderous invaders and had grasped an essential lesson: *Always evade a human's approach.*

Cook had sound reasons to hasten onward from Kerguelen Land. While here, more of his animals, bruised and buffeted by the long, cold sail from Cape Town, had perished, and many more seemed to be suffering acutely. If the surviving animals were going to make it to Tahiti, Cook needed to find good fodder for them. This urgency must have influenced his decision to move on from the Isle of Desolation.

On his way east, he would take some soundings and bearings along Kerguelen's serrated coast and do what cursory charting he could through the fog—naming features along the way for dignitaries and royals back in England or for members of his own expedition: Cape Sandwich, Bligh's Cap, Point Pringle (after the president of the Royal Society). Naming things in this imperious way may have been a silly, pompous exercise, but it was the explorer's prerogative, especially in a place where no Native names were available.

The two ships, nipped by the cold, continued eastward through foggy seas.

13   *Lunawanna-alonnah*

TASMANIA, JANUARY 1777

For days the *Resolution* and the *Discovery* sailed from Kergeulen in
the direction of New Zealand. The two ships were carrying full sail,
while operating "in the dark," as Cook phrased it. By that he didn't
mean literal darkness, although relentless fog cast a flat gloom over
everything; rather, he meant that he didn't know where he was. Cook
couldn't study the seas, and his astronomer, William Bayly, couldn't
study the heavens. With little more to go on than a compass reading,
Cook was essentially sailing by dead reckoning. Yet he had fallen so
far behind on the schedule the Admiralty had set for him—he was
supposed to be in Tahiti by now—that he felt he had no choice but
to take advantage of the prevailing westerlies and deploy every sheet
of canvas he had.

This made for white-knuckled voyaging. The challenge once
again was how to keep the ships moving together without colliding.
For the better part of a week, the two vessels lost sight of each other.
The crews fired guns every half hour, trying to judge the whereabouts of the other by the changing volume of the cannon blasts in
the thick atmosphere. It was blind guesswork, with the highest possible stakes, a tedious but urgent exercise that rewarded those young
men on either ship who were blessed with the sharpest ears.

Shortly before dawn on January 17, a squall snapped the *Resolution*'s fore topmast, along with the main topgallant mast. The crew
spent nearly an entire day sorting through the splintered lumber
that was left tangled and twisted in the rigging. Some of the officers adopted the familiar refrain of cursing the shipwrights at Deptford for poor workmanship and accepting inferior wood. But a few
skeptics on board quietly found fault with Cook's nautical judgment.
Lieutenant King wondered whether Cook had pushed too hard and
risked too much in order to meet an unrealistic schedule. The "shortness of our time" had forced Cook to "carry all sail possible," King

wrote in judgment, noting that the consequent stresses had assuredly "caused the loss of our mast."

The damage done to the *Resolution*, combined with the continuing travails of the animals on board, convinced Cook that he immediately had to find a place to stop. The condition of the cattle was especially acute, but all the beasts were suffering. Some had perished while en route from Kerguelen, and many others appeared on the brink of death. Someone spread the theory that the animals were being poisoned—the meager fodder gathered on Kerguelen, they said, was tainted by penguin urine and feces. Whatever the case, the animals needed fresh, clean hay, and respite from their confinement, the cold weather, and the jolting seas.

The two ships had passed well to the south of New Holland, as Australia was then known, although the continent's southern contours were not understood. Cook couldn't know for sure, but he surmised that he must be approaching Van Diemen's Land, where he thought he could find not only fresh provender for the animals but wood to repair the ship. The Dutch explorer Abel Tasman had been the first European to spot this land, in 1642, and he'd named it after his sponsor, Anthony van Diemen, the governor of the Dutch East Indies. (The island wouldn't be renamed Tasmania until 1856.) In 1773, during Cook's second voyage, Tobias Furneaux's *Adventure*, having become separated from the *Resolution*, had briefly stopped at Van Diemen's Land. Cook recalled that Furneaux had raved about a certain anchorage on the south coast he had named Adventure Bay. It was supposed to be a serene harbor with abundant fresh water and thick forests. Cook made up his mind to go find the spot; he hated hearing about a place he hadn't visited. Although stopping at Adventure Bay would require a slight detour, it might save the king's ailing livestock.

Cook's hunch about his location proved correct: On January 24, the fog having lifted, a lookout caught sight of the notched coast of Van Diemen's Land, its highest points still powdered with snow. A number of whales and grampus dolphins were spotted, and, as Anderson noted, "a shark of uncommon size swam some time about the ship." Two days later the *Resolution* and the *Discovery* were safely moored in Adventure Bay, in twelve fathoms of water, over what Cook called "a bottom of ooze and sand." The place was just as Furneaux had depicted it—a perfect anchorage, the cerulean blue waters ringed by a crescent of white beach that was backed, in turn, by hills cloaked in enormous blue gum eucalyptus trees.

Like Furneaux before him, Cook believed Van Diemen's Land was a southeastern peninsula of New Holland, the great land whose east coast Cook had charted during his first voyage. He didn't realize that Van Diemen's Land was actually a substantial island, for no explorer had yet established the existence of what is now known as the Bass Strait, separating Australia from Tasmania. Furthermore, Cook didn't realize that the shoreline fronting Adventure Bay was part of a smaller island located slightly offshore from Tasmania, a secluded spot today known as Bruny Island, or Lunawanna-alonnah, its Aboriginal name.

In 1642, Tasman had sailed into this same promising-looking bay, but contrary winds had brushed him away. Tasman called it Storm Bay and never set foot there. One hundred and thirty-five years had passed since then. As far as anyone knew, Furneaux and his men aboard the *Adventure* were the only Europeans who had ever been here, walking these same shores (albeit for only two days).

Cook's men wasted no time hoisting the boats into the water and rowing them ashore. The weather was warm and sultry as parties vanished into the interior to hunt for grass and cut wood. Another party set a seine across a lagoon and hauled out a trove of flopping fish—mainly elephant fish, an odd-looking little shark with a plow-shaped snout. Midshipman George Gilbert deemed its rubbery flesh "very indifferent eating," though a welcome change to their diet. Mai, the natural-born angler, grabbed a rod and caught a load of bream.

Parties combing further stretches of the beach encountered a rich variety of life in and along the waters: sharks, rays, crabs, sea sponges, and shellfish. Some of the life forms were bizarre, including a sea hare (an enormous, smelly slug that glurped along the water's edge) and a Medusa's head (an astonishingly intricate kind of basket starfish).

Inland, Cook's men sighted an abundance of animals, too—parrots, snakes, lizards, scorpions, even a marsupial known as a brushtail possum, which was promptly shot as it tried to skitter up a tree. The eucalyptus trees were enormous, "growing to astonishing height and size," wrote Lieutenant Rickman, and "exceeding everything we had ever seen." Rickman guessed that some of the trees "rose ninety feet high without a knot" and claimed that the trunks had girths so massive that "were we to report it, [it] would render the credit of the reporter doubtful." Lieutenant James Burney noted that the forest was infested with "troublesome vexatious insects"—mainly mosquitoes, though Anderson had an unfortunate encounter with "a large black ant whose bite is almost intolerable." (This was *Myrmecia,* the notorious bull ant, whose venomous bite is known to be one of the most painful and toxic in the insect world.)

FOR ALL THE life the crewmen found around them, they spotted no *Homo sapiens,* although humans lived here. On the approach into Adventure Bay, Cook had glimpsed columns of smoke rising from the hills. Furneaux, during his short stay four years earlier, had seen no Natives, but he'd encountered evidence of human activity, including simple structures.

Cook's men stumbled upon a different kind of shelter: The trunks of immense eucalyptus trees had been hollowed out by fire, each one leaving an enclosed circle upon the ground large enough for four or five people to gather about a clay hearth. Anderson was enchanted by the very notion: Here were people who lived inside trees, like creatures from Greek mythology. "What the ancients tell us of fauns and satyrs," he wrote, "is here realized."

Walking deeper into the forest, Cook sensed that the inhabitants were closely watching him and his men from the thickets. In the afternoon, a group of eight men and a boy materialized. They were naked, their black-brown bodies daubed with ocher and crosshatched with keloid scars, repeating half-moon patterns that had been cut into their skin and rubbed with ash. The Natives seemed diffident, but not scared, and not the least bit impressed by Cook's arrival. "They did not express that surprise which one might have expected from seeing men so much unlike themselves," Dr. Anderson wrote. "They seem mild and cheerful without reserve or jealousy of strangers." When Cook offered them axes, knives, and trinkets as gifts, they accepted them with little interest.

This was probably the first time these particular people had encountered Europeans, or, for that matter, members of any other race. The Palawa, the Aboriginal people of Tasmania, had been separated from the mainland of Australia for at least ten thousand years—with the flooding of the Bassian Land Bridge that occurred at the end of the last ice age. And all Indigenous people of Australia, in turn, had been isolated from the rest of the world for at least fifty thousand years, reaching back to the fogs of the Dreamtime and the primordial days of their earliest myths. Yet, judging by the stolid expressions on the faces of these tribesmen, their first encounter with a people so dramatically different from them appeared to be a nonevent.

In his published account, Cook adopted a neutral anthropological tone, evenhanded and remarkably devoid of judgment or religiosity, jingoism or national pride:

> They approached us from the woods, without betraying any marks of fear, with the greatest confidence imaginable. None of them had weapons except one who held in his hand a stick about 2 feet long and pointed at one end. They were naked and wore no ornaments except some large punctures or ridges raised on different parts of their bodies, some in straight, and others in curved lines. They were of common stature and rather slender. Their skin was black and also their hair. Most of them had their hair and beards smeared with a red ointment and some of their faces were painted with the same composition. They received every present we made without the least appearance of satisfaction. They seemed to set no value on iron or iron tools. When some bread was given, as soon as they understood that it was to be eaten, they either returned it or threw it away without even tasting it. They also refused some fish, both raw and dressed,

which we offered them. But upon giving some birds to them they did not return these and easily made us comprehend that they were fond of such foods.

Cook's comments about the Palawa continued in this same matter-of-fact tone; he seemed to view it as his proper place only to observe. He was distrustful of his own prejudices and opinions. Others who encountered the Aboriginal people were far more critical, and more prone to making sweeping pronouncements and invidious comparisons. Take Clerke, for example, who, though charmed by their "harmless cheerfulness," declared that these Natives had "made the least progress towards any kind of improvement... of any people I have ever met." They "lived like the beasts of the forest," asserted Rickman, "without arts of any kind."

Burney added to this derogatory chorus. "Few people may more truly be said to be in a state of nature," he said, noting with some disgust how the inhabitants would urinate in full view of everyone. "In the most natural actions they are without restraint... One of these gentlemen, whether sitting, walking or talking, will pour forth his streams without preparatory action or guidance, or even appearing sensible of what he is doing; and not in the least interested whether it trickles down his own thighs or sprinkles the person next to him."

Despite the simplicity of their implements and their apparent poverty, the Palawa appeared to many of Cook's men to be content. "They have few wants," wrote John Henry Martin, a midshipman aboard the *Discovery*, "and seemed perfectly happy, if one might judge from their behavior, for they frequently burst out into the most immoderate fits of laughter, and when one laughed, everyone followed his example immediately."

Mai tried to converse with them in Tahitian but could understand nothing of their tongue, nor they of his. The only word the Englishmen could get the Palawa people to understand was *kangaroo*, which veterans of Cook's first voyage on the *Endeavour* had learned while among the Aboriginal people of New Holland. Though Cook saw no kangaroos here, some of the Natives wore miscellaneous strips and thongs fashioned from pelts that resembled kangaroo fur. That, plus peculiar animal tracks crisscrossing the forest floor, led him to think that kangaroos must live hereabouts. (They did, along with wallabies, quolls, pademelons, and other marsupials.)

Still, Cook thought the Palawa suffered from a dearth of large animals. As an act of charity consistent with King George's larger mission of spreading useful animals across the nether reaches of the world, Cook decided to donate a sow and a boar from his shipborne stock, in the hope that they would reproduce and populate the interior, thus affording the inhabitants a permanent food source unknown to them now. It would be, in effect, a miniaturized, and *feralized*, version of the animal husbandry program intended for Tahiti.

The concept of "invasive species" was not one that had dawned on Englishmen in Georgian times; nor, it seems, did it occur to Cook that the Palawa might be satisfied with the diet they already had. They were far from starving—their own hunters and gatherers were proficient at procuring all the food they needed.

But a pig is an impressive animal, and when Cook presented two of them, the Natives were captivated. However, they failed to comprehend Cook's scheme that the swine should be allowed to breed. The Palawa seemed to want to slaughter them and eat them right there on the spot. The instant they saw the squealing creatures, wrote Cook, "they seized them by the ears like a dog and were for carrying them off immediately, with no other view as we could perceive but to kill them."

Cook decided that the Palawa were "incapable of entering into my views of improving their country." It was a patronizing turn of thinking—who was Cook to presume how to "improve" a country that was not his?—but he was probably right that the two pigs would die quickly if he just handed them over to the people. As he put it, "I have no doubt [what] will be their fate." For the moment, he decided he'd better hold on to them.

With a series of gestures, Cook prompted a Native who carried a pointed spear to demonstrate its use. The man set up a target on a nearby tree. He was probably not their best spear thrower, for he proceeded to hurl the missile at the target, over and over again, without hitting his mark. Mai, growing impatient with the exercise, soon intervened, perhaps at Cook's suggestion. The Polynesian was eager to show what a proper English firearm could do. As the man stepped aside, Mai picked up his fowling piece and took aim.

When he fired, the Natives were shocked. "The report astonished them all very much," David Samwell wrote. "They stood for some time as if thunderstruck, not knowing what to do." Overcome with fright, the Palawa men dropped the knives, axes, and other gifts Cook had given them and bolted into the woods. Some of the Englishmen ran after them, begging them to come back, but to no avail.

And so, with the crack of a firearm, the historic first encounter between two races of human beings from islands on opposite sides of the globe had abruptly ended. The men cursed the overeager Mai for having spoiled what had been a most convivial gathering. Samwell was sure the incident "would prevent our having further intercourse with these people." The Palawa seemed to have vanished for good.

But Cook was still intent on releasing the boar and the sow into the wild, and with the Palawa scattered, now was the time. Knowing that domesticated swine readily became feral and were "fond of the thickest cover of the woods," the captain thought there was a decent chance they might survive long enough to reproduce. That afternoon, Cook ordered the two pigs to be carried a mile farther into the eucalyptus stands and left beside a freshwater stream.

THE NEXT MORNING, Cook took heart: A group of about twenty inhabitants were seen congregating on the beach, clearly hoping to interact again with the white-skinned visitors. The Natives seemed to have recovered from Mai's ballistics display the day before. "They were convinced that we intended them no mischief," thought Cook, "and were desirous of renewing the intercourse."

Cook promptly went out to meet and mingle again with the

Palawa, this time much more freely than the previous day. Though he was outnumbered, he seemed to have no fear and took no precautions; he walked unarmed among them and engaged in the cryptic, often awkward, and sometimes comical effort of trying to understand an utterly unfamiliar people—bartering and gesturing, smiling and pointing, occasionally making grunts and other strange sounds. The cerebral Cook was far from being a gregarious or voluble man, but he had a knack for these sorts of rough-and-tumble interactions.

This forthright curiosity was an admirable trait, one he'd shown during his previous voyages. Many navigators during the Age of Exploration were content to exploit whatever resources they could quickly locate and move on. Far too many first encounters between Europeans and isolated tribes transpired without the feeblest attempt at cultural understanding—and, sadly, they too often ended in bloodshed.

But Cook's inquisitiveness was genuine. He wanted to know who the Palawa were, what they ate, how they thought and talked and dressed, how they worshipped their gods. One senses that of all the different roles his voyages required him to carry out, Cook derived the most pleasure and satisfaction from playing the part of anthropological observer.

It was strange to Cook how little acquainted the Palawa appeared to be with the sea. Unlike Polynesians, they didn't seem to like to swim, and Cook noted that he did not see a single "canoe or any vessel in which they could go upon the water." They ate mussels and other mollusks but showed no interest in other kinds of seafood; they ran away in seeming horror several times when Cook's men presented fish as a gift. When shown a fishhook, they appeared to have no idea what it was. They seemed curious about, but also fearful of, Cook's small boats moored beside the beach, and though some of the Englishmen tried to coax the Natives out for a short ride in the bay, the Palawa couldn't be persuaded to come aboard. "With all our dumb oratory we could not prevail [upon] any of them to accompany us," wrote Samwell, "though it was easily perceived that one of them was very desirous of going and had a long struggle between his fears and his inclinations."

Cook saw many similarities between these people and the Aboriginal people of New Holland he had briefly encountered in 1770 while sailing the *Endeavour.* Yet there were also many differences, as one would expect, given that the human populations of Australia and Tasmania had been separated for so many eons. Cook thought, correctly, that they spoke a separate dialect. "The language here," he wrote, "appeared to me to be different from that spoken by the inhabitants of the more northern parts of the country whom I met with on my first voyage."

One Aboriginal man in particular, a "much deformed" figure, caught Cook's fancy. He had advanced kyphosis—that is, a severe curvature of the spine. (Cook called him "humpbacked.") But the man seemed to serve as the tribe's comic philosopher and diplomat. Cook was taken by the "drollery of his gestures and the seeming humor of his speeches." Added Samwell: "We could easily see that this little Aesop was the most shrewd and sensible man among them." Mai threw a white cloth over the man's shoulder, in the fashion of Tahiti, and the hunched figure joyously paraded down the beach.

In contrast to the day before, a number of Aboriginal women had joined their men to interact with Cook's party on the beach. They were animated and friendly, but they were covered in lice, some of the men noted with dismay. All their hair had been shorn off, except for a thin band of fuzz that grew along the circumference of the scalp. Their hairstyle reminded Samwell of a tonsure, such that the women "appeared something like friars."

Several crewmen from the *Discovery* tried to make advances on the women, but their overtures "were rejected with great disdain," Cook reported. When the sailors persisted, Cook said, an elderly man, who seemed to carry the authority of a chief, "ordered all the women to retire, which they did." Cook, who was incensed by the conduct of his men, calling it "highly blamable," was relieved by this outcome.

Van Diemen's Land would be one spot where Cook's expedition did not spread the spirochetes of venereal disease. The Palawa were safe for now, but they would soon experience the full brunt of "civilization." The Palawa had no immunity against common European pathogens—they were, as scientists today like to say, "epidemiologically naive." Murderous violence dispatched those whom disease did not. English settlers would hunt down the Palawa like animals, sometimes shooting them just for sport. Within a century of Cook's arrival, they were nearly an extinct race. The last living full-blooded Aboriginal Tasmanian was widely said to be an elderly woman named Truganini, who'd been born on Lunawanna-alonnah. She died in 1876.

Cook admired the Palawa. They lived a simple life, but a stubborn pride suffused their culture. They did not seem to think much of the strangers who'd washed up on their coast, and did not need their metal tools or other advancements. These people, he thought, "live in a tranquility which is not disturbed by the inequality of condition: The earth and sea of their own accord furnishes them with all things necessary for life. They covet not magnificent houses [or] household stuff."

Cook thought it best to bid the Palawa farewell before his expedition could do something to forever besmirch this primeval spot. He and his men had seen and done much in their four days at Adventure Bay. They had repaired the *Resolution* and found some decent grass to feed the still ailing animals. But now it was time to go.

Cook's weather eye noted a light breeze that was beginning to pick up from the west. On January 30, the two ships weighed anchor and sailed east. Leaving Van Diemen's Land behind, the voyagers finally entered the largest body of water on earth, the planet's single largest feature: the Pacific.

This mighty ocean was more than twelve thousand miles across, nearly half the circumference of the globe. It was Magellan, the legendary Portuguese explorer, who had named it the Pacific, but that was only because when he first encountered it, at the tip of South America in 1520, the sea was uncharacteristically calm. Magellan soon found the Pacific to be quite tempestuous and, as the expedition reports put it, "so vast that the human mind can scarcely grasp it." Yet it was in the Pacific, incomprehensible in its immensity, that Cook felt most at home.

14   A Shocking Scene of Carnage

NEW ZEALAND, FEBRUARY 1777

As the two ships heaved across the dove-gray swells in the direction of New Zealand, many a man wondered if their fortunes had turned; they dearly wished they could circle back to the tranquility of Van Diemen's Land. Out on the open Pacific, conditions deteriorated: thick fog, sudden squalls, torrential rain. Then, on the night of February 6, an accident occurred: A marine named George Moody, serving on the *Discovery*, tumbled overboard in the dead of night and was never seen again. Some accounts hint that he may have been drunk, but that's only a guess. To some, the *Discovery*, with her captain growing more sickly, seemed an accursed vessel. The voyage was still in its early days, and yet two men from Clerke's ship had already gone overboard.

The crews didn't know why the two ships were aiming for New Zealand. Cook kept his reasoning to himself and was chary with the details. Reticence was a characteristic of his command style, but especially on the current expedition. "He was very reserved," wrote Heinrich Zimmermann. "When at table with his officers he frequently sat without saying a word." New Zealand was hundreds of miles out of the way, a straight shot east when, according to the Admiralty schedule, which was now well blown, they should be angling sharply northeast and making for Tahiti. Having repaired the *Resolution*, filled the casks, and refreshed the animals at Van Diemen's Land, Cook, it seemed, could accomplish little in New Zealand. But his instruction to Clerke was to rendezvous at an old familiar way station: Ship Cove, deep within the shelter of Queen Charlotte Sound, on New Zealand's South Island.

Cook had a piece of unfinished business to attend to in Queen Charlotte Sound, a matter that dated back to his previous voyage, regarding a dreadful incident that had befallen the men of his consort ship, the *Adventure*, captained by Tobias Furneaux.

———

IN LATE OCTOBER of 1773, Furneaux's ship had become separated from Cook's *Resolution* during a storm in the powerful seas off New Zealand. For weeks Furneaux battled fierce and erratic winds that shrilled through his rigging and frayed his sails. Searching in vain for Cook, he reported to the preassigned rendezvous point at Ship Cove.

On November 30, as the *Adventure* eased into this serene hideaway, Furneaux could see no sign of the *Resolution*. But his men eventually found a gnarled tree root bearing a carving that read, LOOK UNDERNEATH. Digging in the sand, Furneaux's men found a bottle containing a message from Cook dated November 24—just six days earlier.

The buried message stated that Cook was herewith departing Ship Cove, after having waited for Furneaux for several weeks. Cook was headed back into Antarctic waters to continue the search for the hypothetical supercontinent, and he could not say for certain when or where Furneaux might catch up with him in the months ahead. "Captain Cook has not the least hopes of meeting with Captn Furneaux," the note said. Any place of rendezvous, Cook said, would "depend so much upon circumstances that nothing with any degree of certainty can be depended upon."

Furneaux couldn't believe he had so narrowly missed his connection with his flagship. Realizing it was distinctly possible the two vessels might never reunite, he decided to shelter at Ship Cove for a while, to replenish the *Adventure*'s stores, repair her wounds, and let his men recuperate. He thought he would probably have to give up on the voyage and return straight to England.

At least Ship Cove was a place Furneaux knew well—the *Adventure* and the *Resolution* had been here just six months earlier. It was a placid anchorage, with ample food and fresh water and bountiful supplies of hardwood. The local Māori were generally known to be friendly and accommodating.

But this time around, Furneaux sensed, something had changed. The Natives seemed impatient, demanding, and rude. They had put up with Cook and the men of the *Resolution*, but now, less than a week after Cook's departure, another ship full of foreigners had landed on this crescent beach to take up residence. These Englishmen were testing the limits of Māori hospitality—and trying their patience.

FOR MORE THAN two weeks, while Furneaux remained encamped at Ship Cove, he and his men experienced a steady drumbeat of problems. There was much thievery, strange stirrings in the woods at night, and one incident that Furneaux, in a report, cryptically described as a "narrow escape." The tensions were palpable and growing, and many of the men had become thoroughly spooked. As if to underscore the gothic atmospherics, late one evening, William Bayly observed an unusually large meteor rocketing across the night sky, an event some of the more superstitious sailors took as an omen.

Furneaux, sensing that he'd overstayed his welcome, began to make preparations for leaving. At dawn on December 18, he hoisted out the cutter and dispatched a group of ten armed men to sail over to a place called Whareunga Bay to cut wild greens. There was a spot in the bay, which Cook had called Grass Cove, where a species of wild celery was known to grow in abundance. This plant was thought to be an excellent anti-scorbutic.

Furneaux put Jack Rowe, the master's mate, in charge of the grass-cutting detail and gave him strict instructions to return by the afternoon. Rowe and his nine comrades departed Ship Cove at first light. By nightfall they had not returned, and the next morning, with still no sign of them, Furneaux dispatched a detail of ten sailors and marines, led by Lieutenant James Burney, to search for the ten missing men. Mai, who was a passenger on the *Adventure*, would serve as Burney's translator. Furneaux felt a "great uneasiness." He worried that Rowe's party had been swept out into the powerful currents of the bay, and that the cutter had perhaps smashed upon the rocky shores, stranding the men. He had a hunch that the little boat was, as he put it, "stove in among the rocks." So certain was Furneaux in his surmise that he ordered Lieutenant Burney to bring along multiple sheets of tin to repair the damaged cutter.

Burney and his party left Ship Cove in a small boat, enjoying a light breeze. They spent much of the day searching the notches and coves—using a spyglass to scour every inch of the shore—but they could find no sign of the cutter. Repeatedly, Burney had his men fire guns into the air, hoping for a response from Rowe, but they heard only silence.

Farther down the coast, the lieutenant spotted a *waka*—a large double-hulled canoe—hauled up on the sand. He and his men went ashore and searched the Māori canoe. Inside they found a piece of metal. On closer inspection, Burney realized it was part of one of the oarlocks from the cutter. They found a pair of shoes, which were immediately identified as belonging to one of the *Adventure*'s midshipmen, a Mr. Woodhouse.

Burney scanned the shore. Higher up on the bank stood a collection of baskets, about twenty in number, all of them cinched tight with rope. Burney snipped the cord on one of the baskets and found it to be full of fern root, a starchy staple of the Māori diet, which they ate like bread. He cut open another basket and saw that it was filled with roasted meat, still warm from the fire.

Burney continued up the beach and to his consternation found another pair of shoes lying on the ground. Then he discovered something that took his breath away: a severed human hand. He scrutinized it and caught a terrifying detail. Etched on it were the initials T.H. He immediately knew whose hand this was—Thomas Hill, a forecastleman. Some months earlier, while Cook and Furneaux were stopped in Tahiti, Hill had had his initials tattooed on his appendage. Burney had remembered this about the young sailor, and now it filled him with horror. Nearby, he spotted a circle of freshly disturbed ground, some four feet in diameter—probably the preparations for a traditional *hāngī*, an earth oven.

Burney and his men nosed their boat back into the water and followed the coast farther, finally coming to Grass Cove, the place where the wild celery grew thick. There they saw four canoes and hundreds of people on the beach. A large fire crackled on the high land, beyond a scrim of woods. Among the crowd, Burney could hear laughter, celebration, a festive atmosphere. "All the way down the hill," he wrote, "the place was thronged like a fair." These were Māori from the Ngāti Kuia and Rangitāne tribes, who had been living in this part of the sound for centuries.

Some of the Māori men boldly hallooed and gestured for the Englishmen to land—as if to beckon them to the celebration. Burney shook with rage and revulsion, not only because of what he'd glimpsed of his butchered colleagues, but because the Māori seemed to be taunting him and his men, luring them to their own probable deaths. He ordered the marines to fire their muskets at the Natives gathered higher up the bank. After a few volleys, the crowds "began to scramble away as fast as they could, some of them howling," Burney wrote. "We continued firing as long as we could glimpse any of them through the bushes."

Having cleared the immediate vicinity, Burney landed with the marines. On the sand they found two bundles of wild celery, which Rowe and his men had evidently cut the day before. A cracked oar from the cutter was planted upright in the sand, the Natives having tied their outrigger canoes to it. The marines searched the brush in back of the beach but could find no sign of the cutter. Then Burney spotted something. It was, he wrote, "such a shocking scene of carnage and barbarity as can never be mentioned or thought of but with horror."

Scattered about the hillside, glistening in the late-afternoon light, lay a miscellany of fresh human organs and body parts—"the heads, hearts, and lungs," as Burney described it, "of several of our people." They found, roasting on coals or strewn upon the ground, eyeballs, livers, severed feet, and Rowe's left hand, which was easily identified by a recent scar on its forefinger. The hacked head of James Swilley, Furneaux's servant, was spotted nearby. At a little distance, dogs chewed on piles of discarded intestines.

Burney had probably stumbled upon a *whāngai hau*—a sacred ceremony that involved the offering of food to an *atua*, or supernatural being. After a successful battle, some Māori tribes had a tradition of eating the flesh of their vanquished foes. According to one modern New Zealand scholar, it was about "destroying the *mana* [the spiritual life force] of the victims and leaving their kinsfolk bereft of ancestral protection."

Burney and the marines stood for a few moments in disbelief, staring at this abattoir composed of their countrymen's remains. But then they heard the whoops of Māori warriors gathering in the thickets and realized their own lives were in immediate danger. "We could hear the Indians in the woods at high words," Burney wrote, "I suppose quarrelling whether or not they should attack us." He knew that any attempt to avenge the assault on Rowe's party would have been "foolhardiness."

Burney and his men scooped up some of the body parts and scurried back to their boat. They destroyed three Māori canoes but, knowing that they were overwhelmingly outnumbered and that darkness was fast approaching, did not attempt further retribution.

It had started to drizzle, and as they rowed toward Ship Cove, Burney thought he heard an English voice calling in the distance. It was probably his imagination, he guessed, but he had the men lay on their oars. In the twilight, the boat silently glided across the rain-pecked surface. They cried out several times but heard no reply.

Burney returned to the *Adventure* close to midnight to give his terrible report. Captain Furneaux was incredulous. "I had not the least suspicion that our people had received any injury from the natives," he wrote in shock. "How much I was mistaken." Furneaux, deciding that retaliation would be pointless, pulled up anchor and departed Ship Cove early the next morning. Out in the sound, in a hastily arranged funeral, he had his men wrap the salvaged remains of their massacred comrades in a hammock, weighting the twisted bundle with ballast. They were, said Furneaux, "our very best seamen, the stoutest and most healthy people in the ship." Then they were consigned to the deep.

WITH A HEAVY heart, Furneaux set sail. He made a courageous run for a stretch of the southern seas to prosecute a search for Terra Australis on his own, perhaps also hoping to cross paths with Cook, however unlikely that was. Yet, deprived of the wild greens Rowe had cut at Grass Cove but had never been able to deliver, the first signs of scurvy began to set in. Worried about his crew, Furneaux headed for home—a long and arduous journey, for Great Britain lay some twelve thousand miles away.

In the midsummer of 1774, Furneaux limped into Portsmouth, and the lurid news flashed across the country: Ten sons of England had been slaughtered, dismembered, roasted, and eaten by cannibals in the South Seas. (That these men might have done something to provoke the Māori's wrath seemed scarcely to have been considered.) The newspapers were filled with righteous outrage and calls for vengeance, if and when another voyage could be mounted to New Zealand. On the other hand, there were cynics who insisted that the vaunted voyages of discovery, undertaken at enormous expense, accomplished nothing of practical value for England, while putting many of her finest sailors at mortal risk.

THE INCIDENT AT Grass Cove should have taken no one in England entirely by surprise. It was already well known that the Māori were ferocious defenders of their realm, and that cannibalism was a part of their martial culture. But the massacre at Grass Cove still troubled Captain Cook. He felt it demanded an inquiry and a reckoning, however long overdue. It was the most shocking tragedy that had befallen the members of any of his expeditions. Cook wanted a better understanding of how the attack had started, and who precisely was at fault. And so, to the many roles he had played while commanding his voyages, Cook was about to add a new one: homicide detective.

As he headed for New Zealand, Cook's mind was open. "I shall make no reflections on this melancholy affair until I hear more about it," he had written. If he had any preconceived notion, it was that Furneaux's men had likely done something rash and stupid that drew the Māori's ire. "I have always found them of a brave, noble, open, and benevolent disposition," Cook maintained. "But they are a people that will never put up with an insult if they have an opportunity to resent it."

15   The Land of the Long White Cloud

NEW ZEALAND, FEBRUARY 1777

New Zealand's South Island was sighted on February 10, and the two ships worked their way northeast along its emerald coast. It was a land of deep fjords and sprawling beaches of fine black sand, broken intermittently by cold blue rivers of glacial meltwater that raced from mountains more than ten thousand feet high.

New Zealand, or Aotearoa, as some Māori tribal groups called this spectacular country, was the southern point of what has come to be known as the Polynesian Triangle. It is said to have been the last large habitable land on earth settled by humans, and the last of the islands discovered by the Polynesians. New Zealand had been unpeopled for all the eons since it rose from the sea, a fragment torn loose from the ancient supercontinent of Gondwana. But then, sometime during the 1200s, a succession of star voyagers from eastern Polynesia arrived, having sailed their large oceangoing canoes, or *waka,* more than two thousand miles down through the South Pacific. No one knows precisely what motivated or lured them to make such a long trek in the first place—the promise of wealth? resource depletion or environmental collapse on their home islands? a need to escape violence among kinship groups?—but the subsequent voyages seem to have been carefully planned schemes of migration.

Some Māori traditions say the first wayfinder to reach New Zealand was a chiefly fisherman named Kupe, who hailed from Hawaiki, a mythic Polynesian homeland. In a creation story that bears distinct echoes of Melville's Captain Ahab and the white whale, Kupe developed a vendetta against a giant octopus that had consistently stolen his catch within his traditional fishing grounds. Kupe, burning with rage, constructed an immense canoe and, for uncounted days, with a large crew aboard his proud vessel, pursued his eight-legged nemesis far beyond waters familiar to him. The octopus seemed to be leading Kupe onward, heading purposefully toward a destination. One day, Kupe's wife spotted a great unknown land, "like a cloud on the horizon." It is said that Kupe made a tour of the islands, noting that they seemed to be uninhabited by humans but madly aflutter with birds.

According to some of the myths, Kupe returned to his home and shared knowledge of this fabulous land; its existence simmered as a brilliant secret within Polynesian culture. Eventually, seven large voyaging canoes packed with men, women, and children struck out from their Polynesian home islands to relocate Kupe's magical realm to the south. These seven vessels have come to be known as the Great Fleet, and their mythic trek forms the basis of a foundation story whose details are debated among scholars today.

On board, these migrants carried familiar plants and animals, for they had every intention of making Kupe's fabled land their permanent home. The canoes sailed together, but upon reaching Aotearoa, they separated and landed at far-flung locations along the coast. Some Māori scholars say that all the tribal groups of New Zealand can trace their lineages back to the chiefly class of navigators who piloted the seven canoes of the Great Fleet.

These adventurous settlers, who became the Māori, found a dazzling world very different from the tropical islands and coral atolls they had known. Here was a place of sharply variegated landscapes, of sleet and ice and cold mountain lakes, of fierce winters and frequent earthquakes, of fumy rhyolitic vents and rumbling volcanoes mantled in snow. This large kingdom boasted a total land mass more than eight times that of all the other islands of Polynesia combined.

Its wildlife was strange and diverse, too. Sequestered for tens of millions of years, New Zealand had an evolutionary history like nowhere else on earth. Among other creatures that evolved only here was a giant cricket known as the wētā, genus *Deinacrida* ("terrible grasshopper"), which was and still is the planet's largest insect. The world's largest freshwater eel—*Anguilla dieffenbachii,* or the longfin eel—has called New Zealand home for some eighty million years. These sometimes aggressive behemoths can grow to six feet in length and weigh nearly a hundred pounds, with a life span approaching a century.

Until the Polynesians arrived with dogs and rats, New Zealand had no terrestrial mammals other than a small bat. It was a "land without teeth," as biologists have described it. Free of the four-legged predators found on every continent, avian life had flourished to a spectacular extent on New Zealand—but therein lay a future vulnerability, for most birds here had never particularly needed to develop defenses against attackers.

In many ways, this was a land *dominated* by birds, including the Haast's eagle, one of the largest raptors to have existed on earth, with a wingspan of nearly ten feet and enormous talons that resembled a leopard's claws. There was also a certain twelve-foot-tall, quarter-ton ostrich-like creature called the moa, which was the Haast's eagle's primary prey. One species of moa, *Dinornis giganteus,* is believed to have been the tallest bird that ever walked the earth. Its fleshy drumsticks were the size of a moose's haunches, and its eggs were as big as medicine balls.

Europeans would never see these implausible creatures; by the time of Cook's arrival in New Zealand, they were long gone, although their fossilized bones could be found scattered about. The Māori, pursuing the gargantuan land bird for its meat as well as its feathers, hide, and eggs, had hunted the moa to extinction by the 1400s, with the Haast's eagle soon following its favored prey into evolutionary oblivion.

But the Māori thrived here. In a few centuries, they had populated both islands and built a distinct civilization. They were fine hunters, fishermen, sculptors, carvers, and designers. They were Polynesian but had lost touch with Polynesia. They no longer voyaged backwards, to their place of origin, but concentrated their energies on this new place—a place that was actually 680 million years old but completely devoid of human history. Living in isolation, the Māori settled the ranges and coves and valleys, the estuaries and bays, and the rugged interior, too, where the rivers teemed with fish and the canyon grottoes pulsed with glowworms that speckled the night like the stars these brave voyagers had sailed in by.

COOK'S TWO SHIPS rounded the top of the South Island and turned into a crazy fretwork of channels and drowned river valleys that fed down into the long, serene body of water that Cook had named (after King George's German-born wife) Queen Charlotte Sound. On February 12, they nudged into their familiar spot at Ship Cove and dropped anchors. In all his travels, this was the fifth time Cook had stopped here. It was a fine, clear day, and the waters were flat calm. A faint wind breathed through the stands of huge, prehistoric-looking evergreens—known as rimu trees—that climbed the surrounding hills.

Canoes had followed the two ships into the cove, but the Māori paddlers, though curious, were timid and distrustful. Cook recognized some of the Natives—a few were old friends. Using Mai as a translator, Cook tried to convey to them that he came in peace, that he wanted to trade and interact as they always had. But the Māori didn't believe Cook. They were certain he had returned to retaliate for the killings of the Englishmen.

"Neither professions of friendship nor presents would induce [them] to come into the ship," wrote Cook. "It appeared to me they were apprehensive we were come to revenge the death of Captain Furneaux's people." Seeing Mai on board only redoubled the Natives' fears—for they well remembered that Mai had been with Furneaux on the *Adventure*. "They must be well assured that I was no longer a stranger to that unhappy affair," said Cook. "I did all in my power to assure them of the continuance of my friendship, and that I should not disturb them on that account."

The Māori, still not convinced, sang songs of peace, waved strips of white cloth, and kept their distance. Some of the seamen thought the Natives acted exactly as guilty people might be expected to act. "Nothing can be a greater proof of their treachery," reasoned George Gilbert, "than their suspecting it in us." For those who had been part of Furneaux's crew on the *Adventure*, this return to the scene of the incident was haunting. James Burney, who for the past three years had not been able to speak of the killings except in whispers, entered the cove with dread.

COOK'S MEN BEGAN to set up camp on a curve of sand beside the pellucid stream he'd used in previous voyages to fill his casks. The pebbly beach was empty on this brilliant, warm day, but the mood on

shore was eerie. A deafening screech came from the ferny woods—
William Anderson described it as a "perpetual and universal chirping." It was the shrill sound of untold thousands of cicadas.

From the ships, boat after boat crammed with men and supplies
came ashore. Crews erected long rows of tents. The astronomers set
up their observatory. Brewers and blacksmiths tinkered with their
equipment. Animals were ferried across, and soon horses, cows, and
goats were testing their legs and grazing along the margins of the
encampment.

The Māori watched these developments from their canoes. They
seemed dazzled by the scope of the operation, and by the spectacle
of it. They had never seen horses or cattle before. Gradually, their
fascination won out over their fears, and they, too, began to come
ashore, first in small groups, then in throngs. The Englishmen and
the Māori pressed noses together in greeting, as they had during
previous encounters. Out came the "nails, broken glass, beads [and]
other European trumpery," as John Rickman described it—and,
especially, anything made of iron. "There is nothing they will not
sell for iron," he thought, "so great is their desire for that metal."

Word spread to settlements in distant coves, and by the afternoon hundreds of Māori arrived—men, women, and children from
different *hapu,* or kinship clans—hauling their ornately carved boats
onto the beach. Many of them brought portable huts with them, and
erected their own village right beside the English. Cook was amazed
by the abrupt change in the Natives' mood. If they had any lingering
suspicion that he'd come in the role of an avenger, Cook said, "they
very soon laid it aside, for during the course of this day a great many
families came from different parts and took up their residence by us."

By dusk, Ship Cove had the look and feel of a carnival. There was
bantering and bartering, music and bonfires, clanking goblets and
roasting fish. Lanterns and torches burned through the night. Later,
some of the Māori men demonstrated their *haka* dance, which they
usually performed in preparation for battle. Anderson described the
ritual in vivid detail: "They all keep the exactest time, and in a short
space raise their passion to a degree of frantic fury attended with
the most horrid distortion of their eyes [and] mouths." The danc-

ers, added Anderson, "appear more like infernal demons than men." Samwell agreed. The *haka*, he thought, was "admirably calculated to strike terror into their enemies, consisting [of] violent gestures and contortions of their faces and bodies, hanging out their tongues, and staring as if their eyes were ready to start out of their heads."

The Māori dancers, dressed in full regalia, were nothing if not impressive. "Among all the savage sons of war I ever saw, [they] are the most formidable," John Ledyard wrote. "When a New Zealander stands forth and brandishes his spear, the subsequent idea is, *there stands a man.*"

As the night wore on, some of the women offered their favors, but most of Cook's men kept their distance. The memory of what had happened to Furneaux's party of grass cutters seemed to have dampened their libidos. Still, some trysts were reported. A young man on the *Discovery* was said by Ledyard to have fallen for a New Zealander girl, about fourteen years old. "They fell desperately in love," Ledyard wrote, and spent the night "in a kind of silent conversation, in which, though words were wanting, their meaning was perfectly understood; the language of love among all the languages in this sublunary world is the soonest to be comprehended."

But for the most part, Cook's men seemed to concentrate far more on feasting than on lovemaking. The Māori fishermen had brought loads of delicious fresh catch. The lobsters were judged very fine, as were the cockles, oysters, and mussels. There was mullet, tarakihi, blue cod, and mackerel. But by far the most popular was the fish the Natives called moki, which yielded fillets that were incredibly moist and delicate, much like sea bass.

The Māori were expert fishermen—that much was obvious— but the most devout anglers among the English were mystified by their technique. "It is not easy to say by what arts they allured the fish," wrote Rickman, who found their fishhooks laughably inadequate. "But certainly some means were used by them to which we were strangers, nor could they ever be prevailed upon to [reveal] their secret."

The Māori, on the other hand, were weirdly fond of hardtack bread, that dreary shipboard staple. It didn't seem to matter to them how moldy, stale, or bug-infested the old biscuits might be—the Natives still relished them. But the Māori were even crazier about the blubber that some of the crewmen were boiling down from the butchered carcasses of the sea lions that had been shot in the Kerguelen Islands. The Māori, whose diet was lacking in fat, had an insatiable craving for the blubber. "They ate the very dregs of the casks and skimmings of the kettle," noted Cook. They drained oil from the lamps, ate candles, and even consumed the wicks.

Cook's men bedded down, or tried to, but the cicadas kept shrieking, and the Māori drums kept pounding as distant fires flickered through the night. The captain wasn't taking any chances: He'd posted marine sentries at key locations and distributed firearms throughout the camp. He really didn't think these precautions were necessary, but "after the sacrifice which the Natives made of the boat crew belonging to the *Adventure*," he wrote, "it was impossible to totally divest ourselves of apprehensions."

During the night, ominous chants and shouts would erupt from the hills, sometimes followed by what Samwell called "the most dismal cries from different parts of the cove, the cause of which we could not assign." The seamen, restless in their tents, were spooked. Hearing the distant wailings, Samwell said, "we sometimes thought that some miserable wretches were [being] put to death."

YET THE NEXT morning, as the sun crept over Ship Cove, all seemed well. The woods stirred with cheerful birdsong—"the most melodious notes I have ever heard," thought Gilbert. Flitting through the trees were kōkakos, huias, saddlebacks, and other beautiful birds. Among the Māori, there was no indication that anything untoward had occurred during the night. They seemed energetic and mirthful as they bustled into the camp, just as they had the day before, to mingle and trade.

Cook's men were dazzled by the elaborate carvings they saw. The Māori had a powerful gift for pattern and design—one could see it on their boats and structures, on their amulets and tikis, on the greenstone figurines they wore as jewelry. "Their masterpiece seems to be carving, which is found on the most trifling things," wrote

Anderson. "In particular, the heads of their canoes are done in such a manner that not only shows much design but is also an example of their great labor and patience in execution." The surgeon was even more amazed when he considered that the Māori possessed no metal tools. "Their substitute for a knife is a shell, or a bit of flint or jasper," he marveled, "and as an auger to bore holes they fix a shark's tooth in the end of a small piece of wood."

Their proclivity for extravagant design was perhaps nowhere more evident than in the markings that graced the skin of so many Māori. The process of tattooing—or *tā moko*, as the Māori called it—was labor-intensive and painful; the artist punctured the skin with implements made of honed albatross bone, using pigments derived from soot and fossilized resins. The sailors were fascinated by the tradition, and at Ship Cove more than a few sought out the Māori tattoo artists. John Ledyard mentioned a young man from the *Discovery* who wanted "to ornament his person in the fashion of New Zealand"—and who eagerly "submitted himself to be tattooed from head to foot."

Cook had the carpenters stamping through the woods, trimming branches off the rimu trees to make what he called "spruce beer." In vats, the brewers began to boil the long, shaggy needles and boughs, then added liquid malt and sugar, slowly cooking down the decoction. As the boiling progressed, a piney tang issued from the kettles and drifted over the encampment. Later, when the first batches were pronounced ready, the men held out their mugs. Rickman declared it a "wholesome beverage" and felt sure it would "strike at the very root of the scurvy." Anderson said it was "little inferior" to American spruce beer.

Among the Māori habitations nearby, Cook learned that a chief named Kahura was encamped with some of his kin. According to Mai, who conversed with many of the locals milling about the cove, this Kahura was one of the warriors who had killed and eaten Furneaux's men—he was said to be the ringleader of the massacre. Mai had been told that this man was an unpopular chief and a ruthless bully. "He seemed to be a man more feared than loved," wrote Cook. "Many said he was a very bad man, and they importuned me to kill him." Samwell described Kahura as "middle aged, very strong, and of a fierce countenance, tattooed after the manner of the country." Anderson called him "turbulent and mischievous—all the inhabitants concurred in giving him a bad character."

Cook wanted to know more about Kahura, but he wasn't going to execute the man on the recommendation of a few Natives. Wrote Cook: "I believe they were not a little surprised that I did not [kill him], for according to their ideas of equity this ought to have been done."

During his past voyages, Cook had made it his firm policy not to intervene in the political squabbles and conflicts of the Natives he encountered. It was a practice that had stood him in good stead. Maybe he recalled that, more than two centuries earlier, Ferdinand Magellan, one of history's most accomplished explorers, had enmeshed himself too deeply in a local war in the Philippines—and was hacked to pieces in the surf on the island of Mactan. Cook's policy of studied neutrality was particularly prudent in New Zealand, where it seemed to him that tribes and kinship groups were forever warring with one another. "If I had followed the advice of all our pretended friends," Cook wrote, "I might have extirpated the whole race, for the people of each hamlet or village by turns applied to me to destroy the other."

Cook believed that the Māori practice of cannibalism was directly connected to the Hobbesian violence that plagued their fractured tribal society. The people around Queen Charlotte Sound lived under unremitting threat of attack, not only from one another—as multiple independent factions and kinship groups were embroiled in spasmodic bouts of internecine warfare—but also from more powerful tribes from the North Island, who made frequent trips across the strait to collect a prized greenstone found in abundance on the South Island. The raids of these northern marauders created a constant undertow of uneasiness and uncertainty. "From my own observations," Cook wrote, "the New Zealanders must live under perpetual apprehensions of being destroyed by each other. There being few tribes that have not received some injury or another from some other, which they are continually upon the watch to revenge and perhaps the idea of a good meal may be no small incitement."

16   Return to Grass Cove

NEW ZEALAND, FEBRUARY 1777

On February 16, at first light, Cook ventured out with a party of well-armed men in several boats to look for better fodder for the animals—and to do some sleuthing. Among the party was Mai, who would serve as his translator, and several of his most trusted officers, including Clerke. After a few hours of gunkholing about Queen Charlotte Sound, they had succeeded in piling the boats high with fresh hay. Then Cook decided, at last, that it was time to go to Grass Cove, the site of the massacre.

The party pulled the boats up on the sand and disembarked. Though it had once been populated, the area seemed desolate now, with a few half-ruined structures, like a ghost settlement. A group of men were spotted in the distance, and they seemed jumpy at Cook's approach. "I thought they showed manifest signs of fear," Cook wrote. One of the Māori was an old friend—a man named Matahua. Through Mai, Cook put the question to him straight: What had happened here on that day? Why had their countrymen been killed?

Matahua and his companions, shaking off their fears, began to tell the story as they understood it. They insisted that they had not been here when the murders took place, and Cook believed them—he thought they spoke "like people who are under no apprehension of punishment for a crime they are not guilty of." Still, they knew the stories well and were intimately acquainted with everyone who had participated in the affray.

Allowing for a few minor variations in detail, the accounts told by Matahua and his companions more or less jibed with one another. The quarrel had arisen, they said, when one of the Māori stole some trifling item—a few pieces of bread, it was said—from the party of ten English crewmen while they were taking their lunch on the beach some distance from their boat. After a brief scuffle, the one who appeared to be the leader of the party—this would have been Jack Rowe—overreacted: He picked up his loaded musket and, without warning, shot the bread pilferer dead.

The other men in the party were unarmed—they had left their muskets back in the boats. By then, more Māori had arrived on the scene, and Rowe, turning from rage to panic, proceeded to shoot and kill a second Native. Chief Kahura and some of his men overpowered all ten of the Englishmen, clubbing them in the head. Kahura often went around boasting that it was he who had killed the leader, Rowe, with his own hands.

In sifting through the stories, the most important finding for Cook was this: The murders had not been premeditated. By all accounts, it had been a crime of escalating passions. The captain had to conclude that it was largely Rowe's fault—Cook had known Rowe to be an ill-tempered man who detested Natives and was quick to reach for his gun. (One close observer who had sailed with Rowe wrote that the "prejudices of a naval education...induced him to look upon all the natives of the South Sea with contempt.") Cook felt sure that Rowe was to blame. "If these thefts had not, unfortunately, been so hastily resented, no ill consequence [would have] attended," Cook reasoned.

As for the cannibalism part of the story, there could be no doubt of its veracity. Yet Cook saw no point in getting incensed about what happened after their deaths. Call it an enlightened tolerance, or call it moral relativism, but Cook didn't believe in superimposing Christian morality or English ethics on situations he encountered on the other side of the globe. It was well known that Māori warriors consumed the flesh of those they had killed in combat. Anthropophagy was a fact of Māori life, a ritual of their warrior culture. Wrote Cook: "This custom of eating their enemies slain in battle (for I firmly believe they eat the flesh of no others) has undoubtedly been handed down to them from the earliest times and we know that it is not an easy matter to break a nation of its ancient customs."

Cook asked Matahua and his companions what had become of

the boat the grass cutters had rowed into the cove, but he couldn't get a straight answer. "Some said she was pulled to pieces and burnt," Cook reported. "Others said she was carried they knew not where by a party of strangers."

Cook left Grass Cove with a clearer picture of what had happened on that horrible afternoon, but he would keep pressing for more details in the days ahead. If anything, he thought the stories came nearer to absolving the Māori and implicating Furneaux's own men—or at least one of them—in the quarrel that had led to their deaths.

Clerke, on the other hand, was not so sure. "The stories these people choose to tell of such an unfortunate business can very little be depended on," he thought. "I firmly believe them very capable of the most perfidious and cruel treachery."

BACK AT SHIP Cove, it seemed that the attitude of the Māori had changed. In their bartering, they were more forceful, more impatient, more insistent. A new haughtiness had crept into their dealings with the English. "They are much clearer in their demands than formerly," master's mate Henry Roberts noted. "Traffic was greatly altered in favor of the Indian," James Burney insisted. "A nail last voyage purchas[ed] more than an axe or a hatchet would now." John Gore thought something had changed in their outlook—they were "confident of their own power." He thought he knew why: They were starting to realize that Cook was never going to retaliate for the massacre at Grass Cove. "Perhaps," said Gore, "our not resenting with any degree of severity" the murders of Furneaux's men had tipped the scales of power and had only made the Māori more audacious.

Burney had the same idea. "It seemed evident that many of them held us in great contempt," he said, "and I believe chiefly on account of our not revenging the affair of [Grass Cove], so contrary to the principle by which they would have acted in the like case."

This was undoubtedly true. The Māori lived by the principle of *utu*—the concept that social affairs must be regulated by a strict sense of balance and reciprocation. In matters of warfare, a death must be avenged by another death. It was not only expected; it was required.

To sublimate the instinct to avenge the murders of his men, as Cook had done, was a sign of weakness. It was unnatural, a violation of the spiritual laws. In previous voyages, the Māori had respected Cook as a leader. Now they questioned his very essence, his *mana*.

The Grass Cove participants were so emboldened that they started to come out of the shadows and brag about their roles in the incident. "As an instance how much they trusted to our easiness," said Burney, "one man did scruple to acknowledge his being present and assisting at the killing and eating of the *Adventure*'s people."

But no one was bolder than Kahura, the man said to have led the massacre. As Cook began preparations to leave Ship Cove, Kahura had the temerity to venture aboard the *Resolution* several times, mingling with the Englishmen on deck "without showing the last mark of fear," according to Cook. To many, Kahura's very presence on the ship was an act of provocation. This man had killed, butchered, and eaten their comrades, and now here he was, flaunting his power, strutting around the ship with impunity. On one of these visits, Mai pointed Kahura out to Cook and beseeched the captain to have him shot. Mai volunteered to do it himself. Kahura paid so little heed to these threats that he returned in his canoe the very next morning, February 25, with his whole clan—more than twenty in all, including men, women, and children. Mai asked Cook if he should invite Kahura and his kin on board, and Cook, to everyone's surprise, said yes.

When Cook ushered Kahura into his private cabin, Mai was outraged. He tried to intervene, saying, "There is Kahura, *kill him!*" But Cook showed no intentions of violence, and Mai lost all composure. "Why do you not kill him?" he yelled. "If a man kills another in England, he is hanged for it. This man has killed ten and yet you will not kill him." He reminded Cook that many of Kahura's own people wanted him dead. Executing him, Mai insisted, "would be very good."

Cook considered what Mai had said but did nothing. As he later put it, "Mai's arguments, though reasonable enough, [had] no weight with me."

Instead Cook instructed Mai to ask Kahura why he had killed Captain Furneaux's people. At this, the chief folded his arms and hung his head in despair. He "looked like one caught in a trap," Cook thought, "and I firmly believe expected every moment to be his last." Cook tried to soothe him, assuring him of his safety. Kahura's demeanor changed completely. He became chatty and cheerful, as though he'd received a reprieve from his executioner. Still, he would not answer the question Cook had put to him until Mai once again assured him that he wouldn't be hurt.

Finally, Kahura began to tell his variation of the story. He claimed that it all started when one of the ten sailors, while having lunch on the beach, accepted a stone adze, in what was supposed to be a trade, but failed to offer anything in return. From the Māori point of view, the Englishman had effectively *stolen* the adze. This rudeness prompted one of the Natives, in turn, to make off with some bread, and the dispute erupted in violence. "The remainder of his account," said Cook, "differed very little from what we had been told by other people." Cook suspected that the bit about the stolen adze was pure embellishment. "The story," he wrote, "was certainly invented by Kahura to make the English appear the first aggressors."

Cook believed Kahura to be the leader of the massacre—Kahura had even boasted as much—but he thought nothing would be gained by punishing the chief, let alone killing him, all these months later. Clerke agreed with him. Avenging the murders with more murders, he thought, "could answer no purpose." Although Cook could be a stern disciplinarian, he was seldom moved by vengeance. He tried to remain impartial, cognizant of local customs—and he was also considering the ripple effects his actions might have among the Natives. "As to what was past, I should think no more of it," Cook wrote. The massacre had occurred "some time since, and ... when I was not there."

Others among the crew failed to understand his logic; even if Cook had not been physically present during the massacre, it had nonetheless happened during his voyage, to his own countrymen, who were ultimately under his command. Modern critics of Cook have contended that it is a classic trait of authoritarians to dismiss or belittle events that occur beyond their immediate sphere of influence. "For the authoritarian persona," argues Gananath Obeyesekere in *The Apotheosis of Captain Cook,* "the world can be an extension of his own being: If the massacre had happened to his own crew, when he was there, the consequences would have been different."

Cook did instruct Mai to issue a warning to the Māori around Ship Cove: "If ever they made a second attempt of that kind, they might rest assured of feeling the weight of my resentment."

While sitting in Cook's cabin, Kahura happened to notice a portrait that the expedition artist, John Webber, had painted of some unnamed Māori person. Kahura was taken with it—and perhaps felt a twinge of jealousy. Through Mai, he asked if he could get his own portrait made. After all, he was a chief, and seemed to think he was important enough to deserve one.

Cook sent for Webber. Soon Kahura was sitting for the artist, holding a steady pose in silence amid the flurry of Webber's brushstrokes. In some strange way, Cook respected Kahura—or at least was impressed by the bravura of his performance. "I must confess," Cook said, "I admired his courage and was not a little pleased at the confidence he put in me."

In the resulting portrait by Webber, we see a supremely confident, scraggly-bearded man, with a topknot. Feathers dangle from large holes in his ears, and tattoos spiral across his face. The chief wears a Gioconda smile, enigmatic with a trace of impudence, the look of a man who, quite literally, has gotten away with murder.

FEW OF COOK'S men could understand his leniency. They thought he was taking tolerance and restraint to absurd extremes. Cook knew the name of the prime culprit behind the Grass Cove massacre—and still he did nothing. Worse, he had paid the man the supreme honor of inviting him into his cabin, a sanctum few of Cook's own men had ever seen, and then had consented to the killer's request to pose for a portrait.

Where did Cook's loyalties lie? Throughout this voyage, he had repeatedly used the lash on his own sailors, often for minor infractions like drunkenness or sleeping while on duty. Veterans of his previous expeditions had noticed the change and were troubled by it: If he was no longer the benevolent commander they remembered, at least he could be consistent. Cruelty to his own men, compassion for murdering cannibals? This seeming double standard threw many of the ordinary seamen into a rage.

On board the *Discovery*, a small group of sailors vented their frustration in a bizarre and fiendish way. During their sojourn at Ship Cove, a young midshipman named Edward "Neddy" Riou had gotten hold of a kurī—a breed of Polynesian dog that is now extinct—to adopt as his pet. The kurī looked something like a fox; it had a bushy tail, an elongated body, and sharply pointed ears. Instead of a bark, the kurī let out an unsettling howl.

Neddy Riou was proud of his four-legged souvenir from New Zealand, and planned to bring it back to England. But there was a problem: His new pet constantly nipped at the sailors on board. One day, while Riou was on shore, some of his messmates decided they'd had enough of this irksome canine. They hatched a grotesque idea for a prank: They would put Riou's dog "on trial" for cannibalism. They of course had not forgotten Burney's account of the dogs at Grass Cove that were seen gnawing on the entrails of the slain and butchered men of the *Adventure*. Riou's dog, they insisted, was "of cannibal origin, and was completely a cannibal itself, having bit every one of us, and shown every inclination to eat us alive if he could."

So a court-martial was hastily convened, and the kurī was brought before the members of the jury. The verdict arrived quickly—*guilty!* Then came the sentence: capital punishment. The dog was to be put to death and consumed.

It was a sick burlesque, and, in a way, an act of quiet sedition. It was their way of telling Cook what they thought of his decision not to prosecute Kahura or punish any of the Māori.

If the legal "proceedings" were meant as a perverse practical joke, at the same time, these sailors weren't kidding. They had every intention of devouring the poor beast. The dog was promptly killed, cooked, dressed, and eaten—"for we were all so confoundedly hungry," said master's mate Alexander Home. After their feast, the group set aside a portion of the roasted dog meat in a wooden bowl for Riou to enjoy upon his return. Meanwhile, they took the skin of the animal and turned it into a grisly hat. When Riou returned to the ship, the pranksters placed the skin over his head, the animal's bushy tail hanging down his back and its paws drooped over his shoulders.

Riou was horrified. "You're all a set of damned cannibals!" he cried, and went belowdecks, sulking. Home followed him. After grumbling for a while, Riou looked at Home with a baleful expression.

"Damn you," he said. "Did you not even leave me a share?"

"That I did, Neddy, my boy," Home replied, and went to fetch the wooden bowl he had saved.

Riou seemed miserable as he scrutinized the last remnants of his beloved kurī. Then his hunger got the better of him. Said Home: "Poor Neddy munched up his dog, cursing all the while."

COOK WAS UNAWARE of the particulars of this incident, but he was beginning to detect the disaffections of his men. It's also possible that he had started to recognize that the Māori themselves did not respect him for the tolerance he had shown—quite the opposite. For Cook, it was damned if you did and damned if you didn't. If he demonstrated forbearance toward the Natives, many of his own men would criticize him for being too soft and forgiving. But if he visited swift vengeance in a way that Polynesians expected from a man of his stature, others in his crew would say he was cruel and drastic. Whatever the case, his visit to Queen Charlotte Sound became a sharp turning point. For the rest of the voyage, Cook would show far less mercy and patience in his dealings with Indigenous people. Increasingly, he would become a despot, a hard-liner, with a mean streak that was seldom on display during his previous voyages.

There was perhaps another dimension to Cook's change in attitude, the souring of his outlook. In reading his journals, one detects that he was slowly losing faith in the supposed benefits of cross-cultural contact. He was starting to realize that visiting these islanders wasn't good for them. More and more, he doubted whether Native ways of viewing property and trade could really mesh with European ways. The two worlds, the two organizational regimes, were so fundamentally different, he thought, they could never come into true alignment.

On this stop in New Zealand, Cook had sensed an evolution among the Māori, a restiveness and a discontent he had caught only a faint whiff of during his second voyage. It was not the same place it had been when he first set eyes on it in 1769, aboard the *Endeavour.* In less than a decade, through forces of disruption and dislocation that his own visits here had set in motion, the Māori were changed. Cook discerned this—not only the change, but the direct role his voyages had played in it.

"We debauch their morals," Cook wrote, "and we introduce among them wants and diseases which they never before knew." Cook thought the cumulative effect of his stops in New Zealand "serve[d] only to disturb that... tranquillity they and their forefathers had enjoyed. If anyone denies the truth of this assertion, let him tell me what the natives of the whole extent of America have gained by the commerce they have had with the Europeans."

DURING PREVIOUS VOYAGES, Cook had usually shown a shrewd sense of timing, and at least that gift did not abandon him now. After nearly two weeks in Queen Charlotte Sound he knew it was time to leave.

As the two ships readied for departure, Mai had become obsessed with the notion that he should have a servant. If he was going to live as a prince in Tahiti, he needed to surround himself with the proper trappings. He was determined to bring one of the Māori home with him, and he had already selected his candidate: a seventeen-year-old boy named Te Weherua, the son of a respected chief who had recently been killed in battle. Te Weherua had been hanging around the *Resolution,* and all the men liked him. Samwell called him "a good-natured honest young fellow."

Long-distance voyaging, of course, had deep roots in Te Weherua's culture. He seemed enchanted with the idea of visiting Tahiti and its scattered islands. But Cook took a dim view of this development. He scarcely had room or provisions on the ship for another soul. Nor did he think it was fair to this lad to spirit him away, for he would probably never see his native country again. "I was apprehensive Mai had deceived [the boy] by a promise of returning back," said Cook, who made sure Te Weherua and his mother understood that if the boy went away with the ships, he would never return. "But this," said Cook, "seemed to make no sort of impression."

Te Weherua had his own demands. Because he was descended from an eminent family within Māori society, he announced that he would be bringing his own servant. He chose a nine-year-old boy named Koa, whose father presented him "with far less indifference than he would have parted with his dog," said Cook. Not one of Koa's relations "seemed to trouble themselves about what became of" the boy.

On the eve of embarkation, Te Weherua was still very eager to go, but his mother refused to part with her son. The realization that she would never see him again had fully overtaken her. She sobbed uncontrollably and mourned her impending loss by scraping herself with a shark's tooth until the blood coursed down her face. For hours, she held Te Weherua close.

Cook was moved by the scene. "She and Te Weherua parted with all the marks of tender affection that might be expected between a mother and her son who were never to meet again." After some time, his mother regained her composure. "She said she would cry no more, and sure enough she kept her word."

On February 25, after final farewells were exchanged, the *Resolution* and the *Discovery* unmoored and slipped from the cove. They headed down the sound and out to the mighty seaway separating New Zealand's South and North Islands. Cook Strait, it was called, and still is. (Cook hadn't named it that; it's believed that Joseph Banks was largely responsible for getting the name affixed to the charts.)

No sooner had they lost sight of land than the two Māori boys, Te Weherua and Koa, fell into a profound homesickness. The pangs took hold of their hearts, and wouldn't let go, as the *Resolution* and the *Discovery* sailed toward brief stops in what are now known as the Cook Islands, and then longer stays in the Tonga Islands. The two Māori boys "wept both in public and in private," said Cook, "and made their lamentations in a kind of song, which so far as we could understand of it was in praise of their country and people they should never see more."

For days the two boys sat on the anchor chains and gazed at the sea. They wouldn't eat. They wouldn't talk. "They cried most piteously," wrote Samwell, "at the same time singing a dirge in a melancholy cadence." Their longing for home resonated powerfully throughout the ship and seemed to upset the entire crew. Mai did all that he could to soothe them. But the two distraught boys only stared at the endless Pacific.

BOOK THREE

Faraway Heaven

———

Spyglass to the ready,
the Captain speaks, heading for Tahiti.
Ah Paradiso bliss!
These natives are the gentlest, a breezy caress
while my crew
feast on all their senses can thrust and chew...

But don't just thrust and chew,
we're disciplined, we're English
through and through—Venus
is our mission, and exploration
next. We crew for the nation!

—ROBERT SULLIVAN, CAPTAIN COOK
IN THE UNDERWORLD

17 Aphrodite's Island

For days Mai searched the horizon for the first sign of his home islands puncturing the flat calm of the sea. The men on board the *Resolution* watched him and were fascinated by his change in mood. "As we approached his island, Mai became more and more an object of our attention," wrote James King. "His anxiety was equal to ours, and we were glad to observe as he grew nearer, more thoughtful." On August 12, after a passage of four slow weeks from Tonga, the ship's lookout spotted the great volcano, a luminous wispy blue, hanging in the distance.

Finally, the men were about to arrive at the place of their wildest desires: Tahiti. King George III Island. New Cythera, as Louis Antoine de Bougainville had called it when he visited the island in 1768, after the Greek island that was said to be Aphrodite's birthplace. For it had seemed to the French visitors, just as it had to the English crews under Wallis and then Cook, that Tahiti was a place where sensual pleasures were paramount.

No small number of young men aboard the *Resolution* and the *Discovery* had signed on for the voyage simply because they had heard the stories of how lovely Tahiti was and yearned to see the mythic utopia for themselves. The island of love and beauty, where bread grew on trees, plenitudes of fish darted through the turquoise lagoons, and palm trees swayed in the trade winds. On previous voyages to Tahiti, European sailors had found that sex could be had, literally, for the price of a nail.

The *Resolution* and the *Discovery* had been sailing a year and a month, traveling some twenty thousand arduous miles since Plymouth. Cook and his men were entitled to a good "refreshing," as he liked to put it, and Tahiti was one place where good refreshings nearly always happened.

Staring at the ever enlarging island, the men could almost conjure the smell of coconut oil and hibiscus, of pandanus fruit, of hogs slow-roasting in underground pits. Wrote surgeon's mate David Samwell: "You may well suppose the satisfaction mixed with anxious curiosity that was visible in every countenance as we approached by slow degrees this new Cythera, of which we had heard such pleasing, such romantic accounts from other visitors." The people's imaginations, he added, "were heated with the descriptions they had read."

By now, Samwell was starting to emerge as the most engaging, energetic, and eloquent voice of the voyage. The Welshman, in addition to being a physician, was a sensitive observer and a poet who sometimes went by his Welsh "bardic" name, Dafydd Ddu Feddyg, meaning "Black David, the Doctor." More and more, Samwell had become an important and beloved presence on the expedition—one account described him as "tall, stout, black-haired, pock-marked, fierce-looking, [and] wondrous friendly in company."

Samwell noted that Mai "sat all day on the forecastle viewing his native shores with tears in his eyes." They were tears of joy and longing, Samwell thought, but also tears that seemed to spring from more complicated emotions. As Tahiti drew nearer, his apprehensions thickened. He'd been away four years, and he had no notion how his countrymen would receive him. Would he return as a hero? A prince? An ambassador from England? Would the rarity of his recent experiences help him transcend the lowliness of his birth? He had seen so many things no Polynesian had seen before. His powerful friends in England—Banks, Lord Sandwich, King George—held such high hopes for him, and had given him the tools they thought might guarantee his success.

But revenge was still foremost on Mai's mind. He couldn't forget what the invaders from Bora Bora had done to his people on Raiatea, the island of his birth. He couldn't forget how they had murdered his father and seized his family's land. "He would never listen to any plan," Lieutenant King said, "except that of destroying the Bora Bora chiefs and freeing his native Raiatea from its present slavery."

As the *Resolution* skirted the southeast coast of Tahiti, the men thought Mai was focused less on the rapture of homecoming than on the cruder satisfactions of waging a long-delayed war.

LATE IN THE afternoon, on the approach into Vaitepiha Bay, some Tahitian paddlers ventured out in their canoes to meet the two ships. "Who is your captain?" they cried when they drew up near to the *Resolution*.

"Toote! Toote!" Mai yelled back over the gunwales—this was how the Tahitians pronounced Cook's name.

The paddlers understood and seemed ecstatic. *"Maitai! Maitai!"* ("Very good!") they sang out, and pulled alongside. When the Tahitians climbed onto the deck, Cook greeted them effusively. They did not seem surprised that a Tahitian man was sailing aboard the ship of this eminent and well-known captain from "Pretanne." More canoes arrived, and in one of them, by chance, was Mai's brother-in-law. Oddly, the man seemed indifferent to Mai—not the slightest flicker of emotion passed across his face.

Yet when Mai led him below and showed off a collection of red feathers he had obtained in Tonga, a complete transformation came over his brother-in-law. It was as though Mai had shown him a chestful of glittering jewels. Mai gave him a few feathers as presents, and suddenly they were fast friends again. There was something magical about red feathers; the Tahitians found them irresistible. They were emblems of the cult of Oro, talismans from nature in the hue of the gods, signifying blood and fertility. They were more precious than any delicacy or intoxicant, more precious than any tool hewn from iron.

Mai's brother-in-law showed his companions his prized gifts, and soon the Tahitians on deck were in a frenzy. What followed, thought King, was a "farce of flattery and vanity." A lesser chief, who had hardly noticed Mai before, suddenly showered him with fawning praise. "He now began to caress Mai," said King. "He asked him to exchange names in token of friendship, and sent ashore for a hog in return for the precious feathers." Cook became irritated, both by the overtness of their greed and by Mai's eagerness to curry their favor. "It was evident to every one," Cook said, "that it was not the man but his property they were in love with."

WORD MUST HAVE spread quickly along the coast, for early the next morning, outriggers by the score sped toward the two ships newly anchored in Vaitepiha Bay. Feathers, feathers, feathers: The craving was palpable. Their vessels were piled high with pigs, fruits, and other goods with which to barter. One of the canoes cut through the crowd and sidled up next to the *Resolution*. On board, a woman could be heard weeping inconsolably. It turned out to be Mai's sister. She had risen with the dawn to meet her long absent brother.

Mai was overcome with emotion. "His heart was so full that he would hardly speak," said Samwell. He ushered her aboard and brought her into his cabin, for a tearful reunion that Cook found extremely moving. She was gracious and deferential, and before leaving she thanked Cook and his officers for bringing her brother safely back home.

Other women, with less noble purposes in mind, had begun to crowd onto the two ships. The trysts occurred in shadowy hammocks, in dank corners, even in broad daylight right upon the decks. Yet something had changed this time around. "The women are thought to be more friendly than on former voyages," wrote astronomer William Bayly. He realized what accounted for the difference: It was the feathers. "Numbers of fine women have come on board the ship, and would cohabit for nothing but red feathers." But as soon as they had earned a small quantity of the coveted plumes, Bayly observed, they vanished from the ship and rarely came back.

Cook was astonished by how quickly the presence of feathers had skewed the broader economics that had prevailed during his first two voyages. "Not more feathers than might be got from a tomtit would purchase a hog of forty or fifty pounds," he wrote, whereas "nails and beads, which formerly had so great a run at this island, they would not now so much as look at." There was surprising force in this new currency, but Cook feared it might also bring unpredictable results.

THE CAPTAIN HAD a more urgent worry to investigate. Some of the Tahitians on board had shared, through Mai, a distressing piece of news. During the three years Cook was absent from Tahiti, a Spanish expedition had come to claim the island and convert its people to Catholicism. Worse, they had brought a sampling of animals and an assortment of plants, which—assuming it was true—seemed to preempt the Noah's ark operation Cook had been so painstakingly conducting since leaving England. Hearing this report caused "disappointment and vexation" for everyone, Lieutenant King wrote. "We saw that our act of benevolence from its being too long deferred had lost its hour and its reward. We saw the loss of a season and an immense deal of trouble all thrown away to no purpose."

The details and timelines coming from the Tahitians seemed garbled, but Cook had heard enough that he had to go see for himself. He was rowed ashore with Mai and several officers and went to investigate a little house the Spanish had built for their friars close to where the Vaitepiha River flowed into the bay. It was a prefab structure made of planks that had been carefully numbered. Inside, it was mostly empty, just a few spartan sticks of furniture—some stools, a table, a bed, and a mahogany chest filled with some old garments.

Close by the house stood a cross that had been erected to mark the grave of the Spanish commander, Domingo de Bonechea, who had died in 1775 from some unknown disease. An inscription on the cross claimed Tahiti as a Spanish possession, in the name of King Carlos III. The move to annex Tahiti was part of Madrid's long-standing claim, reaching back to the early 1500s and the expeditions of Balboa, that all lands within or adjoining the Pacific Ocean were the sole possession of the Spanish Crown, and therefore *mare clausum*—off-limits to other European powers. The English scoffed at the audacity of their ancient adversary, derisively calling the Pacific the "Spanish Lake." Spain's pretensions to owning an entire ocean were as grandiose as they were indefensible. But South Seas expeditions mounted in recent years by both Great Britain and France had piqued Spain's interest, prompting the Crown to press its own claims on the island paradise.

The mere sight of this brash inscription raised Cook's ire. He immediately took the cross down and had another inscription engraved on the back, noting that the British had been here numerous times, starting with Wallis's initial visit in 1767. The Tahitians cringed at Cook's handling of the crucifix; the Spanish had warned them that they would return and that if anyone so much as touched the cross, or the little friars' house, all the people in the area would be killed.

From what Mai was able to gather by talking to locals, Tahitians around Vaitepiha Bay found the Spanish more impressive than the British. For one thing, their ships—which were frigates—were larger and more elegant than the Whitby cats Cook sailed. What's more, the Spanish were more regal in their bearing and wore spiffier uniforms.

Mai was deflated to learn that at least two Tahitians had sailed away in a Spanish ship to Lima, the capital of the Viceroyalty of Peru, where they had been paraded about as public curiosities, much as Mai had been presented in London. The two Tahitians had been returned and were living nearby. This was devastating to Mai: He was not the only world traveler, not the only Tahitian who had sailed to a distant world and come back.

One of the Tahitian adventurers was located and questioned by Clerke. The young man "had imbued a good deal of that distant, formal deportment of the Spaniard," Clerke found, and "so larded his conversation in 'señors' as to render it unintelligible." He considered Peru to be a very destitute country, mainly because "there were no red feathers there." Further, "when he saw the great abundance of Mai's riches, he cursed the señors very heartily and lamented much, that his good fortune had not given him a trip to England instead of Lima."

Mai learned that Tahitians had been led to believe that the Spanish had obliterated England in a decisive battle. Clerke colorfully elaborated on what a Spanish officer had apparently told the Tahitians. "There was a damned, little...state called England," Clerke wrote, but the Spanish claimed they had "erased the rascally breed from the face of the earth." England, the Tahitians were told, "is now no more and the very name nearly forgot."

The Franciscan friars who had lived here had made no headway in converting the Tahitians to the holy faith. The brothers were described as small, skittish men who rarely left the confines of their prefabricated house. They seemed to have no interest in interacting with the locals, and failed to teach the most basic tenets of Christianity. Not a single Tahitian had been converted. The locals had found the two friars laughable. They had stayed less than a year and then sailed away on another Spanish ship.

Cook was contemptuous of the Spanish desire to win souls for the Catholic faith. He knew that the Tahitians had their own religious beliefs, their own cosmology, their own system of morals. Never in his travels had Cook shown the slightest desire to convert locals or perform for their benefit any ceremonies or customs of the Christian faith. In keeping with the secular ethos of the Enlightenment, he seemed to view it as his duty to observe and document the religious practices of the cultures he encountered, not to proselytize. "He never mentioned religion," wrote one able seaman, "and would have no priests [chaplains] on the ships."

As for Cook's initial fears that the Spanish had preempted his scheme to introduce animal husbandry to Tahiti, further inquiries led him to believe that his worries were overblown. The Spanish had brought a few animals—some goats and dogs, a few Iberian hogs— but they were already scattered about, and no attention appeared to have been paid to breeding them. Cook had also heard rumors about cattle, but the sum total of the bovine livestock turned out to be one Spanish bull that was said to be tethered in a yard on the other side of the island. Cook felt a renewed confidence that the troubles and torments he'd lived through in transporting his animals to Tahiti weren't completely wasted after all.

BY NOW, THOUGH, Cook was starting to worry about Mai. More and more, the young Polynesian was putting on airs, prancing and preening, comporting himself as though he were royalty. One day he was supposed to pay a visit to a juvenile chief who, despite his youth, was the recognized sovereign of the area around Vaitepiha Bay. For the occasion, Mai donned the most pretentious garb one could imagine. Wrote Cook: "Mai, assisted by some of his friends, dressed himself not in English dress, nor in Tahitian, nor in Tongan, nor in the dress of any country upon earth, but in a strange medley of all he was possessed of." The outfit seemed to capture Mai's confused state of identity—for although he was no longer purely Tahitian, neither was he an Englishman. He'd become something in between, a mongrel of cultures and castes. His years at sea had added yet another layer to the complexities of his persona. Like so many hardened mariners who'd traveled around the world, he'd become a creature of shipborne life. He'd been practically everywhere but belonged nowhere. At times he seemed lost, uncertain how to behave, hoping to graft things he'd absorbed in England onto the island life he once knew, but not quite sure how to do it.

Near the mission house, Cook and Mai discovered some grapes the Spanish friars had planted. The vines were in a sorry state, untended, choked by weeds. Mai, who had developed a taste for wine while in England and in Cape Town, had ambitions of starting his own vineyard. He cut a few slips from the Spanish vines to plant wherever he ended up settling.

If Mai hoped to be a vintner, he also aspired to that other gentleman's pursuit: equestrian prowess. The Spanish had neglected to bring horses to Tahiti, so when Cook and Clerke ferried the steeds ashore for some morning exercise, the spectacle made a big impression on the Tahitians. They were amazed by the fleet and graceful animals, all the more so when they discovered that a man could sit upon their backs. In Cook's view, seeing a man ride a horse was more arresting to the Tahitians than a trunkful of red feathers, and it "gave them a better idea of the greatness of other nations than all the other things put together." Samwell agreed: "It is impossible to describe the uproar and confusion there was among the [Tahitians] in crowding to look at them, it being the first time they had ever seen a horse."

Mai wanted to show his fellow islanders that horseback riding wasn't just something Englishmen could do. In the morning, according to the *Discovery*'s Lieutenant John Rickman, Mai put on a full suit of armor—one that had been made especially for him in the Tower of London—and proceeded to mount one of the horses. Brandishing a sword and a pistol, he took off cantering down the beach. When the dumbstruck Natives began to congregate, Mai fired his pistol over their heads to clear the way. The crowds dispersed in terror. Perhaps Mai cut a chivalric figure up there, wearing his medieval helmet and plate armor in the full heat of the tropics, but there was something tragicomical about the whole display. To Rickman, he looked "like St. George going to kill the dragon."

For the returning hero, it was an inauspicious debut. Mai had wanted to dazzle his countrymen, to surprise and impress them, but he had merely scared them away.

18   This Barbarous Custom

TAHITI, AUGUST 1777

Cook had no intention of staying long at Vaitepiha Bay—he had other ports of call in mind, both on Tahiti and on nearby islands. Having decided to his satisfaction that the Spanish colonial experiment here had been a failure, he was ready to set sail. But before he did, he had an important matter to discuss with his men. It had to do with possibly the single most beloved item in the British sailor's regimen: grog.

Grog was a sacred fluid, the one indulgence mariners could count on, the staple that fueled long journeys. It was one part rum to four parts water. Centuries earlier, voyagers had learned that fresh water stored in casks tended to grow foul-tasting and slimy with algae. But mixing water with strong liquor inhibited the formation of bacteria and made it a little more palatable, and over the years rum had become the Royal Navy's mixer of choice.

What Cook proposed to his men was unheard of, something that under other circumstances might provoke a mutiny. Not only did he want to reduce their daily ration of grog; he wanted to eliminate it. Cook's method of accomplishing this dramatic measure was equally unheard of: He wanted his own men to take a vote and *choose* to abstain from their precious drink.

The proposal sounded outré, but Cook knew what he was doing. It may have helped matters that Cook himself was known to be a disciplined drinker. "Moderation was one of his chief virtues," wrote one able seaman. "Throughout the entire voyage no one ever saw him drunk. And if it happened at any time that a man was too drunk to carry out his duties, he was severely punished."

Now, for the first time, to all the men on the *Resolution,* Cook unveiled the ultimate purpose and destination of the mission. In the spring and summer of the following year, they would be headed into the icy waters of the Arctic, in search of a route over the top of North America leading to the Atlantic Ocean. It would be a monumental voyage of huge consequence to the fortunes of the British Empire, and if they succeeded they would garner a reward of £20,000—every single man would receive a portion of the prize. (The total reward would be more than three million dollars in today's currency.) A further prize of £5,000 could be won if the *Resolution* became the first ship to come within a degree of the North Pole.

But here was the rub: Their supply of grog was running out. If they continued to drink their daily ration, they would not have enough to see them through their passage into the hostile waters of the Arctic. He would not dictate the terms. The decision was theirs to make. Drink now and suffer later, or abstain, here in the paradise of Tahiti, secure in the knowledge that once they reached the rigors of the polar regions, they would enjoy the warmth and comfort of alcohol.

Cook must have couched the overture just right, for the vote was unanimous. They would conserve their grog. "It remained not under a moment's consideration but was consented to immediately," Cook wrote with satisfaction. He let Captain Clerke pose the same referendum to the men on the *Discovery,* and their verdict was the same. They, too, would save their spirits for the Arctic. Here in Tahiti, plenty of other hedonistic pleasures could be indulged in.

Many were impressed by Cook's aplomb in bringing off the trick. "The readiness with which they consented to this was a little surprising," Lieutenant John Williamson marveled. "A seaman in general would as soon part with his life, as his grog."

It was the old Captain Cook: solicitous of the health and happiness of his men, engaging them in decision-making, but acutely aware of his stores and the timetable as he projected months and years into the future. Perhaps to reward them for making the right decision, Cook decided on a token allowance. He would permit his men to consume a small portion of grog once a week. To make it even more agreeable, they could concoct their own Tahitian version of grog, composed of rum and coconut milk—which Samwell viewed as "a very rich and agreeable liquor, much better than punch." On Saturday nights, the men could "drink to their female friends in England," Cook said, "lest among the pretty girls of Tahiti they should be wholly forgotten."

On August 23, the two ships pulled out of Vaitepiha Bay and sailed around the island to another harbor, the place where Cook usually made his anchorage whenever he stopped in Tahiti. It was a lovely spot on the north shore called Matavai Bay, a scallop of Curaçao-blue water rimmed by black-sand beaches that gave way to foothills covered in jungles. This was the same place where Samuel Wallis had first anchored at Tahiti a decade earlier, "claiming" the island for King George III, and where the teenaged Mai had been injured by shrapnel. Beyond the steep hills, the island's tallest peak, Mount Orohena, soared seven thousand feet into the clouds.

The next morning, Cook and his officers were rowed ashore in style, dressed in full navy regalia, with the marines beating drums and playing fifes. He'd ordered the boats to be festooned with silk flags and bunting, and Mai wore his natty suit of Manchester velvet. Cook wanted everything to look just so. Having learned on his stop at Vaitepiha Bay that the military polish and sartorial formality of the Spanish had duly impressed the Tahitians, he had decided to conduct his arrival here with more splendor. He wasn't going to let the dons upstage him—at Matavai, he would look sharp and put on a show.

The ruling chief in this area was a corpulent man with frizzy hair named Tu. By some reckonings, he was as close to being the "king" of Tahiti as any chief on the island. Tu had arranged himself on the beach with his retinue to greet Cook. Gifts were exchanged, including heaps of red feathers. Cook also presented Tu with a suit of fine linen, a gold-laced hat, and an assortment of tools. The chief sat expressionless on his portable throne, his minions around him.

Then Mai approached Tu and knelt before him. If he was going to live here at Matavai Bay with any degree of success, Mai would have to endear himself to Tu and insinuate himself into the chief's kinship clan. Cook had it in his mind that Mai might marry one of Tu's family members—a sister, a cousin—and thus assure his standing. Cook wanted to leave most of the animals here on this part of the island, under the care of Tu's people, and he imagined that Mai could serve as Tu's farm manager, as it were, a director of animal husbandry.

At first, Cook was impressed with Mai's behavior. He thought that his friend had "conducted himself with a great deal of respect and modesty." Still, Tu took little notice of him. Despite Mai's experiences and the possessions he had accumulated along the way, Mai was a landless young man without distinction—and nothing, not even Cook's vigorous sponsorship, could change that.

Later, though, Tu began to pepper Mai with questions about English life. Mai launched into an exuberant soliloquy on the riches and marvels of London, and he went a bit over the top. England was an impossibly opulent and dynamic country, he said, and King George's powers knew no bounds. Mai "did not fail to magnify the grandeur of the Great King," Rickman wrote. "He compared the splendor of his court to the brilliancy of the stars in the firmament; the extent of his dominions [to] the vast expanse of heaven; the greatness of his power [to] the thunder that shakes the earth." Tu seemed amazed by this, but he did not like hearing that someone else, however far away, wielded so much more power than he.

The king of "Pretani," Mai went on, had 300,000 warriors at his command, and more than double that number of sailors, with fleets of ships that patrolled the oceans, night and day. Mai said there was one city in England, on the banks of a river removed from the sea, that contained more people than all of Tahiti.

This last statement may have been true, but Tu had lost interest. This impertinent young Polynesian in English clothing, this pretender, was starting to annoy him. Mai, having been stripped of his family's land on Raiatea, was little more than a commoner. During his four years away, he had forgotten his place.

IF TAHITI WAS a second home for Cook, Matavai Bay was the exact spot on Tahiti where he felt most welcome. As far as he was concerned, it was the epicenter of Tahitian life. He intended to stay here awhile, several weeks at least, maybe a month. Nearly all his associations with Matavai Bay were good ones. On his first voyage, on a nearby spit of land, Cook and his astronomer had set up their observatory and witnessed the 1769 transit of Venus—to this day, the place is called Point Venus.

Cook was popular here, a figure of awe among some, and except for the perennial problem of disappearing items, he and his men had rarely run into trouble on this side of the island. Now the tents would come out, the casks would get filled, the carpenters would do their caulking, and the sailmakers would stitch their repairs. But in the balmy Tahitian air, it hardly seemed like work at all. The scenery was exquisite, the bay serene, the weather close to perfect.

And the women: Canoes by the dozens came out to the ships to disgorge packs of young ladies—smiling, fragrant with oils, flowers in their hair. The men couldn't believe their good fortune; it was just like the stories they'd heard in England.

The women "flocked to us," wrote Samwell. "We never wanted [for] fine girls on board." "They are...angels," rhapsodized Thomas Edgar, master of the *Discovery*. "I can without vanity affirm it was the happiest [time] I ever spent."

Lots of theories have been put forward to explain what was really going on here. Some anthropologists, for example, have suggested that the women were merely curious about these interlopers, and perhaps a little bored by the day-to-day monotony of an insular world that experienced few outside distractions. The Englishmen, however grotty and foul, were something exotic, something *other.*

Tahitian society viewed white skin as a sign of chiefly rank—royals never worked and rarely showed themselves in the sun, and sometimes they went so far as to bleach their already pale hides with various treatments. Because of this, other anthropologists have speculated that women of lowborn classes may have reasoned that having sex with Cook's fair-skinned men could confer a higher social status upon themselves, or at least to any children that might result from such a union.

An even more elaborate explanation has been put forward: Perhaps on some atavistic plane of consciousness, the female inhabitants of these isolated islands were thrilled beyond belief by the sudden arrival of new blood that might enliven a gene pool circumscribed by geography.

Whatever the case, it seemed to John Ledyard, the American-born marine, that the Tahitian women could not wait to leap into the men's arms—any place on the ship would do. They were "almost frantic with joy to see us," claimed Ledyard, "and without any ceremony ran down between decks crying out for some of their old acquaintances, many of whom they found and embraced with the greatest affection. The ship was so crowded and confused that we could attend to no duty the remaining part of the day."

ON SHORE, THE next several days were spent in nearly constant ceremony and revelry: songs, dances, and wrestling matches, feasts of breadfruit, yams, and the succulent meat of baked hogs wrapped in plantain leaves. Cook dazzled the crowds with fireworks displays—the night sky popped and fizzed, leaving the locals poised between giggling from wonderment and running in panic.

One night a troupe of Tahitian performers put on an elaborate, frenetic, and (in the estimation of Cook's men, at least) quite erotic dance performed during a festival known as the *heiva.* Most of the men loved it, though a few prudes found it excessively vulgar. Dr. William Anderson, for one, seemed embarrassed by the women's

gyrations. He called it a "dance that rather bespoke an excess of joy
and licentiousness" and seemed shocked by the "young women, who
put themselves into several lascivious postures."

The festive times at Matavai Bay were abruptly cut short when
an alarming rumor arrived that the Spanish had returned to Tahiti
in two galleons—some accounts said four—and were preparing
to make war on Cook's ships. The report first came by way of a
Tahitian messenger from Vaitepiha Bay (where Cook had recently
anchored), who claimed he'd been on board one of the ships. When
Cook insisted on evidence, the messenger produced a blue garment
that he claimed was given to him by the Spanish.

Cook, though skeptical, had no particular reason to doubt the
man, so he erred on the side of caution. For all he knew, Britain and
Spain might be formally at war, so far removed was he from any
news of the world. Methodically, he prepared his ships for hostilities,
hauling up heavy guns and ammunition from below and positioning
them for firing. "The ships were little in a condition to meet with an
enemy of any force," wrote Samwell, "but we were resolved . . . not to
deliver ourselves into their hands tamely."

Cook promptly dispatched Lieutenant John Williamson to lead
a well-armed reconnaissance expedition by small boat around the
island to investigate the messenger's claim. The next day, Williamson returned from Vaitepiha Bay with a report that the Spanish
scare was a hoax. He had found no evidence of the Spanish anywhere. Cook thought the ruse had been concocted by Vaitepiha Bay
residents to draw the two British ships back so they could resume
trading. He sensed it was part of an intra-island jealousy—two rival
coastal fiefdoms competing for access to English wealth.

But a further layer of intrigue presented itself. Some of the chiefs
on Tahiti had been engaged for years in an on-again, off-again war
with Moorea, Tahiti's sister island to the immediate west, and Cook
had arrived at a time when war talk was at a fever pitch. Moorea
was a mere dozen miles away—the captain could see its craggy contours from his anchorage at Matavai Bay. Cook learned that Tu and
some of his allies were planning an attack on Moorea. At that very

moment, war canoes were being assembled. Tu fervently hoped that the English would join the hostilities—siding with the Tahitians, of course.

Cook refused to intervene, however. He had made it his policy to stay out of local conflicts. The Tahitian chiefs were angered and baffled by Cook's neutrality. They thought it strange that Cook, who had always declared himself to be their friend, would not go and fight against their adversaries.

But as he reflected on it, Cook began to suspect that the Spanish scare might have been the work of Moorean agents operating on Tahiti—a gambit to divert Cook's energies and keep the British out of the fight on Moorea. Perhaps they thought the English would quit Tahiti to elude the supposedly superior Spanish galleons. Cook was unable to confirm his theory, but as the Tahiti–Moorea struggle continued to escalate, it seemed to him the most plausible explanation behind the fictitious arrival of the Spanish.

WITH OR WITHOUT Cook's military support, Tu and his allies planned to forge ahead with an assault on Moorea. To ensure success in battle, a chief named To'ofa had made arrangements with priests to stage a special ceremony at a sacred temple, or marae, on the south coast of the island. The purpose of the ceremony was to win favor with Oro, the Tahitian god of war, by sacrificing a human. Tu invited Cook to attend, and because the captain had never experienced a human sacrifice before, he enthusiastically agreed to go. Cook was curious about these sorts of rites and rituals, however cruel they may have seemed—he viewed it as his responsibility to document the mores of the people he encountered on his voyages. He would try his best to remain objective as he witnessed what he called "this extraordinary and barbarous custom."

Cook chose Anderson and expedition artist John Webber to join him, as well as Mai. They took the pinnace and, following Tu and his entourage, made their way down the coast to the marae, where the ceremony was just getting underway. Drummers in loincloths began to tap out a rhythm. Fires had been lit, and veils of smoke drifted through the palm fronds. A few dozen witnesses, all men, sat in rows upon the ground. On a scaffold about six feet high lay the carcasses of two dogs and two pigs, which had been sacrificed some time earlier, for they emitted what Anderson called "an intolerable stench." Placed about the sacrificial mound, Cook counted no fewer than forty-nine skulls—presumably the craniums of those who'd been offered up to the gods in previous ceremonies.

Cook and the other Englishmen removed their hats and took their place at the edge of the marae. Webber sketched away with his pencil. Fortunately, the man to be sacrificed was already dead. He was a middle-aged vagrant—as Clerke put it, "the most worthless, unconnected rascal in the whole district"—who'd been clobbered in the head with a rock some hours before. No one seemed to know who he was or whether he'd done anything to deserve such a brutal end. Cook was later told that victims were "never apprised of their fate till the moment that puts an end to their existence. Whenever any of the great chiefs thinks a human sacrifice necessary, he... sends some of his trusty servants who fall upon him and kill him." The man's corpse, bloodied and bruised about the head, was trussed up to a pole.

The drums grew louder, and the priests sang their songs and threnodies. One of the priests, said Anderson, "seemed often to expostulate with the dead person." The man's left eye was removed from its socket and wrapped in a green leaf, and Tu went through the ritual of ceremonially "eating" it. Tufts of red feathers were offered up to Oro, along with a lock of hair plucked from the corpse. The priests prayed for Oro to help them in their coming battle against Moorea. In due course, a live dog was led into the marae, and attendants promptly snapped its neck. They tossed the animal onto the fire, then cleaved open its belly and roasted the liver, which they placed on the scaffold.

After a time, the attendants dug a shallow grave and dropped the victim into it with what Anderson considered "an air of great indifference," then covered it with earth and stones. Anderson was later told that the god Oro would come in the night as an invisible presence and would "feed only on the soul or immaterial part[s]" until the body of the sacrificial victim "was entirely wasted by putrefaction."

During a lull in the ceremony, a shrill cry resonated through the glade. "It is the god!" Tu exclaimed under his breath. Cook thought it was the screech of a kingfisher, a sacred bird whose call was believed to be the mouthpiece of the gods.

Anderson, for his part, saw nothing remotely sacred about the ceremony; he found the ritual "horrid," rooted in "the grossest ignorance and superstition." He observed that most of the Tahitians in the audience showed no reverence for the proceedings—many weren't even watching. Instead, many in the audience flocked around Mai for much of the ceremony, begging him to recount story after story from his world travels—which, said Anderson, they listened to with rapt attention.

Still, as perhaps the expedition's chief observer and scribe, Anderson was pleased to have witnessed the ritual. Throughout Polynesia, Cook and his voyagers had heard tales of human sacrifice and had seen after-the-fact signs of the practice, but they had never seen the grisly act itself. Now they had what Anderson called "ocular proof." The accounts of the sacrifice that Anderson and Cook wrote, together with detailed drawings produced by Webber, would later shock and outrage Christian sensibilities back in Britain and help spark a movement in the 1790s to send English missionaries to Tahiti and elsewhere in Polynesia to save these heathen souls.

When the ceremony was over, To'ofa, the chieftain who had organized the sacrifice, asked Cook how he had enjoyed it. His reply dumbfounded him. "We of course condemned it," Cook wrote. The captain told the chief that he believed the sacrifice would produce the opposite of its intended purpose. Oro "would be angry with them for it," Cook told To'ofa.

Mai went further, telling To'ofa that in England the ritual would be considered a crime. "Mai," wrote Cook, "put the chief out of all manner of patience" by telling him that in London an individual who put an innocent man to death in this way would be hanged. To'ofa reacted with outrage, finding the thought of a world without human sacrifice horrible to contemplate. To'ofa would not hear another word. In the end, said Cook, "we left him with as great a contempt for our customs as we could possibly have of theirs."

19   Duped by Every Designing Knave

TAHITI, SEPTEMBER 1777

The war canoes crowded the bay in the soft morning light—as many as seventy of the elaborately carved vessels, each one manned by more than a hundred paddlers. The Tahitian men sent up their lusty war whoops in unison as they powered the outriggers this way and that across the deep blue waters. The boats, arranged in serried ranks, were well equipped with spears, clubs, and other weapons, and from each stern competing pennants snapped in the sea breeze. The captains of these canoes, dressed in breast mats and feathered war caps, shouted out their commands so loudly that they could be heard on shore.

Standing at a prominent vantage point, Tu and Cook beheld the dazzling array of boats as they executed their maneuvers. Tu had arranged this review of the Tahitian war fleet, which was preparing for an amphibious attack on Moorea, and he had invited Cook to attend. Throughout the day, drums pounded and crowds massed on shore to watch the races, mock battles, and elaborate displays of naval tactics—affording Cook "a good opportunity to get some insight into their manner of fighting."

Later, Tu and Cook, along with Lieutenant James King, boarded one of the canoes and ventured onto the water to participate in the war games. Mai boarded a nearby canoe, and the two elegant boats skimmed gracefully over the gardens of coral toward deeper waters. "After we were out in the bay," wrote Cook, "we advanced upon each other and retreated by turns, as quick as the paddlers could move them."

Constructed upon the canoes were platforms on which stood crowds of men who "flourished their weapons and played a hundred antic tricks which could answer no other end that I could see than to work up their passions for fighting." After advancing and retreating at least a dozen times, the two canoes clashed. A short stint of "fighting" ensued, and very quickly it seemed that the men on Mai's canoe got the upper hand. "The troops on our stage were supposed to be killed," said Cook, "and we were boarded by Mai and his associates, and that very instant Tu and all the paddlers leaped overboard to save their lives by swimming."

It was all quite entertaining, but Cook supposed that these were pretty much the tactics the Tahitians employed in a real battle. "This method of fighting," Cook said, "was used when they were determined to conquer or die. It was a bloody engagement, and all agreed that they never give quarter."

After the mock battle had ended, Mai pulled on his full suit of armor and stood upon the platform as the oarsmen slowly rowed the "victorious" canoe along the coast so the crowds could feast their eyes upon the champion. The boat made a full circuit of the bay, yet the spectacle of this young man in his sparkling metal suit failed to stir much of a reaction. "Everyone had a full view of him," said Cook, "but it did not draw their attention as might be expected."

IN COOK'S VIEW, as this vignette seemed to illustrate, things were not going well with Mai on Tahiti. At first he had done his best to ingratiate himself with Tu, lavishing the chief with gifts, even throwing extravagant dinners in Tu's honor. But Mai's efforts were in vain. He had no flair for diplomacy. He seemed to live in the moment, a man of raw instinct and pure emotion. He preferred fraternizing with people born to his station in life—ordinary folks, fishermen, laborers. People were drawn to him mainly because of the riches he had acquired in England, but he didn't seem to notice. At the same time, he continued to insist that he be treated as someone special. In addition to the two Māori "servants" he had brought from New Zealand, he had acquired six more attendants on Tahiti. He was putting on airs, with a train of hangers-on following him everywhere he went.

Cook thought Mai was behaving like a "vain and gullible fool." Mai did not have the first understanding of how to conserve his wealth, or how to use it strategically to forge constructive relationships. With the "property he was master of," wrote Cook, "I expected he would have had prudence enough to have made himself respected, and even courted by the first persons on the island, but instead he rejected the advice of those who wished him well and suffered himself to be duped by every designing knave." Cook, fearing Mai wouldn't have anything left to live on, impounded what was left of his possessions, locking them away on the ship. "If I had not interfered," Cook wrote, Mai's opportunistic friends "would not have left him a single thing."

To foster an enduring alliance with the power structure here, Cook had decided that Mai should marry one of Tu's sisters. That way, he would enjoy security, status, and lasting wealth. There were geopolitical implications, too: Such a marriage, Cook felt, would further adhere the British Empire to Matavai and, by extension, all of Tahiti. "It was my wish to fix him with Tu," wrote Cook. "I intended to leave the cattle, poultry, etc. at this island, [and] I thought he would be able to give some instruction about the management of them and of their use."

It was a tidy plan. The only problem was, Mai didn't like Tu's sister. He immediately rejected her. She was too plain-looking, he insisted, and besides, she was living with another man at the time. Cook viewed Mai's spurning of Tu's sister as a direct repudiation of his paternal wishes and well-laid plans. "He rejected my advice," Cook fumed, "and conducted himself in such a manner as not only to lose the friendship of Tu, but that of every other person of note on the island."

Cook's men loved Mai like a brother, but they, too, were distressed by his flighty behavior and were growing genuinely concerned for his future. Lieutenant James Burney worried about Mai's "vanity and extravagance" and noted how he "dressed in the most tawdry manner he could contrive and was constantly attended by a large train of followers whose only motive was ... profit." Samwell echoed the same sentiment: "He chose rather to associate with the black guards of the island, and among these he squandered most of his red feathers and other articles ... He employed much of his time in acting the part of a merry Andrew, parading about in ludicrous masks and different dresses to the great admiration of the rabble."

Mai was far less focused on how he would resettle on Tahiti

than on how he would wage war against the Bora Borans. Some of those "black guards" that Samwell referred to were Mai's old band of refugees and dissidents from Raiatea who had been displaced by the armies from Bora Bora. Like Mai, they were spoiling to fight their sworn enemies and were eager to see what weapons Mai had acquired from England that might be useful in the coming campaign. Mai was incensed to find that enclaves of Bora Borans were living on Tahiti, enjoying Tu's friendship and blessing. At one point, Mai instructed the fat chief to expel them all—a bold demand that only deepened Tu's animosity toward the young upstart.

The real problem Mai had to overcome was his wealth itself, and the covetousness it aroused, the instabilities it engendered, the desires it stirred—in a people who, before the arrival of the European explorers, were by most accounts generally content with what they had and who entertained very different ideas about property. One historian of Tahiti, writing about Mai's riches, observed that in the Society Islands, private wealth could be compared to "a sore on a healthy body: like healing, social forces would eradicate it, and smooth it over until it vanished."

The Tahitian people didn't know how to deal with a young man like Mai, a lowly person who had so many things—more possessions than any chieftain. In Tahiti, real status derived from one's *mana*—a power that, in turn, sprang from deep and largely immutable factors related to one's birth and genealogy, one's station in life, and one's larger networks of family friends and alliances. By returning to Tahiti with all this English paraphernalia that he believed would confer higher status upon him, Mai seemed rather brazenly to be attempting to short-circuit ancient traditions and mores.

Mai was "envied for undeserved riches," thought John Ledyard, "and despised for his obscure birth and impudent pretentions." In describing Mai's predicament, John Rickman was more blunt: "Men sprung from the dregs of the people must have something more than accidental riches to recommend them to the favor of their fellow citizens."

Like a father who broods over a wayward son, Cook did not know what was to become of his Polynesian charge, but he did know this: Mai wasn't going to take root on Tahiti. He had frittered away his options here, he had made foolish decisions, he had made enemies. Cook would have to choose another island on which to install him. The expedition would go farther west, deeper into the Society Islands archipelago, to find Mai a suitable home.

COOK WAS ALREADY sensing that it was time to leave Tahiti. They'd been on the island for a month. His men had made themselves too comfortable here. The trading, friendly and fruitful at first, had degenerated into a thousand glum hagglings and bickerings. The value of things, Cook thought, was all askew—certain worthless items (feathers) were inflated beyond belief, while other items which should be of enduring value (metal tools) were virtually worthless. He noticed how quickly his sailors' presence had changed the tenor of life here. He worried about venereal disease—how his own men were spreading gonorrhea and possibly syphilis among the locals, and how the locals were spreading it back to his own men. Clerke, too, lamented the spread of venereal disease but guessed that not much could be done to govern the urges of sailors on long voyages. "Seamen in these matters are so infernal and dissolute," Clerke wrote, "that for the gratification of the present passion, they would entail universal destruction upon the whole of the human species."

Petty theft, that bane of his previous stops here, had returned. On this visit to Tahiti, Cook had employed a new punishment (some accounts say Clerke first came up with the idea): When he caught a thief, he would shave half of the man's head, or half of his beard. He had noticed that Tahitian men were fastidious about their grooming, and he had a notion that this punishment would leave a stark impression. In this Cook was right. This half-shearing technique made the culprit look ridiculous in the eyes of his peers—it was like a branding, a badge of shame. Shaving a thief caused no harm; it only humiliated him.

Cook knew he and his men had remained too long. They'd begun to quarrel with the locals, and amongst themselves. Two of Cook's men had fought a duel. Lieutenant John Williamson and Molesworth Phillips, commander of the marines, had been butting heads for weeks. One day, the two men met at an agreed-upon spot with their seconds at their sides. Williamson and Phillips drew their pistols and fired. Luckily, each man missed his mark, and a follow-up round produced the same non-result. Their seconds convinced them to halt the proceedings, and each contestant declared his grievance satisfied. Most of the men had hoped Phillips would prevail, for no one seemed to care for Williamson. Wrote ship's corporal William Griffin: "Many persons would have rejoiced if Mr. Williamson, our third lieutenant, had fallen, as he was a very bad man and a great tyrant."

BY THIS POINT in the voyage, Charles Clerke had come to understand that he had tuberculosis. He surmised that he had contracted it during his stay in the dungeons of that London debtors' prison the summer before. He hadn't confided his suspicions to anyone, but his symptoms had only advanced throughout the voyage, having become much more pronounced during the cold, wet passage across the southern Indian Ocean and upon the frigid barrens of the Kerguelen Islands. He was having trouble catching his breath, and during coughing fits he spat up blood. At times he felt like he was wasting away. Clerke had started to wonder, with good reason, how he could possibly survive the coming rigors of the Arctic. He decided to confess his worries to Dr. Anderson, the *Resolution*'s surgeon. Anderson examined him and confirmed the diagnosis.

But Dr. Anderson had his own confession to make: He, too, had tuberculosis. He didn't know how or where he had caught the disease, but Anderson's case was more advanced than Clerke's. Just like Clerke, the doctor had wondered how he could endure the icy dampness of the polar regions.

So the two stricken men hatched an idea. They would ask Captain Cook if they could abandon the voyage and stay on Tahiti. There was little doubt that Alaska was going to kill them, but here they at least had a chance of staying alive for another season, maybe even another year or two. They would spend their last days breathing the balmy air of Tahiti and its neighboring isles, which Clerke viewed as "delectable...as pleasant and happy spots as the world contains." Their quitting the expedition wouldn't be desertion, exactly, for they would secure Cook's permission; they would be transparent in their intentions from the start.

Clerke and Anderson were both crucial men of the expedition, but the voyage could continue without them. John Gore, serving on the *Resolution,* was more than capable of taking over as captain of the *Discovery.* For now, the two officers kept their secret. They would arrange their affairs, get their papers in order. They just had to find the right time and place to broach the idea with the captain.

CAPTAIN COOK WAS having medical issues as well. During his last weeks on Tahiti, he suffered from an ailment he described as rheumatism, but it was more likely acute sciatica—a pinched sciatic nerve. The condition can be utterly disabling, with a tingling, some-times electric pain that can radiate from the lower back all the way down the legs. Some have argued that sciatica might help explain Cook's saturnine moods during this voyage, his uncharacteristic sur-liness, his flights of temper.

The Tahitians were distressed to learn of Cook's malady, and a canoe was promptly dispatched to the *Resolution.* Out hopped twelve women, armed with an assortment of oils and unguents. They were a gang of healers who had come to address his woes. He tried to shoo them away, but they insisted: Captain Cook was about to get his first massage—*lomi lomi* was what the Tahitians called it.

"They told me," said Cook, "they were come to cure me of the disorder that I complained of, which was a sort of rheumatic pain in one side from my hip to the foot." The women arranged a pallet on the cabin floor and had Cook lie down in the midst of the healers. "I submitted myself to their direction," Cook wrote warily. "As many as could get round me began to squeeze me with both hands from head to foot, but more especially the part where the pain was, till they made bones crack and a perfect mummy of my flesh."

Cook was peculiar about his privacy, and not a person who much liked to be touched. He was English, after all. This was an entirely novel experience for him—a dozen women squatting around him on the floor, poking and prodding, mashing and kneading his flesh. He found no pleasure in the exercise, at least not at first. "After being under their hands about a quarter of an hour," he said, "I was glad to get away from them."

However, in the moments afterwards, he had to admit they had done something—their knowing fingers had penetrated to the source of the pain. "I found immediate relief from the operation," Cook conceded. A few hours later, before he retired for the evening, they came back and gave him a second rubdown. "I went to bed and I found myself pretty easy all the night after." The women stayed on board through the night and repeated the treatment the next morning before they went ashore, then returned once more that evening. Cook was astonished. His healing was complete. "I found the pains entirely removed," he said, "and the next morning they left me."

Cook had become a believer in Tahitian *lomi lomi*. He began to entertain a broader curiosity about its efficacy as a remedy and its practice as a cultural tradition. Massage, he noted, is "sometimes performed by the men but more generally by the women." *Lomi lomi* seemed to be a widespread healing art, and almost a form of social intercourse. It was just something Tahitians did, and were good at. Said Cook: "If at any time one appears languid or tired and sits down, they [those practiced in the art] immediately begin *lomi* upon your legs, which I have found to have an exceeding good effect."

Captain James Cook, calcified by a life at sea, must have been one of the tightest men on earth. But that night he slept soundly, and he did not complain of the ailment again.

PERHAPS THE GREATEST cause of tension and anxiety in Cook's daily routine since departing England had been the animals living on board the *Resolution*. Finally, that source of nearly constant aggravation was about to fall away. Cook had made a plan to leave most of the animals with Tu and his kinship group. A few of the beasts, including two of the horses, would stay with Mai, and a few more would stay with the expedition for later use as it headed into the northern hemisphere. But Cook had decided that Tu was in a much better position than Mai to carry out King George's experiment in animal husbandry.

And so, on shaky legs, the world's best-traveled barnyard animals came trotting and waddling and staggering off the ship: cattle, horses, goats, sheep, chickens, peacocks, geese, rabbits, turkeys. Tu was pleased with these gifts that had come so many miles across the ocean. Many of them were life forms he had never seen before. Tu seemed to understand the larger idea behind the operation—that is, not to slaughter and eat the livestock, at least not immediately, but to let the animals multiply.

Cook was relieved to see the animals go—everyone was. "Now I found myself lightened of a very heavy burden," Cook wrote. "The trouble and vexation that attended bringing these animals this far is hardly to be conceived." The racket, the dander, the rank smell of piss and feces, and all the fussing, night and day, over their health and feeding had taxed everyone's patience. Trying to run a floating zoo while exploring the world had been a drain on the crew's attentions.

Still, Cook seemed to think the Noah's ark project had been worth the trouble—or least he thought it prudent to say so, on the assumption that King George would one day read his words. "The satisfaction I felt," wrote Cook, "in having been so fortunate as to fulfill His Majesty's design in sending such useful animals" to the Tahitians "sufficiently recompensed me for the many anxious hours I had on their account."

Cook also showed Tu's people how to lay out a proper English garden plot, planting long rows of pineapples, potatoes, melons, and other crops, as well as two shaddocks (a citrus tree with glossy, dark green leaves). The Tahitians viewed all this effort with good-natured confusion. They could tell Cook was trying to do them a favor, but Tahitians already had a bountiful and healthy diet, healthier than the Englishmen's, with much seafood and pork, as well as the nearly ubiquitous breadfruit and coconuts. Many of the English journals remarked upon the excellent health of the Tahitians, their flawless skin, their luxuriant hair, their straight white teeth. Tahitians were not starving, not remotely—they lived in a veritable land of milk and honey.

After a few weeks, it seemed to Cook that the new crops were taking root, and the animals were in a promising way. Most of the poultry were thriving—two ducks and two geese were already sitting on eggs. And the cows had been turned loose with the enormous bull the Spanish had left behind. Cook was impressed with the Iberian behemoth—"a finer beast than he was, I hardly ever saw," he said. The bull had immediately gone to work on King George's cows, a rare collaboration between the English and the Spanish, and the mating seemed to be a complete success.

But the whole operation would prove to be a bust. Scarcely a single animal from the experiment is believed to have survived on Tahiti, at least in domesticated form. (It's said that some of Cook's goats went feral and thrived in the mountains.) Most of Cook's livestock apparently died during a string of civil wars that would convulse Tahiti throughout the 1780s. When William Bligh returned here in 1788 as the captain of the HMS *Bounty*, he found only a few descendants of Cook's animals, and the garden that Cook had so meticulously planted was gone. All that was left was the two shaddock trees.

Modern critics of Cook, such as Princeton anthropologist Gananath Obeyesekere, have viewed King George's agricultural scheme, well intentioned though it may have been, as indicative of something far larger and more sinister—imperial England's attempt to "civilize" Native peoples by insisting that they adopt a distinctly British way of life. Wherever Cook landed, he planted tidy English gardens. "The act," argues Obeyesekere, "is primarily symbolic, supplanting the disorderly way of savage peoples with ordered landscapes on the English model. Pairs of animals are carefully set loose...to *domesticate* a savage land." In Obeyesekere's view, Cook had taken on a role very much like that of Prospero in Shakespeare's *The Tempest*—that is, an authoritarian "civilizer" who systematically colonizes a remote island and dismisses Natives as savages "given to prelogical or mystical thought that [is] fundamentally opposed to the logical and rational ways of modern man."

THE TIME HAD come for Cook to bid Tahiti adieu. In the last week of September, he began to make his final preparations. The men performed their tearful farewells to friends and lovers on shore. Cook would be sailing west, farther into the Society Islands to find Mai a good home.

On his way, the captain would pay a short visit to Moorea, Tahiti's sister island. Mai, who had acquired a handsome canoe for the small price of some red feathers from Tonga, would be sailing over to Moorea, just ahead of Cook, to prepare the islanders for the coming English ships. Mai had decided to christen his new canoe the *Royal George*, and had it decorated with brightly colored flags, streamers, and pennants, including a version of the Union Jack, a hybrid of British and Polynesian styles that made it an oddly perfect reflection of his identity.

In both superficial and meaningful ways, the English and the Tahitians had mingled their customs and cultures and had influenced one another during Cook's sojourn here. Many of the sailors had adopted Tahitian practices—they'd submitted themselves to the tattoo artists, grown to love traditional dances and food, learned healthy smatterings of the Tahitian language, and thrown themselves into one of the islanders' most venerable amusements: kite flying. They had gone night fishing with the local anglers, catching trevally, bonito, parrotfish, and other species in the guttering glow of torches. Many had traded names with Tahitian male friends, forming a kinship bond called the *taio*.

At the same time, English notions of property ownership had begun to rub off on some of the locals. This became glaringly obvious when, in the week leading up to Cook's departure, Tu begged the captain to have his carpenters construct a box to hold the many belongings he had accumulated from Cook and other European voyagers. Tu wanted an impregnable vault where he could safely store his new treasures. Cook consented, and soon the carpenters were sawing and hammering away. Tu urged them to build it large enough so that two guards could lie on top of it. Some accounts say that Tu had a bed placed inside so that on occasion he could sleep with his treasure.

All of this suggests that Tu had rather suddenly become worried about theft. Traditionally, Tahitians seldom stole from one another—and definitely not from their all-powerful chiefs, who were considered holy. Most property was communal, and average Tahitians had few possessions they could call entirely their own. The thatched houses were open to the air; doors, gates, fences, and walls were rarities; and the very concept of a lock would have seemed strange to most Tahitians. By and large, the culture was not materialistic. People baked their food in the ground, drank from coconut shells and gourds, ate off of plantain leaves, and relied on nature to provide a thousand other tools and implements. Individuals could be rich in land or in animals, but not rich in the sense of owning large collections of inanimate objects. But with all the baubles and beads, the looking glasses and mirrors, the garments and feathers and hatchets that had flooded into the economy, new jealousies had been stirred, and new concerns had risen to the fore.

Tu was thrilled with his new vault, which was fitted with locks and bolts. He began to think of other projects the carpenters could usefully pursue. The king asked Cook if these magical craftsmen could remain on the island—presumably forever—but Cook declined.

Tu had one last favor to ask. He had seen some of the portraits that Webber and the other expedition artists had drawn. Now the king wanted a likeness of Cook, something to remember him by, a parting relic that would forever cement their bond. Cook was happy to oblige, and soon sat for Webber. The completed portrait was framed and packed in a crate, complete with its own lock and key. Tu seemed enormously pleased with the gift. With tears in his eyes, he vowed to safeguard it, and to exhibit it to the captains of any ships that might call here in the future, so as to broadcast the point: Britain and Tahiti were one.

On the afternoon of September 29, an easterly wind began to stir. As the *Resolution* and the *Discovery* stood out to sea, Cook honored Matavai Bay with a salute of seven guns, and the crews whispered their last goodbyes to Aphrodite's Island.

20 *A Kingdom for a Goat*

MOOREA, OCTOBER 1777

The green spires of Moorea sawed at the western sky. The *Resolution* and the *Discovery* inched across the Sea of the Moon toward Tahiti's neighboring island, only twelve miles away. Cook had never been to Moorea, arguably the most beautiful and inviting of all the Society Islands. During previous stops at Tahiti, he'd been led to believe that Moorea had no harbors large enough to accommodate his ships, so the normally inquisitive explorer had dismissed the place.

Moorea, in the Tahitian language, means "yellow lizard"—the name is believed to have derived from a vision experienced by some high priest of yore. Geologists say Moorea is considerably older than Tahiti. The island's multitude of serrated peaks and weird cones, pitched at sharp angles, are the eroded remnants of an ancient volcano.

The two ships made for the north side of the island and, finding a passage through the outer reef, slipped into a turquoise lagoon. Mai, who had crossed over from Tahiti the day before in his sprightly *Royal George,* greeted Cook and Clerke and guided them in. The ships nosed into a bay that narrowed into a long finger of dark blue water. No harbors on Moorea? Cook was astonished how wrong his intelligence had been. This was one of the loveliest ports he'd ever seen—deep, safe, and smooth-bottomed, "not inferior," as he put it, "to any harbor I have met with."

The vessels were warped deep within the bay, to a place where the brackish water became fresh from the commingled flow of several streams spilling from the mountains. Cook anchored in ten fathoms of water and, with hawsers, had the ships fastened to the sturdy hibiscus trees growing along the shore.

It was a stunning landscape, with mountains towering three thousand feet above them. William Ellis, surgeon's mate on the *Dis-*

covery, found it "truly romantic" and "delightful beyond description." He noted the bizarre slabs of basalt "that rise in a variety of forms, appearing like old ruined castles or churches." Near the summit of one of the peaks was an intriguing hole, with daylight shining through, which according to Polynesian myths had been created by the great warrior Pai, who hurled a spear all the way from Tahiti to pierce the mountain.

Cook's men were giddy with surprise, for here was a place possibly even lovelier than Tahiti. There was fresh water aplenty, thick stands of tropical trees where the carpenters could gather wood, and lush aprons of grass along the shore for grazing the few animals that remained in Cook's stock. The flowering jungles skittered with geckos, skinks, and other lizards, and the close air was melodious with birdsong. "It is scarcely possible," thought William Bayly, "for nature to have formed a more complete harbor."

IF THE SPOT seemed idyllic, on closer inspection, the men could glimpse signs of the recent Tahitian invasions: Some of the structures along the shore had been charred and dismembered, and many of the trees were stripped of fruit. "The ruins of war," said Cook, were "everywhere to be seen." The locals on shore seemed scared at first, their natural curiosity over the arrival of these unfamiliar vessels tinged with fear that maybe the vessels had come for *them.*

Mai had done what he could to prepare the Mooreans for Cook's arrival, assuring them of the captain's beneficence and peaceful intent. Though skeptical, the Natives began to crowd along the shoreline to get a better look at these strange, white-skinned travelers. Most of them had not seen Europeans before.

The place where Cook had positioned the *Resolution* was only thirty yards from shore—so close that it gave him an idea. He knew that the rat population aboard the *Resolution* had swelled. The vermin had all but taken over the holds, gangways, and lower decks. The ship, as Cook put it, was "pestered" and "haunted" by this "numerous tribe." He had spars lashed to ropes that were strung from the ship's scuttles over to dry land, creating a swinging bridge for the

"A grave, steady man": James Cook, circa 1776.
This portrait, held in private collections for more than
two centuries, was not rediscovered until 1986.

John Montagu, Fourth Earl of Sandwich.
As the First Lord of the Admiralty, Sandwich was a
principal architect and sponsor of Cook's third voyage.

The Greenwich Hospital and Royal Observatory, located on the prime meridian,
beside the Thames. When voyaging, Cook's chronometers showed the exact time
at Greenwich. Cook was serving as "captain" here when he abandoned a brief
retirement to lead his third and final expedition.

Mai as rendered by Joshua Reynolds in 1776.
In 2023, Reynolds's painting, *Portrait of Omai*, was jointly
acquired by the Getty Museum and London's National
Portrait Gallery for $62 million.

Joseph Banks, the famous field naturalist and Royal Society luminary, was Mai's patron during the Polynesian's stay in England.

King George III, known as "Farmer George," was a staunch supporter of Cook's voyages and donated animals from the royal herds to be transported with Mai to Tahiti.

Charles Clerke, captain of Cook's
consort ship, HMS *Discovery*, pictured
with an unnamed Māori man

The young William Bligh,
master of Cook's ship,
HMS *Resolution*, in 1776

David Samwell, the Welsh poet
and surgeon's assistant aboard
the *Resolution*

The Connecticut-born adventurer
John Ledyard, who served with the
Royal Marines aboard
Cook's *Resolution*

The Swiss-born John Webber, expedition
artist aboard the *Resolution*

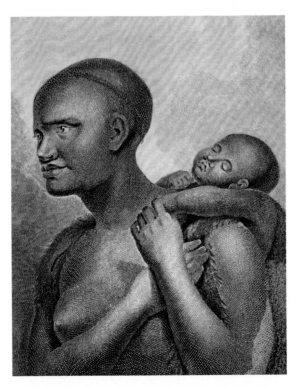

John Webber's portrait of an aboriginal Palawa
woman with her child on Bruny Island, Tasmania.
Within a hundred years of Cook's visit,
the Palawa people would be virtually extinct.

River bathers on the margins of Vaitepiha Bay, Tahiti

Webber's rendering of a human sacrifice ritual witnessed by Cook
and some of his men on Tahiti

Cook's ships anchored at Matavai Bay, Tahiti

The *Resolution* and *Discovery* anchored off the island of Huahine,
where Cook would leave Mai to spend the rest of his days

rats to scurry ashore. In due course, a number of them did find their way across, though not enough for Cook's satisfaction. Still, wrote Lieutenant King, "we were certain that we got quit of a few by this means."

With rats, it only took a few—one male and one female, to be exact—to grow rapidly into a ravening army. And thus what a delightful unwanted gift Cook had bequeathed to the unsuspecting citizens of Moorea, within a few short hours of his arrival: *Rattus rattus*, also known as the black rat, the ship rat, native of prehistoric Europe, perhaps the most invasive of all invasive species. Soon enough these ultra-adaptive and cannily opportunistic omnivores would be swarming over the beaches and the forest floor and even climbing up into the jungle canopy, gorging on everything in sight. Moorea and the other islands in the archipelago already had one species of rat—the Polynesian rat, a smaller and slightly less destructive species that had been brought by ancient voyagers. But today black rats remain a scourge throughout Polynesia and have been held responsible for countless extinctions of plants and animals, erasing millions of years of evolution.

Then a different pest vied for Cook's attentions. It was discovered that a tiny burrowing insect was destroying the ship's casks containing the all-important spirits—rum, port, wine, and other stores of alcohol. Cook had a detail haul the casks up on deck to coat their heads with pine tar, a measure he hoped would deter the tiny wood-eating bugs.

The next morning several outrigger canoes filled with Tahitian women glided into the harbor. Many of them were the sailors' regular girlfriends from Matavai Bay. These young women, who'd been as heartsick as the Englishmen when the two ships pulled out of Tahiti, had gone to some trouble to cross the channel separating the two islands and reunite with their English lovers here.

IN THIS SAME harbor, not far from where the *Resolution* and the *Discovery* lay anchored, a lesser chief, recently deceased, had been set out for public viewing as part of an extended funerary vigil. The atmospherics were solemn. "We could not but admire the piety of these people in showing so much regard for their dead," wrote Samwell, though the Welshman felt the need to report that the corpse, which had been lying in state for some time, was a bit ripe. "Being very near neighbors to it, we often inhaled effluvias whose fragrancy we could very well dispense with."

The ultimate chief of this part of Moorea, a seasoned warrior named Mahine, was still very much alive, but he was nowhere to be found. He'd decided to keep his distance. Doubtless he'd heard that Cook had befriended Tu while on Tahiti, and so he suspected that the Englishmen had come in these formidable craft to make war.

Mahine's fears were unfounded, of course. Cook was determined to maintain his neutrality in the ancestral wars between the two islands, and his alliance with Tu did nothing to prejudice him against anyone on Moorea. Simple curiosity had lured Cook here—he wanted to see how the island differed from Tahiti, and what it offered in the way of provisions, culture, and anchorages. Cook also wondered if Moorea might not be a suitable place to ensconce Mai, since all attempts to resettle him on Tahiti had failed.

It took another day before Mahine presented himself, and even then he did so tentatively. Cook's men had heard so many stories about the chief's martial exploits that they were surprised and disappointed by his thoroughly unintimidating appearance. They had been expecting some stout Polynesian Achilles, and instead they were presented with an old, fat, infirm man, blind in one eye, his body blotched with blemishes and scars—"all which he says are the consequences of the many wars he has been engaged in," noted William Ellis. Not only that, Mahine was bald, a rarity among Polynesians, and he seemed to want to hide the fact by wearing a kind of turban. Cook wondered whether a bald head was "a mark of disgrace with them, or [if] they thought it was so with us."

Despite his unfortunate appearance, Mahine seemed to command the respect and allegiance of this part of Moorea. Though his sovereignty was secure here, the ebb and flow of his power seemed to depend mostly on the machinations of Tu and the on-again, off-again war with Tahiti, which, being the larger and more populous of the twin islands, would inevitably have the upper hand. Mahine hoped to keep has family dynasty in place for generations to come. "He has a son who he intends to succeed him," wrote Ellis, "provided he can become independent; but the people of Tahiti will probably always be too powerful for him, and of course put in a king of their own choosing."

Mahine, along with his mistress and several other local women, came aboard the *Resolution* to exchange gifts: several squealing hogs and mounds of fresh fruit for hatchets, nails, and beads. For some reason, red feathers, so coveted on Tahiti, had scant value here. As a special gift, Cook presented Mahine with a linen gown printed with large flowers, which seemed to impress him. For a half hour, Cook entertained Mahine, and after exchanging names and still more gifts, the chief became convinced that Cook's peace overtures were in earnest and he began to relax.

Amid their onboard pleasantries, Mahine spied a particular animal, cute and weird, with hooves and horns, clomping along the decks of the *Resolution*. The chief had never seen anything like it. It was a creature of this world, but also of some other. He inquired about it and learned its English name: *goat*.

Mahine said he would very much like one—or two, if that was possible. But Cook demurred. The last few goats remaining in his diminished stock were intended for other Edens within the Society Isles.

Mahine was disappointed and likely felt insulted. He had probably heard that Cook had given Tu, Mahine's archenemy on Tahiti, numerous creatures, including goats. Why couldn't the captain spare Mahine just one animal?

THE VERY NEXT day, one of Cook's goats disappeared. The ruminant in question had been out on the grass, grazing. At some point, the sailor who'd been put in charge of the animal took something from a Native without permission or pay. This Moorean man, out of revenge, took the young goat and vanished into the hills.

Cook instantly put the blame on Mahine—"a plan had been laid," he wrote, "to steal what I had refused to give." The captain said he was "fixed in my resolution" that Mahine "should not keep it." He dispatched an ominous message to the chief, demanding both the animal and its pilferer. It took a day to get to the bottom of the larceny, but the thief voluntarily returned to the ships with the goat, unharmed. Though the Native man seemed chastened and apologetic, Cook ordered him put in irons.

But while this was happening, another goat was stolen, this one a nanny goat, big with kid. Acting on some probably flawed intelligence gleaned by Mai, Cook sent two midshipmen to the far side of the island to hunt down the she-goat. That night, when they returned empty-handed, Cook's wrath exploded.

On some level, he seemed to know he was overreacting, heading down a path that would only lead to heartache. There was no compelling reason why he couldn't let the incident go. But locating the animal and punishing its thief had become a matter of principle, of defending property and saving face. "I was now very sorry I had proceeded so far," he confessed, "as I could not retreat with any tolerable credit, and without giving encouragement to the people of the other islands we had yet to visit to rob us with impunity."

Cook asked Mai what he should do. "Without hesitation," Cook wrote, Mai urged him "to go with a party of men into the country, and shoot every soul I met with." That was too much for Cook. "This bloody advice," he vowed, "I could not follow."

Instead Cook decided he would wage war not on the people themselves but on their land, their dwellings, their belongings— leading a scorched-earth campaign across the island. The next day, October 9, Cook gathered a well-armed party of thirty-five men and marched with them over the mountainous interior, aiming for a settlement where Mai had been told the goat was being hidden. The jungle air was buggy and oppressive, and Cook's rancor seemed to intensify with every punishing mile as they climbed over the rugged thumbs of basalt.

When the party reached the coastal village where the goat was supposed to be sequestered, most of the people had fled, and the few residents who remained pleaded ignorance. They had not seen any such animal, they protested. Cook, convinced they were lying, had his men fan out and scour the area. When the goat still didn't turn up, he ordered every house in the village to be torched. Wholesale destruction followed—huts were gutted, crops burned, pigs and dogs slaughtered, and stores of fruits and vegetables confiscated to be consumed later aboard the ships. And this proved to be only the opening salvo of a rampage of arson and plunder.

Several months earlier, when Cook was passing through islands in the Tonga group, he had shown a taste for cruelty that some of his officers found both surprising and alarming. In the face of what he called the "repeated insolence" of the Natives—jackets, shoes, and a pewter basin had gone missing, as had daggers, bayonets, and muskets—Cook's fury smoldered. On Tongatapu and its nearby atolls, he took to flogging Natives far past the daily limit of twelve lashes per man allowed by navy rules; in one instance, he had a Native whipped a sadistic seventy-two times. He cut off the ears of some of the most egregious thieves, and in at least one case, on his orders, a cross was carved into a Native man's shoulder, all the way to the bone.

Yet Cook had never visited on anyone the kind of widespread retribution that he was now unleashing on the people of Moorea—punishing the many for the misdeeds of an individual. It seemed Cook had taken leave of his senses. The wanton destruction of the homes of people he had no proof were actually connected to the theft—this was a first. Although some of his men threw themselves into the vandalistic acts with gusto, most were appalled by the harshness of their captain's orders. They understood Cook's initial frustration over the theft, but his lust for retaliation had grown into something terrifyingly toxic, with no sense of proportion.

"I doubt not," thought one lieutenant, "but Captain Cook had good reasons for carrying his punishment to these people to so great a length, but what his reasons were are yet a secret." It was "all about such a trifle as a small goat," wrote Midshipman George Gilbert. Cook's reprisals "were so different from his conduct in like cases in former voyages."

Later in the day, for good measure, Cook had members of his party stalk down to the water's edge and rip apart every canoe they could find. This was much more than a passing insult. It would be difficult to exaggerate the importance of a canoe in Polynesian society—the labor and craftsmanship it entailed, the utility it provided, the livelihood it advanced. Canoes were transportation, but they were also art. What the horse was to the American West, the canoe was to the Society Islands. To destroy canoes was to strike at the people's independence, their means of sustenance and of getting about, their sense of aesthetics—and, to some extent, their sense of identity, too.

Cook, who surely understood this, persisted through the day, and the day after that: He sent teams of men along the coast to smash up every outrigger they encountered. Some Mooreans filled their beloved vessels with heavy rocks and sunk them in the lagoon shallows, thinking this might deter Cook. It didn't. "The Captain," wrote Lieutenant John Rickman in horror, "ordered the canoes that were sunk to be weighed up and destroyed."

It is extraordinary that the islanders didn't rise in defiance and kill these white-skinned invaders. The Native weapons may have been no match for muskets, but the Mooreans outnumbered Cook's small party by a thousandfold. They could have made quick work of the Englishmen, but for some reason they remained pacific, even as parts of their island were consumed in flames.

ON THE MORNING of October 10, Cook, still convinced that Mahine must be behind the heist of the nanny goat, sent word to the chief that if the animal was not returned at once, his men would obliterate every canoe and every single structure on the island.

Mahine failed to present himself or to reply to Cook's message, and the goat remained at large. So, on Cook's orders, the pilfering and destruction raged for another day. "The damage which the inhabitants . . . sustained," thought the *Discovery*'s coxswain, Heinrich Zimmermann, "could scarcely be repaired in a century."

It was true that no one was killed, or even physically harmed, but the ravages were relentless—and horrifyingly out of scale. There was a deep and tragic irony in all of this: Cook, following his policy of island neutrality, had refused to join the Tahitian chief Tu and his allies in their proposed attack against Mahine. Yet now Cook had visited more punishment on Moorea than even the Tahitians likely had in mind.

Mai's active involvement was one of the most disturbing aspects of the continuing melee. Not only did he join in on the devastation and the looting, but in many cases he led the effort, and repeatedly beseeched Cook for permission to fire on innocent Mooreans as they fled in fear. "Although I am told that our own people showed a mighty satisfaction in what was done," King noted, "in these depredations, Mai was the most active." Many of Cook's sailors wondered how Mai could treat his fellow islanders this way. "We thought it rather extraordinary," wrote Zimmermann, "that Mai himself... executed the greater part of this destruction."

It was hard to fathom Mai's conduct, hard to know what he was thinking, or *if* he was thinking. Maybe he was trying to emulate his indignant captain, and to please him through overzealousness. Anthropologist Gananath Obeyesekere has suggested that Mai and Cook had become codependent, as modern psychologists might phrase it. "Cook and Mai were in a close, almost symbiotic relationship," Obeyesekere argues, "such that one seemed to be the alter ego of the other, each feeding the fragments of the dark side of the other's being."

It's possible that Mai nursed an ancestral grudge of his own against the people of Moorea, some obscure vendetta against a kinship group or faction there—it was plausible, even, that some of the Mooreans he attacked originally hailed from his hated Bora Bora.

Or, far more likely, with the taking of Cook's goat, Mai had glimpsed his own uncertain future. Wherever he settled in the Society Islands, people were going to try to make off with his store of treasures, to pick and chip away at his wealth until he had no wealth at all. By adopting a draconian stance, perhaps he thought he would make a daunting first impression and establish a reputation for himself, throughout the islands, as a fierce and uncompromising defender of his property.

Still, what Mai had done was self-destructive. He had marked himself as a traitor, someone with an appetite for inflicting pain on his Polynesian brethren. One thing was assured: If Moorea had ever been a serious candidate for Mai's relocation, it most assuredly wasn't one anymore.

On the third day, while Cook was out conducting yet another torching raid on another part of the island, the pregnant goat was discreetly returned—still in good health. It wasn't ascertained who had stolen the animal, or where it had been hidden all this time, but Cook would never waver in his belief that it was Mahine's doing.

As the last wisps of smoke settled over Moorea, the *Resolution* and the *Discovery* prepared to leave. None of the sadness or nostalgia that usually accompanied Cook's departures from South Seas islands was evident—the residents were thrilled and relieved to see the Englishmen go, and the Englishmen, having made ample strides in just a few days toward destroying this utopia, were eager to slink away.

Some of Cook's officers defended his terrible reprisals on Moorea, most notably Clerke, who laid all the blame for the incident on the islanders themselves—"these good people, whose ridiculous conduct in stealing those goats, and most absurd obstinacy in keeping them, has brought upon them such damages...as they will not recover from these many months to come." But, Clerke said, "it was wholly their own seeking... The Devil put it in their heads to fall in love with the goats." Clerke thought that Cook had resorted to extreme measures only after "every gentle method" had first been exhausted.

Yet most of the officers on both ships were disturbed by what had happened on Moorea, and shocked by the ferocity of Cook's temper. King wrote that he was not "able to account for Captain Cook's precipitate proceeding in this business." He felt sure that "less destructive measures might have been adopted and the end gained...I doubt whether our ideas of propriety in punishing so many innocent people for the crimes of a few, will be ever reconcilable to any principle one can form of justice." When he considered all the "weighty damages they have sustained," King concluded that the Mooreans "may fear but never love us."

It was one of the more inexplicable episodes in Cook's long career. In his anvil of a biography, J. C. Beaglehole, Cook's staunchest defender, dismissed his actions on Moorea as an aberration, placing them within a behavioral compartment all by itself—an "odd unintelligible phenomenon," he called the episode. One historian would wonder whether the captain had been suffering from a "passing madness," while others would unequivocally describe Cook's dealings as deranged, brutish, and gratuitously cruel. Obeyesekere compares Cook's behavior to that of Colonel Kurtz in Conrad's *Heart of Darkness*. The events on Moorea showed Captain Cook at his nadir, and offered further indication that something had profoundly changed in his outlook, that some sinister force was pulling at his psyche and his soul.

Others—historians, biographers, even forensic pathologists—who've pondered the events on Moorea have argued that, here again, something must have been *medically* wrong with Cook. His behavior was evidence of a "decay of his splendid intellect," suggested Cook biographer Richard Hough. "For such a total transformation, we may have to look for the deepest of causes—changes in the organic structure of the brain. Pathology rather than psychology is likely to be our best guide."

Even Cook seemed to recognize that he'd plunged over a precipice while he was on Moorea. After it was over and he was headed toward the next speck in the Society Islands chain, he wrote, in an uncharacteristically rueful tone: "This troublesome, and rather unfortunate affair ended, which could not be more regretted on the part of the natives than it was on mine."

21   *The Ardor of Inviolable Friendship*

HUAHINE, OCTOBER 1777

The *Resolution* and the *Discovery* sailed west over the blue swells and the next day eased through a gap in the coral reef that surrounded the little island of Huahine. Mai had managed to arrive just ahead of Cook, although his *Royal George* had nearly capsized in a squall during the night.

Huahine was where Cook had decided he would finally install Mai with his retinue and his abundant English cargo. Mai had a history here, and some family ties, and it was enough of an unsophisticated backwater, Cook thought, that his friend's wealth might make a deeper and more lasting impression than it would have on Tahiti. Mai was amenable to the plan, although his preference was still to resettle on the nearby island of Raiatea, his native soil. There he hoped to enlist Cook and his men with their guns to drive out the Bora Bora warriors who had seized his family's land. Mai thought he could recruit large numbers of Raiateans to join them in a revolt against the usurpers. But Cook refused to abet such a scheme. "I neither would assist them in such a design," Cook wrote, "nor suffer them to put it into execution."

On the other hand, if Mai was willing to sublimate his pride, set aside his family vendetta, and pledge permanent peace with the Bora Borans, Cook thought he and Mai could employ a bit of diplomacy to reclaim at least a portion of Mai's ancestral plot on Raiatea. But Mai could not stomach a policy of rapprochement with his bitter foes. "I wanted to reconcile him to the Bora Bora men," wrote Cook, but "he was too great a patriot to listen to any such thing."

With Raiatea out of the question, the fair and friendly island of Huahine would have to do. It was eight miles across and nine miles long, its steep hillsides choked in forests of purau and mape and snarls of tropical vines. Huahine boasted a brackish tidal lake full of shrimp and many species of fish that the Native people had been catching for centuries in elaborate weirs made of volcanic stone. In some of the island's streams lived a rare variety of eel, with translucent blue eyes, that the locals considered sacred. Huahine, which was actually two islands linked by a sandspit causeway, lay a little more than a hundred miles northwest of Tahiti, just far enough to have resisted some of the big island's influences while cultivating its own rhythms, customs, and dialect.

Huahine was a gorgeous island, with a shallow lagoon whose

palette of iridescent colors strained credulity—from cobalt to robin's egg, emerald to aquamarine. Glimpsed from certain angles upon the sea, the contours of Huahine's mountains resembled a recumbent pregnant woman, her face upturned to the sky, the peak of her bosom dipping, then rising again to a swollen belly that tapered down toward her hips. Perhaps in part because of this famous silhouette, Huahine had a reputation for being the garden isle of the archipelago—raw, rural, and reproductive. It was said to be an island with a certain feminine touch, and, in fact, Huahine had been governed by powerful women at various times.

Cook had been to Huahine twice before. In July of 1769, aboard the *Endeavour*, he had become the first European to touch here, and he'd returned in the *Resolution* in 1773. Cook was smitten with the place, though he regarded it as a bit unruly, a cauldron of competing factions and rogue elements without a strong central authority. "I had always met with more troublesome people at this island than any of the others," he wrote. "Anarchy seemed to prevail more here than at any other place."

Part of the "anarchy" had to do with the fact that Huahine was right up against a number of other islands. From Huahine, Cook could gaze toward the west and make out Raiatea and Taha'a and then, farther back in the briny haze, Bora Bora. Depending on wind conditions, each island was usually no more than a day's sail, sometimes less, from the next green volcanic stud in the chain. The regular intercourse this proximity afforded had prompted Cook, during his first voyage, to think of the cluster, including Tahiti and Moorea, as a "society of islands." The local people, he noted, were constantly crisscrossing the waters in their outriggers to trade, visit relatives, and engage in ceremonies, and sometimes to make war. The name Cook placed on his early charts—the Society Islands—had stuck, and it endures today as another name for what is also known as French Polynesia. (Some historians have contended that Cook styled them the "Society Islands" in honor of the Royal Society, but in his journal he insisted that the name had occurred to him simply because the islands "lay contiguous to one another.")

Having nudged into Huahine's harbor and dropped anchor just

off the settlement of Fare, Cook came ashore to meet with the locals. They seemed obsequiously friendly—probably they'd heard what Cook's men had done on Moorea and feared an encore eruption of the captain's wrath.

The sovereign of the island was said to be a boy about ten years of age named Teri'i-tari'a. The juvenile king emerged onto the white-sand beach, attended by two stout young men whose backs he mounted whenever he pleased, as though riding a horse. Cook's men found the young chief surly and spoiled. "A very mean looking boy he is," thought the *Discovery*'s master, Thomas Edgar. It was learned that Teri'i-tari'a's mother was actually responsible for the management of affairs, at least until her son reached maturity. Chiefs from other precincts arrived, lending credence to Cook's belief that Huahine was an island suffering from some measure of political confusion.

After presents were exchanged and religious prayers uttered, Cook explained to the assembled party the reason he had come to Huahine: He intended to leave Mai here, permanently. Mai had voyaged all the way to England, and he possessed considerable property as well as the blessings of the British nation. What parcel of land, the captain asked, would be most suitable for Mai to build a house and live out the remainder of his days?

One of the other local chiefs, probably intimidated by Cook and his ships, stepped forward. Employing grandiose gestures, he said that as far as he was concerned, the magnificent Captain Cook owned *all* of Huahine, so Mai could settle upon whatever tract Cook might choose.

The captain marked off a plot by the beach that was about two hundred yards wide. Then he "purchased" it for the price of fifteen axes and "some beads and trifles." Mai seemed pleased with the parcel, and the carpenters, armed with saws and hammers and awls, came ashore to start constructing a proper English house.

THE SALIENT REQUIREMENT in Cook's ordered design of the structure was that it should be built without nails, or at least as few as possible. By using pegs and mortise-and-tenon joints instead of nails, Cook hoped "there might be no inducement to pull it down."

Mai's house would be twenty-four feet long, eighteen feet wide, and ten feet high, with a small attic for ventilation. It was to be surrounded by a deep ditch, like a moat, and would be constructed largely of planks. Its rooms would be appointed with English chairs, tables, and a bed with a mattress. It would have a basement underneath to store foodstuffs and accept a magazine to be crammed with ammunition. And, most important, Mai's house would feature a front door with a sturdy lock.

The house was to have several outbuildings, including a stable for horses. Mai would need a compound of lesser structures to lodge his dependents and hangers-on, for a brother and numerous cousins and other relatives had arrived, hoping to live under the umbrella of his largesse. In addition, there were six attendants Mai had acquired in Tahiti, as well as Te Weherua and Koa, Mai's two Māori servants.

While the carpenters immersed themselves in their work, Cook and several parties of men crouched around the site, laying out a garden that would include melons, squash, pineapples, and slips from the Spanish grapevines Mai had pruned on Tahiti. Beside the structure, Cook planted a shaddock tree.

As the house began to take shape, other work details embarked upon an extermination project: Both the *Resolution* and the *Discovery* had become infested with cockroaches, a scourge almost as bad as the rats. Cook ordered practically every movable object—chests, trunks, barrels, tents—to be hauled up from the holds and brought on shore while the decks were smoked with gunpowder and brimstone. "The number of cockroaches that infested the ship at this time is incredible; the damage they did us was very considerable," said Cook, reporting that the bread room had become overrun with the vermin. The stores of hardtack biscuits had been soiled with cockroach excrement. The roaches, crawling over every surface of the ship at night, had devoured books, maps, and even some of Anderson's stuffed birds.

"They eat and destroy everything," complained Bayly, the astronomer. "These insects [are] so innumerable on board the *Resolution* that they run in every part of her, so thick you would think the ship alive."

ON THE EVENING of October 22, hundreds of the locals, along with some of Cook's officers, gathered in a large thatched assembly house to watch a series of *heiva* festival dances that were being performed by a troupe of *arioi* from Raiatea. The *arioi* were an order of itinerant dancers, actors, and singer-poets. In some ways, they were the South Seas equivalent of strolling minstrels or troubadours, although they also served an important religious function, helping preserve and celebrate the ancient myths and cosmology of Polynesian culture through their elaborate performances.

In the Society Islands, when the *arioi* arrived upon one's shores, work ceased and the feasts and ceremonies commenced. Their hallowed ranks were composed of both men and women. They enjoyed special privileges, wore unique clothing, lived in separate lodges, and had identifying tattoos inked upon their skin.

In a society that already encouraged decidedly frank attitudes about sex, the *arioi* were expected to lead lives of extreme erotic pleasure. They were not permitted to have children, however, so when a child was born to an *arioi* woman, she either had to leave the order permanently or kill her progeny, usually through suffocation. Infanticide was said to be a not uncommon practice among them. Explorers' reports about the phenomenon would stir horror in the imaginations of English readers and would eventually lead to a movement of missionaries, who by the early 1800s would descend upon Tahiti and her neighboring islands, determined to ban the *heivas* and stamp out the heathen, licentious cult of the *arioi* for good.

On this lovely October evening, the *arioi* were dancing in the flickering glow of the torches. Cook's men found the dances mesmerizing. Samwell was particularly enthralled by the lead dancer. "The principal performer," he wrote, "was a young woman as beautiful as Venus and very elegantly dressed."

Deep into the ceremony, a commotion erupted. Captain Cook, wild-eyed and red with rage, stormed into the gathering. At first the crowds tried to ignore him—he didn't seem to understand that they were in the middle of a sacred *heiva* performance that was not under any circumstances to be interrupted. But Cook persisted, and gradually the drums fell away, the dancers halted their gyrations, and the magnetic energy of the moment dissipated.

In the sudden hush, Cook, speaking with a thunderous voice, made it known that someone had stolen the sextant—some accounts say it was a quadrant—from Bayly's onshore observatory tent. Most likely, the marines who were supposed to have been guarding the observatory had been distracted by the revelries. Cook was resolute: This crime would not stand. The crowd was startled and alarmed, and clusters of people, innocent of the theft, began to back away. Cook tried to reassure them that they had nothing to fear, but they didn't believe him. They peeled off and scattered into the hills.

Cook stomped and thrashed about the crowded assembly house. His face throbbed with spite, and his eyes flashed with an almost maniacal determination to hunt down the culprit. (Cook's men were starting to make a connection between the dances of the *heiva* festival and their captain's strange fits of fury. The dances, they thought, bore a distinct resemblance to the violent motions and stampings of Captain Cook when he fell into his tantrums of anger. From then on, whenever their commander lost his cool, the crew would remark that he was "throwing a *heiva*." What was remarkable about Cook's tantrums, however, was the discipline of his language. Although he was "hasty tempered," wrote one able seaman, he "never swore, not even when in a rage.")

Cook commanded Mai to find the thief, and he did. The perpetrator was in the crowd, just a few feet away, defiant and unapologetic. Mai, learning that the man was from Bora Bora, drew his sword and threatened to run him through. The man was hauled back to the *Resolution*, where he was confined in chains. Mai, with Cook at his side, led an interrogation and eventually extracted from the malefactor not only an admission but a detailed description of where he had hidden the sextant. In the morning, one of Mai's servants located the instrument, concealed in some high grass under a tree about a quarter mile from the tents.

At noon that day, the defendant was put on trial and sentenced. First Cook administered his now customary sanction for theft— ordering the man's hair and eyebrows shaved off. But this time,

Cook went a step further, issuing a brutal sentence that he had experimented with months earlier while passing through Tonga. On Cook's orders, one of the marines approached the prisoner with a sharp knife. Then, as Clerke put it, the Bora Boran was "deprived of his ears."

It was a measure Clerke thought justified. "The extraordinary impudence and audacity of this fellow whilst in confinement on board surpassed everything," said Clerke, who called the islander "the most consummate rascal I have met with." Clerke thought Cook had no choice but to make a "severe example of him. He abused everybody about him, without exception, and frequently declared he was determined upon the destruction of Mai."

The earless man, yowling in anguish, was hurled overboard and left to swim back to Huahine. The man made good on his promise of revenge, however, by trampling Mai's new garden, ripping up the vines that had just been planted, and releasing some of Mai's animals from their enclosures. He swore that once Cook had sailed from Huahine, he would murder Mai and burn his house to the ground.

Something drastic would have to be done with this willful and recalcitrant man, whom Cook regarded as a "hardened scoundrel." Cook had him apprehended again. According to one account, the captain intended to have him marooned on some distant atoll so he would never again pose a threat to Mai. The outrages already committed by the Bora Boran man had left Cook "anxious for the safety of Mai, and fearing that if this man remained upon the island, some mischief would ensue."

Cook had him flogged until, as Zimmermann described it, "particles of his skin came away in shreds." But that night, even though two of Cook's men were guarding him on the quarterdeck, he broke free of his chains and swam ashore, this time tormenting Mai at his half-finished house, which he attempted to burn. (This, noted Clerke, could have been catastrophic; since large amounts of gunpowder were stored inside, a fire would "have blown our poor friend Mai's fortunes to the devil.") Before he could be caught, the man fled into the island's interior.

Cook punished the two guards severely for their negligence.

They claimed they had merely fallen asleep, but Cook suspected they'd taken pity on the mutilated captive and unlocked his manacles. Cook applied the lash to the two guards without mercy—over the next three days, the main sentry, Thomas Morris, was administered thirty-six bites of the cat.

(This had become a well-established pattern of the voyage. Cook's floggings had become far more frequent and severe than on his first two expeditions—far more frequent and severe than the punishments William Bligh would mete out while leading his ill-fated voyage of the HMS *Bounty,* a little over a decade later. "Beatings shall continue until morale improves" is a saying often attributed to Bligh, yet Cook on his third voyage considerably exceeded Bligh's use of the lash.)

In thinking about the Bora Boran man, Cook wondered whether his defiant behavior might be an expression of something larger. The captain was beginning to appreciate the depth of the bad blood that had existed between the Raiateans and the Bora Borans, and he doubted whether much could be done to avert the inter-island clash that Mai had long yearned for and that Cook had tried to avoid. Cook, detecting many ominous stirrings behind the thief's taunts and threats, worried that the complicated project England had pursued, at great expense and nuisance, to transport Mai to London and bring him safely back might be in jeopardy.

ON OCTOBER 26, when the house was nearly finished, Mai started bringing his English treasures and souvenirs ashore from the *Resolution:* the regiments of tin soldiers, the metal helmet and suit of armor, the mechanical Punch and Judy, the serpent jack-in-the-box, the barrel organ that could be cranked by hand. The globe of the earth, the portraits of King George and Queen Charlotte, the illustrated Bible, the "electrifying machine" that could give unsuspecting parties a jolt. The compasses and beads, the mirrors and looking glasses, the menagerie of toy animals. The kettles and crockery, the mugs and cutlery, and case after case of port wine. The saddles and bridles and horse tack. The wardrobe of English clothing—riding boots, velvet jackets, satins and linens, and numerous hats. Last but not least, the

swords and cutlasses, the muskets and pistols, the fowling piece, the
cartridges and pistol balls, and additional kegs of gunpowder.

Mai had wanted far more of these last items; he had originally
asked for enough war implements to outfit an entire army. But Cook
feared that the guns would do Mai more harm than good. "I was
always of [the] opinion," said Cook, that "he would have been better
without firearms than with them."

Mai took up residence in his new digs and seemed happy with
them. The house was a piece of Britain, smelling of fresh-hewn
wood, with a Latin carving over its door meant to signify that its
occupant was under the protectorship of King George III: GEORGIUS
TERTIUS REX. (The locals began to call that part of the island "Pretani," and the name would stick for generations to come.) Whenever
Mai left his cottage—to visit the ships or to ride his horse down the
beach—he locked the front door and dropped the key in his pocket,
just as he had done with the key to his apartment when he went out
on strolls around London.

In the final days, as Cook and Clerke readied their ships for
departure, Mai threw a succession of torchlit parties for the officers,
dining under the stars beside his English house. They drank port
and gorged themselves on fresh-caught fish and barbecued pork.
Some of the chiefs, including the boy king Teri'i-tari'a, joined in
the festivities, while Mai leaped among his guests, grinding his barrel organ. The Huahine people were astonished by the contraption
and smiled in wonderment at the treacly mechanized melodies that
issued from it.

Mai had a modest assortment of animals penned around his
house—a stallion and a mare that was believed to be with foal,
four sheep, a pair of ducks, a pair of rabbits, a pair of peafowl, and
some cats, among other species that the Huahine people had never
seen before. Mai also had a monkey—presumably he had brought
it aboard while in Cape Town, but the accounts are vague on this
point. The locals were delighted by the nimble creature, which they
called "Hairy Man."

On those last nights, members of Cook's crew brought out their
bagpipes, flutes, and fiddles. Mai set off fireworks, and there was

much "mirth and jollity," said Bayly. "We have nothing but good humor subsisting among us."

At other times, Mai seemed pensive and wistful. Perhaps he was apprehensive about his Bora Boran nemesis—no one seemed to know what had become of the earless man, but the assumption was that he would resume his depredations just as soon as the two ships departed Huahine. On several occasions, Mai hinted that he might like to return to Britain, although he understood that it was not a possibility.

Cook noted that several other people on Huahine had volunteered to sail off with the ships—they, too, wanted to visit London and see the sights of Pretani. But Cook declined. The cross-cultural experiment had already been done. Bringing more Polynesians to London would only seem passé. As George Gilbert put it, "The curiosity of the people of England [had] quite subsided," and an encore visitation of Pacific islanders would merely be "a burden on the public."

THE MEN OF the *Resolution* were going to miss Mai. He had annoyed the crew at times, but he had been a loyal and gregarious companion. His work as a Polynesian interpreter and a boatman had been priceless, not to mention his inexplicable talent as an angler. He was "a goodnatured sensible young fellow," thought Samwell, who "was universally liked."

Cook was going to miss Mai, too. His faults, the captain thought, "were more than overbalanced by his great good nature and docile disposition." But Cook entertained profound doubts as to whether any of the tools and implements Mai had assembled would ultimately do him or his countrymen much good. "I cannot avoid expressing it as my real opinion," Cook wrote, "that it would have been far better for these poor people never to have known our...accommodations and arts...than after once knowing [them], to be left again and abandoned."

With respect to Mai's future, Cook went on: "Such is the strange nature of human affairs, that it is probable we left him in a less desirable situation than he was in before his connection with us." Cook feared that despite all that had been done to secure Mai, the future did not augur well for the young man. "It is here as in many other countries," Cook wrote, that a man "richer than [his] neighbor is sure to be envied. This was Mai's fate, and there were numbers who wished to see him upon a level with themselves; from these he had everything to fear."

All Cook could do was issue dire warnings to the chiefs and to the people of Huahine. He admonished the people that he would lay waste to the island and destroy anyone who molested Mai's property. "This," thought Cook, "will certainly have some effect, as they have not a doubt but that I shall return again to the island."

But Cook had no intention of coming back to Huahine. He was leaving for good. The *Resolution* would be stopping for a while in Raiatea and then, briefly, Bora Bora, before aiming for the ice fields of Alaska.

FINALLY THE DAY came, November 2, 1777. Mai boarded the ships to pay his final respects. He was dressed in resplendent garb, with a sword and a pistol at his side. He worked his way down the long lines of officers and supernumeraries, the marines, the midshipmen, and the ordinary seamen, too, and though his eyes brimmed with tears, he held his emotions mostly in check as he kissed and shook hands with his old friends for the last time—expressing, as James Burney described it, "real and unaffected sorrow."

"Mai sustained himself with a manly resolution," wrote Cook, "until he came to me." Suddenly Mai threw his arms around Captain Cook and wept uncontrollably. "In a torrent of Polynesian, broken with a few English words," Cook said, Mai tried "to express his gratitude for all that had been done for him." Mai's "eyes were never dry," Lieutenant John Rickman noted, and his sobs were like the "supplications of a dutiful son to an obdurate father. Mai hung round his neck in all the seeming agony of a child trying to melt the heart of a reluctant parent [and] twined his arms round him with ... the ardour of inviolable friendship."

Still in tears, Mai departed the ship and climbed aboard his outrigger, the *Royal George*. He escorted the two ships as they passed through the gap in the reef. As the winds picked up and the *Resolution* began to spread her sails, Cook saluted Mai with a blast of five guns.

22   *Faraway Heaven*

HUAHINE

On Mai's native island of Raiatea, a certain rare flower, the tiare apetahi, grew high along the volcanic slopes of Mount Temehani. Mysteriously, the flower flourished only in that one specific place, and it was said that any attempts to transplant it to other islands, or even to other spots on Raiatea, would fail. The plant observed a definitive and delicate sense of place; it wouldn't take root anywhere else. The tiare apetahi flower was an eloquent metaphor for Mai's life story. Raiatea was his home, and though he spent much of his life moving around the islands and traveling the world, he was never entirely at peace anywhere else.

There are many stories about what happened to Mai after Cook departed for Alaska. Few of them are reliable. They come down to us through oral history, through European explorers who later stopped in the Society Islands, and through missionaries who arrived generations later to convert the islanders to Christianity. Inevitably, the stories were distorted by their having filtered through language barriers and a thousand nuances of cross-cultural misperception. Suffice it to say that Mai quickly passed into the realm of legend, leaving behind a legacy that was murky and complicated.

What most of the stories agree on is rather tragic: Mai lived only a few years after Cook's departure. He seems to have died sometime in 1780 from a virus—an infection of the throat, it was reported— that was thought to have been introduced by a Spanish ship that stopped at Tahiti. Te Weherua and Koa, Mai's two New Zealand servants, also died around the same time, perhaps from the same disease. Most of the animals perished, too, including the pregnant nanny goat. Even Hairy Man, Mai's monkey, died, after tumbling from a coconut tree.

Mai apparently had no children, so he died without heirs, and his remains were said to have been buried at the site of his house. The structure itself was dismantled, his remaining animals confiscated, his curios looted and dispersed among the people of Huahine.

In 1789, William Bligh passed through the Society Islands aboard HMS *Bounty*, on a voyage that would end in a notorious mutiny. Bligh tried his best to learn the details of Mai's fate, but already, less than a decade after his death, the stories about him seemed dim and distant.

However, there was one story that resonated with Bligh. Shortly after Mai had settled on Huahine, the old war between the people of Raiatea and Bora Bora was rekindled. In a battle that according to some accounts occurred on the island of Taha'a, which lies nearly adjacent to Raiatea, Mai fought bravely and expertly. Employing his muskets and stores of ammunition, perhaps using his horses and armor, too, he made a decisive difference in the fight. Large numbers of the enemy were slain. The people of Huahine were victorious.

The battle did not succeed in permanently dislodging the Bora Borans from his family land on Raiatea, but Mai had finally clashed with his enemy—just as he had said he would.

So, in a sense, Mai accomplished precisely what he had set out to do when he boarded Tobias Furneaux's *Adventure*. He had procured firearms, learned how use them, and, in a brief shining moment, successfully deployed them in battle against his foe. In doing so, he had honored the memory of his murdered father. All his life he had vowed to avenge his family's losses, and to some degree he'd done just that.

When he visited Huahine, Bligh found almost nothing left of the compound where Mai had lived. "The house," he wrote, "was torn to pieces and stolen. The seeds and plants that were sown had been a long time destroyed." Bligh heard that Mai had often ridden his horse up and down the beach, wearing the leather equestrian boots he had brought from England. Bligh noted that a number of Natives bore a curious tattoo on their legs: the image of a man astride a horse.

In England, Mai's memory was kept alive for many years. He was the subject of an enormously popular musical play, *Omai: or, A Trip Round the World,* by the Irish dramatist John O'Keeffe, which opened in 1785 at the Theatre Royal in Covent Garden. King George III saw it twice and was said to have wept at certain scenes. The same year, the acclaimed English poet William Cowper published his masterwork, *The Task,* in which he imagined Mai, the "gentle savage," longing to return to Britain as he strolled the beach at Huahine, wondering if "the surge that bathes" his feet had ever washed upon England's shores.

Many years later, an English missionary named William Ellis spent time on Huahine and heard further stories, which he related in his book *Polynesian Researches,* published in 1829. The missionary noted that after several generations, the spot where Mai's house had been erected was still called Pretani and that the shaddock tree Cook had planted was still growing beside what remained of Mai's garden. Ellis reported that Mai's metal helmet and other parts of his body armor, as well as several cutlasses, were hung on the sides of a newer house that had been constructed where Mai's dwelling once stood. A local chief had some of Mai's artifacts and curios, including a jack-in-the-box. Ellis also found the large English Bible that Mai's tutor, Granville Sharp, had given him as a present. All other evidence of Mai's existence had disappeared.

Local lore concerning Mai is practically nonexistent, so nearly everything that is understood about him comes to us through the anecdotes of English sailors, the descriptions of English observers, and the brushstrokes of English painters. One thing is glaringly missing from the record: Mai's own voice.

Like so many cases of cross-cultural transplantation, Mai's odyssey led him, in the end, to an ambiguous place. His journey served as an allegory of colonialism and its unintended consequences. England, by showing off her riches and advancements and sending Mai back with a trove of mostly meaningless treasures, had doomed him to a jumbled, deracinated existence. Like the tiare apetahi flower of Raiatea, Mai, after all his travels, couldn't take root in other soils.

Polynesian scholars recently located the spot where Mai's house stood and where his remains were buried. It's set back from the shore, on the outskirts of Fare. A modest yellow church called Iehova Saloma, with a corrugated roof of galvanized metal, had been built on the site. In back of the chapel, thickets of tropical trees, laden with fragrant flowers, swayed in the salt breeze.

This would have been Mai's vista from the front door of his house, the only door in all of Polynesia that had a lock. Gazing west past the lagoon and the waves smashing on the reef, he would have had a perfect view of Raiatea, the sacred isle, a snaggy mountain on the horizon, just twenty-five miles away.

Mai had sailed around the world and back again in the hope of returning there, to build a life on the shores of his "faraway heaven." And in his last days, there it stood, right in front of him.

23   Scorched Up by the Heat of the Sun

KIRITIMATI, DECEMBER 1777

For weeks, the two ships pushed north over the blue furrows of the Pacific. The weather was muggy, and through the listless afternoons the sailors could hear only the soft rasping of the timbers, the strain of the ropes, and the waves rhythmically frothing along the hulls. On the night of December 22, the two ships crossed the equator. Thankfully, this was no cause for another silly dunking ritual—the baptism of virgin "line crossers" that had occurred in the Atlantic the year before was deemed sufficient—but it was a notable occasion nonetheless, for this was the first time in all his travels that James Cook had passed north of the equator while in the Pacific.

Venturing into the northern hemisphere brought a change in the tenor of the voyage. Seventeen months after leaving England, Cook was at last pursuing the expedition's true objective: the search for a northwest passage. He believed there was nothing but open sea between the Society Islands and the northwest coast of the American continent. As far as he understood it, they were entering a blue void, an emptiness larger than any on the planet. It would be a perilous haul of some five thousand miles before they saw land again. To cross such an expanse, Cook would have to conserve his water, ration his food, and pray that no storms would wreck his masts—for between here and North America, he was all but certain his carpenters would find no trees with which to make repairs.

So far on this voyage, Cook had largely played the role of a glorified chaperone and delivery man. But now, with King George's animals deposited and Mai installed, the real work of the expedition could begin. This put Cook in a better mood—it seemed he couldn't wait to reach the Arctic and become an explorer once again.

Back home in England, Cook's reputation as a mariner-scientist had only grown. A few months earlier, the account of his second expedition, *A Voyage Towards the South Pole and Round the World,* had been published in London to wide acclaim. The book itself was a work of art, printed in two beautiful quarto volumes, bound in calfskin, with a companion folio volume containing plates, charts, and maps. It was a publishing sensation, all the more so because its author was off at sea, taking new risks on the other side of the globe, on yet another adventurous errand for the country. Within weeks, the first edition sold out, but it would go through three more editions and would soon be published in many other European languages. (Today, copies of *A Voyage Towards the South Pole* in good condition can fetch thousands of dollars at auction.)

Cook was now even more of a luminary figure—across England and Europe, he was a household name. In reviews, some critics ridiculed the book's lack of literary polish, but it was received with overwhelming respect and, in some quarters, a measure of awe. Cook, for all his simplicity of language, had found an Olympian manner of address that carried beyond his superiors at the Admiralty, beyond the British reading public; he seemed to be writing for history, for science, and for cartography. *This is the Pacific,* he seemed to be saying. *This is how it looks. These are its coordinates, laid out in a grid of latitude and longitude. It's all here.*

Cook must have wondered if his book had made it to the printing presses and, if so, how it was faring with readers, and whether there might be any financial windfall for him and his family. But these were developments he would never learn about.

———

AS THE TWO ships continued toward the northeast, the men failed to share Cook's enthusiasm for the Arctic and what was coming next. The joys and amusements of the tropical South Seas were over. They had nothing to look forward to but ice floes and frostbite, nasty weather and drab salted meat. Said George Gilbert: "We left the [Society Islands] with the greatest regret imaginable, supposing all the pleasure of the voyage to be now at an end."

It was strange and incongruous to be worrying about Arctic weather while sailing through sweltering equatorial heat, pushing up through the hot blue latitudes, but the idea of the Arctic, the dread of it, was already pressing on people's thoughts. Preparing for the frigid climes ahead, Cook's quartermasters would issue the wool "fearnought" jackets and other winter gear.

No one, however, was more gripped by trepidations about the polar weather than Charles Clerke and William Anderson. Whether out of embarrassment, personal loyalty to their captain, or a sense of patriotic duty, they had not found a way to speak with Cook about their dilemma—that they were dying of tuberculosis, that if they sailed to the freezing attic of North America they would die up there, and that instead they'd like to live out whatever was left of their numbered days in the healthful paradise of Polynesia.

Clerke had said he needed to get his papers in order before approaching Cook with his request to quit the expedition, but that apparently never happened. Anderson, who was sicker than Clerke, seems to have been similarly unsuccessful in broaching the subject with Cook. It's possible that they did speak with him and Cook refused to let them go, but if so, any documents related to such negotiations are lost to history.

The two sickly men, doubtless after much soul-searching, had decided to stick with the voyage. As the *Resolution* and the *Discovery* slipped steadily north, Clerke and Anderson, in their fits of coughing up blood, realized that whatever the coming adventure in Alaska might entail, it was for them probably a death sentence.

ON DECEMBER 23, something strange happened: The lookouts spotted an island dead ahead. It was a low coral island, but one of considerable extent, surrounded by an outer reef that was bashed by what Cook called "dreadful" breakers.

This crescent of coral and scrub, which Cook would call Christmas Island, is now known as Kiritimati. With a land area of 150 square miles, it's the largest atoll in the world. Polynesian way-finders had used it as a replenishing stop on long odysseys (archae-ologists have found remnants of stone structures), but by the time of Cook's arrival, this forgotten island had been uninhabited for hundreds of years. Starting in the 1950s, British and then American scientists would destroy much of the atoll by conducting a series of nuclear weapons tests.

The ships dropped anchor in thirty fathoms, and Cook ordered boats put in the water to search for a gap in the reef. Eventually Mas-ter Bligh found one, though it was only wide enough to admit small boats—the ships would have to remain anchored outside the reef. Soon parties were sent ashore. The island, thought surgeon's mate William Ellis, "had the appearance of being scorched up by the heat of the sun." Its meager soil, he said, was "composed of sand, stones, and the decayed shells of crabs and other shellfish." Mainly, the atoll appeared to be a refuge for staggering numbers of seabirds, includ-ing colonies of terns, noddies, petrels, boobies, and frigate birds—many of the fowl "so tame," said Ellis, "as to be taken off the bushes."

The island was virtually treeless, with just a few spindly coconut palms rising above the flats of rocky carbonate soil, but the backwa-ters and lagoons pulsed with life. Along the reef, sharks preyed upon swarms of fish. The white-sand beaches were alive with lizards and crabs, and sea turtles abounded in the island's salt marshes.

What was it about Cook's voyages? Time and time again, he had shown an uncanny serendipity for intersecting with islands dropped in the oceanic vastness. Kiritimati had possibly been encountered in 1537 during a Spanish voyage led by Hernando de Grijalva, but the expedition records were spotty, and the atoll's location had not been accurately pinpointed. Now, 240 years later, here was Captain Cook. Whether it was dumb luck or a sixth sense he was able to summon, to have struck this lonesome encrustation of land in the middle of the world's largest ocean was a feat.

Boats were sent to scout for fish. Arrowing through the coral reef were vigorous schools of trevally, but the men, wielding long pikes, had to fight a constant war with sharks to get to the prized fish. "On every side of us swam sharks innumerable," wrote Midshipman James Trevenen, one of the fishermen, "and so voracious that they bit our oars and rudder, and I actually stuck my [sword] into the back of one while he had the rudder between his teeth."

Cook sent out parties to look for fresh water, but the island appeared to be bone dry. "We tried in many places," said Ellis, "but could procure none but what was very brackish, and totally unfit for use." Cook dispatched still other details to hunt for sea turtles, and they found hundreds of them—"a noble supply," thought John Ledyard. Kiritimati, it turned out, was a rich turtle breeding ground; the creatures, which could weigh as much as three hundred pounds and often lived for seventy years or more, thrived in the island's salt marshes and seagrass meadows. Many mariners considered green sea turtle meat a delicacy. The animals were also a bountiful source of lard—a layer of green fat found beneath its shell was the reason for the turtle's name (its outer shell typically sporting hues of olive, brown, or black).

Catching the turtles on land was easy: All the hunters had to do was sneak up on them at night when they were asleep on the beach and turn them over on their backs, then return in the morning with more men to haul them away, flippers still churning, to the ships.

But capturing them in water was an altogether different challenge. At low tide, the coral inside the reef sat in no more than a foot of water, but there were many deep pockets and holes where some turtles would remain until the tide's return. The water in these cavities was so clear that the men could plainly see the hiding turtles. The best swimmers, sometimes working in pairs, sprang into action. They would dive into the holes, noted Trevenen, "and then the sport began," followed by what he called "very many ludicrous scenes."

In deep water, the turtles had the advantage, wrote Trevenen, "but when there was not more than six inches, we could come up with them and catch them by the fins." However, a bigger, stronger

turtle could sometimes drag a man across the shallows before dropping into the next pool—taking the hunter, still holding on to his
quarry, for a ride into the depths. "I have seen one, larger than common, thus taken three times and at last escape through a passage in
the reef into the open sea." The chase was enlivened, said Trevenen,
"with all the vicissitudes of hope and fear...the more so as perhaps
our dinner depended on it." In the end, Trevenen's band of hunters was successful: Within a half hour they had managed to capture
forty-two sea turtles.

Other turtle hunters had a much harder time. Two members of
a turtling party, working on the far side of the atoll from where the
ships lay anchored, got separated from their comrades and became
hopelessly lost. For several days, the two men, Bartholomew Lowman and Thomas Tretcher, wandered the brambly beaches. Roasted
by the sun, chewed by insects, the two sailors clawed at the sand in
a vain search for fresh water. In their desperate thirst, they slit the
throats of some sea turtles and slurped the blood. This, said Samwell,
proved counterproductive—"instead of quenching their thirst," he
wrote, "it made them sick." Finding bird nests here and there, they
cracked eggs and sucked their yolks. One of the men drank his own
urine.

Cook and Clerke sent search parties to scour the island. Perhaps
this place wasn't uninhabited after all, and Lowman and Tretcher
had been captured by hostile Natives? But eventually the search-
ers found the two lost men. By then, both were in severe distress—
disoriented, sun-blind, "speechless through fatigue," and "totally
stupid," said Rickman. Revived with food, water, and brandy, the
two men would slowly recover, but it was a close call.

Cook, like any responsible captain, had fretted about the two
men's welfare, but in the end he reacted to their ordeal with more
astonishment than commiseration. His mind, with all its cartographer's precision, had trouble fathoming how the two young men
could have gotten so lost on a flat and treeless island where, from
any piece of slightly higher ground, the two ships' masts were visible. Cook chalked it up to the fact that most mariners were clue-
less idiots when they ventured upon dry land. "Considering what a

strange set of beings the generality of seamen are when on shore," the captain mused, "instead of being surprised at these men losing themselves, we ought rather to have been surprised there were no more of them."

CHRISTMAS ARRIVED—HENCE Cook's name for the island—and the captain gave all hands the day off "to amuse themselves," wrote Rickman, "and every one had a pint of brandy to make merry and drink health to their friends in Old England." The Christmas dinner offerings were large quantities of roasted fish and shark steaks, vats of turtle burgoo, and platters of broiled seabirds.

It had been exactly one year since the expedition had encamped upon a very different uninhabited island—Kerguelen, that wind-swept barren in the frigid southern oceans. If the Kerguelen Christmas had been cold, sepulchral, and damp, this one was slightly more hopeful, although the weather was almost intolerably hot.

On December 30, Cook and Bayly, armed with achromatic tele-scopes, observed a partial eclipse of the sun. Two days later, the year 1778 was ushered in, and two days after that, Cook left a bottle with the usual note in Latin declaring that King George's ships had called at this place. Then the *Resolution* and the *Discovery*, their larders filled with several hundred green sea turtles, were off again. They headed north, enjoying what Rickman called a "prosperous gale."

24   A New Race of People

KAUA'I, JANUARY 1778

For two weeks, the *Resolution* and the *Discovery* crept across the Pacific, headed north by northeast. Nearly every night, the officers and crew were served stewed Kiritimati turtle. The seas were so calm that Charles Clerke transferred over to the *Resolution* to enjoy a luxurious lunch in Cook's cabin, where the two captains discussed the long voyage ahead.

A few days later, tangled mats of seaweed appeared on the water's surface. As he approached the Tropic of Cancer, Cook was surprised to find more birds in the air, more life in the sea, more timber floating about—sure signs that land was nearby. On the morning of January 18, 1778, off the port bow, the lookout glimpsed a mass on the horizon. It was a substantial volcanic island, dark blue in the early light. As the ships drew closer, Cook realized he was seeing not a single island, but several.

How was this possible? It had to be a mirage, some optical trick of the equatorial atmosphere. Cook hadn't expected to encounter land again until he reached the coast of North America—weeks or possibly months from now. The most experienced navigators he met while in the Society Islands had told him they knew of no islands to the north. The maps the Admiralty had provided Cook showed only a blank space, extending for thousands and thousands of miles.

But now it appeared that Cook had made a "fresh discovery," as the terminology of the times went. Aboard the two ships, the anticipation was palpable. To come upon this new land "excited our curiosity much," wrote David Samwell, who expected "to meet with a new race of people." Crewmen with spyglasses scoured the shoreline and could see that this island was fertile, clad in forests, and riven with streams that spilled from the high mountains.

"We were charmed with its appearance as we came near it," wrote Rickman, "observing it to abound with rivers, and to exhibit a prospect so full of plenty." The timing of this landfall was auspicious, for the ships had run out of green turtles from Kiritimati atoll and were so short of water that they had been forced to use a crude distilling machine, called an evaporator, to tease fresh water from the ocean. "Now that we saw whole rivers before us," Rickman exclaimed, "our hearts were dilated with joy."

THE ISLAND COOK was aiming for was the beautiful hunk of volcanism known as Kaua'i—Cook would call it "Atooi" on his charts— near the western end of the Hawaiian chain. (The first land he had spotted was O'ahu, but the winds had driven the two ships farther west.) Kaua'i was far enough away from the other islands of Hawai'i— far enough in miles but also in style and spirit, and in war and politics, too—that it was sometimes called a "separate kingdom," a realm unto itself.

The Hawaiian chain was the most isolated archipelago on earth, yet it was rather extraordinary that Spanish mariners had failed to find—and establish a permanent presence on—these islands long ago. For nearly 250 years, the Manila galleons, packed with spices and silks from Asia or precious metals from South American mines, had routinely sailed between the Philippines and Acapulco, passing just above or just below the latitudes of Hawai'i. Somehow, in all those epic pool laps across the blue Pacific, the Spanish captains, hewing to the established sea lanes and favorable trade winds, had apparently never strayed far enough or been blown sufficiently off course to intersect with this magnificent constellation of islands.

This point has been disputed by scholars, however. Spanish maps from the 1600s showed an island group, enticingly labeled "Los Bolcanos" (the Volcanoes), in the general vicinity of Hawai'i. Some accounts say that in 1555, Captain Juan Gaetano, a Spaniard sailing from Mexico to the Spice Islands, sighted the Hawaiian archipelago—it is thought that perhaps he was lured by the glow of an active volcano. But if that was so, the Spanish hid their discovery deep within their archives and logbooks, made no attempt to land on the islands, and did nothing to claim or develop them as possessions of the Spanish Crown.

In 1743, a British captain named George Anson had seized a Spanish galleon near the Philippines, and among the many treasures aboard he found a chart showing an island cluster more or less at the latitude of Hawai'i. It was not known whether the specks shown on the map were real or phantom islands, but some have suggested that the Admiralty surely would not have dispatched Cook to explore the North Pacific without equipping his chart room with some version of that tantalizing map. Yet in his journal Cook made no mention of it, and by all accounts, his surprise in stumbling upon these islands was genuine, not an act. To suggest, as some historians have, that he already knew of Hawai'i's existence and that he had steered straight for the island group with the cynical intention of usurping what was rightfully a Spanish exploratory achievement would be to accuse him of a duplicity that was wholly uncharacteristic of him.

In any case, Cook would thereafter be credited as the first European discoverer of Kaua'i and, by extension, the Hawaiian chain. And what a place it was—Kaua'i, this gem of malachite green, thirty-three miles across, with undulating cliffs and razorback ridges sweeping thousands of feet down to the sea. Along with its smaller sister island, Ni'ihau, Kaua'i is geologically the oldest of the archipelago, created five million years ago as the shifting Pacific Plate passed over the Hawai'i Hotspot, causing spasms of magma to spurt from vents some fifteen thousand feet down along the cold, dark ocean floor. Kaua'i's highest peak, Kawaikini, soared more than five thousand feet from the shore into the sky. Although Cook had arrived on the parched side of the island—the leeward side—Kaua'i's highlands, covered in mossy rainforests, were among the wettest places on earth.

FOR HOURS, AS Cook cruised along the southwest coast, near the place where the Waimea River flows into the ocean, he was kept in suspense, wondering whether the island before him was inhabited. But on a closer pass, he spotted cultivated fields, thatched structures, smoke twisting from the thickets. Soon he could see canoes being launched from the shore and hastening toward his ships.

These Natives were muscular and strong, and they powered their canoes swiftly through the water. But they were wary. "None of them would come near enough to converse with us or that we might see what sort of people they were," wrote John Ledyard. The Kauaians paddled slightly closer, and it was noticed that their canoes were heaped full of stones, which they presumably intended to lob at the visitors should hostilities erupt. Already, some of them were striking a bellicose pose, a demeanor reminiscent, to some of Cook's men, of Māori warriors. "They shook their spears at us," said Ledyard, "rolled their eyes about and made a variety of wild uncouth gesticulations."

Some of Cook's sailors who had become conversant in the Tahitian language called out to the Kauaians, and the reaction was incredible: They understood the questions that were put to them. Cook found it stunning to contemplate. This volcanic plug lay out in the blue bulge of the ocean 2,800 miles from Tahiti—separated by forty degrees of latitude. It had taken him five weeks to reach this place, in steady sailing, from the Society Islands. Yet its people spoke the same Polynesian tongue, or at least a related form of it.

Not only was the language similar, but Cook would soon see similarities in dress, facial features, canoe design, and customs. In every sense, these were *Polynesians*. Building upon what he already knew from his travels across the Pacific, he was beginning to grasp the extent of the Polynesian diaspora—from Tonga to Easter Island, from New Zealand to this place well north of the equator. "How," he wondered in his journal, "shall we account for this nation spreading itself so far over this vast ocean?"

Cook had arrived at the apex of what has come to be called the Polynesian Triangle, an area encompassing more than ten million square miles. He could only conclude that in ancient times the Polynesians must have been expert long-distance voyagers, pioneers of the high seas, far more adept and ambitious than he had first realized. Cook admired their accomplishments as only someone who'd traversed those same vast oceans could.

So chasmic were the distances between the different Pacific island groups that some of Cook's officers found it inconceivable that the supposedly primitive Polynesians of long ago, lacking navigational instruments, could have deliberately and repeatedly sailed to so many far-flung places. "It can scarce be imagined," wrote John Rickman, that "they could ever have any communication, being at more than 2,000 miles distance one from the other, with very little, if any dry land between."

Modern archaeologists believe the Hawaiian Islands were discovered in about A.D. 300 by navigators from the Marquesas Islands and that the archipelago was further populated by subsequent migrations from Tahiti, Raiatea, and other outposts in the Society Islands. Humans had dwelled on these islands for some fourteen centuries, unaware of a world beyond the Polynesian islands from which they had originally hailed.

These ancient mariners sailed double-hulled canoes that were lashed together with sennit vines and propelled by sails stitched from pandanus plants—canoes large enough to carry many people and considerable supplies. The navigators relied on the sun and stars, the prevailing winds and currents, and the patterns of swells, clouds, and storms, as well as the routes of petrels and other migratory seabirds, to wend their way across the void. It was not uncommon for these master seafarers to know more than 150 stars by name. A subtle green hue tinting the underside of a distant cloud bank might indicate land; a faint flickering of orange or pink might suggest a belching volcano just beyond the horizon. Some Polynesian navigators were known to bring frigate birds along on their voyages and release them into the skies, for they knew that the frigate bird could not swim and seldom ventured more than fifty miles from land. If a released bird returned to the canoes, the Polynesians knew they were still a long way from land.

The ancient navigators brought stock with them to colonize the Hawaiian Islands—hogs, chickens, rats, the seeds and bulbs of familiar food plants, and saplings of the paper mulberry tree. For generations, the people of the Hawaiian chain remained in contact with the mother islands far to the south. There were voyages in both directions. But at some point, for reasons that aren't clear, the journeys stopped. Knowledge of the route grew fuzzy, then fell away altogether. The inhabitants of the Hawaiian group became a happily marooned people on a happily sequestered chain of islands, and their world lay undisturbed for centuries.

And so it must have been a profound surprise for the Kauaian men, their paddles trailing slack in the water, to hear words and phrases of their own language spoken to them by such strange-looking people, dwelling upon such queer-looking craft.

THE ISLANDERS PADDLED nearer, lit with curiosity yet still on their guard. "It required but very little address to get them to come alongside," wrote Cook, "but we could not prevail upon anyone to come on board."

The stories passed down among the Kauaians say that what the men in the canoes noticed first was the considerable amount of iron attached to the two ships—flecks of the magical stuff seemed to gleam from every surface. They had seen iron before, most likely nails or other scraps of metal attached to driftwood brought on the currents of the ocean, flotsam that perhaps came from wrecked Spanish galleons.

Cook sensed their interest in metal, so he had a few nails and some brass medals lowered to them on the end of a rope. The islanders jettisoned the heavy caches of rocks from their canoes. At last, some of them were persuaded to climb aboard the two ships. They were dumbfounded by the huge floating labyrinths of wood, crammed with so many unfamiliar contents. "I never saw Indians so much astonished at the entering of a ship before," wrote Cook. "Their eyes were continually flying from object to object, the wildness of their looks and actions fully expressed their surprise."

Ledyard noted that at first the Hawaiians seemed uncertain whether members of the crew had normal human body parts. They "ran up to us," Ledyard wrote, "and examined our hands and faces." They pulled back the crewmen's shirtsleeves and opened "the bosoms of our shirts to view such parts of our bodies as were covered by our clothes." They wondered if Cook's men were capable of eating, and when a sailor demonstrated in the affirmative by munching on a biscuit, the islanders ran to the side of the ship and "called to those in the canoes, who hove on board several little pigs and some sweet potatoes."

Samuel Mānaiakalani Kamakau, the Hawaiian historian, noted how surprised the Kauaians were by the sight of crewmen smoking pipes; they did not understand how these people "breathed fire from their mouths" and figured they must be of "the volcano family." The strange beings had sharp-pointed things on their feet. The islanders were also confused by the tricorne hats that Cook's officers wore, and some concluded that these white-skinned people must have three-sided heads.

When the Natives saw strange misshapen pieces of fruit lying about the deck—probably melons—they said, "This is the fruit of a sorceress or mischief-maker of the ocean." Later, they glimpsed the hide of a large animal, probably a cow, and were equally amazed by its implications. "Another mischief-making sorceress has been killed," they said. "Perhaps these gods have come that all the evil monsters might be destroyed."

Lieutenant James King led some of the visitors on a tour of the *Resolution*'s lower decks. They were most impressed by the armorer's forge and mesmerized by how the blacksmiths teased and shaped the substance. Many other items caught their eye as well. "When we showed them beads," King recalled, "they asked if they should eat them, or what was their use. They returned looking glasses, saying they did not know what these things were for. They were quite ignorant of what our china cups were made of, taking them for wood. In their behavior they were very fearful of giving offense."

Almost immediately, the old problem of disappearing items arose on both ships. It had a very different quality from what Cook had experienced in the Society Islands. These islanders were less surreptitious, more forthright but also more casual. Throughout the Hawaiian Islands, light-fingeredness was virtually regarded as an art form. Audacious feats of thievery were celebrated in the local lore, and the best practitioners had their own patron gods.

What the Kauaians wanted most was iron. They were not at all bashful in their desire for it, and they would not be denied. From the start, their attitude seemed to be: *These people have more than enough of this precious metal, so naturally they will be happy to share.* Within minutes, a man absconded with a cleaver. Another man took an interest in the ship's lead and line (a simple but crucial depth-sounding tool composed of a long rope, notched in incremental markings, with an attached plummet usually made of lead). The man swiped the lead and line without asking any questions and began to crawl overboard. When he was stopped, he showed not a trace of embarrassment or guilt. "I am only going to put it into my boat," he explained.

The story was much the same aboard the *Discovery*. Captain Clerke greeted a crowd of Kauaians in his cabin. "My guests," he noted, "were exceedingly curious and very desirous of handling and examining whatever came their way." The windows in the cabin were propped open by iron brackets. When an islander ran his hands over one of these fixtures, presumably intending to take it, it came unlatched and the window slammed shut like a trap door. The sudden noise so frightened the Kauaian visitors that they dived out of the other open windows, breaking glass as they scurried overboard.

Luckily, they were strong swimmers, and their countrymen fetched them in canoes. These people were perfectly at home in the ocean. Cook called them "the most expert swimmers we had met with." He marveled at the sight of women "with infants at their breast" leaping from their canoes and swimming ashore, seemingly without effort, "through a surf that looked dreadful."

Clerke thought the men and women alike handled their boats "with great dexterity" and were "so perfectly masters of themselves in the water that it appears their natural element." Clerke noted the islanders' skill and agility when paddling a certain wooden conveyance about eight feet in length—today's surfers would probably call it a longboard. Wrote Clerke: "They get astride with the[ir] legs, then laying their breasts upon it, they paddle with their hands and steer with their feet, and gain such way through the water that they would fairly go round the best-going boats we had in the two ships, in spite of every exertion of the crew, in the space of a very few minutes."

AS THE DAY progressed, more and more young women arrived in canoes and circled the ships. They were "exceedingly beautiful," Samwell exclaimed, and by employing what he called "lascivious gestures," they made their intentions known. But under no circumstances would Captain Cook allow them aboard, for he did not want his men to communicate venereal disease to these innocent people—who, unlike the Tahitians, he firmly believed had never come into contact with Europeans before.

"Every precaution was taken to prevent the men from meddling with them," observed Thomas Edgar, with a note of disappointment. Cook remained adamant. Anyone who invited a female on the ships would face the severest punishment. Cook's prohibition, said Rickman, "created a general murmur among the seamen, whose pleasure was centered in that kind of commerce."

At first the women were puzzled to be spurned in this way. Then they became outright offended and incensed. As Samwell put it, they were "much chagrined on being refused."

Some of the more resourceful Hawaiian women, egged on by British crewmen, donned European clothing so they could pass as sailors and sneak aboard to consort with the men belowdecks. When Cook discovered this, he was unforgiving. After one sailor, William Bradley, was caught bringing a woman on board, Cook had him disciplined with a dozen lashes. It may have seemed an extreme punishment, but Cook knew that Bradley was, as one officer put it, "injured with the venereal disorder."

LATER IN THE day, Cook sent Lieutenant John Williamson, in command of several armed boats, to hunt for a suitable place to land and take on water. The Kauaians—who paddled their canoes while facing forward—watched in wonderment as the English rowers pulled at their oars while facing the stern of the boat, their torsos bending deeply with each stroke. In one of the oral history accounts, a Native man is said to have exclaimed, "They must be nursing babies, for they lean over like mothers!"

As Williamson, with a small detail, approached the beach, enthusiastic throngs of Kauaians surrounded his boat and steered it shoreward, at times literally lifting it out of the water. More islanders crowded around the boat, some of them grabbing at the oars. The notoriously impulsive Williamson, misinterpreting the Natives' excitement as an attack, began to panic. He spotted an islander, whom he described as a "tall handsome man about forty years of age [who] seemed to be a chief," struggling to steal the boat hook—theft, at least, was how the lieutenant interpreted the man's intent. Williamson attempted to strike him with a rifle butt, but to no avail.

Without any other warning, Williamson snapped off a shot from his pistol—some sources say it was a musket. He later claimed he fired his weapon "with the greatest reluctance." The man slumped into the surf, mortally wounded. The ball had pierced his right side, near the nipple. Recoiling in horror as they saw the water tinged with blood, the Natives collected their fallen comrade and retreated to shore.

The Kauaians did not know what to make of the strange implement that had instantly killed one of their countrymen. They could not comprehend what it was, what substance it was made of, or how it worked. Naturally, they could conceive of it only in terms of materials they already knew. According to Kamakau, they called it a "water squirter," because the smoke that projected from its barrel reminded them of water shooting from a hollow tube of bamboo, or of seawater rushing, geyser-like, through a tidal blowhole—a phenomenon that was not uncommon along the rocky Kaua'i coast. They seemed convinced that their fellow villager had been killed by some high-velocity jet of water.

Lieutenant Williamson was known to be a hothead. At other times during the voyage, he had demonstrated a propensity for violence, and here, while landing upon a new island, in the very opening moments of first contact, he'd shown his true colors again. Williamson later admitted that none of the islanders had designs to kill or hurt him or his crew. His hasty decision to fire, said Corporal William Griffin, was "a cowardly, dastardly action." Astronomer William Bayly agreed, noting that the Natives, while perhaps overzealous, were only trying to help conduct the boat through the breaking waves. "It does not appear that they had any ill intention," wrote Bayly, "but rather the contrary, they being overeager to assist us in landing through the surf."

Williamson would later attempt to justify his actions by claiming that Indigenous people often had to be put in their place, swiftly and decisively, in order to check their "insolence." He believed in what he called "the good effects of at once showing our superiority"—principally through firearms. The best way to handle these types of messy situations was to "do execution," as he called it. An early discharging of a weapon to injure or kill an occasional Native, he said, was a merciful action that saved lives in the end. "These barbarians must be quelled by force," he wrote, "as they afterwards readily believe that whatever kindness is then shown them proceeds from love, whereas otherwise they attribute it to weakness, or cowardice."

After the shooting, Williamson rowed ashore at another location, near the village of Waimea, where he found a clear stream that pooled into a pond that was nicely situated for the two ships to fill their empty casks. Beyond the village, in the foothills, sugarcane and bananas grew in abundance, and the close air was pierced by the caterwaul of roosters.

His reconnaissance complete, Williamson hurried back to the *Resolution* to report his findings. But, fearing Cook's wrath, he elected not to tell the captain that he had killed one of the islanders.

SEVERAL HOURS LATER, when Cook came ashore with some of his officers, he was still unaware of what had transpired. Tromping onto the beach at Waimea, armed with only a cutlass, he was astonished to be met by crowds of hundreds, possibly thousands, of villagers. They parted to create a path for him and prostrated themselves upon the sand. As Cook described it, "The very instant I leaped ashore, they all fell flat on their faces, and remained in that humble posture."

Some of Cook's officers surmised that the islanders did this because they regarded him as a deity, but they probably viewed Cook as something more like a very high-ranking chief. An ancient ritual of the Hawaiian Isles, the *kapu moe*, required commoners to kneel upon the ground in obeisance to the highest chiefs, known as *alii*. (The Kauaians later said that it was easy to identify Cook as the supreme leader of these strangers, for he was so much taller than all the others.)

Cook felt uncomfortable with the spectacle. Laughing heartily, he made signs for the crowd to rise and tried to help a few of the more elderly supplicants to their feet, but most of the people refused to budge.

The prohibitions of the *kapu* system were deadly serious and all-encompassing. A commoner could not stand in the shadow of a holy chief, could not graze his clothing, even accidentally. Other strictures that governed the roles and behavior of the sexes were equally severe. Women were not permitted to take their meals in the company of men, or vice versa, and certain food—coconuts, bananas, pork, some species of red fish—women could not eat at all. A person who broke *kapu* was promptly put to death, either by strangulation or by being burned or clubbed to death. Other culprits were buried alive in an earth oven and baked, as one account put it, "until the body grease dripped."

Presently, one of Kaua'i's numerous lesser dignitaries arrived on the beach, with a retinue of four attendants who held branches of sugarcane over his head, forming a leafy parasol. He took a deep bow, and Cook, in turn, presented him with a mirror and a necklace made of glass beads. Only when Captain Cook and the chief had gone quite a ways inland did the masses feel free to rise to their feet.

The Waimea villagers began to bestow gifts upon Cook and his entourage—hogs, yams, taro roots, and other foodstuffs. They were generous beyond expectation, showing no regard for whether they got anything in return. They presented most of their gifts with plantain leaves, which was understood to be their ceremonial gesture of peace. "I ratified these marks of friendship," the captain wrote, "by presenting them with such things as I had with me."

Cook was enchanted by these islanders. They were, he thought, "an open, candid, active people." They had elegant canoes, lived in well-constructed dwellings, carried finely wrought tools. Theirs was a land of plenty bathed by the trade winds. To Cook they seemed a healthy, handsome race.

Not only that, but in halting conversations with the locals, he was given to understand that this island, fair as it might be, was only one of many in the region, and it was by no means the biggest. On this historic day, out in the immensity of the Pacific, Cook had found a flourishing civilization.

25   In the Land of the Menehune

KAUA'I, JANUARY 1778

The next day, as winds freshened in the bay, Cook was rowed ashore with a contingent of Royal Marines, and once again the crowds parted and prostrated themselves before him. As soon as Cook could persuade them to rise to their feet, a vigorous trade commenced, just as it had the day before. The Kauaians would eagerly offer a fresh hog in exchange for a few nails or a fragment of iron the blacksmiths had formed into a crude chisel. (The metal used in making many of these implements had come from melting down an anchor, once attached to a ship captained by French explorer Louis-Antoine de Bougainville, that Cook had purchased back on Bora Bora.) Other Natives cheerfully helped Cook's men trundle the heavy casks up the beach and over to the stream-fed pond that had been spotted the previous day. The casks, set upon their sides, burbled appreciatively as they filled.

As the provisioning continued, a Native guide caught Cook's attention and led him, along with surgeon William Anderson and artist John Webber, on a leisurely stroll up into the Waimea River valley. Both sides of the river were planted in fields of taro, the staple of the Hawaiian Islands, eaten in many forms, especially as the starchy purple paste known as poi. The elephant-eared leaves nodded in the sun, the stalky plants arranged in paddies, slightly sunken to contain moisture. It was a land of natural plenty, but also of careful sustained engineering, with terraces, ditches, walls, and canals—Cook had the sense that the earthworks here, often constructed of large cut-and-dressed stones, were centuries in the making.

He did not know it, but Cook was working his way up into the mythic world of the menehune, a race of sturdy dwarfs who, it was said, lived in the highlands. As the fables had it, the menehune were extremely industrious, and they labored in concert, in huge numbers, to build great structures—plazas, roadways, fishponds, and aqueducts. It was said they always finished their endeavors in one long night of furious toil—if for any reason they were interrupted or delayed, they aborted the project and abandoned the site forever. They labored only in darkness, and scattered at dawn.

The menehune myth (which would only grow more elaborate as more Westerners visited Kaua'i in the years after Cook) may have been based on kernels of truth. Some anthropologists have surmised that the menehune were actually the first arrivals to the Hawaiian chain, those expert navigators who most likely came from the Mar-

quesas Islands as far back as A.D. 300. These original inhabitants of
Kaua'i were driven into the mountains as a second wave of Hawaiian
immigrants, the stronger, better-armed Tahitians, landed centuries
later and seized the choice coastal lands. The menehune probably
were not a physically smaller people—the term more likely referred
to their diminished social stature as common laborers. As the stories
went, the menehune, urged by the pressures of a more powerful society inching up the slopes, were forced to abide in the rainy gloom
of the forests, where they became builders, tradesmen—a guild of
sorts, but possessed of magical skills.

Mark Twain, who visited the Hawaiian Islands in 1866, described
a large temple that, according to tradition, the menehune had built
long ago, in a single night, in the midst of a thunderstorm. "By the
weird glare of the lightning," Twain wrote, "a noiseless multitude of
phantoms were seen at their strange labor far up the mountain side
at dead of night—flitting hither and thither and bearing great lava-
blocks clasped in their nerveless fingers."

Captain Cook, of course, was thoroughly unaware of these local
fables, but he was impressed with the building prowess, not to mention the sheer backbreaking effort, that must have been summoned
to construct the networks of ponds and retaining walls he saw about
him—the rocks used in these public works projects had been quar-
ried from sites many miles distant. As the three Englishmen climbed
higher into the valley, amid plantings of sugarcane, plantain, and
mulberry trees, they kept encountering field laborers, who seemed
overcome with awe at the sight of these strange-looking foreigners. "Every one whom we met fell on their faces," Cook noted, "and
remained in that position until we had passed."

COOK'S WILLINGNESS TO venture so far upslope from the ships,
unarmed, without bodyguards and surrounded by large crowds, was
a testament to his courage as well as his curiosity. The Kauaians
could have set upon him and killed him in an instant. But no apprehensions seem to have crossed his mind. Moving into the interior,
Cook appeared to be enjoying anew the role of observer and amateur
anthropologist. He was enchanted by the culture before him, taking

note of what he encountered. He understood that, once again, he had stumbled upon a new world.

Cook could see villages nestled along the hillsides, and he inspected some of the houses. They were sturdy, with thatched roofs tightly woven from sugarcane leaves, pandanus, and pili grass. Cook lauded the precise artisanship and solidity of the structures but found the interiors too dark and cavelike for his tastes, and also a bit cramped for a person of his stature.

Even more astonishing to Cook was the intricacy of their tapa cloth, made from thin sheaths of mulberry tree bark. The women patiently beat the bark into a finely textured material and dyed it in dazzling colors derived from charcoal, ocher, and plant pigments. The islanders used bamboo stamps to impress the cloth with elaborate designs. "They have a very great variety ... all glazed and printed with different colors, which are so disposed as to have a pretty and pleasing effect," Cook wrote. Of nearly equal complexity were the tattoos that graced the bodies of so many of the inhabitants. The designs differed in style from the tattoos Cook had seen elsewhere in Polynesia, and were not nearly as bold as those of the Māori, but he found them pleasing and artful nonetheless.

Cook, Anderson, and Webber could see that the men of Kauaʻi were fearsome warriors—there appeared to be internecine conflicts among different parts of the island, and occasional wars waged against the people of other islands down the Hawaiian chain. Cook spotted examples of barbed spears, stone axes, and slings woven from sennit fiber and human hair. There were cords designed to trip an opponent in battle, and smashing clubs wielded by specialists proficient in the art of bone breaking. They had exquisite daggers and other weapons, intricately razored with sharks' teeth, that were used to disembowel an enemy. It was extraordinary to Cook how these people had hewn such formidable implements of war from nothing more than rock, wood, coral, shell, and bone. Cook's journals and those of others on the expedition noted a martial tension, a certain uneasiness hanging in the air. Lovely as this place seemed, it was not a peaceable kingdom—as in the Society Islands, the tranquil cadence of life was punctuated by periodic spasms of warfare.

Still, to Cook's eye, the villagers seemed healthy, well-fed, thriving. He didn't see poverty or much suffering. He was struck by how densely populated the island appeared to be: Based on unclear evidence, he later estimated the population of Kaua'i at about thirty thousand souls. (Scholars now believe it may have been several times that number.) This haggard green volcano was a fertile place, its forests pendulous with fruit, its lagoons shoaled with fish, its thickets scrabbling with pigs, its black soils capable of sustaining a large citizenry.

But more than that, the people of Kaua'i seemed happy. As they went about their daily tasks, they filled the hillsides with joyful rhythms—the pounding of the poi, the beating of bark cloth, the scraping and whittling of the canoe makers, the incessant tapping of the fish-skin knee drums. At night, groups of men, paddling the lagoons by torchlight, sang songs to coax the fish into their boats. The women, too, were constantly singing lyrical chants—Cook found their music "pleasing and tender" and "by no means disagreeable." Their pierced ears were fixed with beautiful clusters of shells. They wore short colorful skirts and little else, and often had wreaths of aromatic flowers on their heads. Nearly everyone, it seemed, adorned themselves in some way—bracelets, necklaces, fetishes, amulets, blossoms tucked fetchingly behind the ear. Except for members of the chiefly classes, who were often morbidly obese, the Kauaians kept themselves athletically fit and clean, bathing several times a day in cool streams and often coating their skin and hair with fragrant oils. Much like the Tahitians, these were a people, men and women alike, who revered physical beauty and had a refined personal aesthetic, a notion that one's body, its motions and movements, its shapes and scents, should be graceful and pleasing to the senses.

YET IT WAS the women, inevitably, that Cook's expedition members remarked upon the most. In some ways, their comments merely repeated the praise they had already heaped on the ladies of the Society Islands. They found the women of Kaua'i desirable in every way. The difference was that, unlike the women of Tahiti, where European vessels had called many times and where the sexual politics had at times sadly degenerated to the level of tawdry commerce, the women on Kaua'i were a blank slate—they had never seen Europeans before.

More and more sailors went ashore—at least the ones who'd been cleared by the surgeon. Almost immediately after the men waded onto the Waimea beach, they found themselves accosted, albeit agreeably so, by young women. "They were determined," explained one lieutenant, "to see whether our people were men or not." Thomas Edgar, master of the *Discovery*, claimed not to have taken part, but he dutifully noted the many couplings about him. "The women used all their arts to entice them into their houses," Edgar wrote, "and even went so far as to endeavor to draw them in by force."

But unlike on Tahiti, the women did not demand or seem to expect payment for their favors—at least not at first. In many cases, the copulation began straightaway, without preliminaries or a search for some private place to rendezvous. During the proceedings, the women rubbed noses with the sailors but refused to be kissed, seeming to find the act revolting in the extreme. The men were amazed by the extent to which they employed their hips to pleasing effect— one account praised the finesse of their "rotatory movement."

Modern-day scholars have made a formal study of Hawaiian sexual mores before the arrival of the missionaries. Collecting accounts reaching back nearly to the time of Cook's landing, Milton Diamond, a University of Hawai'i professor of reproductive biology, cataloged some of those practices in an almost comically detailed 2004 monograph, "Sexual Behavior in Pre Contact Hawai'i: A Sexological Ethnography." Children were not at all awkward or bashful about discussing or imitating sexual acts, Diamond noted, and even before puberty they engaged in a frank style of sexual humor. Starting at a tender age, Hawaiian boys and girls were encouraged to play erotic games together and were instructed, usually by a knowledgeable aunt, in the arts of lovemaking.

"A young female was taught how to touch and caress a male and move her body to please them both," wrote Diamond. "She was taught how to constrict and rhythmically contract her vaginal muscles. Several of the informants who were interviewed remember being so instructed. One adult female told of being instructed on how to get her vagina to 'wink.'"

In their journals, Cook's and Clerke's men frequently mention the women's subtlety of technique. (Conversely, there are no stories passed down through Hawaiian oral history that speak of British sexual prowess.) The sailors could not believe their good luck. They had resigned themselves to a cold and dreary passage across the North Pacific to the ice fields at the top of the world, and now, completely unexpectedly, they had found another land of Aphrodite.

THE ACCOUNTS WRITTEN by Cook's officers are emphatic in asserting that Cook himself remained sexually abstinent while on Kaua'i—just as he had at Tahiti and everywhere else—despite opportunities that were offered to him. Nonetheless, a story took root in Kauaian lore that contradicted the English version of events. An account gathered in the 1830s and '40s by David Malo, a Native Hawaiian historian educated by American missionaries, says that while Cook was anchored off Waimea, the highest-ranking chiefs held a council. The more bellicose among them advocated that they immediately attack the *Resolution* and the *Discovery,* kill Cook and his men, and plunder the contents of the ships. But others argued that they should placate the visitors with gifts and with the charms of their women. This latter course was pursued, and according to Malo's story, Kamakahelei, the highest-ranking chiefess on Kaua'i, decided to offer one of her daughters to Cook as a concubine. Her name was Lelemahoalani.

In researching his account, Malo interviewed a number of elders who were said to be eyewitnesses to Captain Cook's arrival, and they insisted that Lelemahoalani was brought aboard the *Resolution* and that she slept in Cook's cabin that night. Malo's story became enshrined in local oral history and persisted for generations. In the 1870s, Abraham Fornander, a Swedish-born ethnologist and author, seemed to reconfirm the story in an influential book, writing that among "the last generation of Hawaiians it was openly said, and never contradicted, that on that night Lelemahoalani slept with" Cook.

But English-centric historians have dismissed the tale as a pre-

Native boats gather around the *Resolution* and *Discovery* in Alaska's glacier-rimmed Prince William Sound.

A hunting party shooting walrus—Cook called them "sea horses"—along the ice shelf off the Alaskan coast

King Kalaniʻōpuʻu and his royal retinue greet Captain Cook in
Hawaiʻi's Kealakekua Bay, as depicted by the Hawaiian artist-historian
Herb Kawainui Kāne.

A kāhuna priest and his paddlers in the waters of Kealakekua Bay

Webber's rendering of a young woman
of Kealakekua Bay

A Hawaiian chief of Kealakekua,
with feathered helmet

Unfinished painting, c. 1795, by Johan Zoffany,
depicting Cook's death on the shores of Kealakekua Bay

Enlightenment hero: after his death, Cook was lionized in England and widely viewed as one of history's greatest explorers.

YOU ARE ON NATIVE LAND

IN MEMORY OF
THE GREAT CIRCUMNAVIGATOR.
CAPTAIN JAMES COOK, R. N.,
WHO
DISCOVERED THESE ISLANDS
ON THE 18 OF JANUARY, A.D. 1778
AND FELL NEAR THIS SPOT
ON THE 14 OF FEBRUARY, A.D. 1779.
THIS MONUMENT WAS ERECTED
IN NOVEMBER A.D. 1874 ~
BY SOME OF
HIS FELLOW COUNTRYMEN.

More recently, Cook has been reassessed, and his monuments have become controversial. This is how the obelisk at the site of his death looked when the author visited Kealakekua Bay in January 2022.

posterous canard, claiming that it has roots in American hostility to the British dating back to the Revolutionary War and the War of 1812. There *was* a princess named Lelemahoalani, but scholars who've worked out the genealogy assert that she was a young child at the time of Cook's arrival, probably no more than eight years old. The American missionaries, these scholars say, did everything they could to bash Cook and deliberately conflated the behavior of some of his men with that of Cook himself.

Whatever Lelemahoalani's exact age, there is no written suggestion from any of the crew that such a girl boarded the *Resolution*, let alone that Cook led her into his cabin. Cook's officers and men, even some who were otherwise critical of him, went out of their way to underscore the point of Cook's absolute chastity. Typical of the commentary was a remark from coxswain Heinrich Zimmermann, a German by birth. "Never," Zimmermann asserted, "was there a breath of suspicion in regard to Cook's dealings with women. While we were at Tahiti and Hawai'i, where all the men allowed themselves to be led astray by the attractions of the Native women, he alone remained clean and uncontaminated."

Men on all three of his expeditions remarked that Polynesian women ridiculed and even insulted Cook for his steadfast abstinence. Cook "never had any connection with any of our fair friends," wrote a lieutenant who took part in the second voyage. "I have often seen them jeer and laugh at him, calling him old, and good for nothing." Modern critics of the captain, taking a Freudian view, have even gone so far as to maintain that his thoroughgoing chastity during the voyage generated a complex that led, in turn, to his later erratic and irrational behavior while in Hawai'i.

IN HIS FURTHER exchanges with the islanders, Cook began to realize that the people of Kaua'i were more familiar with iron than he had at first supposed. A Kauaian man came forward with a scrap of metal that appeared to have been part of a barrel hoop, and another man presented an edging tool that seemed to have once been a piece of a sword. A midshipman from Clerke's *Discovery*, meanwhile, met a Native who possessed a blade resembling a cutlass.

"It has by no means the appearance of a modern acquisition," Clerke wrote, and "it looks to have been a good deal used and long in its present state." When the midshipman asked where it came from, the Native pointed toward the southeast and said it had been found on an island in that direction. (Archaeologists would later speculate that the blade in question was likely a Japanese fishing knife, although how it might have reached the Hawaiian Islands was anyone's guess.)

These examples of metal set Cook to wondering again whether his was the first European ship to call here. Had the Spanish beaten him to this ambrosial isle? The thought nagged at him. It was possible that Spaniards had landed here but, meeting with some calamity on the high seas, had never returned home to report what they had found. It's a question that has intrigued scholars ever since.

Much of the speculation has centered on a certain Spanish ship that was dispatched by Hernán Cortés from Mexico in 1527 and never heard from again. According to some rather nebulous local legends, the ship wrecked off the Kona coast of Hawai'i's Big Island. It was said that some of the Spanish mariners survived, swam ashore, intermarried with local islanders, and lived the rest of their lives on Hawai'i. Stories passed down through the centuries spoke of locals born with reddish-brown hair—descendants, supposedly, of those first Spanish castaways. To this day, amateur archaeologists, treasure-hunting divers, and beachcombers operating metal detectors continue to look for signs of ancient Spanish, Dutch, or other European shipwrecks among the Hawaiian Islands, but little in the way of hard evidence has surfaced.

Whether or not the Spanish had a prior presence here, Cook suspected that his having pinpointed the Hawaiian Islands on the map would probably benefit Spain more than it would England, since the Spanish still jealously regarded the entire Pacific as *their* ocean, and since the regular trade between Manila and Acapulco, though waning in importance, was very much alive. Cook's observation was aimed at his superiors back in England—Sandwich, Palliser, and others connected with the Admiralty—who were attentive to how a discovery might play into the larger imperial contest. Although

Cook would christen them the Sandwich Islands, he did not formally claim the archipelago for England, nor did he plant a flag in Hawaiian soil, as he had done on other islands. He already seemed to nurse a defeatist notion that the Hawaiian Islands would end up in Spanish hands.

COOK'S HOSTS LED him deeper into the valley until they came to a heiau—an open-air grouping of religious structures very similar to the marae temples he had seen in New Zealand, Tonga, and the Society Islands. The heiau was a sprawling complex with four-foot walls of tightly constructed volcanic rock and an intricate wooden oracle tower that climbed high into the sky, the plaza lined with palm trees whose waxy fronds clattered in the breeze. There were god houses, elaborately carved wooden images, a drum house, and numerous graves. Webber, the artist, worked furiously at his sketchbook. Cook seemed to feel at home here, as though he were back in Tahiti. "These people," he wrote with confidence, "have nearly the same notions of religion."

When Cook and his small party hiked down the slopes and returned to the beach, he found that the men had finished filling the casks. Guarded by the marines, they had taken on some nine tons of fresh water, and with nothing more than an assortment of nails and a few gobbets of iron as currency, they had procured about seventy pigs, some nice fowl, and a huge mound of potatoes, plantains, and taro corms.

Cook returned to the *Resolution*, but he found that contrary winds and powerful currents were sweeping the ship westward from its anchorage. He had wanted to meet one of the several high-ranking chiefs who were said to reign over Kaua'i, but the ship was fast shearing away from Waimea Bay and driving toward Kaua'i's smaller sister island, Ni'ihau. It was as though the gods were drawing him away. Some of his crew would go ashore at Ni'ihau, where they would interact with Natives there, sexually and otherwise, and procure a large supply of sweet potatoes, but Cook would never get back to Kaua'i.

However, Captain Clerke's *Discovery* was in a more protected spot within Kaua'i's Waimea Bay, and from his more secure anchorage he was able to arrange a meeting with a chief, probably named Kaneoneo, who was reputed to be the sovereign on this part of Kaua'i. (In his notes, Clerke erroneously referred to him as "Tamahano.") A large double canoe bearing Kaneoneo pulled up to the *Discovery*. He was a young handsome man in his twenties, nearly six feet tall, clothed from head to foot. He had smooth copper skin and black hair grazing his collarbones and was accompanied by a young woman thought to be his wife.

His minions lay down within the ribs of the canoe to form a sort of human carpet, and Kaneoneo, rising to his feet, trampled over their bodies as he clambered toward the ship. Some of the chief's attendants guided him onto the *Discovery*'s gangway, while others, locking hands, formed a tight protective ring around him. Kaneoneo made motions as though he wanted to step onto the deck, but, according to William Bayly, "his people would not let him stir an inch farther."

Captain Clerke presented himself and employed his considerable charms to persuade the chief to come aboard and make himself at home. Yet Kaneoneo's escorts showed trepidation and would not let him proceed any farther than the gangway. "I said all I could," wrote Clerke. "I was very desirous of laughing them out of these ridiculous fears."

Still they would not budge. When the ever affable Clerke stepped forward and tried to embrace Kaneoneo, taking him by the hand while clapping him on his shoulder, the young chief's bodyguards intervened. "They gently took away my hand," Clerke said, "and begged I would not touch him." Were a commoner to commit such an egregious transgression of the ancient *kapu* laws, he would likely be put to death.

Perched on the edge of the ship, the captain and the chief kept their meeting necessarily brief. Kaneoneo presented Clerke with a carved bowl made for serving kava, the viscous plant-root concoction Hawaiians drank as a sedative, often during sacred ceremonies. Clerke gave Kaneoneo a few trifles, including a swatch of bright red baize cloth. It was a paltry gift, but Kaneoneo seemed pleased enough with it. Kaneoneo invited Clerke to come ashore the next day. Then his bodyguards led him back to the canoe and his strong paddlers whisked him to the beach. Thus concluded the first encounter between European and Hawaiian "principals"—an awkward meeting, but at least one without incident.

Clerke's *Discovery* would reconvene with the *Resolution* closer to Ni'ihau, and the two ships would promptly set sail for North America and points north. But both captains fully understood that they had stumbled upon something remarkable here, something that would change the maps of the world and likely have substantial ripple effects on trade and the larger imperial competition.

Still, Cook did not make any effort to explore the other islands in the Hawaiian chain. Some have suggested that the younger Cook—the Cook of the first two voyages—would have tried to get a glimpse of those other islands, at least long enough to fix them on his chart. It was a seeming dearth of curiosity, on his part, a dimming of the exploratory instinct, that had cropped up several times before on this voyage. While in the Tongan archipelago, for example, he had heard about some significant islands nearby—Fiji and Samoa, it turned out—but he didn't show any inclination to investigate. Those findings could have been significant additions to his cartographic triumphs. And O'ahu, Maui, and Hawai'i, if he had sailed by them, could have been trophies as well. But Cook, acutely aware of deadlines laid out in his Admiralty instructions, was not interested. He sailed determinedly north.

There was a ruefulness in the journals of his officers, indicating that they wished the ships could have stayed longer and suggesting that, if possible, they would like to find a way to return. But Cook's focus was already on a frigid world thousands of miles from this island paradise: *Alaska.*

BOOK FOUR

New Albion

───◆◆◆───

It has become customary ... to damn the ancestral frame of
mind that ravaged the world so fully and so soon ... But God,
to have viewed it entire, the soul and guts of what we had
and gone forever now, except in books and such poignant
remnants as small swift birds that journey to and from the
distant Argentine and call at night in the sky.

—JOHN GRAVES, SELF-PORTRAIT, WITH BIRDS

26 *Foul Weather*

The men scoured the eastern horizon for the first suggestion of land. They knew it had to be there, off in the cold haze. For days they'd seen the telltale signs: waterlogged stumps floating on the surface, glops of seaweed, bulbs of kelp, the occasional visitation of a shorebird. They saw whales spouting in the distance, and pods of porpoises. They were even seeing a few seals, their heads popping up alongside the ships, curious looks on their whiskered faces. There were subtle changes in the color of the water. There were supernatural signs, also, or at least signs some of the men took to be auspicious. On one night, the skies shimmered and danced with the aurora borealis. On another, the water around the ships was speckled with bioluminescent creatures. John Gore, mesmerized by the sight, described them as "a great number of little sparks which exhibited a fiery light and swam about briskly."

If Gore seemed suddenly giddy in his biological musings as the ships approached American shores, perhaps it was because he was an American himself—Virginia-born—and may have felt a sense of homecoming to return to his native continent, although the coastline here lay several thousand miles away from his birthplace. John Ledyard, the Connecticut Yankee, definitely felt those sorts of sentiments. "It was the first time I had been so near the shores of that continent that gave me birth from the time I at first left it," Ledyard wrote. "Though more than two thousand miles distant from the nearest part of New England, I felt myself plainly affected: All the passions incident to natural attachments and early prejudices played round my heart."

Gore and Ledyard could not have known that on the other side of North America, the revolt against England had deepened into a bitter war that showed no signs of abating. At that very moment, British troops were occupying Philadelphia, while George Washington's bedraggled army was beginning to stir from its winter quarters at Valley Forge. The war was taking on an international flavor. Shortly after the *Resolution* and the *Discovery* left the Hawaiian Islands, Benjamin Franklin and two other American commissioners had signed a treaty in Paris that intimately bound France to the rebellious colonies. With the stroke of a pen, France became the first nation to recognize the United States as a sovereign country. An outraged Britain would soon declare war on France, thus fully bringing the French into the American conflict.

Despite all of this, Benjamin Franklin would later make a point of lobbying among his colleagues for Captain Cook and the *Resolution* to be granted special immunity not afforded to other British ships. Should American vessels encounter Cook anywhere on the high seas, they were to give him leeway and clemency. Cook was on an assignment of transcendent importance for humanity, Franklin's proclamation asserted, one too important to be detained by squabbles between nations. Franklin made his remarks in what he called a "passport" addressed to the captains and commanders of all American ships. In case Cook's vessel should "happen to fall into your hands," Franklin advised, "you should not consider her as an enemy, nor suffer any plunder to be made of the effects contained in her, nor obstruct her immediate return to England." Americans, he said, should "treat the said Captain Cook and his people with all civility and kindness, affording them as common friends to mankind, all the assistance in your power which they may happen to stand in need of."

The Spanish, who would soon be joining France in declaring war against England, were already well aware that Captain Cook was supposed to be somewhere in the Pacific, headed for the northwest coast of America—and they were highly displeased with

England's encroachments upon the region. They had informed officials in Mexico to keep a lookout for Cook and, if possible, to intercept and arrest him. Spanish shipwrights were constructing two new vessels—one in Mexico, another in Peru—for a voyage that aimed to halt and overtake Cook while reasserting Spanish claims in the Pacific Northwest.

Cook and his men had been sailing northeast from the Hawaiian Islands in perfect ignorance of these developments. Over the previous five weeks, the *Resolution* and the *Discovery* had made a journey of nearly 2,500 miles from Kaua'i. It had been a mostly uneventful plod. Perhaps the most notable thing that had happened in all those many miles was that a young sailor named Thomas Goodman had slipped from the fore shrouds and had smashed onto the deck. The poor boy broke his collarbone and was badly bruised but would eventually recover—a standard nautical accident, in other words, cursorily mentioned in the ship records.

Sleet and snow began to fall, the decks became slippery, and out came the woolen Magellan jackets. The enveloping cold was a matter of existential significance for Clerke and Anderson. We don't have a record of their day-to-day health, but their symptoms likely included night sweats, exhaustion, chills, and the hacking up of phlegm and blood. "We are all shaking with cold here," Clerke wrote. "Lord knows how we shall make ourselves acquainted with the frozen secrets of the Arctic."

CARTOGRAPHICALLY AND IN every other way, the land that Cook was approaching was only dimly understood by Europeans. Some of the maps were fantastical, with monsters and whirlpools and other strange features, while other charts, humble in their ignorance, simply showed a blank space. Still others depicted California as a massive island. An elegant and widely circulated map, published in Paris in the 1750s, definitively showed that not far inland from the Pacific Northwest coastline was an enormous sea, far larger than all the Great Lakes combined; the French cartographers labeled this nonexistent super lake Mer de l'Ouest—the Sea of the West.

Given how little was known about the region, it made perfect sense that Jonathan Swift, in his 1726 satirical tale *Gulliver's Travels*, decided to place his mythic fantasyland, Brobdingnag, in the Pacific Northwest. He said it was a realm of giant people and mammoth insects, where grass grew as tall as a tree.

There were rumors, probably false, that Russians may have nosed down this way from Alaska. Over the centuries a few Spanish galleons, while making the regular spice run from the Philippines to Acapulco, had been blown off course and ended up in these parts—in recent years, beachcombers have found ancient timbers, shards of Chinese porcelain, and chunks of beeswax with Spanish markings along the Oregon coast. Throughout the 1600s and 1700s, a succession of Spanish explorers, launching from Mexico, had sailed up this way but whatever they may have learned about the country, they had kept to themselves; the Spanish usually shrouded their voyages in secrecy.

It was known that in 1579, the English privateer Francis Drake had ventured somewhere in this vicinity. On his infamous expedition around the world, Drake had sailed through the Magellan Strait and into the Pacific, defying Madrid's claims that the world's largest ocean was off-limits to any other country. Working up the shores of South and Central America, Drake attacked a number of Spanish treasure ships as well as coastal settlements, in a spree of wholesale plunder. As he continued up the Pacific coast, his ship, the *Golden Hind*, struggled from the weight of all his pillaged ingots of silver and gold.

Drake had proven to be an excellent pirate with phenomenally good luck. But he was no cartographer, and he lacked the talent or inclination to account for his movements with any precision. It's not clear just how far north he went, for his own chart and journal disappeared. He almost certainly reached northern California—traditionally, most scholars have argued that he anchored at what is now Point Reyes National Seashore, near San Francisco—but more recently, historians have surmised that Drake probably pushed farther north, at least to a place along the Oregon coast very near to where Cook's ships were now headed.

Drake had the cheekiness to christen all of this area "Nova Albion"—Albion was a quaint Roman name for Britain. In other words, he had proclaimed the uncharted area north of Spanish California to be "New England" some fifty years before the Puritans landed at Plymouth Rock. Drake conjured the name and placed it on his maps to rile the Spanish, or anyone else who might have designs on these far margins of the continent.

In a direct sense, the Admiralty regarded this part of Cook's voyage as a continuation of Drake's explorations—an encore of a sort. It was almost as though two hundred years of history hadn't happened; Cook would be picking up right where the last Englishman had left off, thereby reinforcing the British claim that all of this distant coastline was rightly theirs. *New Albion!* The mere act of sailing past it conferred a patina of ownership—such were the bold posturings of the imperial game. Whether Cook subscribed to this way of thinking is hard to say, but in his journal and charts he did perpetuate the name New Albion for the shores he now approached.

By the end of Francis Drake's far-flung voyage, he had become the first Englishman to circumnavigate the globe. Unlike the Portuguese navigator Magellan, who died before his expedition ended, Drake made it safely home to accept the plaudits of his empire. After returning to England in 1580, he became fabulously wealthy and a favorite of Queen Elizabeth I, who promptly knighted him.

In those days, an explorer was expected to capture loot, win glory, and bring home something hard and tangible for the Crown— and that's what Drake had done. For him, the exploring part was a collateral enterprise. But in Cook's time, the imperatives of modern exploration required a voyager not only to pursue nationalistic ends but also to document, measure, chart, collect, and eventually publish, in order to advance, more generally, the cause of science. A captain had to come back with data, soundings, relics, narratives, artist renderings, barometric readings, and carcasses of unknown species swimming in alcohol.

Now, two hundred years after Drake, Cook was ready to bring the Enlightenment to the northern Pacific coast of America, to punc-

ture the myths and sort through the garbled legends. With one eye
on his nebulous charts and one eye on the horizon, he pressed ahead.

BUT NORTH AMERICA, it seemed, did not want to reveal her
secrets. Just as Cook was nearly upon New Albion's doorstep, the
Pacific brewed up a storm. There was a confusion of winds, slanting sleet, and swirling fog. Visibility closed down to near zero. The
two ships frequently lost sight of each other in the heaving swells.
Powerful winds were driving the *Resolution* toward the unseen land.
For Cook, the exhilaration of approaching North America was thus
replaced by a reasonable fear that he might fatally smash into it.

It took some touch-and-go sailing and the utmost vigilance to
keep the ships from running aground on sharp rocky reefs or crashing into each other. Cook wanted Clerke to stay close but not too
close, so periodically each vessel would fire guns, beat drums, ring
bells, or hoist bright torchlights—known as "false fires"—into the
high rigging to alert the sister ship. They also sometimes used
devices called speaking trumpets—a kind of megaphone—to call
out to each other. As the two vessels climbed over the whitecaps,
there was frantic shouting through the mist, the whine of the ropes,
the skeleton clatter of lumber. In the stentorian voice he was capable
of summoning, Cook barked his orders and the ashen-faced young
men, scared for their lives, did exactly as he said.

On the morning of March 7, the drizzling clouds parted just a bit
to reveal a vista of snow-dusted land, somewhere along the central
coast of present-day Oregon. Beyond the white bloom of the gray
surf, the foothills were a hazy olive drab, clad in spruce and pine.
David Samwell found the coastline "high and craggy" and noted the
"prodigious flocks of birds flying about."

One of the first physical features Cook made note of was a basalt
outcropping some five hundred feet above the sea. The captain, often
more literal-minded than imaginative when conjuring toponyms for
his charts, named the spot Cape Foulweather, a name that sticks
today. It is a place of stark majesty known for its powerful storms—
winds in excess of one hundred miles an hour are not uncommon

here. The late American naturalist writer Barry Lopez, who lived in Oregon, visited Cape Foulweather often and wrote eloquently about its peculiar energy. He spoke of the "faint barking of sea lions in the air, the nearly impenetrable groves of stout Sitka spruce . . . the moss-bound creeks, the flocks of mew gulls circling schools of anchovies just offshore."

Cook didn't get close enough to see people on the coast, though some of his men later thought they spotted "smokes" rising from foothills farther inland. This part of the Oregon coast was populated by the Alsean and Tillamook tribes, who had been living in the area for some three thousand years. They fished the ocean and nearby rivers, gathered oysters along the estuaries, and hunted black-tailed deer as well as marine mammals. It's not known whether any of the Alsean or Tillamook people spotted Cook's ships—there's no mention of it in their oral histories—but Lopez tried to imagine the scene from the Natives' point of view. "Ashore, perhaps a few Alsean hunters studied the thing that had come so close," Lopez wrote. The *Resolution* "emerged first as a pindot on the horizon," then grew "in a few hours into a full-blown three-masted square-rigger . . . Cook's ship, close-hauled a few miles offshore, was plunging and yawing through cross seas."

THE SEAS SOON grew even crosser, the weather even fouler: For four days, squalls blew with such force that Cook had to retreat more than a hundred miles to the south, roughly parallel with what is today the Oregon–California state line, and he often had to tack far out to sea, such that he lost visual contact with land. Cook thought he had to take this backward, crabwise course to keep from being driven into the rocky shores. Bayly, the astronomer, surmised that if they had collided with the coast, "it's highly probable all [would have] perished." Master's mate Henry Roberts claimed to have seen a waterspout, suggestive of a tornado. Ledyard declared it "the ruggedest weather" of the voyage. "The gales of wind were successive and strong, and sometimes very violent," he wrote, adding, "Our ships complained."

The stress on the vessels was alarming. The forests of interconnected wood—masts, yards, sprits, spars, and booms—strained to the breaking point. Shrouds hummed, ropes snapped, sails frayed. The men could hear structures cracking and splintering. Cook would have to figure out a way to get the *Resolution* and the *Discovery* into a snug place where they could be examined and repaired.

On March 16, the crew of the *Discovery* found themselves driving toward a jagged shelf of submerged rocks. "Looking ahead," John Rickman said, "we saw a large reef, not above two cables in length before us. We fired a gun as a signal to the *Resolution,* and had just time and room to escape the danger." It was one of several close calls.

If Cook was disturbed by these trying seas, his journal didn't show it. He merely called the weather "unsettled" and resented that his ships were being "unprofitably tossed about." As usual, Cook was more worried about timelines and maintaining fealty to the larger mission. Clerke echoed his frustrations. "It is really a rather lamentable business," the *Discovery*'s captain wrote. "We can neither forward our matters by tracing the coast, nor have the satisfaction of getting into a harbor to take a look at the country." Clerke complained that "we can do nothing we would wish to do, but are reduced to the old remedy, patience."

FINALLY COOK CAUGHT favorable winds from the south and began to crawl back up the Oregon coast, making up for lost time. He was too far offshore to see the mouth of the Columbia River and its extensive bars and shoals of sediment. Cook's critics have scoffed at him for missing such a prominent feature, and some have argued that it was yet another sign that he was not at his best during the third voyage. But in a sense, it was a good thing that he missed the Columbia. While discovering the mighty river would have been yet another feather in his exploratory cap—the American explorers Lewis and Clark would not lay eyes upon the mouth of the Columbia for another twenty-seven years—Cook might have wasted his energies investigating a waterway that, however impressive, did not connect to the other side of the continent. Just trying to navigate the Columbia's notorious sandbar might have proved lethal; today it is considered one of the world's most dangerous bar crossings and is widely known as the Graveyard of the Pacific.

Exploring the Columbia also would have been a violation of Cook's orders: His Admiralty instructions specifically advised him against probing any rivers or waterways this far south. Apart from any necessary stops along the way to "recruit your wood and water and procure refreshments," the instructions stated, Cook was "not to lose any time in exploring rivers or inlets, or upon any other account, until you get to the latitude of 65 degrees." On all of Cook's voyages, but particularly on the third, he often felt a tension between a pure desire to explore as his whims and circumstances suggested and a countervailing imperative to remain true to the strategic purposes and deadlines laid out by his superiors in England. Now more than ever, he was a man in a hurry to get somewhere else.

But several days later, still crawling northward, Cook also missed the large strait, now known as the Strait of Juan de Fuca, that leads to Puget Sound. Once again, some scholars of exploration history have wondered how the great James Cook could have overlooked such a significant hydrological feature. The simplest explanation is that Cook passed by it at night, in stressful sailing conditions and in stormy, foggy weather. But if it had been daytime and the visibility crisp and clear, he probably would have been lured into the bewildering labyrinth of Puget Sound and its adjoining Strait of Georgia, with their many hundreds of coves and interconnected fingers. As with the Columbia River, it would have been another fantastic accolade of discovery for the master navigator but one that might have resulted in a months-long goose chase. It could have meant yet another year before he reached Alaska.

27 Soft Gold

NOOTKA SOUND, MARCH–APRIL 1778

At last, the battered ships found solace from the angry seas. On March 29, an opening in the coast, just a few miles wide, revealed itself, and Cook seized his chance, gliding into a protected inlet where the winds were calm and the water was a tranquil limpid green. Snow-covered peaks rose above dense walls of hemlock, spruce, cedar, and fir. At the tops of the trees, bald eagles stirred in their nests. Close to the rocky shoreline, harlequin ducks dived for clams. Harbor seals and sea otters left a playful cursive on the smooth surface.

It seemed like a lovely hideaway, but Cook didn't know where he was. His charts shed no light on the matter. Was this place an island, the tip of a peninsula, or part of the North American mainland? Was it inhabited? Was it Russian territory? No one knew. "We were now so far advanced to the northward," said Rickman, "as to have reached that void space in our maps, which is marked as a country unknown."

Deeper within the sound's embrace, the winds dwindled to a dead calm. Boats were hoisted out to tow the ships farther into the inlet. The *Resolution* and the *Discovery* found themselves surrounded by Native canoes—thirty-two in all—that were filled with curious young men from the immediate area. They were dressed in the skins of animals, and many wore cloaks made of pounded bark. They had high cheekbones and broad, flat faces that were painted in a thick paste. Most of them had pierced septa, with ornaments made of snippets of baleen or fishbones dangling from their noses. Their hair was long and shaggy, and some of them had wisps of ceremonial eagle down powdering their heads.

To Cook they seemed "mild and inoffensive," and because they showed not "the least mark of fear or distrust," he strongly suspected that they had seen European vessels before. (He was correct in his surmise; four years earlier, the *Santiago*, a Spanish ship under the command of Juan Pérez, had briefly passed by here, though he didn't come ashore, and thus his contact with the region's First Nations people was limited.)

There are differing explanations for how Cook came to name this place Nootka. According to one version, while Cook was hunting for a safe place to anchor, some Natives in a canoe hollered at him, *"Nootka-a, nootka-a"*—which meant "Go around, go around." Most likely they were just trying to tell him there was a better anchorage around the bend. Or maybe they were trying to convey the opposite meaning: "Keep going around ... and don't come back!"

Whatever their intent, Cook misinterpreted the Natives' refrain to mean that this whole area was *called* Nootka, and that therefore the people here might rightly be termed "Nootkans." Nootka is the toponym still found on maps today to describe this remote and beautiful sound, with its many crabbed fingers that claw into the central west coast of what we know as Vancouver Island.

Although later European visitors, having read Cook's reports, would continue to refer to these people as "Nootkans" for more than a century, they are actually known as the Mowachaht, "the People of the Deer," a proud band of hunter-fishermen who have lived in this sound for at least four thousand years. For most Mowachaht, Cook's arrival was their first up-close encounter with Europeans. According to oral histories passed down through the generations and recorded with Mowachaht elders a half century ago, the local people were utterly astonished by these sallow-skinned creatures who arrived in what the Natives referred to as "floating houses."

At first the Mowachaht decided that the visitors were a species of salmon that had transmogrified into human form. "Those people, they must have been fish," one Native said. When the paddlers noticed that one of Cook's sailors had a hooked nose, they exclaimed, "He must have been a dog salmon!" When a stooped man emerged from the *Resolution*'s galley, another of the Mowachaht replied, "Yes! They've come back alive. Look at that one, he's a humpback salmon."

Cook's men, in turn, tried to sort these unfamiliar Natives into some anthropological category. They could already tell that the "Nootkans" did not seem related to any of the island peoples they had encountered thus far on the voyage. Their facial features seemed vaguely Asian. To those of Cook's men who had spent time on the lakes and rivers of Canada or in the American colonies, these people were reminiscent of Native American tribes living on the continent's east coast.

With the Natives still following in their canoes, the towed ships reached an enchanted cove with a rocky beach where a freshwater stream poured from thick woods. On his orders, the men moored the *Resolution* and the *Discovery* to a few of the stout trees growing on shore.

At dusk, the two ships were treated to a more formal greeting ceremony, led by a shaman, who scattered bird feathers upon the water and began to work up a song. As the canoes made a slow, deliberate circuit around the ships, this dignitary stood in his vessel, stretched out his arms, and shook rattles made of clamshells and deer hooves. He began to sing an incantation, plaintive and ethereal. The Natives kept the beat of his serenade by tapping their paddles on the sides of the canoes.

The song was so charming and sincere that Cook's sailors decided they had to reply. Presently, two musicians broke out their French horns and blew a slow, soft tune. As the music resounded over the cove, the Mowachaht stayed silent in their canoes, seemingly dumbstruck. After the hornsmen breathed their last notes, the Mowachaht answered with another song, just as beautiful as the first. In this way, the two cultures put each other to sleep. The evening ended, and many of the Natives paddled off into the dark. But just as many remained for the night, falling asleep as they bobbed on the tides of the cove, their canoes gathered in a cluster.

THE NEXT MORNING, Cook's carpenters had a chance to investigate the condition of the ships. The gales they'd encountered along the coast had sorely tested the *Resolution* and the *Discovery*. A masthead was found to be rotten. A mizzenmast had to be replaced. Sails needed mending. The leaky hulls of both vessels had to be thoroughly recaulked, which would require careening them. The scope of the repairs infuriated Cook, who was already annoyed by the slow pace of his northward progress and acutely conscious of the need to reach Alaska in order to take full advantage of the short summer season. But as the ships' flaws and wounds were tallied, Cook realized he would have to stay put for weeks, maybe a month, to complete the necessary work.

Luckily, he had a forest at his fingertips, some of the finest timber on earth: healthy Sitka spruce and Douglas fir, straight as arrows and mostly devoid of knots, burls, or other imperfections. Soon his best woodsmen were stumbling into the thickets with their ropes, axes, and saws, hunting for just the right trees to cut down.

It was a piney, feathered world of shadows in there, carpeted in moss, shaggy with ferns, spattered with moisture. In these somber jungles, sounds were strangely muffled and the atmosphere, cool and still, felt like an ancient temple. Some of the massive fir trees here were five hundred years old or more, and often, where an elder tree had fallen, rows of saplings had opportunistically risen from its dead trunk. The saturated ground was soft and springy underfoot, but also studded with slick boulders and crisscrossed with gnarled roots. Cook's workmen found it exhausting to travel a dozen yards into the interior.

But eventually Cook's sawyers, assisted by the Mowachaht, hauled out the timber they needed, and work on the ships could begin in earnest. The cove bustled with activity: Crews were filling the casks with water, brewers were cooking up kettles of spruce beer, blacksmiths had set up their forge, and Bayly had erected his observatory, high on a rock outcropping that overlooked the cove. Cook sent Bligh out in one of the shore boats to explore and chart the sound. As usual, the *Resolution*'s able if insufferable master turned in excellent work, and even today, the spot where the two ships anchored is known as Bligh Island.

Those who weren't working spent their days engaged in an almost frenetic trade with the Mowachaht, who arrived every morning in their long canoes eager to do business and share aspects of their culture. Nearly all the expedition accounts marvel at the beauty and elegance of the Nootka Sound canoes. The Mowachaht spent much of their lives in these substantial, all-purpose water taxis: They fished from them, fought from them, slept in them. The steady canoes could handle the swells of the open sea, where they were sometimes used to hunt whales and tow the carcasses homeward, but the same sleek vessels could scud easily through the shallows of the inland channels, where the emerald-green water was as smooth as glass. Edward Curtis, the celebrated American photographer, visited Nootka in the early 1900s and captured haunting sepia images of these formidable vessels. The canoes were works of art, a nearly perfect union of utility and aesthetics. Master builders had painstakingly hollowed them out from the hulks of single trees, then artisans had carved the gunwales in elaborate animal designs and filigreed the bows and sterns with mosaics of shell and human teeth. Some of the vessels were large enough to accommodate fifty paddlers.

At the cove, Cook's people found that the Mowachaht were savvy about commerce, and very hard bargainers, and they seemed to know a lot about metal. Some of them had knives. Their weapons were headed with iron, and there were innumerable examples of copper among them—ornaments, mostly, dangling from their necks or fixed in their ears and noses. Cook attributed the presence of so much metal not to direct contact with a few European ships but to a more sustained trade that must have worked its way up the coast from the Spanish mission settlements of southern California or overland from the fur trade of the Hudson's Bay Company.

"Nothing would go down with them but metal," Cook wrote. "Whole suits of our clothes were stripped of every button." In return, the Mowachaht had loads of desirable commodities to offer, including skins, furs, and smoked fish. Most popular of all were bladders full of a rich oil that had been rendered from whale and seal blubber. The men, wrote Rickman, "greedily purchased" the bladders and used the contents to make a sauce to enliven their salted fare—"no butter in England was ever thought half so good."

The Mowachaht were gifted artists and craftspeople, and Cook's men purchased a museum's worth of their exquisite works—totemic sculptures, masks, bowls, baskets, hats, carved clubs, hooks, and harpoons. But a few of the sailors bought curiosities of a more gruesome variety: human skulls and severed hands. The best guess was that these were trophies from some recent battle against a neighboring tribe. Ledyard, who often displayed an affinity for the exotic, could not stifle his curiosity when he was presented with a roasted human arm. "I have heard it remarked that human flesh is the most delicious," he wrote, "and therefore I tasted a bit, and so did many others without swallowing the meat or the juices." But he claimed to have found it repulsive. "Either my conscience or my taste," he said, "rendered it very odious to me."

Cook's sailors, predictably, were on the lookout for one other commodity. At first the Mowachaht men refused to share—or prostitute—their women, and the few females encountered seemed quite shy and retiring. But Cook's men, after repeated promptings, got the message across and the Mowachaht began to bring to the ships a procession of young women who could be had for a price.

At first, however, many of the Englishmen were dismayed that the Native women had covered themselves in a thick red ocher paste (which in Mowachaht culture was a form of adornment), and it seemed that they had not bathed in years. This complaint was rich with irony, given how filthy and foul the sailors were. Then someone came up with the idea of bringing out tubs of hot soapy water and bathing the young women on the decks. Samwell called it a "ceremony of purification." The women went along with the ritual scrubbings, but it seemed strange to them, Samwell thought, for "in order to render themselves agreeable to us, they had taken particular pains to daub their hair and faces well with red ochre, which to their great astonishment we took as much pains to wash off. Such are the different ideas formed by different nations of beauty and cleanliness."

The Mowachaht men proved to be tough negotiators: For each rendezvous with one of their women, they demanded one pewter plate. Cook's people considered this highway robbery but agreed to the price. In this way, the Mowachaht, wrote Samwell, "found means at last to disburden our young gentry of [our] kitchen furniture." Upon leaving Nootka, Samwell and many of his comrades could scarcely "muster a plate to eat our salt beef from."

AS THE WEEKS slipped by, relations between Cook's men and the Mowachaht remained friendly, and, if the journal descriptions are any indication, Nootka Sound was a comfortable interlude. Though often dreary and wet, spring could be a magical time of year in this part of the world, misty and cool on the sound but with snow still dusting the higher peaks. Water lilies, salmonberry bushes, and snapdragons were starting to bloom, and migrating hummingbirds had recently arrived from Mexico—some of them, like Cook, would be traveling all the way to Alaska.

In the Mowachaht view, everything that lived and grew around the sound—every tree, fish, berry, and bird—was theirs. They would gladly share the bounty with Cook, but he would have to pay a price for anything he took. "I have nowhere met with Indians who had such high notions of everything the country produced being their exclusive property," wrote Cook. "The very wood and water we took on board they at first wanted us to pay for."

One day Cook sent some of his men to cut grass for the few animals he still had on board the *Resolution*. He had no idea the Mowachaht would object to this, especially since they didn't seem to have domesticated animals of their own. But they did object— and quite strenuously. "The moment our people began to cut, they stopped them and told them they must *makook* for it, that is, first buy it."

Cook understood and even respected their mercantile acumen, up to a point, but he complained that "I very soon emptied my pockets with purchasing." It seemed to him that they haggled over every blade of grass, and he likened their demanding nature to the revolutionaries in Boston. According to Ledyard, one of the Mowachaht got so disgusted while negotiating with Cook that he grabbed the captain by the arm and thrust him aside, "pointing the way for him to go about his business." Cook was astonished, recounted Ledyard, "and turning to his people with a smile mixed with admiration, exclaimed, 'This is an American indeed!'"

LATE ONE MORNING at the cove, the Mowachaht began behaving strangely. Scores of their men had hauled their canoes up onto the gravelly beach and were trading and bantering as usual with some of Cook's people when suddenly there was tension in the air. Their body language stiffened. The Natives started to pile stones on the shore. They broke out their bows and spears and clubs. Anxious expressions overtook their faces. It looked as though they were preparing for battle.

Cook immediately ordered his people to take precautions. Weapons were ferried from the ships to the men on shore, muskets were loaded, the four-pounders were readied. Marines were sent to guard

Bayly's observatory. Someone draped a large sail over the exterior of the *Resolution*'s cabin to protect the ornate band of windows, should the Mowachaht start hurling rocks at the ship. Cook's men, fingers on the triggers of their guns, waited and watched.

On shore, the Mowachaht only became more agitated. "We judged from every appearance that the Indians meant to attack us," said Samwell. But no one could figure out why; nothing had happened that should have provoked them.

At about noon, a large number of canoes glided into the cove, packed with armed Natives who paddled briskly and in perfect time, with the lead man in each canoe making a little flourish with his paddle every fourth stroke. They were strangers—none of Cook's people had seen them here before. "Their number was alarming, not less than 300 of them in their war canoes," Rickman guessed. Cook's officers began to suspect that this was a well-planned scheme to encircle the ships and launch an attack. "As we did not know whether this might not be a stratagem contrived between them to fall upon us with joint forces," Samwell wrote, "we kept upon our guard."

The Mowachaht on shore began to sing their battle songs, and the men in the canoes, drawing nearer to shore, did the same. It was, said Samwell, an "engagement of tongues," which to him was reminiscent of the fishmongers at Billingsgate market in London. Then the babble subsided. On shore, a man stepped up to the water's edge and, brandishing his spear, began to shriek at the assembled canoes, "sputtering his words with the utmost vehemence and throwing out saliva from his mouth, seemingly in the most violent rage and agitation," wrote Samwell. The harangue continued for a long time. Finally, his fury spent, the man marched back to the rest of his party and sat down, cool and composed, as if nothing had happened.

Throughout the diatribe, the paddlers out in the cove had remained silent and still. But now one of them stood up in his canoe and, clutching a weapon of his own, made his retort. He heaped abuse upon the Natives on shore, employing, as Samwell put it, "the same violent actions and gestures as the other had done." The tribesmen on the beach seemed to listen respectfully.

Cook's men, their heads swiveling from one aggrieved party to the other, were not sure what to make of this tournament of alternating tirades. It was both amusing and alarming, for it was unclear whether the two groups of Natives were preparing to engage in battle with each other or were disagreeing on the fine points of how they were going to attack Cook's ships and carve up the spoils.

They kept at it for a long time. It became obvious to Cook that this was an altercation between enemy tribes, and equally obvious that his presence in the sound was its proximate cause.

Eventually both groups exhausted their energies, and the visiting fleet of men, who were probably from the rival Muchalaht tribe, paddled back into the sound, to be seen no more. Later, Cook was given to understand that the standoff was all about commerce: The Mowachaht wanted Cook's vessels to themselves. They viewed these pale foreigners—and whatever opportunities attached to them—as theirs, and they had the strength and stature to fend off other tribes who sought access to the ships. As Cook observed, "The strangers were not allowed to have any trade or intercourse with us. Our first friends seemed determined to engross us entirely to themselves."

The episode suggested to Cook and his men two significant things about the Mowachaht: They were zealous in defending their trade relationships, and they lived in a world where emotions ran high and violence could arise at any moment. There were those human hands sold as curios, which seemed to be evidence of local warfare. Several times, Cook's sailors saw severed human heads, presumably also trophies from battle, fixed on the prows of Mowachaht canoes. One day the Natives offered a little boy for sale. Though Cook declined the offer, it seemed to all present that the scared child was not of the Mowachaht but rather had been taken from some vanquished tribe. "We saw plainly," as James King gingerly phrased it, "that the different parties in the sound were not cordial friends."

BY LATE APRIL, with the ships in their last stages of repair, Cook felt he could turn away from the intensive work long enough to go on an explore. With the midshipmen rowing two boats, Cook, accompanied by Clerke and the artist Webber, made for distant parts of the sound. First they visited the village of Yuquot, a jumble of wooden houses, surrounded by racks of drying fish, that stair-stepped down the hillside toward a rocky beach choked with canoes. The village was the epicenter of the Mowachaht world, a gathering place and a locus of ritual, where a strange and splendid shrine had been erected to honor the dangerous lives of heroic local whalers. (In 1904, at the direction of the famous anthropologist Franz Boas, this sacred whalers' shrine, with its many intricate carvings, was "purchased" under less than transparent circumstances, then deconstructed and shipped to New York City's American Museum of Natural History. Some of the Mowachaht are still trying to get it back.)

The people of Yuquot received Cook and his entourage cordially. They invited the Englishmen into their homes and allowed Webber to make detailed drawings of their dwellings. They prepared a meal, boiling chunks of porpoise meat in a wooden trough filled with oily fluid that was kept simmering by a succession of red-hot stones pulled from the fire. Cook, the notoriously unpicky eater, consumed what he was served, but he was especially impressed with another dish: herring eggs, which the Mowachaht preserved dry on small pine boughs. He pronounced it a "very good caviar."

Cook was touched by the Mowachaht's hospitality, although he thought their homes were as "filthy as hog sties," observing that "everything in and about them stinks of fish oil and smoke." Captain Clerke was harsher in his assessment of the local housekeeping: "Their houses have a most disagreeable effluvia about them." But Clerke had to admit that they were warm and congenial hosts and seemed, for the most part, content. He noted also that they were "happily ignorant of all modes of intoxication... Their only beverage is pure water."

Cook and his group left Yuquot and rowed toward other settlements in the mazelike sound. For the young midshipmen, it was a long and tiring day—all told, they pulled at the oars for more than thirty miles—but it was also a rare and memorable experience. They enjoyed being with their captain in such intimate circumstances. In a small boat, free from the distractions of the ships and the vexations of command, Cook seemed a different person. He told stories and interacted with them with little regard for protocol or rank. Midshipman James Trevenen, who was only eighteen years old, noted that Cook "would sometimes relax from his almost constant severity of disposition and condescend now and then to converse familiarly with us." It was a side of Cook's personality the midshipmen had seldom seen. But the moment didn't last. "As soon as we entered the ships," Trevenen said, "he became again the despot."

One of the midshipmen who accompanied Cook that day was George Vancouver. He was only twenty years old at the time, and he very much viewed Cook as his mentor. Nootka Sound, with its innumerable coves and fogbound notches, must have left a deep impression on Vancouver. Fourteen years later he would return to the sound while in command of an ambitious expedition to further explore and chart the Pacific Northwest. In the end, the significant island that Nootka Sound fingers into would bear Vancouver's name, as would the largest city on the west coast of Canada.

COOK'S MONTH AT Nootka Sound would have far-reaching impacts—and not only in terms of establishing England's early presence in the region that would eventually become British Columbia. Of the many ripple effects emanating from Cook's visit here, perhaps the most consequential had to do with a single vulnerable creature: *Enhydra lutris,* otherwise known as the sea otter. These marine mammals, affectionate and mischievously cute, flourished here, feasting as they did on the huge populations of urchins and shellfish found throughout this extensive waterway. Sea otters appeared to lead a charmed existence, most of it spent cavorting on their backs.

But the trait that made them so beautiful, their thick, glossy coat, was also their curse, for in certain parts of the world—Asia, especially—the pelts were considered "soft gold." Affluent Chinese men coveted sea otter cloaks as a status symbol and would pay astronomical sums for them. The lustrous fur was soft but also resilient, and it could be brushed in any direction, a result of its incomparably high fiber count—sea otters produce upwards of six hundred thousand hairs per square inch, twice the density of the fur seal.

During those heady days of the Manchu Dynasty, the market for pelts was becoming frenzied, akin to the tulip mania that gripped Holland in the 1630s. The potential profits staggered the imagination. Up until that time, most of the sea otter pelts that found their way into Chinese ports came from the Russian Far East and from the first, tentative Russian forays into Alaska. But stories from Cook's visit here would lure crass armies of European and American fur hunters to Nootka and nearby locales, setting in motion a brutal industry that became so wildly competitive it would nearly ignite a war between England and Spain to control access to the sound.

Relentless hunting of sea otters, combined with the fact that they are slow breeders—typically producing only one pup every other year—meant that within a few decades of Cook's arrival they would become virtually extinct. The fur trade springing up around Nootka Sound would doom the sea otter and cause enormous dislocations among the Mowachaht and other tribes living here—for the Europeans brought the deadly triad of alcohol, guns, and disease, which in short order would cast the Native cultures into a tailspin.

In their trading with the Mowachaht, Cook's men procured many hundreds of sea otter pelts. The sailors called them "sea beaver," and they well understood, as Midshipman George Gilbert put it, that their fur "is supposed to be superior to any that is known." At the time, though, the men were not scheming to earn fortunes in Asia. They simply thought the velvety furs would come in handy in the Arctic—and, indeed, they would fashion the pelts into handsome greatcoats, caps, and gloves that would see them through many an Alaskan cold front. "To us who were bound for the North Pole," said Samwell, the pelts "were extremely valuable articles and every one endeavored to supply himself with some of them."

The *Resolution* and the *Discovery*, thoroughly refurbished, were towed out of the cove on April 26, 1778. Mowachaht men, keening songs in their canoes, accompanied the two ships almost to the mouth of the sound. As a parting gift, a chief bestowed upon Cook a handsome cloak made of "soft gold," a fur raiment that nearly reached down to Cook's ankles. In return, the captain presented the chief with a fine broadsword with a brass hilt—which, Cook thought, "made him as happy as a prince." The Mowachaht implored the

Englishmen to return soon. "By way of encouragement," Cook wrote, the chief promised that he and his people would "lay in a good stock of skins for us, and I have not the least doubt but they will."

The two ships, their sails rapidly filling, turned out of the sound and into the open sea.

28   In Bering's Wake

SOUTHEAST ALASKA, MAY 1778

Captain Cook could feel the breath of a storm. Soon after the two vessels slipped from the sanctuary of Nootka Sound, the clouds began to churn, snarly and dark, and the squalls built to a howl. With the barometer plummeting, his better instincts told him he should turn around. Yet he kept going, north by northwest, sailing out into the deep Pacific. By the next day, the storm had become what Cook called a "perfect hurricane." The *Resolution*'s jib shredded and blew to pieces. Visibility had shrunk dangerously close to nil—even in daylight, Cook's men often could not see the ship's bow through the swirling mists.

The men aboard the *Discovery* were similarly distressed. "Our danger," said Lieutenant Rickman, "was equal to any we had hitherto met with in the course of the voyage." The seas were so great and the winds so powerful that at times Cook and Clerke decided to stop sailing and ride it out. "I judged it highly dangerous to run any longer before [the storm]," Cook wrote, "and therefore brought the ships to, with their heads to the southward under the foresails and mizzen staysails."

It was at this most inopportune moment that Cook found out the *Resolution* had sprung a dangerous leak. How his workers had missed the defective spot after all their caulking and care while at Nootka was hard to understand, but there was a glaring gap in the ship, several inches wide, along the starboard quarter, near the waterline.

The discovery of a serious leak while in uncharted waters during the most severe storm of the voyage alarmed Cook "not a little," as he put it in his journal. Down in the bread room, Cook could hear the seawater surging in, and the fish room was found to be several feet deep in sloshing water, with the casks afloat and butting into one another with each violent pitch of the ship. At Cook's direction, his men worked frantically, bailing and pumping through the night and into the next day, until they got the problem tolerably under control.

Not a little. That this existentially dangerous situation concerned Cook only that much says something about his penchant for understatement, but more generally about his calmness in a crisis. Perhaps this was the most impressive quality Cook possessed: In clutch situations, he always seemed to know what to do—Cook the master mariner, who in 1770, on his first voyage around the world, had crashed into an underwater projection of the Great Barrier Reef. The collision caused what was surely a mortal gash; his *Endeavour* would have sunk but for some fast thinking on his part. He ordered the crew to hurl cannons, casks, and stone ballast overboard so he could float the ship and employed a spare sail to essentially wrap the hull's wound—a technique known as "fothering." Then he limped the *Endeavour* into a river mouth on the Australian coast to repair her injuries.

Throughout this voyage, and especially here on the stormy west coast of North America, Samwell had repeatedly noted the same qualities in Cook. He was, said Samwell, "cool and intrepid among dangers, patient and firm under difficulties and distress, fertile in expedients, and ... original in all his designs." Cook's competence in dire situations instilled in his crew the sort of awe that can come only from the recognition that, on seas like these, one man literally holds the company's fate in his hands. There was a charisma bound up in the discretion of his command style—in what he *didn't* say, what he *didn't* do, how he *didn't* react. He believed in minimal exertion of energy or explanation: Make the tiny correction and leave it alone. He had a refined sense for judging gradations of imminent calamity. Wrote one able seaman: "When no one else had a suspicion of danger he often came up on deck and changed the course of the ship because land was near. This was so pronounced that every one believed he had some secret source of foreknowing ... Such occasions were frequent when he alone was sensible to the existence of land; and he was always right."

For nearly five days the storm continued to bludgeon the two vessels—"with very little intermission," complained Ledyard. People were astounded by how calm Captain Cook remained during this uncertain and tempestuous stretch—he spent most of his time lodged in his cabin and displayed not a concern in the world. "On the unknown coast of America," wrote Zimmermann, "the ships ran on foggy nights under full sail, and the captain slept peacefully all the while. In the moment of greatest danger, he was at once the most merry, the most serene, and the most steady. His main object was to establish a calm state of mind on the ship, and in this he succeeded so well that all eyes were usually turned toward him."

ON APRIL 30, the winds finally abated. Cook began to angle closer to the shores of southeast Alaska. By the time he could make out coastal features and take a good reading of his position, he found that he had raced northward a full six degrees of latitude. Evidence of so much forward progress was encouraging to Cook. Yet it was also frustrating, because he had wanted to get clarity about a cartographic feature that was supposed to be located—or, as he suspected, *not* located—along the very coastline he had just passed.

More than a century earlier, in 1640, a Spanish admiral named Bartholomew de Fonte was said to have made a voyage to this coast, all the way from a base in Lima. At approximately fifty-three degrees north he claimed to have discovered a passage leading from the Pacific to the Atlantic—the very thing Cook's entire expedition was dedicated to finding. According to the stories, Admiral de Fonte had sailed into a strait, then far up a river he called the Río de los Reyes, which communicated with a large lake. Somehow, sailing beyond this lake, he had negotiated his ship past waterfalls and through several more interconnected lakes. Deep within the continent, de Fonte had encountered an American ship that had sailed westward from Boston. The body of water he claimed to have found was shown on many maps as the "Strait of Admiral de Fonte."

But the fabulous story, which had been published in 1708 in a not highly reputable English periodical, was pure fiction—an imaginative account of an apocryphal voyage led by an invented captain. Cook knew it had to be a hoax. Nonetheless, de Fonte's "discovery" had persisted in the margins of the literature for decades. Cook was eager to resolve the question beyond a shadow of a doubt with his own eyes and thus obliterate the legend forever. It would have been another accolade of "negative discovery" he could have added to his portfolio.

As Cook put it, he regretted having passed the spot "where geographers have placed the pretended Strait of Admiral de Fonte. For my own part, I give no credit to such vague and improbable stories that carry their own confutation along with them. Nevertheless, I was very desirous of keeping the coast aboard in order to clear up this point beyond dispute."

So Cook had passed by the mouth of the Columbia River and the large strait leading to Puget Sound, and now he had "missed" the (nonexistent) Strait of Admiral de Fonte. This entire coast was such a crazy pattern of fjords and islands and capes, often obscured by miasmas of mist and fog, that it would have taken several lifetimes to explore all the rivers and inlets to see where they led and whether any of them progressed toward the Atlantic Ocean.

All of which spoke to the untenable scope and procedural complexity of the mission the Admiralty had assigned to Cook. He was supposed to follow and chart the trend of the coast for thousands of miles and note anything promising, but also not waste any time on fool's errands. He could not allow himself to be enticed by every opening that presented itself, yet there always lingered the nagging possibility that he could miss something significant. It was an expedition that required perpetual vigilance cut with perpetual skepticism.

In a way, his exploratory goal was the opposite of what it had been during his previous voyages, and it was a much harder one. Before, he had been asked to look for signs of a huge landmass, or the absence of one, but here he had been told to hunt for a mere thread of water leading *through* a landmass. As one maritime historian aptly phrased it, "Instead of the looming haystack of a southern continent, Cook was searching for the slim needle of a Northwest Passage."

In Cook's chart room were stored maps that, based on little more than folklore and willful imagination, depicted Alaska as a very large island completely separated from North America, with a clear waterway leading due north from Cook's current location to the Arctic Ocean. Other maps showed Alaska protruding like a massive proboscis from the American continent. Still other charts showed Alaska to be a confusing hodgepodge of smaller islands. Cook had been sent here not just to find a passageway through it, or over it, but also to try to make sense of the dog's breakfast of theories that had accumulated over the years, obstructing an accurate understanding of what was there.

COOK'S TWO NORTHERING ships fell in along a coast that was staggering in its beauty. The sawtooth peaks, the deep bays, the glaciers of translucent blue crunching down from the glittering heights—it was a landscape made for giants, a landscape on a scale Cook had never seen before. The ice-cold waters teemed with mighty runs of fish, the skies overhead were a chaos of birdlife, and the men frequently saw enormous whales spouting and sometimes breaching the surface.

The weather had turned crystalline and clear—a welcome change but for the fact that now, with hardly any wind at all, the two ships crawled like sluggards up the shore. "We are forwarding our business in tracing the coast," wrote Clerke, "but our breeze enables us to get on but very leisurely." Day after day, the sickly captain noted with relief how refined the atmosphere was; the glorious sun was warm and bright on his skin, and he could see for miles in all directions, with scarcely a cloud in the sky. His damaged lungs seemed grateful for the good, clean air: Maybe Alaska wouldn't kill him after all?

"We continue to have most extraordinary fine weather, with such gentle breezes that we just crawl along shore," Clerke rhapsodized. "I never in my life before in any climate whatever saw for such a length of time the air so perfectly serene, the sea so perfectly smooth. The happy influence of the pure atmosphere was apparent in every countenance."

Free of navigational worries, the men turned their sights on the natural smorgasbord around them. "All hands were employed, officers as well as men, in fishing, shooting, or chasing the seals and sea lions that played about the ships," wrote Rickman. "Great quantities of fine cod were caught, which furnished a high treat to both ships' companies; and some ducks and sea-larks, and four sea parrots [puffins] were killed by the fowlers."

THE NAVIGATOR IN whose wake Cook was following, and would continue to follow in circuitous fashion for the summer, was the formidable Vitus Bering, a Dane by birth who had led two epic expeditions in the employ of the Russian navy. Cook was steadfast in recognizing Bering's legacy; it was one of his virtues that he paid homage to the voyagers who had come before him, to honor their accomplishments and sacrifices.

Bering's second odyssey known as the Great Northern Expedition, had happened nearly forty years earlier. Before his voyage began, he and a huge army of grunts performed an overland journey of nearly nine thousand miles, hauling mountains of material by packhorse and sledge, from St. Petersburg to the shores of the Kamchatka Peninsula, where they built their ships from scratch. In the summer of 1741, Bering's newly christened ship *St. Peter,* along with a sister vessel, *St. Paul,* captained by Aleksei Chirikov, sailed from Kamchatka toward Alaska with the goal of ascertaining whether Asia and America were conjoined or disconnected landmasses. Early on, the two ships lost sight of each other in a storm. Precisely where Bering and Chirikov went in their separate courses along the Alaskan coast is debated among scholars, and the maps that emerged from the expedition proved to be full of errors, hypothetical features, and curious lacunae.

These cartographic imperfections probably had their origin in official Russian secrecy, and also in the unfortunate fact that Vitus Bering died—likely of scurvy, along with twenty-eight of his men—before he could return to St. Petersburg to write about what he had seen and where he had traveled. Though an intrepid and long-suffering explorer of hard-won achievements, Bering was nowhere near the mapmaker Cook was, nor did he have access to the advanced navigational tools and instruments that were available to Cook.

Aleksei Chirikov's journey proved nearly as tragic as Bering's. On the extreme southeastern coast of what is now Alaska, at a place called Cape Addington, Chirikov dispatched a longboat with eleven men to reconnoiter the shore for water and wood. When after a week they hadn't come back, Chirikov sent a second longboat with four more men to search for the lost party—and they, too, failed to return. A distraught Chirikov lingered awhile but sailed on. The fate of his fifteen lost men was never learned, but most scholars believe that Tlingit warriors attacked and killed them all.

For these reasons, it was perhaps inevitable that the haunted wanderings of Bering and Chirikov had remained shrouded in mystery and misunderstanding. It was twenty years after Bering's death that the first English edition of a report detailing his voyage was published in London. Compiled by Gerhard Müller, a German-born historian affiliated with the St. Petersburg Academy of Sciences, the account featured not only descriptions but also maps, rendered in the most impressionistic of brushstrokes, that were full of the afore-mentioned distortions and errors.

Müller's spotty volume was the main source Cook had to go on, although he also had a map, published in Russia in 1773, that purported to incorporate new information gleaned from more recent Russian-led voyages to Alaska. From here on out, Cook would constantly find himself staring at headlands and other prominent features along the Alaskan coast and trying, usually in vain, to square them with Müller's dubious cartography. "The account of that voyage," Cook complained, "is so very much abridged and the chart so extremely inaccurate that it is hardly possible by either the one or the other, or both together, to find out any place that [Bering] either saw or touched at all." After days of scrutinizing Müller's map, Cook decided that it led to far more confusion than illumination. A bad map was worse than no map at all; he would have had much easier voyaging if he'd left it at home in London.

But on May 5, Cook glimpsed an unmistakably grand landmark he felt confident *was* a place described in Müller's account: an imposing massif that Bering had sighted on July 16, 1741, and on his charts was given the toponym "Mt. St. Elias." The imposing snowcapped eminence, eighteen thousand feet high, swept steeply down from the frigid heavens to the deep blue sea. Still named Mount St. Elias today, the peak is notable for its extreme vertical relief; it's the second-tallest mountain in the United States, after Alaska's Denali, and one of the tallest coastal mountains in the world. This lordly Olympus was bigger than any mountain Cook had ever seen—it was so high and broad-shouldered that it appeared to abide within its own weather system. "A vast promontory," Rickman called it, "that seemed to cover its head in the clouds." For many days, Mount St. Elias would serve as Cook's orientation point as he continued up the coast, sketching and charting as best he could along the way.

ON MAY 11, 1778, Cook, having come upon a promising island out in the Gulf of Alaska, decided to land in search of a good spot to repair the *Resolution*'s leak. He was rowed ashore and found a stark, windswept realm, choked with salmonberry shrubs and stunted fir and spruce trees. The island appeared to be uninhabited—today it's known as Kayak Island. As an attestation of his short stay here, Cook stuffed a bottle with a note and some silver coins dated 1772 and placed it at the base of a lonely tree.

What was remarkable about Cook's having stopped here at all was that coincidentally—and unbeknownst to him—Kayak Island was also the first place where Vitus Bering had anchored when he sailed in these waters thirty-seven years earlier. Bering had not gone ashore, but Georg Steller, the expedition's brilliant young German naturalist, had. Bering allotted him only ten hours for a survey of the island, so Steller, aware of the ticking clock, moved quickly to collect a trove of specimens, becoming, in the process, the first non-Native to set foot on Alaskan shores and the first scientist to study Alaskan plant and animal life. Steller would go on to describe numerous species in the region that still bear his name—including the Steller's jay, the Steller's sea lion, and the

Steller's sea cow, a kelp-grazing Arctic variety of manatee that is now extinct.

While on Kayak Island, Steller did not encounter any people, but unlike Cook, he did determine that the island was inhabited—in the summer season, at least—for he stumbled upon a recently vacated camp with still-smoldering coals. After examining the camp's miscellany of contents carefully and discovering a nearby underground cache of goods, he astutely guessed that these people were directly related to Native people he had already studied on the Kamchatka Peninsula. He advanced the groundbreaking hypothesis that the ancestors of these people had migrated across what we now call the Bering Sea from Asia. Georg Steller's ten-hour stint on Kayak Island was one of the most efficient and productive sojourns in the annals of natural science.

Captain Cook, for his part, occupied himself for only a few hours on Kayak Island. Determining that this scrap of sand and rock would not be a good place for his punctured ship to anchor for repairs, he returned to the *Resolution* and shoved off for points north.

The next day, the two ships nosed into a large bay that seemed to stretch toward the north. Although Cook still wasn't at the prescribed sixty-five degrees north latitude—he was five degrees shy of it—this opening was too enticing to ignore. Investigating it would be a slight violation of his orders, but as he had once written, "I believe that he who learns only how to obey orders can never be a great explorer."

Could this be the grail they'd been seeking all along? It was too hazy to tell where this waterway led, but it was big and wide and seductive. Samwell seemed to rouse from the torpor of his diary, writing, "Our hopes of a passage were revived."

The crews on the ships began to buzz with excitement. Many of the sailors became giddy with thoughts of a quick return home to an appreciative Mother England, and with dreams of how they might blow their portion of the £20,000 prize that awaited them. Midshipman George Gilbert captured the elation nearly everyone seemed to feel. "On the 12th of May, about noon," he wrote, "we discovered an opening which had a very promising appearance. Having a favorable wind, we bore away for it immediately, flattering ourselves with the hope of having found the passage we were in search of."

Corporal Ledyard echoed Gilbert, noting that as they turned into this mysterious sea lane, they were "not without hopes of the dear passage, which was now the only theme."

29 *Deep Water and Bold Shores*

PRINCE WILLIAM SOUND, ALASKA, MAY 1778

Almost as soon as Cook's ships entered the promising waterway, currents began to push against them, chunks of brash ice bobbed on the surface, and a blanket of cold mist obstructed the view ahead. As Clerke described it, the thick fog rendered "our endeavors to delineate matters here almost abortive" and caused "a most unhappy retardation of that business we are now so anxious to forward."

Warily, Cook crept northward, slipping into what appeared to be a spacious bay. He had entered what we now know as Prince William Sound, on the glacier-carved flanks of Alaska. It would take Cook several days with the clearing of the fog before he could begin to understand the sound's intricacy and extent. More than two thousand rivers and streams fed into this protected inland sea, and more than twenty glaciers chiseled their way down from the Chugach Mountains to the cold water's edge.

As they descended, the glaciers pried boulders from the bedrock, tumbling and pulverizing them into a powder known among glaciologists as "rock flour." This fine talc was full of iron, nitrates, and phosphates, and as it spilled into the coves and bays it became suspended in the sapphire seawater, giving it a ghostly hue—scientists today call the phenomenon "glacial milk." The mineral-rich rock flour generated prodigious blooms of plankton and krill, which, in turn, nourished large populations of whales, porpoises, seals, and other sea mammals, not to mention some of the world's largest concentrations of fish. Groups of orca whales resided here year-round, but there were transient orcas as well, which would fin in unannounced to prowl the rich waters and beat up the local orcas, like street-gang thugs, drunk on the sound's nutritional soups.

Prince William Sound was a churning biological incubator—Cook's men had never seen so much life crammed into one place, and right at the time when spring was coming on fast, with tendrils of green popping up from thin spots in the mushy snow. The men caught monster halibut and salmon and herring and cod, they shot ducks and geese, and along the mossy shores of spruce and alder they encountered foxes, wolves, bears, and mountain goats. High on the sheer cliff walls were chattering rookeries of kittiwakes, guillemots, puffins, and other seabirds, while in the lagoons and tide pools, communities of starfish, urchins, anemones, and blue mussels clung to the barnacle-splotched boulders.

Nearly all the journals remark upon the sound's astonishing variety and superabundance of wildlife. "An incredible number of whales and seals sporting around us," William Ellis noted, while Clerke grew nearly jaded by the sightings. "It now becomes almost tautology to mention the whales, seals, and numberless fowl that surround us," he wrote, "but really the quantities are amazing." James Burney seemed to think he'd found a piece of heaven, calling the place a "little Mediterranean Sea."

The constant extrusions from the surrounding amphitheater of glaciers had over the millennia created a coastline endlessly broken and notched. With so many fjords and indentations, the shore of Prince William Sound was longer than the entire coast of California. It was a complicated topography to survey and put down with any accuracy on maps, and one senses Cook's growing frustration but also his fascination. Over the course of a full day, it could be tedious and mentally stressful work, squinting to distinguish the insular from the peninsular; keeping a hawk's eye on the outpouring rivers as they worked in advancement or retreat against the inrushing tides; discerning salt water from brackish and brackish from fresh; worrying over the not infrequent gravel bars and submerged moraine boulders that might be strewn in the ships' foggy path; and all the while scouring the snow-mantled landforms, in their shifting angles, for the elusive opening that may or not be there, lurking beyond the next turn of the land.

Cook decided to call this magnificent place Sandwich Sound—as though the First Lord of the Admiralty hadn't already achieved sufficient immortality by way of the voyage's charts. Cook was running out of ideas for toponyms, or perhaps he'd just lost patience with the rigmarole of naming things. Sandwich Sound was framed by two large barrier islands that Cook, in further redundancy, also named in honor of Sandwich: Montague Island (after Lord Sandwich's family name, Montagu) and Hinchinbrook Island (the name, variously spelled, of Lord Sandwich's estate). The two islands still bear those names today, but the Admiralty, at Sandwich's insistence, would negate Cook's appellation for the sound and would instead name it after King George III's son, Prince William, who would much later ascend to the throne of England and become known as "Silly Billy."

BEFORE COOK COULD search for passages deeper within the sound, he needed to address the troubling and potentially catastrophic leak the *Resolution* had developed during the recent storms. He found a nearly perfect place in which to make the repairs, a cove he called Snug Corner. As the *Resolution* was being heeled over to expose the leaky patch, Cook decided the ship should be secured with a stream anchor. But the sailor who plopped the anchor in the water, a young man named William Austin, got a leg entangled in the rope. The poor fellow was yanked overboard and pulled to the bottom of the cove, many fathoms deep. Miraculously, down in the frigid murk, Austin had the presence of mind to extricate himself from the rope and swim to the surface. He would live, but his leg was horribly fractured and he required the close care of the surgeon.

Finally, though, the carpenters could attack the leak in earnest. Pulling back sections of the ship's copper sheathing, they found a gaping hole more than two inches wide—far too wide for simple caulking. The workmen had to wedge a thick piece of tar-saturated rope into the gash and slather on a patch as best they could.

While the *Resolution* had fallen under the carpenters' ministrations, canoes full of Indigenous Chugach men came to visit. The Chugach-Alutiiq people had lived in the region for more than 4,500 years, and they'd built a thriving civilization on the sound's shores. It's possible that some of these people had met Russians before, but more likely this was their first contact with European vessels. They wore the skins and furs of animals and mittens fashioned from bear paws. Their ears and noses were adorned with shards of bone, and most of them had horizontal slits between their lower lips and chins, through which they frequently would thrust out their tongues—giving some of Cook's men the alarming initial impression that these people had two mouths. Cook thought they were a "thickset, good-looking people" but noted that he had "nowhere seen Indians that take more pain to ornament, or rather disfigure, themselves than these people."

The Chugach seemed surprised by Cook's ships but were by no means awed by their presence. The Natives almost immediately commenced trading. They placed exorbitant value on glass beads, particularly blue and green, and would gladly give up a priceless velvety sea otter pelt for just a few beads. Ellis thought they were a "fat and jolly" people who looked "as if they lived well."

Cook's people were most impressed by the little boats the Chugach arrived in—sleek lozenges that darted about the cove. The lightweight, narrow craft, made of sealskin stretched over skeletal frames of alder limbs and whalebone, were quick and responsive, and they had an incredibly shallow draft. The occupant, wielding a double-bladed paddle, sat on the ribbed floor of the vessel, his torso emerging from a round hole that was made waterproof by a tight-fitting skirt. To Cook's eye, man and boat functioned here almost as one. The accounts that Cook and his officers wrote were among the first detailed descriptions of a kayak found in the literature of the Pacific.

To guard against the nearly constant drizzle, the Chugach wore an ingeniously designed covering made from the intestinal membranes of marine mammals stitched together with sinews. These diaphanous gut parkas, called kamleikas, were completely waterproof and featured hoods that could be drawn up around the face and neck. Midshipman Trevenen thought the Native jackets vastly superior to the smelly, cumbersome rain gear the sailors had been issued—clammy garments made of canvas duck cloth coated with linseed oil and paint. Trevenen insisted that the Chugach people's foul-weather jackets "are indeed much better, being lighter, stronger, and answering equally well the purpose of keeping out the wet."

Cook correctly guessed that these people were "not the same nation" as the Indigenous tribes who had populated the shores at his last stop, Nootka Sound. Their language was different, their attire was different, and so were their tools and artworks. Some of Cook's people thought the Chugach had distinctly Asian features—Samwell wrote that they were, "we conjecture, descendants from some Chinese who may have been cast away here in some distant age."

But other expedition members felt the Chugach in every sense resembled the Inuit tribes found along Baffin Bay and Hudson Bay—not just in appearance but in displays of their material culture. For example, the same nimble watercraft, the kayak, was well known along the shores of Greenland. As Cook tentatively phrased it, these Alaskans bore "some affinity to ... the Greenlander." John Ledyard, the American, was more forceful in advancing this point. "The inhabitants bear a very striking resemblance if not an exact one to the Esquimaux," he asserted. "Their skin-canoes, their double-bladed paddles, their dress and other appearances of less note are the same as on the coast of Labrador and in Hudson's Bay."

There was much truth to this—the cultures were similar and in many ways related, including genetically—but there was also much wishful thinking behind Ledyard's comment. Like so many of Cook's men, he dearly wished to believe the similarities between these Alaskans and the Inuit on the Atlantic side were the result of the same transcontinental passageway Cook's expedition was searching for. If these were the same people, it would seem to argue in favor of a clear and unimpeded waterborne communication of ideas and designs across the top of North America. How else to explain so many coincidences of cultural correlation across so many thousands of miles?

Here was a case of "confirmation bias" at work: Ledyard was hop-

ing for a compelling piece of evidence that pointed to the existence
of the voyage's grail. The general excitement over a possible passage
quickened when some of Cook's sailors engaged in discussions with
the locals. These conversations were nothing more than rudimentary
sign language, punctuated with grunts, but the Chugach seemed to
suggest that there were precisely two ways out of this sound—one
toward the south (that is, back to the Gulf of Alaska, from whence
Cook had come) and one toward the north. "We thought we understood from them," Cook wrote, "that we should find a large sea to
the north, but it was more probable that we misunderstood them, for
all the conversation we could have with them was by signs." Samwell agreed with Cook's dubious assessment and was willing to put
a wager on it: "Tis ten to one that the Indians knew no more of what
we were inquiring after than we knew of this supposed passage."

Confirmation bias was not one of Cook's weaknesses. His doubts
were mounting that this magnificent basin possessed a northern exit.
As the fog burned away, all he could see was bulging mountains and
ice fields crowding in on every shore. "The land seemed to close
and left us with little hopes of finding any passage to the northward,
or indeed in any other direction," he wrote. He feared this sound
was an enormous dead end and that he would only be wasting time
by venturing deeper into it. On the other hand, maybe through the
garbled language and wild gesticulations, the Natives had provided
important clues.

Cook doubted it. But with his ship repaired again, he felt com-
pelled to try.

THE TWO SHIPS sailed north until they came to a place where the
sound appeared to fork into two major arms. Cook decided to hoist
out a couple of boats to explore further. He assigned Gore to lead a
party of rowers up one arm while Bligh and his team would follow
the other. Cook made sure both detachments were well armed—he
did not want a reprise of whatever had befallen Chirikov's ill-fated
shore parties nearly four decades earlier. The crews of the *Resolution*
and the *Discovery*, remaining in their anchorage, would wait for tidings from Gore and Bligh.

Artist John Webber used the day to make sketches of the scenery, and the mountains that seemed so out of scale, dwarfing the ships. It would have been a splendid morning, too, for Anderson to observe wildlife and do some botanizing along with Nelson. But such work was no longer possible for the consumptive surgeon and naturalist. Since leaving Kaua'i, Anderson's condition had deteriorated so far, so fast, that he was little more than skin and bones. The Scotsman had no energy for exploration and had long since stopped writing in his journal. The cold, damp weather of Alaska seemed to be hastening his demise. He had drawn up a will, noting that he had been "for some time past in a bad state of health" and "without any prospect of recovery."

Yet throughout his sufferings, Anderson remained stoic and even cheerful. "His decline was too rapid," Lieutenant King wrote of his friend, "not to be observable by all. He...knew that his lungs were affected" and, as a well-informed physician, he had "foretold for a year the different stages of his disorder. And yet so very little an alteration had this on the equality of his temper, and the serenity of his mind, that his messmates knew nothing of his complaints until his very emaciated body gave ocular proofs of them. So much true fortitude in such a trying situation I will venture to say will never be surpassed."

When the two boats returned that night, Cook was eager to debrief Bligh and Gore. Bligh was negative in his report. It was his firm opinion that the arm he had investigated merely "communicated with the one we last came from." Gore, on the other hand, was more sanguine and seemed to think there was merit in exploring further. He claimed that he had seen "deep water and bold shores."

Bligh's pessimistic assessment was the accurate one. He could be dour and misanthropic, but he was almost always correct. Among other things, Bligh's explorations that day resulted in Cook's permanently honoring him on the charts, which still show a Bligh Reef and a Bligh Island. It was just west of Bligh Reef that, in 1989, the tanker *Exxon Valdez* ran aground and spilled eleven million gallons of crude oil into the sound, a cataclysmic event from which the complex webs of life here are still recovering.

Cook had heard enough. He decided to turn around for the open sea. He had explored the sound for eight days, which he felt was more than sufficient. "I resolved to spend no more time in searching for a passage in a place that promised so little success." As he continued his journey along the Alaskan coast, he figured he would find many more promising waterways, ones that, as he put it, "would be less equivocal than any we had seen in this sound."

Cook was at least able to reflect that his expedition had made historic first contact with the Native people here without any untoward incidents, without sexual encounters that might have spread venereal disease, and without violence. "We had the good fortune to leave them as ignorant of firearms as we found them," he wrote. "They never saw, nor heard, a musket fired."

30   Possessed

COOK INLET, ALASKA, MAY–JUNE 1778

For nearly a week, upon angry seas, the ships crawled down the coast of the Kenai Peninsula, threading through its mazes of rocks and jumbled islands. This stretch of the Gulf of Alaska is famously dangerous water, subject to diabolical storms and freak waves. What made the high-wire sailing more distressing for Cook was that the coast seemed to be consistently trending toward the southwest, exactly the opposite of the direction he hoped to be taking.

But on May 25, through wisps of fog, another gap was spotted in the coast to starboard, an opening perhaps more enticing than the one that had led Cook into Prince William Sound the previous week. It was an impressive gateway, bold and deep and wide, nearly sixty miles across. On seeing it, Ledyard thought the channel was "a vast river, having a strong southerly current ... It gave us hopes again of a passage."

The sighting presented Cook with a familiar dilemma: Explore or ignore? Although he was still four degrees shy of the sixty-five-degree north latitude decreed in his official instructions, he suspected that the Admiralty lords would probably chastise him for passing by an opening of this magnitude. "If I had not examined this place," Cook wrote, "it would have been concluded, nay asserted, that it communicated with the Sea to the North." But if he decided to explore it and it didn't lead anywhere, the officials would criticize him for wasting more time in Alaska's brief summer calendar. "The season," Cook fretted, "was advancing apace."

Cook decided to nose in. For the first few days, the inlet continued to show promise. It remained wide and deep—sounding at twenty-four fathoms, with a bottom of fine dark sand—and it seemed to the men like the formidable sort of seaway the Scots liked to call a *firth*. Encouragingly, salinity tests showed a consistent presence of salt water. As the ships pushed inward ten, twenty, now thirty miles, the men's spirits revived. Maybe this *was* the Passage after all—the same one that was shown on some of the Russian maps.

It seemed, thought Clerke, "a fine spacious opening" with multitudinous "crooks and corners." The cold waters were full of herring, smelt, sablefish, and cod. Beluga whales, ghostly white creatures with bulbous heads, glided through the murk, hunting for squid, clams, and sandworms. The ships passed snow-dusted capes and islands. Then a succession of prominent volcanoes shifted into view— Rickman called them "burning mountains"—including two that were more than ten thousand feet high and wreathed in sulfurous vapor, peaks known today as Mount Iliamna and Mount Redoubt.

Villages of the Native Dena'ina people were spotted in the distance, with campfire smoke curling into the sky. The Dena'ina were an Athabaskan people who had made south-central Alaska their home for millennia. They kept away from the ships, but occasionally a brave soul would venture out in a kayak and trade a few items with Cook's men, then quickly paddle to safety. This was probably the Dena'ina's first encounter with European people, and they were bewildered by the strange vessels. Dena'ina stories passed down through the generations and captured in a classic work of oral tradition built around the stories of Shem Pete, a celebrated elder and historian, vividly capture the Native point of view upon Cook's arrival. To the Dena'ina, the *Resolution* "was like a giant bird with great white wings." At first the villagers were terrified. "All the people were very frightened and ran and hid in the woods, except one brave man. He paddled out in his *baidarka* [kayak] to see what it was. The strange people on the boat traded him some of their clothes for what he was wearing. When the courageous Native returned to the shore he was a hero to his people, and the costume he brought back with him [probably a sailor's uniform] was faithfully copied down through the years, to wear in ceremonial dances."

AS SIGNIFICANT A waterway as this was, Cook, curiously, didn't bother to give it a name. In his journal, he merely jotted the word "River" and left a blank space in front of it, which he presumably meant to fill in at some point in the future. Admiralty officials would later decide to honor the captain by calling the unnamed waterway Cook's River. But since it *wasn't* a river, properly speaking, George Vancouver, during his survey of coastal Alaska in 1794, amended the name to Cook Inlet—which is what it's called today.

As Cook sailed deeper into the seaway, he was discouraged to find it steadily narrowing. Little by little, the land was closing in, the channel growing shallower, clouded with silt and choked with sludge and waterlogged timber. Worse, the next salinity tests showed an increase of fresh water—a persuasive indication that this was likely an inlet fed by rivers, glaciers, and snowmelt, not a navigable channel that communicated directly with northern seas. The findings of the salt tests, wrote Clerke, were "a discovery I was sorry to make, for I think it a very cogent argument against this being a strait betwixt two seas."

Yet another discouraging sign was the wildly fluctuating tidal range. When the tide was going out, surging back toward the Gulf of Alaska, Cook's ships could not advance an inch; the outrushing current was so strong that they had to set anchors to keep from drifting backwards. At the tide's lowest ebb, Cook often found himself in danger of running aground on shoals and mudflats. Yet when the tide returned, the inrushing rip was almost too strong and swift for the ships to absorb. The tidal edge arrived in the form of a stout, frothy wave that in some places crested to more than six feet in height and, depending on conditions, might race along at speeds of more than twenty miles per hour. (Today, a subculture of surfers has figured out how to catch the wave and ride it in journeys that can last for many miles.)

Cook could see that the hydrology of this place was exceedingly mercurial and dynamic. In fact, the inlet experiences one of the most powerful bore tides in the world and has one of North America's most drastic tidal differentials, with a range of nearly thirty feet between ebb and flood—a tidal flux almost as pronounced as that of Nova Scotia's famous Bay of Fundy.

COOK KNEW HE was on a snipe hunt, but he continued to press forward. In his journal, he claimed that the only reason he was doing so was to indulge some of his officers—especially John Gore, who still held out hope, based on no particular evidence, that this could be the waterway after all. Wrote Cook: "I was fully persuaded that we should find no passage by this inlet and my persevering in it was more to satisfy other people than to confirm my own opinions." To Cook it had all the signs of being an estuarial river, including "low shores, very thick and muddy water, large trees, and all manner of dirt and rubbish floating up and down with the tide."

Still, something about this landscape was pulling Cook in, despite his best instincts. It was a big, wild dominion coming into the full throb of summer life, with a climate, he thought, "as favorable for settlement as any part of the world under the same degree of latitude." Cook's stubborn sense of thoroughness may have triggered a compulsion to finish the puzzle at all costs and pursue this watery thoroughfare down to its last tapering source. Some of his junior officers seemed to agree that the task, however quixotic, had to be completed. "After all our pains," as Lieutenant King put it, "to have left it a doubtful matter would have been vexatious indeed."

Cook wanted to make something useful and conclusive out of this otherwise extraneous sojourn before quitting the place—while answering in advance the armchair geographers in England who might criticize him for a flagging diligence. "As we had proceeded so far," Cook wrote, "I was desirous of having stronger proofs and therefore weighed with the next flood and plied higher up."

FINALLY, MORE THAN 150 miles into the inlet, the two ships arrived at a place where the waterway split into two distinct branches. Cook anchored near this fork; the shores rising to the east would one day become Alaska's largest city, Anchorage.

Salt tests showed that the water here was perfectly fresh—another bad sign—but Cook was still curious about the two arms and how far they penetrated into the interior. Accordingly, he sent Master Bligh in a boat to explore the larger arm, the northeastern one, while dispatching Lieutenant King in another launch to explore the southeastern arm. The fact that Cook didn't accompany either detail shows how little confidence he held in their finding anything worthwhile. In his mind, this was merely a mopping-up operation to end this unsatisfying probe into the Alaskan interior.

Over the course of his two-day exploration, the ever competent Bligh learned a lot about the northeastern arm. It was a significant and beautiful stretch of water, fed by two tributary rivers supplied, in turn, by large amounts of snowmelt from nearby mountain ranges; those twin rivers are today known as the Knik and the Matanuska. Bligh could see the hulks of the Alaska Range rising in the north, and it's possible that in back of the jumbled mountains he may have caught a glimpse of Denali, North America's highest peak, at more than twenty thousand feet, looming some 150 miles farther inland. Bligh could see enough of this magnificent territory to grasp that it was continental in scale—not an island at all, as the Russian charts showed, but an extension of the North American landmass. Bligh had seen no signs of a convenient waterway leading through it. Today the branch of water Bligh explored and cursorily charted is known as Knik Arm.

When Master Bligh returned to render his disappointing assessment, Cook threw up his hands. "All hope of a passage," he wrote, "was now given up."

Lieutenant King, on the other hand, hadn't been able to make much progress in the southeastern arm. Sometimes he had to fight against the powerful tides, while other times he was stymied by quagmires of mud and quicksand. But it was King's strong sense that the arm dwindled into a river, or several rivers, that may or may not be navigable. In any case, he concluded, there was no possibility of a passage in this direction. King, like Bligh, had to turn around and work his way back to the ships—which led to the name "River Turnagain" being placed on Cook's charts. Today this body of water is still known as Turnagain Arm.

With both reconnaissance reports now in, Cook grew furious with himself for having exhausted a week exploring yet another dead end—and his fury only deepened when he contemplated the more than 150 miles he would have to retrace to reach the open sea. He cast his ire again upon the deeply flawed maps of the Russians and their "late pretended discoveries." He was convinced that the North American continent extended much farther west than any of these fanciful maps indicated—and that he was still a very long way from reaching any opening to the north.

His anger fairly seethed from the pages of his journal. "If the discovery of this river should prove of use, either to the present or future ages, the time spent in exploring it ought to be the less regretted, but to us who had a much greater object in view, it was an essential loss," he wrote. "Nothing but a trifling point of geography has been determined."

It's ironic that the Admiralty officials chose to name this long channel after Cook, because he hated this place—for how it had drawn him in, and for all the time it had consumed, prevailing over his initial doubts. Perhaps it was this contempt that explains why he never filled in that blank in his journal, leaving it to William Bayly, the astronomer, to come up with his own, and perhaps a more fitting, name for the inlet: *Seduction River.*

TRIFLING THOUGH THE geographical details may have seemed to him, Cook was sufficiently impressed by the surrounding country to believe that the Crown would want him to stake a formal claim here. It was prime real estate, in his estimation, and so the old imperial jousting match nudged into his thoughts. He surmised that the

French, the Spanish, maybe the Dutch, or most likely the Russians someday would have designs on this place. So before he left the inlet, he decided to arrange one of his periodic ceremonies of "possession."

Cook wouldn't lead it himself; he would send others on that chore. One senses he had grown tired of the flag-planting ritual, and perhaps understood how absurd it was to claim ownership of an already inhabited land—in this case, a land so very far from Mother England, and so very different. Nonetheless, his Admiralty instructions required him, when finding desirable domains, to perform the ridiculous solemnities, with their quasi-religious overtones, invoking His Majesty's name.

It was June 1, 1778. Cook would remain on board the *Resolution,* making final preparations to sail, but he sent Lieutenant King, with a party of junior officers and midshipmen, to land on a marsh marked only by a few runty spruce trees. A dozen Dena'ina men, well armed and surrounded by a pack of snarling dogs, emerged on the sand and confronted the strange interlopers. (According to *Shem Pete's Alaska,* "The people of the village saw Cook's men coming and thought it might mean war, so they got their spears and weapons ready and went down to meet the English.")

Lieutenant King ordered his men to lay down their muskets. The Dena'ina, still suspicious, stashed their spears in the scrub nearby. Haltingly, the two groups of men began to mingle and barter goods. King offered the Natives a few pieces of iron, while the Dena'ina made a gift of some salmon fillets and two dogs.

Though the interactions seemed cordial enough so far, the Englishmen remained antsy, knowing that the numerically superior Dena'ina could set upon them at any moment. In his skittishness, John Law, the *Discovery's* surgeon, hatched a cruel little plan, seizing one of the dogs that had been gifted to the Englishmen. According to one account, the cur was so vicious that the men had already decided they would make a dinner of it rather than keep it as a pet. The surgeon now dragged the poor hound to the boat, picked up a musket, and shot the animal dead in front of all the Dena'ina. Dr. Law wanted to acquaint the Natives with the lethality of a British firearm and, as one witness phrased it, "to prevent any evil intentions they might form."

The Dena'ina did not run away or show any sign of fear or concern at this completely gratuitous act of violence, but they seemed quite surprised by the flash of the gun and its stark and immediate results.

It was time for the possession ceremony to begin. Lieutenant King planted a staff in the sand, raised the Union Jack, and poured bumpers of good English porter all around. They hoisted their chalices high and toasted to the health of George III, His Britannic Majesty. Three of the Dena'ina tried to repeat some of the proclamations King had uttered.

Later, as discreetly as possible, King buried a bottle containing some coins and a note on parchment, composed in English and Latin, stating that the two ships had anchored here, with dates and other details. King said he put the bottle "not in a conspicuous place, but under some rocks by the side of a stunted tree, where if it escapes the Indians ... it may puzzle the antiquarians."

The fine print of the Admiralty instructions stipulated that Cook's expedition could take possession of lands only if the Native people gave their "consent," which the Dena'ina had not done. The inhabitants, watching in bemused silence, had little notion that they had been made the subjects of a bewigged monarch on the other side of the planet. Throughout the ceremony, they "behaved very friendly," thought Midshipman George Gilbert, "but had no idea what we were doing."

The rites now complete, King and his party said their goodbyes and rowed back to the ships. On the next high tide, the *Resolution* and the *Discovery* headed back toward the sea.

Today, beachcombers still hunt for a buried bottle in the sands at Point Possession—for as far as anyone knows, King's relic was never found. Most likely the Dena'ina dug it up shortly after Cook left the inlet, yet stories about the bottle lived on in the tribe's legends. For generations afterwards, small children of the village, if they found a jar, a can, or a bottle floating among the flotsam of the tides, would wonder if it was from Captain Cook's visit and would immediately bring it to their elders to scrutinize.

31   Risen in a New World

BERING SEA, JULY–AUGUST 1778

At last, an opening revealed itself, this one leading irrefutably to open waters. Cook's ships had worked past Kodiak Island, the Shumagin Islands, and the first volcanic scraps of the Aleutian chain. Sailing in thick fog, Cook's *Resolution* had narrowly averted a disaster, nearly crashing into unseen rocks. But the fogs lifted at a propitious moment, and on July 1, at a place known as Unalga Island, he saw a way through.

Cook's instincts must have been sharp that day. He easily could have missed it—or, upon seeing it, he easily could have mistaken it for yet another cul-de-sac. If he had, his mission might have been over for the season, for the Aleutian chain extends toward the southwest in a great thousand-mile scimitar of more than sixty windswept islands, stretching toward Russia's Kamchatka Peninsula. Cook scarcely knew a thing about the archipelago's configuration or its expanse, for the Russian maps were all a jumble. If he had continued to follow the chain and had missed further gaps between the islands, he would have exhausted the summer window.

But the *Resolution* and the *Discovery* came out on the other side, entering a body of water of nearly a million square miles: the Bering Sea. Cook was like a bird sprung from its cage. He was free to move north and east, the two cardinal directions of strategic interest to his mission.

It would be a long summer of rain and fog and gales, a summer of midnight sun dimmed by constant clouds. But steadily, determinedly, through the month of July, Cook traced nearly the entirety of Alaska's west coast. He poked deep into Bristol Bay (which he named), then into Kuskokwim Bay, before strong winds forced him to edge off the coast for a week and venture back out into the Bering

Sea. Angling closer to Alaska again, he passed the extended plume of silt that discharges from the delta of the Yukon River. Continuing north, he followed the great curve of Norton Sound (which he also named). There were foggy stretches where only the sound of booming surf alerted Cook, almost too late, to the presence of treacherous rocks. The ships lost sight of each other for days—the captains had their men constantly ringing bells and blasting guns to announce their location. Along the way, the crews intersected with the Yupik people—most of whom had not met Europeans before—but these were brief and cursory encounters. Cook was too busy to make many stops, moving too fast over too large a sweep of the sea, with his eye anxiously on the summer clock.

Following the arrowed, dotted lines found on modern maps depicting the route the *Resolution* and the *Discovery* took that summer, one is struck by the sheer ambition of their cruise, the hundreds of little correctional zags, the thousands of questing miles as Cook, in bad weather and on dangerous seas, traced the complicated contours of Alaska's coast. He did not find a passage, but he found and charted something unimaginably wonderful and grand, an entire subcontinent of huge extent.

He was finally doing what he loved and knew best: serious cartographic fieldwork, on a big scale, in an unfamiliar place. There wasn't time for laying down much precision—the minute details would have to be filled in by later explorers—but the general idea of Alaska, its outline, was coming into focus. For the first time in history, on charts that would emerge from this hasty summer survey, Alaska would assume the shape and proportions we recognize today.

Little by little, Cook was destroying the cartoonish maps of the Russians and replacing them with a respectable first draft of geographic reality. He was astounded at how inaccurate the so-called Stählin map turned out to be. With a mixture of irritation and outrage, Cook wondered what possibly could have induced the Russians "to publish so erroneous a map...in which many of these islands are jumbled in regular confusion without the least regard for truth." It was, he said, "a map that the most illiterate of illiterate sea-faring men would have been ashamed to put his name to."

Cook continued north, into the month of August, aiming for the Bering Strait. Much of the time, the men were eating like kings—feasting on salmon and halibut hooked fresh from the bone-chilling water, or on wild currants and berries they found growing in abundance along the shores.

Spirits were running high on both ships when, on August 3, the expedition suffered a misfortune. At half past three in the afternoon, in the middle of the Bering Sea not far from St. Lawrence Island, the *Resolution*'s beloved surgeon, William Anderson, died. Tuberculosis had thoroughly ravaged the body of the Scotsman, who was only twenty-seven years old. Cook wrote that Anderson was "a sensible young man" and "an agreeable companion," adding that he wished "it had pleased God to have spared his life."

Charles Clerke called the surgeon a "much esteemed member of our little society." He was a polymath, nearly fluent in Tahitian, and the most accomplished natural scientist on the voyage. Given Anderson's many skills, Lieutenant King thought the expedition had suffered a significant setback: "If we except our commander, he is the greatest public loss the voyage could have sustained."

After a brief service on deck, Anderson's body, wrapped in sacking, was committed to the deep. Watching the ceremony, Clerke, who was suffering mightily from the cold, had to have wondered if his own time was drawing near.

A WEEK LATER, on August 10, the nearly perpetual summer fog lifted, and for the first time in many days the sun shone brightly, turning the matte-gray seas a sparkling blue. The tundra of the Alaskan coast popped with color. "The enlivening rays of the sun," wrote Clerke, "give even this barren country a most pleasing appearance. We all feel this morning as though we were risen in a new world."

Cook had reached a headland that he guessed—correctly, it turned out—must be the westernmost point of Alaska. He named it Cape Prince of Wales, yet another of his toponyms still in use today. Having reached mainland Alaska's western extremity and marked its coordinates with precision, he had accomplished something even more substantial, giving cartographers a measurement that would inform and refine all future maps and atlases of the world: He had determined, down to the minute, the width of North America.

From Cape Prince of Wales, Cook could look west across the Bering Strait and clearly see what he believed to be the eastern extremity of Asia. The view was enchanting; Cook wanted to set foot on the Asian continent, something that in all his travels he had failed to do. And so, before sailing any farther north along the American coast, Cook decided to make a dash for the world's largest continent. It wasn't far—a little more than fifty miles—and on this calm, radiant day the sailing was easy. Still, there was a curious tag-you're-it quality to Cook's errand. He had no important agenda to pursue on the other continent, no need for supplies, and no time to contemplate staying overnight. He just wanted to go there.

The two ships passed by the Diomedes, twin islands only two miles apart that are stuck like bottle stoppers in the middle of the strait. Vitus Bering had sighted and named them in 1728. Today, because the International Date Line runs between them, these dismal rocks are also known as Tomorrow Island (Russia's Big Diomede) and Yesterday Island (the United States' Little Diomede).

Crossing over to the Asian side of the strait, the two ships slid into an inviting body of water called St. Lawrence Bay. On the bay's north shore was a small Native settlement composed of about fifteen stilted houses huddled near a creek. Although we don't know its name today, it was a village of the maritime Chukchi, an ancient tribe with an extensive range across northeastern Siberia. They were a tough, resourceful people who lived mostly off marine mammal hunting and who had valiantly resisted Russian attempts to control them. Bering, in 1728, had passed near this spot on his first voyage, but besides an occasional visit from Russian fur traders, the people of this particular village had rarely seen Europeans.

Cook was in a buoyant mood to match the cheerful weather, and he seemed eager to meet the Chukchi. The *Resolution*, with the *Discovery* close behind, made straight for the village. Here was the explorer of former times, animated, ready for something different: a new people, a new continent. But as the vessels approached the settlement, Cook could see with his spyglass that the Native Siberians were apprehensive. The women and children were scrambling for safety. "The sight of the ships," Cook wrote, had "thrown [them] into some confusion or fear, as we could see some running inland with burdens on their backs."

Still, Cook had every intention of visiting these people. He stepped into the stern of his pinnace and, accompanied by two more launches full of officers and Royal Marines, was rowed toward shore. When the three boats drew near to the gravelly beach, three Native people came down to the surf, doffed their caps, and bowed their heads. Cook and his men replied by doing the same.

But when Cook disembarked, he was confronted by about fifty Chukchi warriors, dressed in animal skins. They probably thought Cook and his men were Russians, with whom the Chukchi had long differences; earlier in the century, on orders from St. Petersburg, Russian Cossacks had mounted several attempts to exterminate the Chukchi as a people.

By all appearances, the warriors were expecting a battle, and had girded themselves for one. They had drawn their bows taut. Other Natives clutched shields and spears tipped with iron. Strewn on the rocky shore were the carcasses of a number of freshly killed dogs—"perhaps," guessed David Samwell, "as an offering to their gods to implore their assistance in defense of their country, which they must have supposed we were going to invade."

Now would have been a prudent time for Cook to read the signs and back away. He had no need to provoke these people, and they had made their displeasure with his presence clear. Instead, Cook did something peculiar. He commanded his men to wait by the boats at the water's edge. Alone, he walked slowly up from the shore toward the assembled Chukchi, with his arms outstretched to show them he came in peace and had no weapons.

The Natives, still bellicose and untrusting, could have killed him in an instant, and they showed every willingness to do so. But Cook was determined to win them over. He advanced, step by careful step. As he did, the Chukchi cautiously backpedaled, their bows still drawn. The leather quivers slung over their shoulders were full of arrows pointed with barbed bone. Other warriors, wrote Cook, held their spears "in constant readiness, never once quitting them." When Cook approached one of the Natives and laid a friendly hand on his shoulder, the man recoiled in alarm and kept his distance.

Higher along the beach stood a ceremonial arch constructed of two curving whale jawbones dug into the soil. The Natives drew a line on the ground between the two bleached bones, as though to mark a boundary that Cook was not to cross. Still, he kept moving forward, practically daring the Chukchi to attack him.

Cook had performed iterations of this risky minuet on previous voyages, in assorted beach scenarios, striding ashore alone and unarmed. It was a kind of theater of first contact he had perfected. On one level, it involved a bravery and a confidence that bordered on recklessness. Behind it, though, was an optimism. He believed cultures could be made to understand one another: If he used the right tone and body language, if he looked them in the eye and showed proper respect, the chasm between radically different peoples could be bridged.

The marines at the shore boats, however, were not so sure, and they kept their loaded muskets at the ready.

THE CROSS-CULTURAL FACE-OFF lasted quite some time, the suspicious Chukchi not knowing what to do with Cook. Finally one of the village elders stepped forward to get a better look at this strange, tall, white man who had arrived unbidden from the sea. Something in Cook's steady eye and forthright demeanor must have gained the man's trust. Perhaps he decided that Cook wasn't Russian after all. In any case, his mood softened. Cook draped a necklace of beads around the man's neck and presented tobacco to him, and he, in turn, gave Cook two fox skins and a couple of walrus tusks.

Having ascertained that Cook was not a threat, a few more Chukchi approached and joined in the trade. A few of Cook's men strode up from the boats and began to mingle, taking animal skins for beads and small folding knives. The crowd erupted in giddy laughter. Some of the Chukchi took their garments off and performed a vigorous dance to the beat of drums. Something like a carnival atmosphere was in the offing, with many of the Natives buzzing on nicotine. "Their chief demand with our people," wrote Clerke, "was for tobacco and snuff, but that sovereign herb now begins to run very short in both ships."

Cook's men were amazed and relieved. His strategy for addressing the Chukchi had worked after all. The Natives, though still cautious, welcomed Cook into the village. They treated him and some of his men to a lunch of whale meat and onions. They showed him their dwellings, their kayaks, their dog sledges, their hunting implements. Cook described the Chukchi as "long visaged, stout-made men" who "possessed a degree of ingenuity far surpassing anything one could expect amongst so northern a people." They wore the skins of reindeer, dog, and seal and ornamented their pierced ears with colorful glass beads. They spent much time at sea, pursuing whales and also walrus—which Cook referred to as "sea horses." Samwell noted a recently killed walrus that had been dragged up onto the gravel to be butchered. The Chukchi used every part of these enormous animals and carved beautiful, intricate ivory figurines from their tusks.

Cook and his men had a splendid three-hour visit in the Chukchi village. In the afternoon, when they returned to the ships, the captain wrote up his observations with a verve and a level of anthropological detail that was reminiscent of his earlier voyages. He had spent only one day in Asia, but it was a glorious one.

32   Big with Every Danger

AUGUST 1778, THE ARCTIC OCEAN

The week that followed was not only the high point of the expedition—literally, figuratively, even emotionally—but a time of epic zone crossings that happened in quick and dizzying succession. By August 11 Cook had crossed back over from Asia to North America. The same day, he passed north of the Bering Strait, which meant that he had slipped out of the Pacific Ocean and into the Arctic Ocean. The next day, he traversed the sixty-fifth parallel, the line of demarcation specified in his Admiralty instructions as the point at which he should begin searching in earnest for the Northwest Passage. Two days later, he passed the Arctic Circle. And three days after that, he crossed the seventieth parallel.

Measured day by day, it was an exhilarating flurry of attainments. Not that a "day" had any particular meaning this far north, where the summer sun never set and time seemed to blur. Cook had the open sea before him, and not a hint of ice. To his left was Asia, and to his right was the roof of North America—with a clear path over the top of it, toward home. Coasting through waters that were rich with chum salmon, pink salmon, and arctic char, Cook could see that the Alaskan landscape to his starboard was low and unmenacing—and, to his surprise, completely free of snow and ice. It was a mosquitoey country of sandy spits and lagoons rising to a sprawling, featureless tundra.

Cook had entered a vast space where no European explorer, not even Bering, had been. What's more, Cook had become history's uncontested master of the Pacific: He had ventured farther to its south than any known navigator before him, and now he had crossed that great ocean's northernmost limits into unknown waters. He was the first captain—and the *Resolution* the first vessel—to cross both the Antarctic and the Arctic Circles. Something marvelous appeared to be happening for him. The stars were aligning, the landforms relenting, the waters inviting him onward. All the signs were auspicious. For Cook and his men, the puzzle seemed to be coming together just as the Admiralty had hoped it would. "It was as if they had threaded together the whole world," wrote British maritime historian Richard Hough, and it seemed "that the secret of the earth's geography had been revealed to them in this one magic moment of suspension between the continents."

Never before during the voyage had the men's emotions soared quite so high. The crucial moment was at hand. All that they had lived through and suffered the past three years came down to this day. "We are in high spirits in seeing the land to the northward of these extremities trend away so far to the northeast, which bespeaks of an open sea free of land, and we hope of ice," wrote King. "All our sanguine hopes begin to revive, and we are already beginning to compute the distance of our situation from known parts of [Greenland]."

But, inevitably, a note of caution entered the picture. Cook noticed it first—a descent of atmospheric thickness, as though a heavy curtain had been lowered. In his journal he noted a sudden "sharpness of the air and gloominess of the weather."

Then came the next distressing sign. Off in the distance was an eerie white gleam, faintly flickering, in the low sky. Cook instantly knew what it was; he'd seen it many times in his passes through the far southern oceans. He'd possibly also seen it during his summers in Newfoundland. Under certain conditions in the high latitudes, sunlight could reflect off a large ice pack, illuminating the undersides of distant clouds. The phenomenon was known as iceblink. It was an unmistakable sign of ice ahead, a kind of early warning system that Inuit paddlers had long used to anticipate trouble while navigating near the floes.

Cook noted it matter-of-factly. "Some time before noon," he wrote, "we perceived a brightness in the northern horizon like that reflected from ice, commonly called the blink. It was little noticed from the supposition that it was improbable we should meet with ice so soon." By "so soon" Cook meant that a number of Arctic explorers on the Atlantic side were known to have sailed as far as the eightieth parallel before encountering any significant pack. Yet, dismayingly, Cook was only at the seventieth.

A FEW HOURS later, the cause of the weird light was confirmed. Cook was not a man who cursed, but the dread sight of it must have given him the temptation: Without warning, without even a few stray bergs to act as emissaries, a rampart of ice appeared ahead. Ice as far as the eye could see, crunching and groaning, reacting to the pressures of current and wind. The cold sea splashed at its edges, carving out cavities, kicking up spray. The ice, Cook wrote, was "compact as a wall and seemed to be ten or twelve feet high at least. But farther north it appeared much higher, its surface extremely rugged."

How could this be? There wasn't supposed to be ice like this in August. According to Daines Barrington's theories, Cook should be experiencing clear seas and balmy weather. Ice only discharged from rivers, the prevailing wisdom went, yet this pack seemed to be oceanic in origin and scope, gyring down from the far north, where there was supposed to be only a wide open sea. It was apparent to Cook that this ice had been subjected to tremendous forces. There were fissures and pressure ridges, blocks and crusts, anvils and hummocks. It was an expansive field grinding on itself, creating an incessant noise of shudders, ticks, sighs, and creaks. Cook thought the ice "was quite impenetrable."

Still, he kept sailing east by northeast, hoping to find an end to the pack, some way through or around it, a lead, or what the Russians called a *polynya*. On August 18, he reached seventy degrees, forty-four minutes. It was as far north as the expedition would venture, near a spot along Alaska's northern shore that Cook named Icy Cape, about 130 miles down the coast from present-day Barrow (also known by its Native name, Utqiagvik). If he could have kept on going, he soon would have passed over today's Prudhoe Bay, Canada's Yukon Territory, and then the delta of the Mackenzie River.

But Cook could already see he was in serious trouble. The ice pack was shifting, closing in toward the shore, slowly ensnaring the *Resolution* and the *Discovery* in dangerous shallows. As Cook put it, in a tone that for him sounded dire indeed: "Our situation was now more and more critical; we were in shoaled water upon a lee shore and the main body of the ice in sight to windward driving down upon us."

Cook knew he had to make a fast exit, backing out the way he came. "This was what I...most feared," he wrote, for "the wind was right in our teeth...It was evident if we remained much longer between [the ice] and the land it would force us ashore. The only direction that was open was to the southwest."

Cook made signals to the *Discovery* to follow him and then, gingerly, he began his retreat from this ever tightening vise, skirting the edge of the pack all the way. As he made his escape, he must have sneered at the Admiralty's decision, upon Barrington's advice, not to reinforce the *Resolution* or the *Discovery* for the enormous pressures of the pack. His two ships were vulnerable, and they were sailing blind. The fog grew so thick that at times the only way Cook could guess the location of the ice was by listening intently for the braying of unseen herds of walrus that were hauled up on the shelves, resting in great masses. It was a strange and nerve-racking way to navigate, but time and time again, the belching choruses of "sea horses" saved the two ships.

With the ice pressing in from the north, the temperature dropped like an untethered weight. A cloud of freezing fog descended on the ships. "The frost set in so hard that the running rigging was soon loaded with ice," wrote Lieutenant John Rickman. "The ice was seen hanging at our hair, our noses and even at the men's finger's ends... Hot victuals froze while we were at table."

BY AUGUST 21 the two ships had slipped from the trap and made it back to the safety of the Chukchi Sea, just north of the Bering Strait. But it had been as dangerous a situation as Cook had faced in all his years of sailing. Here came a turning point in the voyage that illuminated much about the stubborn and persistent personality, the Quakeresque diligence, of James Cook. Most commanders at such a moment, fresh from near disaster, would have given up. They would have conceded that the ice had defeated them and, without needing to feel the slightest hesitation or guilt, they would have turned back toward home—which, even if things went well, was still an arduous six months' journey around the Cape of Good Hope.

Cook would have been well within his rights to take such a course. He had done enough. He'd performed his duty and beyond. He had proven that most of the Russian maps were hopelessly, perilously, and probably, in many respects, intentionally wrong. Instead of finding a passage, he had found a gargantuan wall of ice, and in so doing he had shown that the idea of a reliable trade route over Canada was a fantasy of the armchair geographers. The Admiralty might elect to characterize it as another laudable achievement of "negative discovery," just like Cook's finding that the southern supercontinent didn't exist. Even if there *was* a continuous waterway, somewhere out there, somewhere up there, the menacing ice floes would make navigation impractical, if not impossible—and extremely dangerous, especially in ships not strengthened to withstand the extreme pressures exerted by the pack. What more did the Admiralty need to know? What more did his country expect of him?

But Cook didn't capitulate, and he didn't turn home. To the surprise and dismay of his men, he decided to head west, to follow the edge of the ever-shifting pack as far as he could go. He would look for promising gaps and weak spots. Perhaps the ice he had just escaped from above Alaska was only an aberration of this particular season, or of that particular sector of the sea. Perhaps if he sailed west toward Siberia, he could find a way through. Or maybe, when he reached Siberia, he could sail up and over it—over the whole continent of Eurasia and all the way back to England. It was unlikely, but he was determined to try.

So the two ships worked their way west, limning the pack, close but not too close, zigging inward when a lead presented itself, zagging outward if the pincers of ice began to close in on his vessels. He kept at this dangerous dance for many days and for hundreds of miles, passing up and over the headlands of the Chukchi Peninsula. It was an endeavor that required the utmost alertness and not a little white-knuckled piloting.

Through this period, James Trevenen was astounded by Cook's "boldness of daring and skill." No difficulty, the midshipman said, "had the power of turning away his thoughts from his object." Sailing along the ice edge like this was a project "big with every danger," he wrote. The two vessels, under Cook's care, were "so active and vigorous in their operations" that they seemed to be "actuated," as Trevenen put it, by a "sublime and soaring genius."

As he groped along in the freezing fog, staring at the impervious pack, Cook thought long and hard about the mechanics of ice formation. He was beginning to question the doctrine that sea ice couldn't freeze. An ice pack of this breadth, height, and solidity could not be explained solely as having been exhaled from a few frozen rivers. Some other factor or factors must be at work, Cook said, and he challenged any "closet studying philosophers" who would doubt him. (This snide remark was probably intended for Daines Barrington.) Lieutenant King was fascinated to watch Cook grappling with the ice and constantly refining his ideas. "Captain Cook," wrote King, "whose opinion respecting the formation of ice had formerly coincided with that of the theorists we are now controverting, found abundant reason, in the present voyage, for changing his sentiments."

DURING THE LONG westward sail along the ice, Cook kept some of his men busy hunting walrus, the very creatures whose barks had periodically been his salvation. Cook had an idea that walrus meat could provide fresh, antiscorbutic food to supplement his dwindling store of salt meat, and he thought the animals' blubber could be rendered into lamp fuel. He sent out armed men in boats to bear down on the hapless pinnipeds as they nuzzled and snored upon the ice. Pacific walrus were an unknown species to Cook's men—some Russian accounts mentioned them, but otherwise Europeans had never described them in detail. They were, wrote Ledyard, "large, unwieldy sluggish animals [that] swim very swift and are very active in water though exceedingly clumsy out of that element."

Cook was amazed by the walrus and went on at some length about them in his journal. They gathered, he said, "in herds of many hundred upon the ice, huddling one over the other like swine, and roar and bray very loud." Cook noted that, while most of the herd slept, a few would stay awake and serve as sentries. At the approach of trouble—such as Cook's hunters—the guardians would "wake those next to them and these the others, so that the whole herd would be awake presently." Cook admired how fiercely protective the female walruses were of their pups. The mothers, he wrote, would "defend the young one to the very last...whether in the water or on the ice; nor will the young quit the [mother] though she be dead; so that if you kill the one you are sure of the other."

After a protracted and bloody engagement at the ice's edge, Cook's men managed to harvest nine walruses. Then began the ordeal of towing the huge blubbery creatures, hoisting them on deck, butchering them, and rendering their fat into oil. Some of them weighed more than a thousand pounds.

The windfall of fresh meat meant that Cook's men could take a break from their grim and unhealthy diet of salted fare. Cook tried to set a conspicuous example by eating walrus with gusto—knowing that sailors could be stubbornly intolerant about novel introductions in their diet. Cook genuinely seemed to like walrus, calling their fat "as sweet as marmalade" and praising their steaks as a form of "marine beef." Clerke agreed. "For my own part," he wrote, "I think them pleasant and good eating; and they doubtless must be infinitely more nutritive and salutary than any salt provision."

But most of the men on both ships found the taste of walrus nauseating and at first refused to eat it. Ledyard called it "an ill reward" for all the work entailed in getting the meat to the table. He noted that Cook "set the example himself by making it his constant food. The people at first murmured, and at last ate it through mere vexation."

Midshipman George Gilbert had stronger words for walrus flesh. He described the elaborate procedure the men improvised to make the "disgustful" meat palatable. "We let it hang up for one day that the blood might drain from it," Gilbert wrote. "After that, we towed it overboard for twelve hours, then boiled it for four hours, and the next day cut it into steaks and fried it. And even then it was too rank both in smell and taste to make use of except with plenty of pepper."

BY THE END of August, Cook had come to a desolate spot along the Arctic coast of the Russian Far East known today as Cape Schmidt. From the point on the Alaskan side where he had been forced to turn around to here, he had traveled an astounding four hundred miles along the edge of the pack. But Cook knew he had come to the end. The ice was closing in on the shore, just as it had when it nearly pinned him above Alaska.

Cook studied the pack closely. There were a few gaps here and there, but he decided it was impossible. "It was a matter of doubt whether a ship could get through it or no," he wrote, "and I had no motive for making the experiment." He did not think it "consistent with prudence to make any further attempts to find a passage this year in any direction, so little was the prospect of succeeding." Not only that, but he feared that the weight of the ice that had been accumulating in the rigging and masts might cause the ships to break apart, or even capsize.

It was time to depart, at least for the season. But Cook decided he would remain in the Pacific through the winter and return to Alaska in the spring to try all over again to find the passage. He feared that he had arrived much too late in the boreal summer, having been detained by all his unsuccessful but time-consuming early probes along the Alaskan coastline. If he returned to the Bering Strait earlier in the season—in June or early July instead of late August—he thought he just might find the Arctic Ocean free of ice. Should all attempts fail, he had already decided he would dedicate his energies, during his trek homeward, to making a running survey of the Japanese islands, another part of the Pacific that was only hazily understood by European navigators.

But now Cook would extricate himself from these dangerous northern waters. He spread the word to his men. "The Captain informed the ship's company that he should leave the ice as fast as he could," wrote King. "Those who have been amongst ice, in the dread of being enclosed in it, and in so late a season, can be the best judge of the general joy this news gave."

Cook had to figure out where to spend the winter. "It was high time to think of leaving these northern parts," he wrote, "and to retire to some place where I could procure refreshments for the people and a small supply of provisions." His Admiralty instructions indicated that the Kamchatka Peninsula might be a good place. Its best port, Petropavlovsk, was the hub of the Russian fur trade and the locus of military and economic power, such as it was, on that volcano-studded peninsula. England enjoyed amicable relations with Russia, and, for a price, Petropavlovsk could probably furnish most of the supplies Cook needed to see his men through until spring.

But Cook didn't like the idea of his men shivering through the winter, huddled in some tiny Russian outpost with little to do but sip vodka, snort snuff, and stare at snowdrifts. In his journal, Cook mentioned the "great dislike I had to lay inactive for six or seven months, which must have been the case had I wintered in these northern parts." He wanted to spend the winter making "some improvement to geography and navigation."

After some thought, Cook announced that instead of Petropavlovsk they would be headed far to the south—to the Sandwich Isles, as he called the Hawaiian archipelago, the remarkable place they had stumbled upon back in January. His crew wholeheartedly concurred. Why overwinter in cold, foggy Kamchatka when, with just a little more effort, they could be in a tropical paradise—one that, as they had already seen on Kaua'i, was full of pigs, produce, wood, fresh water, and friendly people?

Beyond that, Cook wanted to see more of the sweep of the Hawaiian Islands, get a sense of their layout, commit more details to the chart. The people he'd met on Kaua'i had led him to understand there was an expansive chain of islands in the region. He knew the Admiralty would be interested in what was (to them) an entirely new find, and that the lords would want maps and reports from the whole cluster.

It was one of Cook's strengths to try to salvage something from defeat, and that seems to have been his thinking here. Having failed to find the Passage, perhaps he could compensate for it by doing some solid reconnaissance work in Hawai'i, an area he realized he had passed over too hastily. His men admired this trait in their commander. "If he could no longer pursue his first great object," wrote Midshipman James Trevenen, "he immediately began to consider how he might be most useful in prosecuting some inferior one."

So, on August 29, 1778, Cook turned south. As the two ships cruised through the Bering Sea, the sailors could look back over the long, hard summer with pride. "Upon the coast of America, we had seen and suffered a great deal," wrote John Ledyard. "We had, however, the agreeable reflection of having explored the greatest parts of the unknown coasts of northern and western America, and of having ascertained and fixed the exact limits to the whole of it, as well as the northern and eastern coasts of Asia."

But Ledyard hated the idea of returning to the Arctic the next summer and thought it was foolish of Cook to make a second attempt to find the Passage. "We were well convinced already of its non-existence," wrote Ledyard. "Cook alone seemed bent upon a second trial."

BOOK FIVE

Apotheosis

———◆◆◆———

A man who is deified cannot live longer, and must not live longer, for his own and for other people's sake.

—GOETHE, ON LEARNING OF
THE DEATH OF CAPTAIN COOK

33 *Pathway of the Gods*

THE BIG ISLAND OF HAWAI'I, JANUARY 1779

A sparkling bay, sheltered from the wind. A volcanic cliff, hundreds of feet high, rising over the shores, its layered rock pitted with secret caves. The water a crystalline blue-green, so clear one could see far into its depths. Moray eels and parrotfish slipping through the coral crevices. Spinner dolphins at play on the swells.

The place was called Kealakekua—the Pathway of the Gods. Approaching it from the ocean, the bay, with its massive stone walls, had the feel of a grand arena, an amphitheater. It was a place of deep *mana*. Mark Twain, who visited Kealakekua a little over a century later, would describe it as "a little curve like the last kink of a snail-shell, winding deep into the land." Over the millennia, rivers of molten lava had glopped down the flanks of the Mauna Loa volcano, depositing tongue upon tongue of sloping dark rock at the water's edge. One day approximately 120,000 years ago, a massive expanse of the Big Island collapsed into the sea here, leaving this considerable notch in the coastline and unleashing a tsunami that barreled across the channel, sweeping shards of coral more than a thousand feet up into the high country on the island of Lāna'i, which lies 120 miles away.

Kealakekua had long been the place of royal authority on Hawai'i, the residence of the god-kings. The pockmarked cliff face here was a mausoleum where many generations of the island's leaders had been entombed. When an important dignitary died, priests would conduct ceremonies to bake the body and remove the flesh from the bones; a commoner would be sent down the cliff by ropes to hide baskets filled with the late chief's skeletal remains, along with relics, deep within one of the many alcoves. After he had safely stashed the bones in a promising place, the commoner would crane his neck and flash a sign to the priests waiting above, who would sever the taut ropes, dropping the poor burial servant to his immediate death upon the stones below. In this way, the bones were protected from looting or desecration.

If Kealakekua was the seat of royal power, it was also a nerve center for Hawaiian religion and cosmology. It was the home of Lono, the god of peace, rain, and fertility. A temple—a heiau—had been built on the shores of the bay to honor this important deity and to offer him tributes, including human sacrifices.

On January 17, 1779, the *Resolution* and the *Discovery* entered this beautiful harbor on the Kona Coast of Hawai'i. A strange and magical serendipity had guided Cook to stop here at this ancient, powerful, and ominous spot. It seemed the people here were already prepared to receive Cook and his men—that, in fact, they had been waiting in anticipation of his arrival. Vast crowds had assembled, on shore and in the water—as many as ten thousand people, with more than a thousand canoes gathered around. "I have nowhere in this sea seen such a number of people assembled at one place," Cook wrote, noting that the shore "was covered with people and hundreds were swimming about the ships like shoals of fish."

What was more, the Hawaiians appeared almost deliriously happy. On land, in the water, and in the canoes, faces shone with a peculiar joy. People were singing, laughing, chanting, and beating drums, creating a din that reverberated off the lava cliffs. The energy was frenetic, ecstatic, Dionysian. Cook could tell that something special and peculiar was going on here, a revel of some kind. But he couldn't imagine what it was about.

So many Hawaiians tried to climb aboard the *Discovery* that it started to heel over from the weight and seemed in danger of capsizing. The islanders wanted the same things they had always wanted, at nearly all of Cook's stops throughout Polynesia: trade, diversion, spectacle, cultural contact, and, most of all, iron. But it felt as though everything had been ratcheted to a manic level, as though the familiar themes of the voyage had here become strangely amplified.

John Ledyard, the Connecticut American, tried to capture the wild scene: "The shouts of joy and admiration proceeding from the sonorous voices of the men confused with the shriller exclamations of the women dancing and clapping their hands, the cries of the children, and hogs that were . . . squalling," he wrote, all mingled to form "one of the most tumultuous and most curious prospects that can be imagined."

Just like the Native Kauaians of the previous year, the Hawaiians were astounded by the visitors and tried to understand them in terms of the world they knew. According to oral history, when they saw the sailors smoking, they compared them to volcanoes, and were baffled by the vapor that seethed from their mouths. They thought the Englishmen's speech sounded like the song of the ʻōʻō, a beautiful bird native to the island that is now thought to be extinct.

A special canoe, ornamented and imposing, threaded though the many hundreds of vessels clogging the bay. The canoe carried a kāhuna whose name was Koa. The holy man was very old, shriveled, and shaky, with peeling skin, probably from too much consumption of kava, but the Hawaiians seemed to fear and respect him. Koa boarded the *Resolution* and introduced himself to Cook with much ceremony, presenting a welcoming gift that included a small pig, some coconuts, and a swath of delicate red cloth, which Koa carefully wrapped around Cook's shoulders like a cape. Cook's men noted a quality of reverence that made them uncomfortable. Something in Koa's demeanor, in his voice and movements, went far beyond hospitality or the mere paying of respect. His chants were more like litanies; the encounter seemed to be invested with deep religious ceremony.

Koa invited Cook to come ashore, and the captain accepted. While he got ready, the frenzied songs and shouts of the crowds surrounding the *Resolution* and the *Discovery* continued to swell. It was bedlam now. There was an urgency behind their desires and expectations that seemed to have been building for a long time. If this was true of the Hawaiians, it was also true of Cook's men, who had endured quite a hard journey to get here from the Arctic and had been waiting for this moment for what had seemed to them like an eternity.

Lieutenant James King thought the Hawaiians "expressed the greatest joy and satisfaction, by singing and jumping, of our coming to anchor," but added, "nor was the pleasure less on our side, [for] we were jaded and very heartily tired."

TO REACH THE Hawaiian chain, the two ships had sailed south from the Bering Sea, retracing the coast of Norton Sound, but this time in much greater detail. They had made a lengthy stop for supplies at Unalaska, one of the Aleutian Islands. There, Cook met not only Native Unangans but also a small company of Russians who operated a fur-trading outpost. In late October, after several weeks at Unalaska, Cook sailed south. For more than a month and 2,400 miles without a stop, the ships plodded down the Pacific. Each degree of southward progress brought a corresponding degree of temperature rise. Slowly, the men started to loosen and thaw, working the Arctic out of their systems.

Shortly after departing Unalaska, Cook had turned fifty years old, though his birthday was not marked with any particular celebration. By the standards of navy captains, he was getting old and creaky, too old to be this far out at sea, this far from home. Apart from some terrible gales, the long trip was mostly uneventful, although one day, on the *Discovery,* a freak gust of wind flung a young Scottish seaman named John McIntosh down the main hatchway, killing him instantly.

On November 26, a lookout spotted the north coast of an island, which, they would later learn, was called Maui. The sight was stirring. The island had all the familiar features—velvety green slopes, fringing reefs, clouds swirling at its volcanic top, and a succession of "beautiful cascades," as King noted, plunging "down the cliffy coast."

But just as he was approaching Maui's Kahului Bay, just as Native canoes were launched to greet the *Resolution* and the *Discovery,* Cook made preparations to turn the ships around. He had devised a quite unusual plan to skirt the Hawaiian Islands, to ghost around them, in a pattern of contact that might be described as prolonged flirtation. He did not seek to land, but to dance just offshore, to draw the Mauian canoes toward him for the purposes of necessary trade, while keeping relations at arm's length.

Cook's refusal to land after such a long, hard voyage from the Arctic infuriated his men, all the more so because Maui was so manifestly perfect. They thought it was some torture Cook's diabolical mind had concocted. His strategy mystified his officers, and would later mystify more than a few historians as well.

Yet the rationale behind Cook's unorthodox plan made sense. His first concern, once again, was to avoid spreading venereal disease to islanders. This was not a passing concern; it was a constant theme in his journal. He knew the ship doctors were reporting fresh cases from liaisons the men had had while in Unalaska—the Russian fur trade was rife with venereal disease. Here, in the Sandwich Isles, Cook thought that if he could keep a slow cruise going just offshore, fewer young ladies would present themselves, fewer temptations would arise, and the plague wouldn't spread.

Standing offshore, he also thought, would minimize the problem of theft and diminish the chance of misunderstandings that might escalate into violence.

Finally, he reasoned, forcing the islanders to come out in their canoes would afford him a measure of control over key items of trade. Cook, a natural economist, understood the laws of supply and demand. "Captain Cook had observed that in a harbor, it was always either a glut or a scarcity, particularly in respect to vegetables," wrote King. By cruising off the coast, the lieutenant noted, Cook "had it in his power to proportion the quantity, and keep up the value of his iron."

So instead of anchoring close by in a bay, Cook would create a highly regulated bazaar at sea. David Samwell, who was now chief surgeon on the *Discovery,* called it a "maritime market," and although he saw some of the merits of the setup, he was frankly disappointed by it. "It must be confessed," Samwell wrote, "that it is rather irksome to cruise for such a long time within sight of land."

Captain Cook was trying to delineate and enforce a border, a cordon sanitaire, between these two very different worlds, to keep the relationship limited, transactional, and antiseptic. The strange enterprise worked, at least at first. The Mauian canoes arrived, with men who were ready to carry on a brisk trade, but not so brisk as to get out of control. Hogs, yams, sugarcane, breadfruit, taro, loggerhead turtles, and fish arrived each day, in manageable quantities, and in exchange the English offered the Native people daggers that the blacksmiths had hastily fashioned from Bougainville's recovered anchor and from any last vestiges of scrap metal they could find lying about the ships. Women came alongside the *Resolution* and the *Discovery* as well, and immediately made known their intentions, but Cook forbade them from boarding.

From the first day of contact off Maui, the validity of Cook's fears about venereal disease were all too clearly demonstrated. The Maui men who vacated their canoes and climbed on board seemed to know that Cook had stopped at Kaua'i and its sister isle, Ni'ihau, the previous year, and if Cook understood them, they believed that the white visitors had left behind a disease that had quickly spread from Kaua'i across all the Hawaiian Islands. The physicians examined some of the Maui men who complained of the malady, and sure enough, they were infected with gonorrhea.

These men were in "great distress," wrote King. "They had [the] clap, their penis was much swelled and inflamed." They appealed to the surgeons for help and were treated with whatever limited medicines were on board—probably mercury or silver nitrate. But many of Cook's men were chastened to realize, as Midshipman Edward Riou of the *Discovery* put it, that they had communicated "to a set of poor harmless and innocent people...an eternal and everlasting curse."

THE TWO SHIPS continued their tacking course around the northeastern coast of Maui, opening up their "maritime market" each morning and for the most part adhering to Cook's strange if exasperating plan of semi-separation. But by then another island, far larger and more dramatic than Maui, had slid into view: the Big

Island of Hawai'i. To Cook's astonishment, the summits of this formidable volcano were covered in snow—the island's inhabitants,
mused Cook, must "know all the climates from the torrid to the
frigid zones."

Hawai'i's highest point, the peak of Mauna Kea, soared into the
sky nearly fourteen thousand feet above sea level. Apart from the two
landmasses of New Zealand, this was the largest island Cook had
ever seen in Polynesia—and, in fact, it was larger than all the other
Hawaiian Islands combined. Not only was it the tallest and most
extensive of what Cook called the Sandwich Isles, but it was also the
youngest—and still growing, for it was home to several active volcanoes, with lava constantly spewing from various vents and calderas.
When measured from its base, on the deep ocean floor, to its highest
ramparts, Mauna Kea could also be considered the largest mountain
in the world. Cook, of course, could not know any of this geographical trivia, but he was so taken by the island's looming presence that
he abruptly changed his course. He left Maui, crossed the channel,
and made straight for Hawai'i.

His intention was to cruise along Hawai'i's shores in the same
on-again, off-again fashion, taking a clockwise direction around the
island. He would chart its coastline, regularly replenishing his ships
with fresh food—while keeping the women at bay.

That, at least, was the plan, but as the *Resolution* and the *Discovery*
passed by a succession of coastal villages, the canoes came out in
such numbers, and the Native women assailed the ships with such
resourcefulness and determination, that Cook eventually relented.
"It was not possible to keep [them] out of the ship," he wrote in disgust, "and no women I ever met with were more ready to bestow their
favors." With Cook's reluctant tolerance, all a sailor had to do was
wave at a particular woman waiting in a nearby canoe—whereupon,
as Samwell described the ritual, "she immediately jumps overboard
and swims to the ship, where we receive her in our arms like another
Venus just rising from the waves."

Cook's one stipulation was that any sailor whom the surgeon
determined to have the "venereal distemper" would not be allowed
to consort with the Hawaiian women. Anyone who violated this

order would be severely flogged—and ship records show that Cook repeatedly carried out his threat.

Cook would not relent, however, in his stubborn scheme of staying offshore. His officers kept wondering when they would land, but Cook remained silent on the question. In truth, for much of his circuit around the Big Island, Cook would have found it extremely difficult to land, even if he had spied a suitable harbor. The seas around these islands were rough sailing, with strong currents, huge swells, and what Cook called a "dreadful surf" that constantly smashed and frothed over the rocky coastline. "I have nowhere within the tropics met with so high a sea as we have had since we have been about these islands," he wrote.

With seas so rough, Cook's men were amazed at how effortlessly the Hawaiians swam about the ships, far from shore, seemingly without fear. To heighten the danger, the waters were sometimes infested with large sharks, but the locals appeared blasé about them. Lieutenant James Burney described a touch-and-go moment when an older Hawaiian man, swimming alongside, narrowly escaped the attack of a shark, approximately seven feet long, that crewmen could see from the decks. The shark was seen gnashing its mouth and turning on its side to take hold of the man's thigh. "Being called to and advertised of his danger," wrote Burney, "he immediately turned round and with his hand struck the shark on the head, which frightened him away."

Other marine life caught the men's attention as well. In the seas around Hawai'i, the ships frequently encountered whales—probably humpbacks that, just like Cook and his men, had migrated all the way from cold Alaskan waters to warm up for the winter. Samwell wrote of a whale "playing so near to the ship that he spouted water in our faces on the quarterdeck."

On and on, Cook continued his slow and erratic cruise around the island. Two weeks, three weeks, four weeks, five, six. They sailed by lush jungles, roaring waterfalls, and sprawling deserts smothered by lava. He seemed to have no intention to land. His men felt like prisoners, just a few miles from paradise. Their minds churned with mutinous thoughts. Ledyard captured the spiteful spirit on board,

writing, "This conduct of the commander in chief was highly repro-
bated by the people on board both ships, as it appeared very manifest that [it] was wholly influenced by motives of interest, to which
he was evidently sacrificing not only the ships, but the health and
happiness of the brave men who were weaving the laurel that was
hereafter to adorn his brows."

All the while, the seas stayed high, and during a spell of bad
weather, the *Resolution* and the *Discovery* lost sight of each other.
Separations had happened a number of times during the expedition,
but never for so long—the two ships remained apart for thirteen
days, the men of each vessel racked with worry that something catastrophic had happened to the other.

WHEN COOK AND Clerke joyfully reconnected, still off the coast
of Hawai'i, both men realized they had to land somewhere, and soon.
So much intense maneuvering, for so long, in such bad weather,
had tattered the sails, sprained the rigging, and frazzled the men's
nerves. Many of the ropes had frayed, too, so that all spare hands
were constantly occupied in knotting and splicing together scraps
of cordage. They needed fresh water and access to timber. They had
to find a port—even Cook admitted it. Only a few days after that, on
January 17, the *Resolution* and the *Discovery* coasted into Kealakekua
Bay.

It was as though Cook had stepped into an ancient script for
a cosmic pageant he knew nothing about: The two English ships
had entered the bay at the very height of a festival known as the
Makahiki, when the revelries were at a fever pitch. They had come
to the place most resonant and sacred to the god who lorded over
this festival, Lono—a place of special reverence for his cult and his
priesthood. They had arrived in the direction that Lono was always
supposed to follow—circling the island in clockwise fashion. Finally,
the tall masts of their vessels, with spars and flowing sails, closely
resembled Lono's symbolic shield, a kind of escutcheon that was
known as the long god.

So many people had viewed Cook's slow circuit around Hawai'i
that by the time the two ships turned into the sacred bay, the word

had spread across the island. Their enthusiastic reports had aroused an anticipation that was palpable, and seemed to be building toward a crescendo.

34   Approaching Adoration

THE BIG ISLAND OF HAWAI'I, JANUARY 1779

Captain Cook stepped into the waiting boat, followed by William Bayly, the astronomer, and Lieutenant James King. By now King had become Cook's right-hand man. Gradually, over the days they'd spent scouring the cold coast of North America, Cook had placed more and more faith in the fair-haired young man. He was Cook's honored assistant and sounding board. Wherever Cook went, King could usually be found at his side. He was winsome, well read and broadly educated, and a natural diplomat. He was also a perceptive writer, if at times a bit precious on the page.

The boat shoved off from the *Resolution,* and as the oarsmen pulled across the translucent water toward shore, the traffic jam of Native canoes effortlessly parted, their occupants showing a strange deference and awe. These people had been lingering in the bay all day, trailing their paddles, waiting to see this powerful man. Finally some were able to get a glimpse of him. A Native Hawaiian historian who collected some of the earliest oral history concerning Cook's arrival wrote that the people in the canoes saw "a fair man with bright eyes, a high-bridged nose, light hair, and handsome features. *Good-looking gods they were!*"

Cook's boat reached the shore, and the captain planted his feet upon the gray-black sand of Hawai'i. Koa met him at the shore and took him by the hand, with King and Bayly following. As they marched inland, the crowds prostrated themselves before Cook, chanting, *"Lono. Lono. Lono."*

The soft incantation was the only sound other than the soughing rise and fall of the surf. Priestly acolytes, their ceremonial white wands tipped with dog hair, led the procession through the crowds toward a small village and, beyond it, to the temple dedicated to the god these people apparently thought Cook was. *Lono. Lono. Lono.*

King was amazed but also disturbed by what he called "the very abject and slavish manner in which the commonality showed their respect." The people's treatment of Cook, King thought, "seemed to approach to adoration." Each time Cook shifted his gaze, the crowds within his purview suddenly dropped to the ground and covered their faces with their hands. It was an odd and slightly comical thing to watch from afar, as John Ledyard did from the beach. "If Cook happened to turn his head or look behind him," wrote Ledyard, "they were down again in an instant and up again as soon [as] his face was reverted to some other quarter." It was amusing to consider, Ledyard thought, that "this punctilious performance of respect in so vast a throng [was] being regulated solely by the accidental turn of one man's head."

Finally, the procession reached the hallowed place, an open-air court paved with lava rocks, much like the marae temples Cook had seen elsewhere in his Polynesian travels. This spot, known as Hikiʻau Heiau, was regarded as Lono's most sacred haven, his holy of holies. A rickety, scaffolding-like tower loomed over the court, beside an offering platform where a decayed hog carcass lay upon a bed of fruits and vegetables. A fire smoldered near the center of the court. Ranged around the heiau were carved wooden statues depicting a pantheon of Hawaiian chiefs and gods. Twenty human skulls grinned from perches along the fencing pales—skulls that, Cook's men would later learn, had belonged to Maui warriors the Hawaiians had captured in a recent battle and sacrificed to Lono.

(Mark Twain, who visited Hikiʻau Heiau in 1866, would describe it as "well sprinkled with pagan temples and stocked with awkward, homely idols carved out of logs of wood." He was told that it was sacred to the god Lono in olden times—"so sacred," Twain wrote, "that if a common native set his sacrilegious foot upon it it was judicious for him to make his will, because his time had come.")

The kāhuna Koa had brought Cook here to make him the centerpiece of a ceremony that would last several hours. More prayers and incantations were sung. Koa presented a small live pig to the captain. The kāhuna took the animal by its hind legs and smashed its head on the lava rocks, then held it over the fire, singeing off the hairs, until the pig finally stopped writhing.

Koa led Cook up the ladder of the tower. This was the place, closer to heaven, where the priests traditionally communicated with the gods. Standing up there, looking so awkward, Cook seemed both a dignitary and a captive—the reluctant protagonist in a ritual he did not understand. He didn't know whether he had been brought up to this platform to be worshipped or sacrificed, or if this was just part of an unusually extravagant greeting. But he acquiesced, with a patient stoicism, and not a little curiosity. Cook "was quite passive," King thought, "and suffered Koa to do with him as he chose."

The holy man recited a long string of litanies, then sacrificed yet another hog. After that, Koa led Cook on a slow procession to greet, one by one, the tall carved images representing assorted Hawaiian gods. Koa kneeled before one of the images and kissed it. At Koa's urging, Cook did the same.

Another priest mashed and chewed the pulp of a coconut and rubbed it onto a cloth, which he used to anoint Cook's head, face, hands, and arms. As attendants prepared a feast—peeling vegetables, cracking coconuts, slicing up barbecued pork—Koa and Cook slurped kava beside the fire. When the food was presented, Cook thought the pork was fetid, and politely declined to eat it. Koa, misunderstanding, thought Cook must only be hinting that the meat was too tough, so the priest took a portion, chewed it for a while as though to tenderize it, then spat it out. Koa tried to place the masticated morsels into Cook's mouth, in the way one might feed a baby. The captain knew Koa meant this as a gesture of hospitality, but he couldn't bring himself to choke it down.

Later that afternoon, after more kava drinking, the feast ended and the rites and observances were complete. Cook, King, and Bayly, no doubt still mystified by what had just happened, were led back to shore. King thought that it had been a "long and rather tiresome ceremony, of which we could only guess at its object and meaning." So much had transpired during this recondite service, and so many strange things had been uttered. Yet because the three Englishmen knew but a smattering of pidgin Tahitian, they understood only the smallest fraction of what Koa and the other priests had said. If only Mai had been here to translate, they might have gathered more nuances.

As the oarsmen rowed toward the *Resolution* in the twilight, a now familiar chant carried over the water: *Lono. Lono. Lono.*

ANTHROPOLOGISTS HAVE SPILLED lakes of ink arguing over whether the average Hawaiian that day really thought Cook was the god Lono. Some have insisted that the Hawaiians didn't view him as the actual deity but rather someone playing the *role* of Lono—an actor, in other words, an impersonator, a performer in a choreographed theological drama. Others have said that Koa and the other shrewd priests at Kealakekua must have perceived their own benefits in associating with Cook and in declaring him to be the living god. Lono's return not only made for good theater; it was also a spectacular metaphysical event that could give their priesthood, and its supporting cult, a ringing validation.

Many other explanations have been proposed to describe what was going on. The Hawaiians, some say, may have thought Cook was a commanding figure they wanted to align themselves with—it was about power and politics, they suggest, not religion. The Hawaiians knew about Cook's stop at Kaua'i a year earlier and doubtless had heard about the potent weapon his men carried that seemed to breathe fire and had instantly killed a Native man. It was a weapon they wanted to know more about—and possibly utilize in the ongoing wars with the neighboring isle of Maui.

Or the Hawaiians at Kealakekua may have just been doing what they were told to do by the great and fearful chiefs and priests who ruled over them. They had no experience with these white-skinned visitors, so maybe they thought it prudent to go along with the narrative of Cook's godhood until they could learn more about who these people really were.

The final possibility is the original one, the one that has been the largely accepted theory for more than two centuries: The Natives at Kealakekua, most of them at least, really did believe Cook was the returning god Lono. Hawaiian oral history strongly suggests so. The Hawaiian historian Samuel Mānaiakalani Kamakau, who collected stories from elders around Kealakekua in the mid-1800s, believed his research was clear on this point. "When Captain Cook appeared they declared that his name must be Lono," Kamakau wrote, "for Kealakekua was the home of that deity...and it was a belief of the ancients that he had gone to Kahiki"—a distant, dimly remembered place of Polynesian origin—"and would return. They were full of joy, all the more so that these were Lono's tabu days [the Makahiki]. Their happiness knew no bounds; they leaped for joy [shouting]: 'Now shall our bones live...He has returned!'"

Many of Cook's officers and men were similarly convinced that the crowds regarded him as the living god. In their accounts, they used words like *veneration, devotion, reverence, divinity*. Lieutenant King wrote most eloquently on the subject, insisting that the Hawaiians called the captain Lono but reserving some doubt as to whether the Englishmen fully understood the meaning of the term. "Captain Cook," he said, "generally went by this name [Lono] among the Natives of Hawai'i; but we could never hear its precise meaning. Sometimes they applied it to an invisible being, who, they said, lived in the heavens. We also found that it was a title belonging to a personage of great rank and power in the island, who resembles...the ecclesiastical emperor of Japan."

However the name Lono was parsed, the idea that Cook may have allowed himself to be treated as a deity did not sit well with some of his own God-fearing crew—nor would it sit well with many of his sanctimonious countrymen back in England. After the voyage returned home, stories about Cook's behavior at his Hawaiian welcoming ceremony would raise more than a few eyebrows. For those of a more conservative religious persuasion, it sounded distinctly as though Cook had not only permitted but *encouraged* the Native Hawaiians to bow down to him, and that he, in turn, had worshipped the pagan gods of these heathen people, kneeling before a series of graven images, even kissing them.

Christian missionaries who arrived in Hawai'i several decades later would take the story further, accusing Cook of the most egregious heresy and sacrilege. The influential American missionary Hiram Bingham, for example, would denounce Cook for his "direct encouragement of idolatry, and especially for his audacity in allowing himself, like the proud and magisterial Herod, to be idolized."

Did Cook himself think the Hawaiians had mistaken him for a god? And if so, why did he play along? Most likely he wanted to show respect for island customs—and to placate the priests. The anthropologist in him must have been a little curious about what the ceremonies meant. But the most obvious reason for his accepting the Hawaiians' seeming veneration was purely practical: He and his men needed things from these people and from this island—wood, water, protein, produce. He needed their goodwill and cooperation. If their regarding him as an august figure or possibly a supernatural being helped in that cause, then all the better.

Still, it was the first time in all his wanderings that Cook had found himself not only witnessing a Polynesian ritual but becoming the central figure in one.

IN THE mid-1980s, two prominent American anthropologists breathed new life into the old matter of whether the Native Hawaiians really believed Cook was a deity, while also hotly debating the thornier question of how the modern world can ever really know what Native people may have thought and felt in those early moments of first contact. These two academics—Marshall Sahlins, from the University of Chicago, and Gananath Obeyesekere, from Princeton—went directly at these themes, hammer and tong, for more than a decade. It became a vicious personal feud, and a cause célèbre within the cloistered world of anthropology.

Sahlins, who had a deep expertise in Hawaiian anthropology, argued that, yes, the evidence was overwhelming and irrefutable that the people of the Big Island thought Cook was Lono and that, yes, modern anthropologists generally do have the tools and techniques to figure out how Indigenous people thought back then, at such places as Kealakekua.

But Obeyesekere, arguing that his island upbringing on Sri Lanka gave him a unique perspective on the matter, begged to differ: The Hawaiians weren't naive or gullible, he argued; they knew that Cook was human right from the start. To suggest otherwise, he said, was racist, imperialist, and paternalistic, evidence of the "god complex" that Westerners felt, and perhaps still feel, in relation to supposedly primitive peoples. Obeyesekere finally vented his contempt for Sahlins's views in a book called *The Apotheosis of Captain Cook*. Some years later, Sahlins replied with his own blistering polemic, packed with intricately detailed appendices, bearing the slightly sarcastic title *How "Natives" Think: About Captain Cook, for Example*.

As is true of many academic disputes, the ferocious but largely esoteric smackdown between Obeyesekere and Sahlins probably generated more heat than light. But it did touch a raw nerve, exposing the passionate ideas and feelings that swirl around larger questions about first contact, and how two very different cultures can possibly understand one another. What transpired on that supercharged day that Cook stepped ashore at Kealakekua will never be precisely known, but surely it was a fraught and compelling moment of cultural encounter.

There is one firsthand witness whose perspective, ironically, is absent from the events of that afternoon and all that followed: Captain Cook himself. This is because his journal ends on the very day he walked ashore. The last line of his journal, from January 17, 1779, reads: "Koa took me by the hand and conducted me to a large marae. Four or five more of the natives followed." It was a most peculiar thing; the moment he stepped into the role of Lono, he went silent. Whatever else Cook may have thought and felt during the last month of his life is lost to history.

Did Cook really stop putting pen to paper? It seems highly unlikely. He'd always been a regular and diligent diarist—why would he go quiet on such a momentous day, and not resume his writings? Naturally, over two centuries, questions and conspiracy theories have abounded. If Cook kept writing his journal entries, what happened to them? Did they go missing while the expedition was still in Hawai'i, or was it officials within the Admiralty who later lost them—or, possibly, destroyed them? And if so, what compromising details could the missing pages have contained that marked them for censorship? It remains a mystery to this day, an unsettling void in the historical record.

35   Golden Days

THE BIG ISLAND OF HAWAI'I, JANUARY 1779

The fortnight that followed was a halcyon period, a time of loveliness, as tranquil an interval as Cook and his men had experienced on the whole voyage. It was as though they'd returned to all the things they loved about Tahiti. The Hawaiian people welcomed the visitors with generosity and grace. The food was tasty and plentiful, the weather balmy, the sea breeze fresh and sweet. The bay was full of fish. Manta rays glided through the water in search of plankton. Cook's crews landed without resistance to do their work—carpenters, sailmakers, blacksmiths, coopers. "Every article that wanted either to be reviewed or repaired was sent on shore, and not the least interruption was given," wrote Lieutenant Rickman. "On the contrary, no strangers were ever more hospitably received."

Some accommodating locals vacated a thatch-roofed shack near the beach and permitted Cook to use it as an infirmary to house some of the expedition's sick. William Bayly was allowed to set up his observatory tent in a fenced sweet potato garden that one of the priests then declared *kapu,* thereby ensuring that his scientific instruments would be safe from theft. The carpenters and sailmakers also made their encampment within the tabooed space and were pleased to know they could do their work without interruption.

Kealakekua was a nearly perfect anchorage, the only inadequacy being the supply of water, which stood in a stagnant and slightly brackish pool set back from the beach. As Clerke described it, "The water of the pond has so strong a twang of the salt as to be very disagreeable to the palate and I believe obnoxious to the bowels." But those willing to hike miles up into the country could find mountain streams that ran cool and fresh and tasted, said one of the Royal Marines, "like a kind of nectar to us."

The locals still viewed Cook as Lono—at least they continued to call him that and to prostrate themselves before him every time he ventured ashore—but the hysteria generally seemed to have abated. More and more of Cook's men came ashore, and the usual island pastimes commenced: Baubles were traded, friendships formed, stories swapped. The Hawaiians were amazed by Cook's men. At times they seemed to view the visitors as something like aliens— creatures, quite literally, from outer space. "They observed that the color of our skins partook of the red from the sun," wrote Ledyard, "and the white from the moon and stars." They didn't bow down to the sailors, as they did for Cook, but they did show an absolute astonishment. "It is very clear that they regard us as a set of beings infinitely their superiors," thought King, though he suspected that their enchantment would "wear away from familiarity."

The Hawaiians were astonished, too, by some of the gifts the sailors offered. Someone gave a young woman a small mirror as a present, and, like a Polynesian Narcissus, she became thoroughly engrossed by her own image. Samwell observed that she "took great pleasure in admiring herself at the glass, and it seems was much struck with her own beauty. With all the simplicity in the world, she cried out, 'A very fine woman am I!' "

Here, as on Kaua'i, the sex was rampant—on the ships, on the beach, and farther inland. Often as not, the women expected no payment in return, although a metal button or a nail was always appreciated. Other times, a man would come forward to negotiate the favors of one of his immediate family members. An only halfway disgusted Samwell wrote that "a married man here would as soon let you lie with his wife as his daughter or sister, and so long as he got the [payment] into his possession, it was a matter of perfect indifference to him on which of his family your choice might light."

As always, the preferred trade item was any form of iron. The Hawaiians' desire for it was as insatiable as it had been throughout Cook's Polynesian travels, and it remained the basis of all commerce, including the sex trade. The armorers set up their forge on the beach and continued to crank out daggers and hatchets to serve as trade items, but they were fast running out of the scrap metal they needed for raw material.

The Hawaiians, excellent swimmers all, were constantly diving beneath the two ships and, with a small tool, prying out the nails from their hulls. "These people are so eager after our iron," worried Samwell, "that they pick the sheathing nails out of the ship's bottom. And our men pull as many as they can on the inside to give to the girls, so that between them both, was there not a strict eye kept over them, we should have the ships pulled to pieces at this place."

Captains Cook and Clerke were not without some assistance in policing the nearly constant thefts. The Hawaiians had their own enforcers. In particular, there was a strapping young chieftain named Parea who would ruthlessly track down anyone who pilfered from the ships. In one instance, Parea jumped overboard in pursuit of a thief and caught up to the man. The two thrashed about underwater for quite some time, until Parea finally surfaced, gasping for air. The thief, he proclaimed, was dead. Parea had choked the life out of him and his limp form had sunk to the bottom of the bay.

Every last shard of metal was in danger of being snatched, it seemed, *except* for the intricate metal instruments Bayly used in his observatory on shore. The *kapu* that the priests had decreed upon the sweet potato field was foolproof: No Native Hawaiian, male or female, no matter how metal-crazed, would dare cross the line into the forbidden space. As a precaution, Cook had assigned a few marines to guard the tent around the clock, but he needn't have bothered. When some of the marines tried to persuade women to sneak into the enclosure and sleep with them at night, their entreaties were ignored. "No women will on any account come to them," Samwell wrote in amazement. As a bribe, they "offered a large bible to the priest to let a girl or two come in at night, but he informed them that if any of the [girls] were seen in the place, they would be killed."

THE GOLDEN DAYS at Kealakekua Bay flew by. Cook's men were having the time of their lives. They found the Hawaiians engaging, friendly, and physically impressive. They wore beautiful bracelets and necklaces made of boar tusks. They were vibrant and muscular and clean from constant swimming in the sea. At night, there were feasts and entertainments, the Hawaiians showing off their talents for drumming, boxing, and, most interesting of all, dancing—this was Europeans' first encounter with the beautiful, sinuous hula, and the descriptions running through the voyage accounts marked the hula's first appearance in literature. Cook's men had little to reply with to capture the Hawaiians' awe—except for a fireworks display that dazzled but ultimately terrified most of the locals. Rickman wrote that "with the rising of the first sky-rocket," the people "fled precipitately and hid themselves in houses, or wherever they could find a shelter."

The Hawaiian landscape was as beautiful and impressive as its people. Their terraced farms sprawled across the face of the volcanic incline—breadfruit, taro, and yams, mostly, but also turmeric, plantains, and sugarcane. Just like Kaua'i, this island was a land of plenty, with ashen soils that, with just a little coaxing, could grow practically anything. In the upland forests was a towering tree called the koa that was hard and reddish and intricately grained, something like mahogany. The islanders used its massive trunks to build their finest outrigger canoes. Today the stately koa is considered one of the most valuable hardwoods on earth.

The koa forests were alive with brightly colored tropical birds— "some of a very sweet note," thought Samwell. The surgeon bought several live specimens from the bird catchers who were constantly employed in the woods snaring honeycreepers and other species whose iridescent plumage was used in the elegant cloaks, capes, and headdresses worn by Hawaiian dignitaries. The trappers had devised cunning methods to invade the avian haunts. Having learned the calls of their prey, they lured the birds into fine nets, woven from strands of human and dog hair, that were strung up between trees. Other times, they smeared a long wooden rod with "bird lime," a tacky emulsion made from breadfruit and the viscous juice of a shrub, then they would deftly insert the rod between the tree branches until one of their feathered quarry adhered.

AFTER A FEW days relaxing on shore, many of the men grew restless to venture farther afield—after all, they'd been cooped up on
the ships for months and there was a massive island to explore, with
a mountain, wrote Rickman, "of stupendous height, whose head was
covered with snow." Crews of carpenters went on excursions into a
nearby forest, with local guides, to fell trees they needed to repair
the ship. John Gore went on a fishing expedition. John Webber paddled and traipsed all over Kealakekua, making detailed and beautiful sketches, and William Bligh conducted a meticulous survey of
the bay.

The American John Ledyard secured Cook's permission to
ascend much farther up the slopes of the Mauna Loa volcano in
the hope of reaching its cold summit. Ledyard, accompanied by the
young midshipman George Vancouver, the botanist David Nelson,
and several others, set out from Kealakekua, hiking up through networks of sweet potato farms, then entering a wild, ferny forest.

But Ledyard's party got no more than a dozen miles from the
coast before realizing the futility of the quest. The snowy heights
were just too far up there in the mist, the paths too steep and, as Ledyard complained, "impeded by such impenetrable thickets as would
render it impossible for us to proceed any further."

David Samwell, meanwhile, was spending time down at the
beach, studying the local teenagers as they played in the powerful breakers. He was amazed at how eagerly they engaged with
giant waves English sailors wouldn't think about getting anywhere
near. One amusement in particular caught the Welsh surgeon's
fascination—and led him to pen what historians of surfing think
may have been the first detailed description of the sport. Samwell
was eloquent yet also comically exacting as he tried to dissect the
surfers' movements; it was as though he didn't think readers back in
England would quite believe the astonishing athletic performances
he had witnessed unless he formally broke down the biomechanics in
minute detail. "They provide themselves with a thin board about six
or seven foot long and about 2 foot broad," Samwell wrote.

On these they swim off shore to meet the surf. As soon as they see one coming they get themselves in readiness and turn their sides to it. They suffer themselves to be involved in it and then manage so as to get just before it or rather on the slant or declivity of the surf, and thus they lie with their hands lower than their heels laying hold of the fore part of the board which receives the force of the water on its under side, and by that means keeps before the wave which drives it along with an incredible swiftness to the shore. The motion is so rapid for near the space of a stone's throw that they seem to fly on the water, the flight of a bird being hardly quicker than theirs... Sometimes they fail in trying to get before the surf... and after struggling awhile in such a tremendous wave that we should have judged it impossible for any human being to live in it, they rise on the other side laughing and shaking their locks and push on to meet the next surf... Thus these people find one of their chief amusements in that which to us presented nothing but horror and destruction.

36   A Welcome Overstayed

THE BIG ISLAND OF HAWAI'I, JANUARY 1779

The whole time the *Resolution* and the *Discovery* had been anchored at Kealakekua Bay, the men kept hearing about an all-powerful figure named Kalani'ōpu'u. He was a king who lived hereabouts and who ruled over the entire island of Hawai'i. But throughout Cook's stay, and all through the revelries of the Makahiki, this monarch was nowhere to be seen. It was said that Kalani'ōpu'u and his retinue of attendants and bodyguards were over on Maui, where the king had been prosecuting a vicious war. Rumor had it that his fortunes on the battlefield had not gone well.

But the Hawaiians insisted he would return any day now, and they seemed often to be consulting the ocean for a glimpse of the royal armada. What the Natives weren't able to convey to Cook's people was that when the king returned, the Makahiki was supposed to be over, the calendar reset. A new season would begin, one ruled over by an entirely different deity— Kūka‘ilimoku, or Kū, the god of war and politics.

Finally the day came. On January 26, 1779, on a cloudy afternoon, the royal canoes coasted into the bay, and when they did, the festive atmosphere around Kealakekua almost instantly sobered. The monarch, whose full name was Kalani‘ōpu‘u-a-Kaiamamao, was an *ali‘i nui*, a supreme high chief, whose genealogy reached back to the time of creation. He was a god-king who inspired fear and awe in his subjects. In a sense, Kalani‘ōpu‘u was the personification of the god Kū. His royal fleet was a formidable sight—Rickman reckoned it consisted of more than 150 large war canoes, powered by crews of brawny paddlers. The king's own vessel, sixty feet long, was "most superb," Rickman wrote, ornamented with "four idols, two at each end, representing men of a monstrous size, covered with mantles of feathers."

Cook's men were quite surprised when the canoes drew nearer and they were finally able to lay eyes on the king. From all they'd heard about him, they were expecting a commanding figure, perhaps a morbidly obese one, like so many of the powerful chiefs they had encountered elsewhere in Polynesia. But Kalani‘ōpu‘u was scrawny and in poor health, his gray hair thinning, his eyes tired and inflamed. He was, thought Ledyard, "an old man and very feeble." Samwell described him as "seemingly much emaciated by debaucheries…He totters as he walks along, and his skin is very scurfy and his eyes sore from drinking kava."

Despite his debilitated state, Kalani‘ōpu‘u had an unmistakable charisma—something in his demeanor and facial expressions was magisterial. "He had a countenance very expressive of conscious dignity and merit," observed Ledyard, and he carried himself like a "worthy ruler of the people." There was no doubt about the military power the king could summon. "He gave us to understand," wrote Rickman, "that he had six thousand fighting men, always at readiness to war against his enemies."

Kalani‘ōpu‘u wasted no time in greeting Cook, and when

they came face-to-face, the captain was shocked to realize that he had already met this man. While the *Resolution* and the *Discovery* were cruising off the coast of Maui on their return to the islands, Kalani'ōpu'u had interrupted his war designs and had come out in a canoe to see what the strange ships were about. The king had boarded the *Resolution* for a visit, but Cook assumed he was only some lesser chief of Maui; he had no idea this decrepit and sickly man was actually the omnipotent ruler of the Big Island, and, in the eyes of many, a god.

On the shores of Kealakekua, the king presented Cook with an exceptional gift. His attendants removed the resplendent feathered cloak he was wearing. Then Kalani'ōpu'u took the sumptuous garment and delicately wrapped it around Cook. He was literally giving Cook the shirt off his back, but what a shirt it was. The cloak was composed of deep vermilions and yellows that seemed to fluoresce in the sunlight. The king had Cook remove his tricorne hat so that he could place a beautiful feather helmet upon the captain's pate—a crested headpiece that was shaped like the war helmets of the ancient Spartans. Unlike the dowdy uniform Cook wore underneath, with its knee breeches and tired frock coat, *this* was an outfit for a commander.

CEREMONIAL RAIMENTS LIKE these were often composed of hundreds of thousands of tiny feathers, extracted from tens of thousands of birds caught by the king's armies of skilled snarers (like the ones Samwell had met earlier) who prowled the upland forests. Each cloak represented untold hours of human toil, not only on the part of the bird hunters but also by the many men and women who painstakingly cleaned, trimmed, stitched, and otherwise fussed the tufted garment into perfection. The cloak was a work of artisanship so refined, it far surpassed the smoothest velvet. It was probably the most exquisite gift Cook had received in all his travels. Some of his men thought so. "A more rich or elegant dress than this," wrote Samwell, "the arts of Europe have not yet been able to supply."

As a sartorial clincher, Kalani'ōpu'u casually laid six more feather cloaks at Cook's feet, further gifts from the bottomless royal wardrobe. It was as though the king was saying, in back of his generosity, *Look at how many well-trained peons I have, on the shore and up in the hills, doing my bidding.* Cook had nothing so wonderful to offer as a gift in return—at least not then and there—but he later would present the king with an entire chest packed with fine metal tools.

The two men would become quite friendly over the next few days. They exchanged names, in the time-honored Polynesian tradition, and greeted each other by pressing noses. Sometimes Kalani'ōpu'u would come on board the *Resolution* and dine in Cook's great cabin—often the king's young sons would accompany him and play about the ship. Other times, Cook would visit the king on shore at the royal village, a place called Ka'awaloa that was set back from the water, beyond the lava flats, at the north end of the bay.

Living in the king's court at Ka'awaloa were many lesser chiefs, whom Ledyard described as "stout, comely, and bold-looking." One of them was the king's young nephew, a shrewd and formidable warrior named Kamehameha, who would go on to become the most powerful man in Hawaiian history, uniting the islands after a series of brilliant if ruthless military campaigns.

Kalani'ōpu'u lived here at Ka'awaloa with his wives and kids, as well as several concubines. The king also had a number of *aikāne,* or male lovers. Throughout the Hawaiian Islands, powerful chiefs and kings commonly kept a harem of men for their pleasure—it was an honored tradition, and they did nothing to hide it. Some of Cook's crewmen, when they realized what was going on, were aghast at the practice. "The cohabitation is between the chiefs and the most beautiful males they can procure about seventeen years old," Ledyard wrote. "These youths follow [the chiefs] wherever they go and are as narrowly looked after as the women. They are extremely fond of them."

The king and his attendants made their way over to Bayly's observation tent to inspect the astronomical instruments there. Of course, Kalani'ōpu'u could transgress the taboo the priests had put in place—*he* was the supreme law of the land. The king seemed to think, at first, that Bayly's telescopes and other instruments were weapons, like the guns he had learned Cook's men had fired while on

Kaua'i the previous year. "They had heard what terrible things our guns were," wrote Ledyard, "and therefore were particularly apprehensive of our two telescopes that stood elevated above the rest."

Kalani'ōpu'u was also enchanted by the sextants, quadrants, and chronometers he saw, and inquired about their purpose. After much discussion of the moon and sun and the constellations in the sky, the king seemed to have concluded that Cook and his men had "so much to do with the sun and the rest of the planets," wrote Ledyard, "that we must have come from thence, or be some other way connected with those objects."

AFTER A FEW more days, Kalani'ōpu'u started to ask when Cook might be leaving Hawai'i. The queries became more and more pointed, indicating that Cook perhaps had overstayed his welcome. Hawaiian hospitality had its limits. One hundred and eighty ravenous Englishmen were starting to try the king's tolerance and to tax the largesse of his land. There were only so many hogs snuffling through the forest, only so much tuna and mahi-mahi, lobsters and crabs, to be plucked from the sea. "It was supposed," acknowledged Lieutenant King, "that we had drained Kealakekua pretty well."

But the thrust of Kalani'ōpu'u's concern was not about his shrinking resources. It was about respecting tradition and the flow of the sacred calendar. Cook may or may not have been Lono, but there was one sure test, for Lono was supposed to know his season and his place. The Makahiki was over and it was time for Lono to move on.

Cook sensed the king's impatience, and he was eager to go. His ships were ready. His men were tanned and rested. The carpenters and sailmakers had finished their work. The observatory tents had been struck. And the quartermaster had salted down and put in storage several months' worth of Hawaiian pork, more than enough to see the two ships back to Alaska. There was only one problem, a most unexpected one, at a most inopportune time: One of Cook's men had died.

His name was William Watman, a gunner's mate. He was a middle-aged man who had accompanied Cook on his second expedition. Watman had gone into early retirement at Greenwich Hospital, but he was so fond of Cook that he decided to forgo the easy life there and join his beloved captain for one last hurrah. Though Watman had been sick for some time, his death was sudden and quite a shock to his mates, for he was universally liked, known for his "good and benevolent disposition." The cause of his death was variously listed as a nervous fever and a paralytic stroke. Watman had lived a hard life and had served as a marine in the Royal Navy for twenty-one years. Cook was particularly regretful when he heard Watman had passed. The captain, too, had a soft spot for him and knew that the deceased man had a wife and family back in England.

With the full concurrence of the king and the priest Koa, Watman's body was brought ashore in one of the boats and taken to the sacred heiau. The Hawaiians dug a grave about four feet deep and layered its bottom with tropical greenery. Watman's corpse was lowered inside, and the chiefs who attended the funeral placed a baked hog beside Watman's head, and another one at his feet, with offerings of breadfruit, plantains, and bananas deposited all around the body. Captain Cook read the funeral services, following both navy protocol and the traditions of the Church of England, and the grave was covered over.

The next three nights, local priests continued to pay their respects, singing prayers and incantations, in their own tradition, beside the grave. The Hawaiians showed more emotion and solemnity at Watman's death than his own countrymen did.

The funeral had been tender and respectful, and the observances that followed showed the abiding goodwill of the Hawaiian people. The event of Watman's passing tangibly connected Hawai'i and Britain forever, for a son of England was now buried at a sacred spot in Hawaiian soil. But Watman's death must also have set in motion a train of doubts among the people. It showed, loudly and unequivocally, that Cook's men were not supernatural beings, and that Cook himself probably wasn't one either. They were as vulnerable and mortal as anyone else. The god Lono surely possessed the power to prevent the death of one his attendants. So maybe Cook wasn't Lono after all.

WITH WATMAN IN the ground, Cook hurriedly made his final preparations to leave. It was then that Kalani'ōpu'u approached Lieutenant James King with an unusual request: He implored the young officer to stay behind on Hawai'i. Kalani'ōpu'u had taken a shine to the lieutenant. He seemed to think that King was Cook's own son, and perhaps he reasoned that by adopting him as a member of his extended royal family, he could seal a relationship with England that would be strategically valuable (and maybe lead to the procurement of armaments useful in his war against Maui). Or, as King himself seems to have hinted at, was it possible that the monarch sought to install him in his stable of *aikāne* lovers?

Either way, the stubborn Kalani'ōpu'u wouldn't take no for an answer. His subordinates discreetly approached Lieutenant King and laid out clandestine plans for spiriting him inland and grooming him to be a powerful leader. "I had proposals by our friends to elope," King wrote, "and they promised to hide me in the hills till the ships were gone, and to make me a great man." But King had no intention of deserting Cook and the expedition. He suspected that all Kalani'ōpu'u wanted was to make him his personal pet—that, as King put it, he had "no better motive than what actuates children to be possessed of a curious plaything."

Finally, Kalani'ōpu'u made a direct overture to Cook, beseeching him to leave his trusted young officer behind. Cook was taken aback by the request, which seemed to border on a demand. But he didn't want to anger Kalani'ōpu'u, whose yearning for King had grown into something like obsession. Cook's reply showed that he hadn't lost his gift for diplomacy. He told Kalani'ōpu'u that, unfortunately, he needed the young lieutenant for his coming voyage to the north; but then, dissembling, he said he would circle back soon and that when he did, he would deposit King on the island. As Lieutenant King described it, "The Captain, to avoid giving a refusal to an offer so kindly intended, told them that he could not part with me at that time, but that he should return to the island next year and would then endeavor to settle the matter to their satisfaction."

Cook's solution seemed satisfactory to Kalani'ōpu'u, but just barely—the king was not used to having his wishes denied.

AS COOK PREPARED to depart, one other development may have left a sour taste in the mouths of the local authorities. Cook had noticed that the wooden fence around the heiau was in a dilapidated state. Though it was not much to look at, he realized that it would make for superb kindling for his shipboard furnaces and galley stoves. Cook sent King ashore to ask Koa if the entire fence could be purchased and hauled onto the ships. The captain seemed to have forgotten that the heiau was a sacrosanct place and failed to recognize the impropriety of his request. "I must confess," wrote King, "I had at first some doubts about the decency of the proposal, and was apprehensive."

Yet Koa seemed amenable to the idea. He refused payment for the wood, but Cook insisted that the priest accept a gift of some metal tools. Whether the kāhuna's acquiescence was genuine, we will never know. But if Koa truly believed that Cook was Lono, then he may have reasoned that the captain was within his rights to take what he wanted—after all, it was Lono's temple, expressly dedicated to him. If he wanted to dismantle his own shrine, that was his choice.

Presently, a crew of Englishmen ripped up the fence palings and ferried the load of splintered lumber across the bay to the ships. But in the process, the large wooden statues of the gods that decorated the heiau were also removed—some of Cook's men apparently thought the exotic relics would make terrific souvenirs. In Hawaiian eyes, this theft was a blatant act of impiety. Cook's men might as well have taken the Shroud of Turin. When Koa discovered that the godly figures were missing, he politely asked King if a few of them, the statues most important to him, could be returned—and they promptly were. But once again, the Englishmen had grated on local sensibilities and ignored crucial boundaries.

John Ledyard noted that a "considerable concourse of the natives" had watched these "sacrilegious depredations," as he called them, and that "the poor dismayed chiefs" were outraged "to behold the fence that enclosed the mansions of their noble ancestors and the images of their gods torn to pieces by a handful of rude strangers." In Ledyard's view, it was further evidence that the expedition had stretched Hawaiian generosity to the breaking point. "Cook," he thought, had become "insensible of the daily decline of his greatness and importance in the estimation of the natives."

The priests at the heiau had much work to do to cleanse the sacred space and prepare it for the changing of the season. On the night of February 3, Cook's men were surprised to see a large fire on shore. The structures beside the heiau, where the sailmakers and carpenters had set up their encampment, were crackling in flames. Cook's men figured the blaze was an unfortunate accident. But in all likelihood, as one prominent Hawaiian anthropologist has proposed, the priests "were ritually purifying the ground on the eve of Lono's departure."

THE NEXT MORNING, February 4, the ships in Kealakekua Bay weighed anchor. From the Hawaiians, the alohas were heartfelt, but also strained—*Thank you for coming, but thank you for leaving, too.* One could almost hear the collective sigh of relief as Cook ordered his vessels to be turned around to catch the next promising breeze—relief on both sides, really, for everybody seemed to have a sense that this visitation, this episode of cultural interchange, needed to come to an end. It had been extraordinary, intense, weird at times, and also beautiful. But it was over.

On shore, thousands of Hawaiians cheered, many of them waving white cloth, bidding farewell to the figure they still believed was Lono. Many canoes escorted the two ships out of the bay.

Before heading for Alaska, Cook planned to keep threading through the Hawaiian Islands, to see what they were about and place them on his charts, and also to locate better water than the brackish, sandy stuff they'd siphoned from Kealakekua's ponds.

For several days, the two ships eased out into the sea and worked their way up the west coast of the Big Island. But as they drew near to the northernmost tip of Hawai'i and prepared to cross the 'Alenuihāhā Channel toward Maui, a squall started to build. The channel, whose name means "great billows smashing," was thirty miles across and six thousand feet deep, and it is notorious among today's sailors for its huge swells and its powerful wind funnel. The squalls grew into a gale that left many seasick on both ships.

On February 8, with little warning of its intensity, a tremendous gust split the *Resolution*'s foremast, which was probably already rotten. It was a catastrophic problem, immediately apparent to all. Cook seethed with fury. There was no way the voyage could continue to Alaska. He had to find a place, with good timber and friendly relations, to repair his mast. He thought about trying to reach Maui but then decided to revisit the only safe anchorage he knew.

So the *Resolution* and the *Discovery* turned back, through storm-tossed seas, toward Kealakekua. "All hands chagrined," wrote Lieutenant King, "and damning the foremast."

37   The Water's Edge

THE BIG ISLAND OF HAWAI'I, FEBRUARY 1779

At first light on the morning of February 14, Lieutenant James Burney, who was on watch duty aboard the *Discovery*, gazed out over the waters of Kealakekua Bay and felt a sudden stab of worry. The cutter, a large boat that had been moored to a buoy beside the ship, was missing. On closer inspection, Burney discovered that the thick rope had been hacked with some tool. There was little doubt what had happened: Under cover of darkness, someone had snuck up beside the boat and chopped the hawser securing it, probably with one of the daggers—*pahoas,* the Hawaiians called them—that the blacksmiths had been churning out as gifts.

Burney went straight to Captain Clerke's cabin and roused him from his sleep. Clerke was feeble and desperately ill that morning, but he sprang into action, for he immediately understood how serious the situation was. He dressed as fast as he could, and by six o'clock he'd been rowed over to the *Resolution* in the small "jolly" boat to confer with Captain Cook.

The news sent Cook into one of his *heivas*. Clerke had never seen

Cook so angry. Since the *Resolution* and the *Discovery* had anchored again here in Kealakekua Bay, four days earlier, the Natives had treated the Englishmen very differently. They were surly, suspicious, mean-spirited. The atmosphere had changed. The emotional valences of the place had flipped, as though someone had thrown an electrical switch. The people couldn't understand why Lono had returned so soon. He was out of sync; it wasn't his season anymore. Not only that—the real Lono wouldn't have a broken ship, would he? And if he did, he would use his supernatural magic, his *mana,* to heal its wounds. He wouldn't go backwards. Counterclockwise was not his direction.

John Ledyard eloquently captured the profound change in mood at Kealakekua. "Our return to this bay was as disagreeable to us as it was to the inhabitants, for we were reciprocally tired of each other," Ledyard wrote. "They had been oppressed and were weary of our prostituted alliance. It was evident from the looks of the natives as well as every other appearance that our friendship was now at an end." King Kalani'ōpu'u, when he met with Cook, seemed very distressed. "He was very inquisitive, as were several of the chiefs," Burney noted, "to know the reason of our return, and appeared much dissatisfied."

Cook's carpenters had managed to unstep the *Resolution*'s split foremast and haul it on shore, and Bayly erected his astronomical tent once again. As before, Koa, the old kāhuna, had tabooed the same patch of land near the heiau so Cook's crews could perform their work in peace. But just like Kalani'ōpu'u, Koa seemed confused and troubled by Cook's return.

The Native acts of thievery, which before had mostly possessed a sportive and mischievous quality, had turned blatantly provocative and in some cases violent. For Cook, policing and punishing these acts had become a nearly all-consuming task. The previous day, a set of blacksmithing tongs had gone missing, then were returned, then promptly went missing *again.* Cook ventured ashore to chase down the perpetrator. Mad with rage, he marched along Kealakekua's coastline, sometimes breaking into a full run, sweat pouring from his brow. The locals merely laughed at him, and often gave him false information, sometimes to throw him off the scent, other times just to flummox him. The tongs were eventually returned, but not until after some of Cook's men engaged in a bruising fight with a large group of warriors. Cook's people were lucky; the melee easily could have escalated into a massacre.

And now the Hawaiians had stolen one of Cook's boats—in fact, the largest boat he had.

He would need the cutter in Alaska, would rely on it daily; the shore boats, and especially the large cutter, were indispensable workhorses, and in certain situations they could spell the difference between life and death for his crew. Cook viewed the cutter not as *his* property but the property of the Royal Navy, something naval regulations required him to do his utmost to defend and protect. Cook and Clerke surmised that the perpetrators had probably taken the vessel not so much for the craft itself but for the miscellaneous metal it contained—tackle, hooks, and oarlocks, not to mention the nails holding it together.

Cook, trying to think through his fury, began to devise a plan. Quickly, before the sun climbed over the cliffs and the Native people began to stir, teams composed of Cook's most capable men, armed with muskets, would hurry in the remaining boats toward the several villages clustered along the bay. These parties would attempt to blockade the entire curve of Kealakekua's shoreline and impound as many canoes as possible. Should a Native vessel attempt to slip through the cordon, Cook's men were to give chase, seize the canoe, and arrest its occupants. The men in the boats should not hesitate to fire upon any Native who defied their orders—and they were free to use ball instead of shot. Cook hoped the blockade and seizure of so many Hawaiian watercraft would be so crippling to the locals' livelihood and economy that they would quickly produce the stolen cutter.

THE PLAN WAS set in motion. Within minutes, boats commanded by Lieutenant John Rickman and Master William Bligh sped southeast toward the bayside villages of Kalama and Waipuna'ula to enact the blockade.

After Clerke had left the *Resolution* and returned to the *Discovery*, Cook, in his deepening rage, was seized with an extremely rash idea, one that he chose not to share with Clerke. Secrecy had often been one of the peculiar and exasperating hallmarks of Cook's command style—and in this case he surely must have suspected that Clerke would have tried to dissuade him from executing his audacious scheme.

This was his plan: Cook would personally pay a visit to the king, Kalani'ōpu'u, at the royal village of Ka'awaloa. He would greet Kalani'ōpu'u, just as he had many times before, and invite him aboard the *Resolution* for a friendly meal. But once the king was safely on the ship, Cook would inform him that he was under arrest. Kalani'ōpu'u would not be released until the stolen cutter was returned.

In other words, Cook had decided to abduct the king of Hawai'i for ransom. He didn't intend to harm him in any way, but rather to confine him on the *Resolution* until favorable results could be obtained. Kidnapping was a technique the captain had employed a number of times before on his voyages, often to good effect. When something was stolen, he would seize a person of consequence—a chief or a priest—and as often as not, the missing object would turn up rather quickly.

The difference here was that Kalani'ōpu'u was no mere chief. He had large armies of seasoned warriors around him, many thousands in number. The villagers, already agitated by Cook's hasty return, were disposed to distrust Cook and his men. These people revered Kalani'ōpu'u. Their loyalty to him was unshakable. He was one of their gods.

Cook's idea, which he appears to have dreamed up in the heat of the moment, entailed enormous risks. But he felt confident in the depth of his friendship with Kalani'ōpu'u—they had traded names, after all, in the Polynesian fashion, and had spent many cheerful hours together on his ship as well as on land. The captain saw no reason why his plan shouldn't work.

AROUND SEVEN O'CLOCK, Cook descended the *Resolution*'s gangway and stepped into his waiting pinnace. He would be accompanied by the stout Irish lieutenant, Molesworth Phillips, and nine of his red-coated Royal Marines, all heavily armed. Two more boats would be in the vicinity to offer support: a small cutter, piloted by master's mate William Lanyon, and the launch, piloted by Lieutenant John Williamson. All hands in these other boats would be well armed as well.

The pinnace was rowed straight for the tongues of lava that fronted the royal village, just a hundred yards or so from where the *Resolution* lay anchored. Cook and Phillips stepped out of the boat onto the slick rocks and marched inland, with most of the marines following behind. A number of double-hulled canoes were pulled up on the rocks, and a group of women sat together by the waterside, cheerfully eating their breakfast. Cook was greeted by the king's attendants and some of his children, who were alert and chipper in the fresh morning air. The young princes knew Cook well and seemed happy to see him. It was still early, maybe a quarter past seven, sunlight filtering through the shaggy palm fronds. The village was just beginning to rouse from its slumbers.

From his previous visits, Cook had become such a familiar sight in the royal court that his marching ashore like this did not excite suspicion among the bodyguards. There was nothing unusual about his presence, except for the early hour of his arrival and the fact that today he was armed with his double-barreled flintlock shotgun, while Lieutenant Phillips carried a musket.

The two men strode through the central pathway of the royal village. Several people prostrated themselves, apparently still certain Cook was Lono, but the captain cordially bade them good morning and guided them back to their feet.

Cook and Phillips reached the king's thatch-roofed hut, which was situated about a hundred yards from the water. For all the pomp and regalia associated with the monarch, Kalani'ōpu'u's quarters were quite modest: a simple shack on stilts, dim and shadowy inside, its entrance open to the air. Cook and Phillips waited outside while an attendant went in to rouse the king. After some time had passed,

Cook asked Phillips to duck his head into the hut and learn what was
happening. Phillips found Kalani'ōpu'u still lying on his mat, just
beginning to stir. The lieutenant indicated that Captain Cook was
waiting outside, and the king, groggy from his sleep, slowly rose and
fastened on his cloak. He stumbled to the doorway, squinting in the
morning glare.

The king seemed pleased to see the captain and showed no
sign of apprehension. Cook, trying to conceal the true purpose of
his visit, led him by the hand and made casual conversation in his
best pidgin Polynesian. He invited Kalani'ōpu'u to come on board
the *Resolution,* and the king accepted. They moved outside the royal
residence. In a neutral tone, Cook mentioned that a boat from one of
his ships had gone missing during the night, but he tried to hide the
depth of his wrath over the incident. Kalani'ōpu'u seemed to have
no knowledge of the theft. Either his ignorance was genuine or he
was a talented bluffer. Cook turned to Phillips and indicated that he
thought Kalani'ōpu'u was entirely innocent of the crime.

Around this time, the marines closer to shore and the men bobbing out in the bay in the other vessels became aware of a strange
and ominous sound emanating from the rocky palm groves behind
the royal village. They described it as a murmur, an anxious drone
that grew in volume and intensity. It was the sound, they decided, of
hundreds, maybe thousands, of angry people gathering in the distance. To them it sounded like warriors preparing for battle.

But the king seemed unaware of the sound. Cook, sensing that
time was of the essence, tugged at Kalani'ōpu'u's arm and asked
him to accompany him to the *Resolution* straightaway. The king gave
his assent, with no inkling that he was about to be taken hostage.
Kalani'ōpu'u started walking toward the pinnace, which was still
riding in the surf beside the lava flats.

It was a gorgeous, warm morning. Light swells washed over
the rocks. The bay was a deep blue, but along its rim, coral gardens shimmered beneath the surface. One of the princes, whose
name was Keōua, ran ahead, swam out to the pinnace, and excitedly
crawled aboard—he was looking forward to another day playing on
the *Resolution.*

As Cook, Phillips, and the king walked together toward the water's edge, they could see the *Resolution* lying placidly at anchor close by, the *Discovery* a ways beyond it. But the rising drone in the coconut groves at their backs had become deafening. An unmistakable tension was building in the air; even the king seemed to be aware of it.

What had provoked this outcry among the Native people was an incident that had happened, less than a half hour earlier, on the far side of the bay: Lieutenant John Rickman had fired his musket at a canoe that had attempted to break through his blockade. Rickman's gunfire had killed one of the Hawaiians—an important chief, it turned out, named Kalimu. Word of Kalimu's death had traveled quickly. Most of the warriors who lived in and around the royal village had received the news. Shocked and dismayed, they were in an avenging mood.

They were good and done with Cook and his men and their thousand impertinences. Why wouldn't the Englishmen leave? Didn't they have someplace to go? These pasty-skinned *haole* had used enough, eaten enough, taken enough, run roughshod over all manner of ways and customs. They had fornicated with the Hawaiian women and brought disease. They didn't belong here. They showed no respect. Now they were trying to make off with the god-king of this ancient island domain. If the events on the other side of the bay offered any indication, it seemed likely to the Hawaiians that Cook intended to harm the king, or possibly even kill him.

COOK AND PHILLIPS, accompanied by Kalani'ōpu'u, had nearly reached the shore when a woman ran to his side and threw herself at the king's feet. It was Kāneikapōlei, one of his wives, sobbing with emotion. She had probably heard about Kalimu's death. Shrieking and crying, she begged her husband to halt. She thought Kalani'ōpu'u was in imminent danger. As Phillips later described it, "With many tears and entreaties, she begged he would not go onboard."

Two burly young chiefs joined her at the king's side. They grabbed Kalani'ōpu'u and forced him to squat on the rocks beside a large double-hulled canoe that had been hauled up on shore. They insisted that he proceed no farther. Cook flared with rage at this—just like the king, Cook was not accustomed to having his intentions frustrated by anyone. The king, sitting in the dirt, did not know what to say or do in the midst of this strange tug-of-war, and he seemed deeply uncomfortable to be put in such an awkward and undignified position. Phillips thought he looked "dejected and frightened."

From the coconut groves, warriors began to stream out into the open—scores, hundreds, possibly a thousand. Most of them wore nothing more than loincloths, though some had vests of body armor, woven from coarse fibers and the sinews of animals. They were jostling, bellowing, shaking fists, brandishing *pahoas*. Some wielded clubs, while others blew conch shells to summon reinforcements.

Phillips, who, though brave, had a reputation for being a bit thickheaded, was only now sensing danger. "It was at this period," he later said, "we first began to suspect that they were not very well disposed towards us." Cook, for his part, seemed to cling to the notion that they were only arming themselves in a defensive posture—that is, to protect their king and prevent his seizure.

Then, in a bizarre twist, a priest appeared and tried to insert himself into the situation. The wizard began to chant a song while making an extravagant offer of breadfruit to Cook. Phillips thought he was nothing but "an artful rascal," and the two men tried to ignore him. Perhaps he was the village idiot—or perhaps the village sage—but the energy of the crowds and the sense of imminent danger had stirred him up. Maybe he understood that something terrible was about to happen. It wasn't clear whether he was trying to de-escalate the situation or to distract Cook and Phillips, to allow the gathering multitude more time to gird for battle. Finally, Lieutenant Phillips put his hand to the old man's mouth to try and shut him up, but he kept singing his lugubrious chants.

Phillips asked Cook if he should order the marines to draw up on the rocks and assume a tight battle formation along the shore so that they might execute a swift exit. Cook absent-mindedly nodded his assent but was otherwise paralyzed with indecision. He stood scowling at the roaring throngs as they assembled around him. He was strangely calm.

"We can never think of compelling him to go on board," he told Phillips, "without killing a number of these people." It was an odd thing to say, its meaning opaque. Was he saying that they *should* kill a number of these people and get on with the plan? Or was he expressing repugnance at the very idea of killing, while finally admitting that the plan had failed? Within a few moments, the point had become moot—for the bodyguards were already moving the king back into the village, out of harm's way.

IT SHOULD HAVE been obvious to Cook and Phillips that they should retreat to the pinnace immediately. Their lives depended on it. But Cook wouldn't budge. Perhaps he didn't want to lose face, didn't want to appear undignified or cowardly. Perhaps, from all his years spent among Polynesians, he thought he understood their tides of emotion, their body language, their mentality. Or perhaps, for the first time in his life as a commander, he genuinely didn't have a clue what to do. He had drifted into another world that left him insensible to the dangers pressing in on him.

But a warrior broke forward and pulled Cook from his reverie. The man charged at him and raised his *pahoa* in the air. Cook didn't miss a beat: He leveled his double-barreled flintlock and fired at him, point-blank. But because the first barrel was loaded with small shot, the discharge hadn't penetrated the thick matted armor the man was wearing. Cook's shot, Phillips thought, "had no other effect than further to provoke and encourage them, and I could not observe the least fright it occasioned."

Seconds later, another warrior came at Phillips, but the lieutenant drove him back, hitting him hard with the butt end of his musket. As others rushed forward, Cook swiveled his flintlock and fired again; this time the barrel was loaded with ball, and it instantly killed one of the Hawaiians. As far as is known, this was the first person Cook had killed in his life.

More combatants were advancing, and stones were flying in the air, hurled with great force by Hawaiians who stood farther back, armed with slings. Finally Cook gave the order for the marines standing on shore to open fire. They immediately did so, and the volley dropped a line of warriors, perhaps a dozen. The Hawaiians were shocked by the flash and report of the muskets and the nearly instantaneous carnage. There were a few moments of silence as they crouched in disbelief to try and help their fallen comrades, whose blood freely spilled upon the lava rocks.

It was during this short lull that Cook yelled out, "*Take to the boats!*" There was still time for him and Phillips to make a run for it, still a chance to reach safety. But Cook ignored his own order. He stood steadfast, glaring at his antagonists. The Hawaiians, having recovered from their initial shock at the marines' fusillade, erupted in a bloodcurdling, deafening cry—a din, said Phillips, "far exceeding all the noise I ever came in the way of."

Phillips began to backpedal toward the water while frantically reloading. Then a stone smacked him square in the head. The lieutenant was regaining his balance when one of the fighters stabbed him deep in his shoulder with a long spike. Phillips turned and shot his attacker dead.

It was at about this time that Keōua, the young prince, who had been patiently waiting in the pinnace for his father to come on board, became so alarmed by all the noise and violence on shore that he wisely decided to dive into the water and swim to safety.

In all the adrenalized pandemonium, Phillips had lost track of his captain. He had assumed Cook had made a dash for the pinnace, but he hadn't. He still stood stubbornly in the pathway, confronting his attackers, taking their insults. Cook seemed to think he could face them down through the sheer force of his stature and authority.

Some of his men also thought he had far too great an estimation of the psychological power of gunfire to scatter the Hawaiians— even now, well after events had proven otherwise. "Had Captain Cook come down to the boats directly, he most probably would have saved his life," thought the *Discovery*'s master, Thomas Edgar. "But he too wrongly thought that the flash of a musket would disperse the whole island. Led on by these ideas, he hearkened to no advice, till it was too late."

Men watching the unfolding events from the boats or, through spyglasses, from the decks of the ships could not understand the rationale, if there was one, behind Cook's delay. It seemed to proceed from a misplaced confidence, as though perhaps he thought the Native people still believed he was the god Lono and thus, in the end, they would stop short of seriously harming him. "By an infatuation that is altogether unaccountable," wrote one of his men, Cook "continued to trifle away his time on the shore."

Another factor that may have prevented him from moving to the water more expeditiously was this: Like so many navy officers, Cook couldn't swim. The water did not present itself to him as potential salvation, but rather as a danger and an impediment. The pinnace had drifted some number of yards away from the foreshore, and the sea bottom dropped off precipitously at that point into a turquoise world of coral and fish. Perhaps Cook, knowing he might drown in there, simply couldn't see an easy way to reach his comrades.

The captain turned his head and gazed toward the pinnace and the two other boats bobbing in the faint swells beyond. He raised his hand high in the air, a commanding but ultimately unclear gesture that most of the men in the vicinity interpreted to mean *Come in closer and render aid.*

The men in the small cutter piloted by Lanyon did just that. Drawing nearer, the boat's occupants kept firing their muskets as fast as they could reload, and their fusillades did help to keep the attackers at bay. But the other vessel, Lieutenant Williamson's launch, inexplicably lingered far offshore, beyond musket range. Williamson, frozen with fear, showed no intention of rowing closer to the bloody fray to help his threatened comrades. On the contrary, he had his men row *away* from shore. His main goal seems to have been to stay just beyond the range of the stones the people were hurling with their slings. Later, Williamson would conveniently claim that he had interpreted Cook's hand signal to mean *Hold your fire, it's no use—pull away and save yourselves.*

Williamson's reading of the situation, craven as it was, would later help inform the romantic view, which would become popular in England, that Cook was an authentic martyr—that in his final gesture the captain was acting humanely, that, having relinquished any thought of his own survival, he was concerned primarily for the safety of his men, but also did not want to see the Hawaiians suffer any more bloodshed. It's doubtful that this was true, but the scene had descended into such panic and confusion, it was hard to say what Cook's intentions might have been, and what his cryptic hand signal meant.

THE MARINES, STANDING beside the water near the pinnace, had fallen under attack. Many of them hadn't had time to finish the laborious, multistep process of reloading their muskets. The people on shore had been lobbing rocks at a furious rate—the missiles rained down, slamming into bodies, pelting the boats, splashing in the water around them. It was, Phillips said later, "a most miserable scene of confusion."

Other warriors had rushed in to attack the marines close in, with spears, blades, and truncheons made of wood and whalebone. They sliced Private John Harrison nearly to ribbons with their *pahoas*, but somehow he got away and was saved. Private Tom Fatchett wasn't so lucky: He was knocked down in the water and bludgeoned to death. Corporal James Thomas had just finished reloading when an attacker ran a blade through his abdomen. Mortally wounded, Thomas collapsed into a tidal pool. Then Privates John Allen and Theophilus Hinks fell dead after they were repeatedly clubbed.

The Hawaiians were closing in on all sides, as many of the marines floundered in the water. "They never gave the soldiers time to reload their pieces," said Phillips, "and would have killed every man of them had not the boats by a smart fire kept them a little off and picked up those who were not too much wounded to reach them."

Phillips had clambered over the slick rocks and jumped into the shallows when yet another rock smashed into his head, nearly knocking him unconscious—the projectile, he said, almost "sent me to the bottom." With blood streaming down his scalp, he started swimming toward the pinnace.

Then a Native man hurled a spear into Private John Jackson's face. It penetrated deep into his cheekbone, just below his eye. Yowling, Jackson tried to yank it out, but the stem broke off just in back of the spearhead. Bleeding profusely, he stumbled into the surf and probably would have drowned had Phillips not turned back to save him. Grasping him by a hank of his hair, Phillips snatched Jackson from the water and tumbled him over the gunwales into the pinnace—incredibly, the young private would survive.

Phillips swam over to Lanyon's cutter and managed to climb aboard. "All of my people," he would report, "were totally vanquished and endeavouring to save their lives by getting to the boats."

Through all of this tumult, in a prolonged dereliction of duty, Lieutenant Williamson continued to loiter in the middle distance, doing nothing. He commanded his men to lay on their oars and wait. Some of them, sickened and outraged by the grisly massacre transpiring on shore, ignored him. They grabbed their muskets and aimed at the attacking Hawaiians. But Williamson halted them, vowing that he would kill them if they defied his orders. Molesworth Phillips, observing his colleague's strange behavior from some yards away, was so disgusted with Williamson that he later said he "thought of shooting him on the spot."

AT LAST COOK turned from the wall of seething Hawaiians and began to walk toward the pinnace. He assumed a stately gait, seeming to think it was unbecoming for him to run. He carried his spent flintlock under his right arm and, with his left hand, tried to shield the back of his head from the hailstorm of stones. A few times, he turned and used his gun as a bat to fend off his assailants.

He was at the water's edge when a man separated from the crowd and raised a club high in the air, as though to test the proposition *Can we kill the god?* He retreated, then, emboldened again, lunged a second time at Cook's head. "If he be a god, he will not make a noise," an onlooker said, according to one oral history. "If a man, he will cry like ourselves."

At this, the attacker delivered a devastating blow that Cook didn't see coming. As the oral history has it, when Cook groaned in pain, "the multitude immediately shouted, 'He is no god. Let us kill him. He is only a man.'"

Stunned by the blow, Cook slumped onto a hand and a knee. His flintlock slipped from his grasp and clanked on the ledge beside him. The king's personal attendant, a man named Nu'a, crawled onto Cook's back and, riding him like a doomed animal, drew a *pahoa* from his feathered cloak. Nu'a drove the dagger deep into Cook's neck. The captain tried to scramble to his feet, then collapsed into a tide pool, where the water was knee-deep. While others held Cook's face down in the seawater, Nu'a kept stabbing him with his blade.

(Oddly, Cook's officers, eager to blame a familiar nemesis, would later observe that the French had a hand in this violence, too—for it was remembered that the ship's blacksmiths had fashioned the *pahoas* from Bougainville's melted-down anchor. Other sources have it that the blade that did the most damage to Cook was a locally made dagger constructed from the bill of a swordfish.)

Cook, struggling defiantly, managed to raise his head one last time. He was trying to yell something to his men in the nearby pinnace when, wrote Samwell (who was watching in horror from the railings of the *Resolution*), "a fellow gave him a blow with a large club and he was seen alive no more."

The scene was one of unbelievable slaughter. Blood was smeared on the rocks, muskets strewn about, wounded Natives coughing on the ground, women wailing in the distance. In addition to Cook, four marines lay dead, and as many as twenty Hawaiian warriors.

The Hawaiians fell upon Cook's corpse in a frenzy. Some cracked his head with stones or pierced his body with spears. Those who had no *pahoa* would seize the weapon of a comrade, apparently hoping to deliver a finishing blow. "As soon as one had struck him," said Samwell, "another would take the instrument out of his body and give him another stab."

Lono, if he was ever Lono, was quite dead—killed on the shore in a manner eerily reminiscent of Ferdinand Magellan's death, 258 years earlier. But Cook's attackers weren't done. Working together, a number of them hauled the captain's corpse up from the tide pool, foaming pinkish red, and dashed his head against the lava flats, over and over again.

38   The Bones of Captain Cook

THE BIG ISLAND OF HAWAI'I, FEBRUARY 1779

The *Resolution* opened up with her big guns, heaving balls into the crowd above the lava flats. Cries of terror went up, and the Hawaiians scattered into the palm groves, leaping into ditches, hiding behind thatched houses and rock walls.

The ledges where the fighting had taken place were now clear, affording a brief opportunity for the men in the boats to come ashore and retrieve the bodies of Captain Cook and the four dead marines, which lay twisted about, half in and half out of the water. But Lieutenant John Williamson wouldn't allow it. He would never be able to explain his thinking to anyone's satisfaction, but he seemed to believe the dangers were too great. The men in his boat seethed with anger at his cowardice and his obstinate refusal to do what everyone else understood was required in the situation. If they didn't go in now, the Hawaiians would move the bodies up into the country, where further indignities might be visited upon Cook's already mutilated corpse.

Williamson ordered his rowers, to their utter shock and consternation, to turn the boat around and head for the *Resolution*. As they drew beside the gangway, the young men were sobbing. One of them was heard crying out, "Our father—we have lost our father!" On board the ship, people were so stunned they couldn't speak or think. "Everyone," said the German-born coxswain, Heinrich Zimmermann, "was stricken dumb, crushed . . . nearly all of the crew shed tears."

"Grief was visible in every countenance," wrote Midshipman George Gilbert. "A general silence ensued throughout the ship, it appearing to us somewhat like a dream that we could not reconcile ourselves to."

The silence gave way to bitter recrimination. The men wanted to flog Williamson, put him in irons, have him court-martialed; others wanted to kill him. Williamson was already the most hated man on the voyage—his hot temper, fanatical ideas, and irritating personality had gotten him into trouble many times over the past three years. But what had happened this morning was beyond contempt. He had, said Zimmermann, "remained a mere spectator" to the slaughter of his countrymen. Many thought Williamson could have saved Cook, or at least saved some of the marines; and if that was unrealistic, at least he could have brought off their remains. Samwell caught the depth of everyone's rancor, writing, "To have come away at such a time as this and forsaken the body of Captain Cook cannot be thought on without feeling the keenest anguish and indignation."

Molesworth Phillips, who had already fought one duel with Lieutenant Williamson on Tahiti, would later challenge his nemesis to another one for his cowardly inaction on the day of Cook's death. Phillips's disdain for Williamson was matched only by William Bligh's. A disgusted Bligh summed up Williamson's behavior this way: "The whole affair from the opening to the end did not last ten minutes, nor was there a spark of courage shown in the whole business."

FROM THE DECK of the *Discovery,* about a quarter mile away, Captain Charles Clerke had watched the grotesque scene on shore through his glass. From that distance, with all the thrashing of bodies, he hadn't been able to make out too many details, calling it a "confounded fray." But he got the gist of it, and a boat from the *Resolution* was sent over with eyewitnesses who supplied him with the grisly facts.

Clerke would conclude that "this most unhappy disaster" was not a premeditated act on the part of the Hawaiians, but the result of numerous miscues and misunderstandings that had escalated in the heat of the moment—"an unfortunate string of circumstances," as he phrased it, "tending to the same unlucky point." And, Clerke was sad to say, his friend Captain Cook had largely brought it on himself by succumbing to his temper and firing point-blank, though the first shot was nonlethal, at a Native Hawaiian. "Upon the whole," Clerke later wrote, "I firmly believe matters would not have been carried to the extremities they were had not Captain Cook attempted to chastise a man in the midst of this multitude."

When one thought about it, what was perhaps more surprising than Cook's violent death was that it hadn't happened earlier, at some other island. For how many times had he landed upon unfamiliar shores—alone or nearly alone—a stranger, surrounded by thousands of understandably suspicious Indigenous people who could not know his true intentions? Over the years, across the hundreds of thousands of oceanic miles, how many opportunities had there been for disagreements to erupt? Cook had cheated death so many times, at so many of his anchorages, that it was a wonder he had lived this long.

Still, a flood tide of emotion must have overtaken Clerke as the news slowly sank in: dread and revulsion at the shocking manner of Cook's death, followed by an impulse to seek immediate revenge for the loss of his friend and comrade with whom he'd thrice traveled about the world. But then came a fearful realization that he, Captain Charles Clerke, was commander of the expedition now, in spite of a debilitating illness that had robbed him of his former vitality and turned him into a ghost. "I cannot help lamenting my own unhappy state of health," Clerke wrote, "which sometimes is so bad as hardly to suffer me to [stay on] deck and of course incapacitates me for succeeding so able a navigator as my honored friend and predecessor."

For so many years, Clerke had wanted to lead his own voyage, but now, in the most dreadful of circumstances, for the most terrible of reasons, he was finally commanding one. He had to summon the strength and clarity to make a series of crucial and timely decisions. This was not a moment to grieve or to strike back at the Hawaiians or to analyze the precise sequence of events that had led to the tragedy. He had to sublimate his passions and focus on supremely practical matters close at hand.

He crossed over to the *Resolution* and assumed command of the expedition's flagship, proclaiming, in turn, that John Gore, the Virginia-born American, would become captain of the *Discovery*. By this time, as nearly everyone had feared and predicted, the Hawaiians had slipped down to the shore and removed the dead bodies, along with the assorted weapons and belongings of the fallen. Men watching from the *Resolution* could see the Natives hauling the corpses into the interior of the island. Clerke realized that recovering the remains of his countrymen was going to be a tricky proposition at best.

But he would come back to that. Clerke's first order of business was to send Master Bligh with a heavily armed detail over to the tabooed area by the heiau on the south side of the bay. There, using musket fire to fend off Native attacks, they retrieved the *Resolution*'s foremast, which still hadn't been fully repaired. They also struck the observatory tent and collected the all-important instruments and chronometers. The men who had been stationed there were promptly moved to the ships—astronomer Bayly, Lieutenant King, their helpers, and the crews of carpenters, plus the small contingent of marines who had been assigned to guard them.

Clerke's idea, in essence, was to turn his two ships into floating castles and pull up the drawbridges. "The safest and best method we could take," he wrote, was "to get everything from the shore to the ships, where we could work at our leisure and [the local people] could not possibly annoy us without inevitable destruction to themselves." The carpenters laid the rotten mast lengthwise along the *Resolution*'s decks and, laboring in cramped conditions, tried to finish their work as best they could.

Clerke's next task was to send Lieutenant King ashore in a small boat to begin negotiations for the return of Cook's body. King had natural diplomatic skills and a decent grasp of Polynesian languages, but he had another mark in his favor: Some of the Hawaiians still thought King was Captain Cook's son. Those Natives who still believed Cook was Lono therefore viewed King as something like Lono's heir, his next incarnation. Clerke thought the lieutenant could capitalize on that perception, and perhaps use it as leverage.

King accepted his assignment, went ashore, and, from a cautious distance, spoke to some of the chiefs. What little he was able to learn was discouraging: They would do what they could, but Cook's body, the chiefs said, had already been taken far into the hills. Lieutenant

James Burney held a separate parley with Koa, the elderly kāhuna, who promised he would do all in his power to track down Cook's remains.

That night, Clerke had armed boat patrols constantly circling the ships, for he feared that the Hawaiians planned to cut the anchor cables, tow the ships toward shore, and attack them en masse. The patrols discovered nothing untoward, but throughout the night, the hillsides around Kealakekua crackled with bonfires and echoed with the plangent songs of the Hawaiians mourning their dead. "Women were heard howling and crying ashore," wrote Samwell, "over their deceased husbands and friends."

King guessed that some of the fires were "most probably the bodies of our slain countrymen" being incinerated. Midshipman James Trevenen agreed: "By the light of the fire, we could plainly perceive the Indians in motion about them, and this sight joined to the awful solemnity and stillness of the night now and then interrupted by their horrid cries and yellings was finely calculated to make an impression on our already agitated feelings."

THE NEXT DAY, one of Koa's lesser priests came out to the *Resolution* bearing a bundle. Clerke, with some his officers, unwrapped it in his cabin. They were sickened to find a slightly charred hunk of bloody tissue that the priest said had been cut from Cook's leg. They guessed it weighed about six pounds. "It smelled strong," said Samwell. "It was a large piece of human flesh, being the whole of the upper part of a thigh, with the bone taken out."

The priest smiled awkwardly, for he could see that Clerke and his officers were displeased. Samwell asked the priest if they had a tradition of eating the flesh of their enemies. "This," said Samwell, "he strongly denied." When Clerke inquired about the whereabouts of Cook's head and the rest of his body, the priest replied that the head had been smashed to pieces, the body and limbs burned. Cook's bones, he explained, were in the possession of King Kalani'ōpu'u, but Koa would try to collect them. Kalani'ōpu'u had departed the royal village and was in hiding. It was said that he and his attendants were living in one of the grottoes up in the cliffs behind the town, for they feared that Clerke had every intention of killing the monarch to avenge Cook's death.

The priest was not able to understand the importance the English attached to having the remains—preferably the *whole* remains, undisturbed and intact—of their dead. Hawaiian funereal rites were different from the Christian traditions of Europe. Often, particularly if the deceased person was a figure of high consequence, a formal ceremony would be held in which the body was burned and dismembered, with any remaining flesh carefully scraped away from the bones. In their view, the bones, particularly the long ones, as well as the skull were where the spiritual force, the *mana*, was located. The bones would be distributed among the high chiefs, who would preserve and honor them as powerful relics.

To this day, Hawaiian elders have insisted that no part of Captain Cook was eaten, that cannibalism was just as abhorrent to their society as it was to European cultures, and that Cook's remains were treated with the same respect and dignity accorded to the most revered chiefs of the island.

CLERKE, WHO SCARCELY knew anything about Polynesian burial customs, was nauseated by the sight of what was purported to be his former commander's flesh. Clerke wasn't convinced that the piece of meat was from Cook's body, but he promptly had it buried in the sea. That day, another series of events only deepened his queasiness as well as his resolve to seek, at the right moment, revenge against these people. A group of Hawaiian men on shore taunted Clerke's men by waving flags that, upon closer inspection, proved to be articles from the uniforms of the deceased marines.

Later, a Native man paddled a canoe over to the *Resolution* and provocatively spun Cook's tricorne hat on the tip of a stick. Laughing, the "impudent rascal," as Clerke called him, stood up in his canoe, placed Cook's cap on his head at a jaunty angle, presented his bare buttocks to the ship, and smacked them in glee. For quite some time, as Burney phrased it, the man kept "making many flourishes and antic gestures expressive of defiance and derision." Yet another of the locals flaunted the very knife that Cook had worn on his person the day before, while some of his fellows "even danced around us," wrote Zimmermann, "dressed up in Captain Cook's clothes."

For Clerke, this pageant of mockery was "too gross an insult to bear with any degree of patience." Samwell, finding it "intolerable," wrote that "the circumstance of the hat being shown to our people, like the mantle of Caesar to the Romans, inflamed them even to madness and nothing was heard among them but a cry for revenge."

Clerke tried to ignore his men's cries for retribution. The captain's "plan of operations for the present," as King phrased it, "was to stifle our resentment till we were ready for sea."

Many of the Hawaiian warriors seemed eager for another fight, yet most of the people were pleading for peace. A poignant example came in the afternoon, when two boys swam over to the *Discovery*, each with a spear in his hand. They reached the stern and, treading water, began to sing a solemn chant to the people up on deck. The men couldn't make out all the words, but the song concerned Lono and his recent death. It was a dirge, soft and plaintive and elegiac, and it went on for more than ten minutes.

The crewmen were touched by the heartfelt beauty of this serenade and invited the two boys to come on board. When they did, the youngsters presented their spears, to show that they came in peace. Samwell was moved by their forthrightness and bravery, writing, "It is difficult to guess what could induce these boys to put such confidence in us as to venture on board at this time at the hazard of their lives." Later, the boys hopped overboard, swam ashore, and were never seen again.

FINALLY THE INEVITABLE clash occurred. Clerke, alarmed that the two ships were running out of water, sent armed details under Lieutenants Rickman and Harvey to a known water source to fill as many casks as possible. To provide cover for the operation, the *Discovery* was warped closer to shore so that her cannons could be trained on the hills above.

Shortly after the watering parties landed, warriors began to harass them, lobbing rocks and tumbling boulders down upon them. The Englishmen were already in a truculent mood, and when several were injured, the hostilities escalated quickly. The men under Rickman and Harvey went on a rampage and, within minutes, committed many savage acts. They put scores of thatched huts to the torch and shot anyone who tried to escape. Villagers who stayed in their shacks were run through with bayonets. Some of the sailors decapitated their victims and stuck their heads on poles, "as trophies of their vile victory," wrote a disgusted John Law, now the surgeon on the *Resolution.*

The Hawaiian warriors fought back bravely, many of them jumping into the fray wearing mats saturated with water in order to douse what they believed was a form of fire that was being flung from the muskets.

But Native stones, spears, and body armor were no match for guns. In the end, it was a massacre, pure and simple. "Our people in this day's transactions did many reprehensible things," admitted Lieutenant King, "in excuse of which it can only be said that their minds were strongly agitated at the barbarous manner in which the Captain was treated, and they were very desirous of taking ample vengeance."

The pugnacious William Bligh, always a hard-liner in such situations, thought the atrocities were completely justified. "If this had not been done," he contended, "they would never have been brought to submission."

IN SOME PERVERSE way, Bligh may have been right: The Hawaiians, having seen the full homicidal power of musketry, cannon fire, and steel bayonets, sued for peace. They floated strips of white cloth and offered bounteous supplies of food as gifts, even sending breadfruit, piled on a surfboard, across the water. They wanted things to be as they had been before, and many times they asked when Lono would return. Many still believed that Cook was the god and that therefore he had the power to reincarnate himself. Some people feared there was a curse on Kealakekua Bay, and that Lono would come back in a spirit of retribution and spite.

The Hawaiians seemed to have received the message about returning Cook's remains. In a few days, another parcel was delivered to the *Resolution,* this one a good deal larger than the one that had arrived before. Again Clerke led some of his officers into his cabin. They opened the package, which was wrapped in a beautiful cloak made of black and white feathers.

Samwell described the bundle's contents in forensic detail. "We found in it the following bones, with some flesh upon them, which had the marks of fire: the thighs and legs joined together, but not the feet... the skull, with all the bones that form the face wanting, with the scalp separated from it, which was also in the bundle with the hair on it cut short; both hands whole, with the skin of the forearms joined to them. The hands had not been in the fire, but were salted, several gashes being cut in them to take the salt in."

Clerke and his officers had little doubt that these were, in fact, Cook's remains, but one specific feature clinched it: On the right hand was a large scar, between the thumb and forefinger, that everyone recognized. It was the scar left by the accident he had suffered in Newfoundland in 1764, when a powder horn exploded in his hand.

Everyone in the cabin stared at the jumble of bones and tissues, revolted but also relieved that they had at least recovered something. Wrote Samwell: "Such was the condition in which those who looked upon Captain Cook as their father, and whose qualities they venerated almost to adoration, were doomed to behold his remains."

Later, other items belonging to Cook trickled in—including his knife, part of his hat, and the barrels of his flintlock, which had been beaten flat in a botched effort to turn them into daggers. The remains of the four marines who had died, sources told Clerke, were spread all over the island of Hawai'i and thus were impossible to reclaim. So, too, was the stolen cutter, whose theft had led to all the violence: On the day after Cook's death, it was learned, the cutter's new owners had broken it to pieces to get at its iron.

A FEW DAYS later, on February 21, Cook's funeral took place on board the *Resolution,* whose mast had finally been repaired and rerigged. The priests, out of respect, had tabooed the entire bay for the occasion. The ships were warped out to where the water was much deeper. At four in the afternoon, the ensigns on both ships were dropped to half-mast and, in the old navy tradition, the yards were crossed.

Cook's clothes and most of his personal effects had been auctioned off among the officers or otherwise distributed to the crew, according to established custom. To hold Cook's physical remains, such as they were, the carpenters had built a modest casket for this solemn day. There was much anguish aboard both vessels, and tears on nearly every face. The *Resolution* had a dead commander and now, with Clerke, a dying commander. James Trevenen observed a "universal gloom and strong sentiments of melancholy." The men bowed their heads and, despite the horrors of Cook's death, tried to accord his burial all the decency and ceremony they could muster. Lieutenant King, looking out over the bay, thought that Kealakekua had become a haunted body of water. It was, he wrote, "a place become too remarkably famous, for the very unfortunate and tragical death of one of the great navigators our nation, or any nation, ever had."

Clerke, though seriously sick, read from the New Testament, the First Epistle of Paul to Timothy: "We brought nothing into this world, and it is certain we can carry nothing out."

With the pealing of the *Resolution*'s bell, the weighted coffin was lowered over the side and committed to the deep. Then came the booms of the cannon, every thirty seconds—ten of them. Their concussions carried over the turquoise water, past the ancient heiau of Lono, finally reverberating off the lava cliffs of the god-kings.

Many of the officers, stricken with grief and doubt, wondered how the expedition could carry on without Cook. "I had been so used to look[ing] up to him as our good genius, our safe conductor, and a kind of superior being," wrote Midshipman Trevenen.

Samwell echoed those sentiments. "In every situation, he stood unrivaled and alone," the Welshman said. "On him all eyes were turned. He was our leading star, which at its setting left us involved in darkness and despair."

39   The Long Concealed Arrangements
of the Almighty

The two ships left Kealakekua Bay on February 23, 1779. Captain Clerke, so weak and frail that he remained in his cabin, left the navigating entirely to William Bligh. The ships threaded through the Hawaiian Islands—Maui, Lānaʻi, Molokaʻi, Oʻahu, then Kauaʻi and Niʻihau, conducting, in abbreviated fashion, the running survey that Cook had said he wanted to perform for the Admiralty. In mid-March the ships left Niʻihau and turned north for the Arctic. Spirits were exceedingly glum as the two vessels inched back up to the freezing North Pacific. The men were participants in what was little more than a stillborn, pro forma mission: returning to a place they dreaded, to search again for a passage that few believed existed, to honor the wishes of a deceased captain, while knowing the search would certainly kill the moribund captain who had replaced him. In what seemed an ill omen, Cook's trusty K1 chronometer suddenly stopped working. The leaky ships lurched northward through sleet and snow and freezing rain, the men constantly having to pump and bail the holds.

In late April, the *Resolution* and the *Discovery* sailed into Avacha Bay, on Russia's Kamchatka Peninsula, and anchored near the dreary settlement of Petropavlovsk. Captain Clerke became friends with the governor there, Major Magnus Carl von Behm, who lavished the English visitors with kindness and generosity. Before heading into the dangers of the Arctic, Clerke decided to leave copies of the ship's journals and other important papers with von Behm, who offered to carry the documents westward across the entirety of Russia and on to St. Petersburg. Von Behm gave his personal assurance that the packet would reach London.

In June the ships left Kamchatka and continued northward into the Bering Sea, through the Bering Strait, and back to the northwesternmost shores of Alaska—where, in mid-July, in nearly the same place they had been halted the previous summer, the ships again encountered an implacable wall of ice. Clerke made his best effort to probe and prod the edge of the pack for any leads, but to no avail. Cook had surmised that by arriving earlier in the Arctic season, one might find ice-free seas; now that hypothesis had been proven false.

Admitting defeat, Clerke turned the vessels around and headed south for home. His condition had deteriorated to such an extent that, on August 10, he dictated a farewell letter to his old friend Joseph Banks. "The disorder I was attacked with in the King's bench prison has proved consumptive," the letter read. "It has now so far got the better of me, that I am not able to turn myself in my bed, so that my stay in this world must be of very short duration."

Less than two weeks later, on August 22, Clerke died on board the *Resolution* and was buried at Petropavlovsk. He was thirty-eight years old.

John Gore assumed command of the *Resolution*, while James King took the helm of the *Discovery*. After repairs and resupply at Petropavlovsk, the two vessels left Kamchatka on October 9 and headed south by southwest along the coast of the Kuril Islands and Japan. They passed Iwo Jima and then Taiwan, and in December anchored off the coast of China at the Portuguese colonial port of Macau. There, the astronomical sums they were able to fetch for the sea otter pelts they'd obtained at Nootka Sound gave many of the men an idea: Why not return to North America immediately and obtain *more* pelts? Greed had so completely overtaken some members of the expedition that there was serious talk of mutiny—or at least of deserting the voyage and locating another ship to take them back to the land of "soft gold." Captain Gore did his best to quash these seditious thoughts as he prepared the ships to sail onward toward Cape Town.

THE *RESOLUTION* AND the *Discovery* were still anchored at Macau when Magnus von Behm's package, after an overland trek across the steppes of Russia, finally reached the Admiralty in London. Among other things, the parcel contained a letter from Captain Clerke bearing the sad tidings from Hawai'i.

The next day, January 11, 1780, *The London Gazette* carried the news. The letter from Charles Clerke, the newspaper reported, "gives the melancholy account of the celebrated Captain Cook, with four of his private Marines having been killed on the 14th of February last at the island of O'Why'he, one of a group of new discovered islands, in an affray with a numerous and tumultuous body of the natives."

London officialdom was shocked and devastated by the report. King George III wept when he heard the news. The lords of the Admiralty were crushed, none more so than Hugh Palliser, Cook's longtime friend and mentor. In a eulogy, Palliser said that Cook's voyages "have enlarged natural philosophy, have extended nautical science, and have disclosed the long concealed and admirable arrangements of the Almighty in the formation of the globe."

Clerke's letter had not delved into much detail, so the public was left to imagine the precise circumstances that had led to Cook's demise. Many of the newspaper commentators struck a tone of righteous indignation at the "savages" of Hawai'i—some demanded a return voyage to exact revenge. But other writers made more nuanced attempts to view Cook's death from the Native perspective. "Had we been born on an island in the South Seas, we should perhaps have called [Cook] an invader, a pirate," wrote a contributor to *The Morning Chronicle.* "Were a body of strange beings, with strange arms and a strange language to land at Plymouth, we should...kill them unless they went away."

WHILE IN MACAU, Captain Gore learned the distressing news that not only was the American Revolution going badly for the English, but both France and Spain had declared war on Britain. Consequently, for the voyage home, facing the danger of seizure or attack, his two ships would remain on a war footing.

The *Resolution* and the *Discovery* left Macau in January 1780, stopping briefly south of Vietnam and then in the Sunda Strait, between Sumatra and Java, not far from the seething volcano on Krakatoa. By April, the vessels were anchored in False Bay, near

Cape Town. In early August, as the two ships approached England, contrary winds forced them far to the west. Gore had to make a long, awkward circuit around Ireland and over Scotland's Orkney Islands. The vessels plied down the east coast of Britain, finally arriving in London on October 7, 1780. The *Resolution* had been gone from England for 1,548 days. At the time, it was believed to be the longest exploratory voyage—in terms of both miles and duration—ever undertaken on the high seas. And yet, despite the odyssey's historic length, once again, not a single person on either ship had died of scurvy.

Lord Sandwich, under intense stress for the disastrous progress of the war against the rebelling colonists, was devastated by the deaths of both Cook and Clerke. For the Admiralty lord, the shock of losing his two friends on a mission he had endorsed was compounded by a personal tragedy from which he was only slowly recovering: In April of 1779, Martha Ray, his longtime mistress, had been murdered outside the Royal Opera House in Covent Garden. The murderer was Ray's jealous suitor, a man named James Hackman, who was hanged for the crime after a scandalous trial that rocked London. Sandwich retired from public life a few years later. He died in 1792 at his beloved Hinchingbrooke House.

IN 1784, FOUR years after the voyage returned home, the official published account of the expedition was finally released to British bookstores. Subsidized partly by the Admiralty, it bore the grandiloquent title *A Voyage to the Pacific Ocean, Undertaken by Command of His Majesty, for Making Discoveries in the Northern Hemisphere.* The monumental publication ran to 1,617 pages, divided into three quarto volumes, along with a separate folio atlas containing exquisite maps and eighty-seven plates of artwork. Despite its formidable heft and exorbitant cost—five pounds—*A Voyage to the Pacific Ocean* sold out in a single day. With both Cook and James King listed as its authors, the epic work was dedicated to "the memory of the ablest and most renowned navigator this or any other country hath produced."

———

AFTER RETURNING TO London, the Americans on board the ships had to face the difficult decision whether to cast their loyalties with Britain or find their way back to their native-born colonies and take up the cause against the mother country under whose flag they had been sailing for the past four years. Because he was still a member of the Royal Marines, John Ledyard was promptly sent to Canada to fight for the British in the waning actions of the American Revolution. He deserted, returned to his native New England, and in 1783 published an unauthorized account of his travels with Cook that became the first written work protected by copyright in the United States. In 1786, not done with epic traveling, Ledyard embarked on a trek of more than six thousand miles, mostly on foot, across Europe and Russia in an attempt to reach Alaska, but he was arrested in Siberia under orders from Catherine the Great. Ledyard died in Cairo in 1788, aged thirty-seven, while preparing an expedition to search for the source of the Niger River.

Ledyard's fellow countryman John Gore, on the other hand, had no interest in returning to the land of his birth. The Admiralty appointed him as one of the captains of the Greenwich Hospital, the same position Cook had vacated when he embarked on his final voyage. Gore served ten years at Greenwich. He was a popular figure among the old salts and died there in 1790.

ELIZABETH COOK NEVER remarried and remained a widow for fifty-six years. Sadly, she outlived all of her children, none of whom had children of their own. In October of 1780, the same month the *Resolution* and the *Discovery* returned to England, Nathaniel Cook, a midshipman serving on the HMS *Thunderer,* went down with more than six hundred other souls in a massive hurricane off Jamaica. He was only sixteen. Thirteen years later, in 1793, Hugh Cook perished from scarlet fever while at Cambridge, where he was studying to be an Anglican minister. Only a month after that, the eldest of the Cook boys, James, drowned near the Isle of Wight. The shock of losing her last two sons in such rapid succession proved too much for Elizabeth—it was said she spent almost three years confined to her bed.

At least, thanks to Lord Sandwich, she received a pension of £200 each year from the Admiralty, which, together with her husband's share of the royalties from the publication of his voyage accounts, saw her into old age. "She kept her faculties to the end," wrote Elizabeth's cousin Canon Bennett, describing her as "a handsome and venerable lady, her white hair rolled back in ancient fashion, always dressed in black satin. She wore a ring with her husband's hair in it, and she entertained the highest respect for his memory, measuring everything by his standard of honor and morality. Her keenest expression of disapprobation was that 'Mr. Cook'—to her he was always Mr. Cook, not Captain—'would never have done so.' Like many widows of sailors, she could never sleep in high wind for thinking of the men at sea."

Elizabeth Cook died in 1835, aged ninety-three.

MARITIME HISTORIANS BELIEVE that in 1782, a year after her return to England, the HMS *Resolution* was captured by the French while on a voyage in the East Indies. Renamed *La Liberté*, she became a whaler, and is thought to have run aground and sunk in the shoals of Newport Harbor, Rhode Island, in 1793. In 1971, a sliver of oak taken from the ship went to the moon and back with NASA's Apollo 15 mission. Coincidentally, the remains of HMS *Endeavour*, Cook's flagship from his first voyage, rest near the *Resolution* at the bottom of Newport Harbor.

FOR DECADES AFTER Cook's death, people around Kealakekua Bay still wondered when Lono would come back. A cache of Cook's skeletal remains (those that had not already been handed over to Captain Clerke) were kept in the heiau at Kealakekua. By 1801 it had been reported that Cook's bones had been moved from the temple and "were divided amongst the chiefs." Kamehameha the Great, who in 1810 united the Kingdom of Hawai'i after several decades of brutal warfare, is said to have introduced the tradition of parading a coffin containing Cook's bones around the island as part of the annual Makahiki procession. Many people still seemed to believe that Cook's personal relics contained powerful *mana*.

But American missionaries, who began to arrive in Hawai'i in the 1820s, were horrified by all this heathenish talk of bones, graven images, and strange gods. The missionaries taught the local people not to worship Lono or any of their other deities. The missionaries also impressed upon the Hawaiians the view that Cook was an idolater and a heretic. The heiau at Kealakekua began to fall into disrepair, and the royal city where Kalani'ōpu'u had lived was abandoned.

Kealakekua seemed eerily desolate when Mark Twain visited the place shortly after the Civil War. (After studying the angles and talking to the locals, he declared Cook's death to be "justifiable homicide.") Twain noted the spot where a coconut tree had been cut down by one of the *Resolution*'s cannonballs—leaving only a "monumental stump." Locals told Twain a disturbing old story about some Native youngsters who, the day after Cook died, had encountered some of the captain's visceral remains. Cook's heart had been "hung up in a native hut," Twain wrote, "where it was found and eaten by three children, who mistook it for the heart of a dog." At first Twain seemed skeptical of the story, until he was convincingly told that "one of these children grew to be a very old man, and died in Honolulu a few years ago."

Despite their conversion to Christianity, many people around Kealakekua, especially the elders, clung to their traditional beliefs. Twain was told that the people here "always expected Lono's return" and that "some of the old natives believed Cook was Lono to the day of their death."

A FEW YEARS after Twain's visit, the British consul general bought a tiny plot of land a few dozen yards back from the rock ledges where Cook was slain. Princess Likelike, on behalf of the Kingdom of Hawai'i, deeded the spot to England for one dollar. In 1874, the English erected a tall white obelisk here that stands today, on land that is still considered British soil and maintained by the Royal Navy. It's a difficult part of the bay to get to, reachable only by kayak or by a steep hike down through thickets of bamboo and sugarcane, past herds of feral goats and the volcanic rubble of the old royal village. Nonetheless, thousands of people make the trek here each year to swim and snorkel in the sparkling blue water and to see the place where Cook met his end.

The obelisk reads: IN MEMORY OF THE GREAT CIRCUMNAVIGA-TOR, CAPTAIN JAMES COOK, R.N., WHO DISCOVERED THESE ISLANDS ON THE 18TH OF JANUARY, A.D. 1778, AND FELL NEAR THIS SPOT ON THE 14TH OF FEBRUARY, A.D. 1779.

Lovely though the seaside surroundings may be, it's clear this place is contested ground—not only because of the monument's presence, or the bloodshed that happened here long ago, but because of the uneasy truth that the monument stands on a sliver of real estate still technically claimed by the British. On the day I visited, the obelisk had recently been vandalized—a frequent occurrence, I learned. Protesters had dribbled and splotched the monument's substantial plinth, Jackson Pollock style, with copious amounts of blood-red paint, and just above Cook's name someone had written, in bold letters: YOU ARE ON NATIVE LAND.

He went like one that hath been stunn'd
And is of sense forlorn:
A sadder and a wiser man
He rose the morrow morn.

—Samuel Taylor Coleridge, *The Rime
of the Ancient Mariner*

Epilogue: Lono's Tears

KEALAKEKUA BAY

Lono had been around since the world was born. He was older than time itself. With a large net, he had pulled up the sun and the moon from the ocean depths and placed them in the sky. He was a gifted athlete and would slide down to earth on a rainbow from time to time to perform supernatural feats of strength and prowess—like sprinting up to the frigid summit of the volcano and hauling down to the sultry shores a massive snowball before it could melt.

He was the god of music and of the rains. He made things germinate and he made things grow. He was the people's deity, the fire-keeper, the virile-pig god, the god of spear-throwing and lovemaking. He was mercurial, distracted. Arrogant at times, at other times brooding with doubts and regrets. He was mostly peaceful, and yet he had a temper, sometimes a violent one.

This was how he had lost his wife, Kaikilani. She was young and mortal, and so beautiful that he often grew sick with jealousy. One day, believing that Kaikilani had been unfaithful and not remembering his own strength as it related to mortals, he killed her in a fit of rage.

Lonesome and distraught, Lono tried to repent for his violent act. That's how the Makahiki came to be. To honor Kaikilani's memory, he created a four-month festival timed to the start of the rainy season and the appearance of the Pleiades star cluster in the night sky. Hawaiians were told to halt all unnecessary labor and set aside their arms, for war was *kapu*. It was a time of feasts, songs, and sporting contests—a time of renewal and redemption.

After the Makahiki had been established to his satisfaction in those long-ago times, Lono built a great canoe and prepared for a long journey. He would be gone for many eons, but he vowed to come back to Hawai'i in the distant future. Then he and his beautiful vessel vanished over the horizon.

For centuries, every winter the Makahiki was held. When the seasonal showers came, Hawaiians said they were Lono's tears—he was still consumed with guilt, they said, still grieving for his bride, living a melancholy life of exile on the high seas.

At the start of the festival each year, Lono's priests led a pilgrimage along the entire seacoast of Hawai'i. The procession always began and ended at the heiau at Kealakekua Bay, and always moved in a clockwise direction. Marching from village to village, the priests collected the season's tributes—pigs, yams, turtles, feathers, taro, breadfruit, coconuts, sugarcane.

As they walked, an attendant carried an emblematic shield that was universally recognized as Lono's symbol: a tall pole with a crossbar, festooned with banners of white cloth. A large outrigger canoe, piled high with offerings, was towed from the bay and set adrift in the open ocean, in the hope that it might reach Lono, wherever he might be wandering.

Year after year, the priests prophesied that the day of his return was coming. When Lono approached, they said, he would circle the island in his formidable canoe, with the land always at his right.

Then, at last, he would glide into Kealakekua Bay—reuniting with his people, at his exalted place. His eternal home.

Acknowledgments

Writing about a far-flung journey requires many far-flung journeys of one's own, and certainly this project involved more miles of travel than any of my other books, with so many kind people to thank for helping me along the way. For simplicity's sake, since this was a project of many stops, I will sing my songs of thanksgiving by region and by country.

United Kingdom: I'm most grateful for the friendship of the extraordinarily knowledgeable Cook scholar and historian Cliff Thornton, a former president of the Captain Cook Society, who helped me in a thousand ways as I burrowed into this sprawling subject. Cliff cheerfully disabused me of many a misconception, helped me run down countless pieces of information no matter how extraneous, and read my manuscript with vigilance and enthusiasm. It was through Cliff that I became acquainted with the Captain Cook Society (I'm now a card-carrying member). This stalwart organization maintains an exceptional website (www.captaincooksociety.com) and regularly publishes an erudite newsletter, *Cook's Log,* which proved to be an indispensable resource throughout this project. In Cook's boyhood hometown of Whitby, I had the privilege to get to know another esteemed Cook scholar, Dr. Sophie Forgan, a long-time trustee of the world-class Captain Cook Memorial Museum. My thanks to Sophie for generously commenting on my manuscript. Thanks also to anthropologist and historian Nicholas Thomas of the Museum of Archaeology at Cambridge, to Nigel Rigby of the National Maritime Museum at Greenwich, and to the good folks at Hinchingbrooke House, Lord Sandwich's old estate in Huntingdon, Cambridgeshire. Richard Connaughton, author of *Omai: The Prince Who Never Was,* gave freely of his time and perspectives, as did Frank McLynn, author of *Captain Cook: Master of the Seas.* My dear friends John and Tanya Young were gracious hosts, as was my editor at Penguin in London, Rowland White. Thanks also to Ruth Rogers of the River Cafe.

New Zealand and Tasmania: In Hamilton, I had the good fortune to meet John Robson, a luminary of the Captain Cook Society and author of many papers and books, including *Captain Cook's World* and the *Captain Cook Encyclopedia.* Sue Hirst, Special Collections Librarian at the J. C. Beaglehole Room, Victoria University of Wellington, was tremendously helpful. Thanks to our friends Jill Cooper Udall and Tom Udall, U.S. Ambassador to New Zealand and Samoa. Thanks also to Rucky and Leslie Barclay, as well as Rodney Russ of Strannik Ocean Voyages Ltd., in Christchurch. My gratitude to Christina Thompson, author of *Sea People* and editor of the *Harvard Review,* for her insights on New Zealand and the Māori. In Tasmania, Don Defenderfer offered perceptive thoughts and comments.

French Polynesia: Frank Murphy, executive director of the Tetiaroa Society, was a generous host and resource throughout this project. Hinano Teavai-Murphy, an expert on Polynesian history and ethnobotany and a cultural consultant for the Disney animation film *Moana,* provided valuable knowledge. On Tetiaroa, conservation biologist David Ringler-Veillon shared his research into the problems of invasive species and their devastating effect on island biodiversity. On Huahine, Dorothy Levin-Lubin squired me around the island, tapping into her rich understanding of Huahine's cultural heritage, natural history, and lore. On Raiatea, my gratitude to the caretakers of the marae complex at Taputapuātea, a UNESCO World Heritage Site. Special thanks to Susan and Bill Banowsky, as well as Cindy and Britton "Captain Crunch" Banowsky, for arranging an adventurous cruise through the Society Islands by catamaran while Covid descended upon the world.

The Pacific Northwest, British Columbia, and Alaska: A tip of the hat to Dave Nicandri, former director of the Washington State Historical Society and author of the excellent book *Captain Cook Rediscovered,* for his ardent insights and companionship during an excursion to Cape Flattery. Jim Barnett, author of *Captain Cook in Alaska,* was an energetic sounding board and a keen reader of my manuscript. My gratitude to the ever-perceptive Professor Jim Warren in Fairbanks for his thoughts on these pages. Special thanks to Harry Stern of the University of Washington's Polar Science Center and to the late Arctic research scientist Kevin Wood. In Seattle, my appreciation to Bill Messing and Luisa Perticucci. In Vancouver, exploration historian and maritime scholar Robin Inglis gave generously of his time and graciously read sections of the manuscript. Karen Duffek of the Museum of Anthropology at UBC was enormously helpful. For their warm hospitality, I thank Nora Vaillant and John Vaillant, award-winning author of *The Golden Spruce* and *The Tiger*. On Vancouver Island, my appreciation to the wilderness guides at the remote Moutcha Bay Resort on Nootka Sound, and to Yuquot elder Ray Williams, the very last First Nations man living on Nootka Island, who shared fascinating stories about this historic seaside village.

Hawai'i: On O'ahu, the acclaimed Polynesian anthropologist and archaeologist Patrick Kirch cordially met with me to discuss this project. Thanks also to the curators at the Bishop Museum in Honolulu, and to Marcus and Emma Boland for generously offering their guest house. Hawaiian art historian and artifact dealer Mark Blackburn kindly showed me a small sampling from his trove of Cook artifacts. On Maui, I thank antiquarian book dealer Lou Weinstein and his wife Laura for their hospitality and for sharing their extensive library of vintage titles of exploration history and early Hawaiiana. On the Big Island, University of Hawai'i botany professor Orlo Steele was an exuberant and gracious guide. Special thanks to Big Island historian Maile Melrose, author Nancee Cline, Hawai'i Tourism Authority CEO John de Fries, and the irrepressible Hawaiian enthusiast and musician Jack Kotz. Hinahina Gray offered valuable insights into native Hawaiian culture. Finally, my gratitude to Chris and Patti Webster for a delightful stay in their gorgeous home overlooking Kealakekua Bay.

The late nonfiction writer Tony Horwitz, Pulitzer Prize–winning author of a beloved book on Captain Cook titled *Blue Latitudes,* gave early inspiration to this project and was collegial in sharing his thoughts and insights. After his untimely passing in 2019, his wife, the novelist Geraldine Brooks, invited me to come peruse and abscond with titles from Tony's extensive Cook library at their home on Martha's Vineyard. I thank Geraldine for her welcoming spirit.

While working on this book, I was fortunate to be offered a writer's residency by the Aspen Institute's "Aspen Words" program. My fruitful stint in Colorado was made possible by Isa Catto, Daniel Shaw, Marie Chan, Elizabeth Nix, Caroline Tory, and Ellie Scott. Thanks also to photographer Pete McBride and Jamie and Patty Morris.

My friends and colleagues at *Outside* magazine supported this project by subsidizing my trip to Tahiti to write a feature about the nearby atoll of Tetiaroa, a Pacific research laboratory and home of the world-famous Brando resort. My thanks to *Outside* editors Mary Turner, Chis Keyes, and Alex Heard. My friends Mark Bryant and Laura Hohnhold were instrumental in helping me publish an early e-book adaptation from this work for Scribd Originals, a project titled "The Exotic."

In Virginia, big thanks to Jim and Toni Brown for kindly offering their guest house as an occasional refuge and writing garret. At home in Santa Fe, I first must thank McCall Sides for his well-honed digital editing skills. Thanks also to Clay Wilwol, my razor-sharp research assistant in the early going, who doggedly discovered where most of the bodies were buried and set me on my course of international wanderings. I must also express my appreciation to David Lamb for gifting me a full set of the published volumes from Cook's third voyage—I'm honored to have those great musty tomes, sumptuously printed in the 1780s, parked like anvils on my office shelves. The hawk-eyed Will Palmer worked wonders on these pages. Massive thanks also to author and maritime historian Revell Carr, former director and president of the Mystic Seaport Museum, for reading my entire manuscript and offering his expertise on all things nautical. Any maritime mistakes found in these pages are my fault; whatever I got right was thanks to Revell.

Special thanks to Khari Dawkins, Maria Carella, and John Fontana at Doubleday. With my agent Sloan Harris, my publicist Todd Doughty, and my editor Bill Thomas, I have an unstoppable dream team that has ferociously supported me and my scribblings for more than two decades. From the bottom of my heart, I can't thank my Dynamic Trio enough.

And another trio: my three amazing boys (young men now) Griffin, Graham, and McCall, as well as their intrepid ladyfolk, accompanied me on several of the sojourns of this book and gamely put up with my fascination with a certain eighteenth-century British voyager. Then, of course, Anne, my best friend and favorite traveling companion over the wide wide seas of this wondrous and precarious earth.

Notes

Prologue: And Louder Grew the Shouting

3 "trembling and frightened": Westervelt, *Hawaiian Historical Legends*, 63.

3 "What are those branching things?": Kamakau, *Ruling Chiefs of Hawaii*, 92.

3 "not an ordinary thing": Westervelt, *Hawaiian Historical Legends*, 63.

3 "marvelous monster": Ibid.

4 "shouting with fear": Ibid.

4 "their skin is loose": Subin, *Accidental Gods*, 360.

4 "bodies are full of treasure": Ibid.

4 "harbor resounded with noise": Kamakau, *Ruling Chiefs of Hawaii*, 92.

Book One: The First Navigator of Europe

1 Negative Discoverer

8 "fall to destruction among the stars": Mercator, quoted in Thompson, *Sea People*, 26.

8 "executioner of misbegotten hypotheses": Beaglehole, quoted in Nicandri, *Captain Cook Rediscovered*, 132.

8 "If I have failed": Cook, quoted in Barnett and Nicandri, eds., *Arctic Ambitions*, 29.

9 "farther than any man": Williams, *Death of Captain Cook*, 1.

10 "coarsest that ever a mortal": Nicandri, *Captain Cook Rediscovered*, 255.

10 "most ungrateful food": Gascoigne, *Captain Cook: Voyager Between Worlds*, 53.

10 "Action was life to him": Nicandri, *Captain Cook Rediscovered*, 267.

10 "On land, he was at the mercy": Collingridge, *Life, Death, and Legacy*, 332.

11 "His inner thoughts": MacLean, *Captain Cook*, 3.

11 "There were depths": McLynn, *Captain Cook, Master of the Seas*, 282.

11 "no natural gift": Beaglehole, *Life of Captain James Cook*, 545.

12 "plain and sensible man": Ibid., 451.

12 "studiously wrapped up": Gascoigne, *Captain Cook: Voyager Between Worlds*, 40.

2 Proto-Anthropologist

14 "seemed to be drawn to land": Hough, *Murder of Captain James Cook*, 78.

15 "manned by violence": Collingridge, *Life, Death and Legacy*, 44.

16 "disagreeable smell below": Kippis, *Life of Captain Cook*, 80.

19 "the greatest piece of mechanism": Gilbert, quoted on the Larcum Kendall page of Wikipedia.

19 "Mr. Kendall's watch": Beaglehole, *Life of Captain Cook*, 438.

19 "our trusty friend": Andrewes, *Quest for Longitude*, 252.

3 A Human Pet

21 "silent stroke": Author interview with Polynesian cultural historian Hinano Teavai-Murphy, April 19, 2021.

21 macabre serape: See Connaughton, *Omai: The Prince Who Never Was*, 37.

24 "spoilt children of fortune": See Thompson, *Sea People*, 69.

24 "He is very brown": Connaughton, *Omai: The Prince Who Never Was*, 115.

24 a "valuable acquisition": Alexander, *Omai: Noble Savage*, 78.

25 "a private gentleman": Beaglehole, *Life of Captain James Cook*, 447.

25 "I do not know why": Connaughton, *Omai: The Prince Who Never Was*, 61.

27 "How do King Tosh!": Alexander, *Omai: Noble Savage*, 74.

27 "Sir, you are king of England": Ibid.

4 A Fine Retreat

28 "I was in hopes": Collingridge, *Life, Death, and Legacy*, 325.

29 "petted children of the nation": Hawthorne, quoted in Aslet, *Story of Greenwich*, 166.

29 "It is a fine retreat": Collingridge, *Life, Death, and Legacy*, 325.

29 "My fate drives me": Hough, *Captain James Cook*, 265.

31 "The *Resolution* will soon be sent": Nicandri, *Captain Cook Rediscovered*, 164.

31 a "lusty extrovert": Obeyesekere, *Apotheosis of Captain Cook*, 29.

31 "there was hardly a man": Cowley and Deacon, *In the Wake of Captain Cook*, 36.

32 "did not possess that degree": Nicandri, *Captain Cook Rediscovered*, 353.

32 "When a certain line of action": Hough, *Murder of Captain James Cook*, 18.

33 "limitless ambition": Rodger, *Insatiable Earl*, 68.

34 the voyage's "grandeur and dignity": Kippis, *Life of Captain Cook*, 86.

35 "Captain Cook was so fired": Ibid.

35 "sheathed and filled and fitted": Hough, *Murder of Captain James Cook*, 14.

36 "that blessed creature": Ibid., 17.

36 "I know not what your opinion may be": Hough, *Captain James Cook*, 273.

36 "If I am not so fortunate": Beaglehole, *Life of Captain James Cook*, 505.

5 A Natural Politeness

37 "Omai has now got through": Alexander, *Omai: Noble Savage*, 75.

37 "without becoming a show": Ibid., 77.

38 "seemed to shame education": Connaughton, *Omai: The Prince Who Never Was*, 131.

38 "The novelty of his figure": Clark, *Omai: First Polynesian Ambassador to England*, 72.

38 A bull was a "man-cow": Alexander, *Omai: Noble Savage*, 124.

38 it was a "soldier bird": Connaughton, *Omai: The Prince Who Never Was*, 127.

38 "Nothing could be better dressed": Alexander, *Omai: Noble Savage*, 126.

39 "popped at all the feathered creation": Ibid., 124.

39 "He had a sense of mission": Ibid., 99.

39 "His eye sparkled": Clark, *Omai: First Polynesian Ambassador to England*, 61.

39 "turned away from a sight": Alexander, *Omai: Noble Savage*, 84.

40 "He succeeds most prodigiously": Ibid., 83.

40 "irregular old house": Rodger, *Insatiable Earl*, 69.

40 "venerable elms": Ibid.

40 "good house for the robust and the jolly": Ibid., 85.

40 "vied with each other": Alexander, *Omai: Noble Savage*, 82.

40 "king of all the ships": Connaughton, *Omai: The Prince Who Never Was*, 127.

41 "deception, a masquerade": Ibid., xv.

41 "He liked to wander around": Alexander, *Omai: Noble Savage*, 82.

41 "child of Nature": Ibid., 130.

41 "What kind of animal": Ibid., 131.

41 "Nothing can be more curious": Burney, *Journals and Letters*, 66.

42 "I am grown so used to him": Rodger, *Insatiable Earl*, 207.

6 The Problem of the Ice

44 "geographical romantics": Beaglehole, quoted in Nicandri, *Captain Cook Rediscovered*, 165.

45 "In the seas near the Pole": Barrington, *Possibility of Approaching the North Pole Asserted*, 132.

46 "did not meet with any ice": Ibid., 34.

46 people from Holland "are not commonly jokers": Ibid., 35.

46 merely a temporary "assemblage": Barrington, quoted in Nicandri, *Captain Cook Rediscovered*, 180.

47 "There is unquestionably no country": Barrington, *Possibility of Approaching the North Pole Asserted*, 139.

7 No Tutor but Nature

48 "a most daring spirit of resistance": George III, quoted in Salmond, *Trial of the Cannibal Dog*, 297.

48 "What a rustling of silks!": Damrosch, *The Club*, 144.

49 "Do you think I should be conquered": Connaughton, *Omai: The Prince Who Never Was*, 141.

49 "There is so little of the savage": Alexander, *Omai: Noble Savage*, 104.

50 "the lion of lions": Burney, quoted in Connaughton, *Omai: The Prince Who Never Was*, 131.

50 "no tutor but nature": Burney, *Journals and Letters*, 33.

50 "committed not the slightest blunder": Ibid., 31.

51 "to pour the light of divine truth": Alexander, *Omai: Noble Savage*, 142.

51 "Thou shalt not commit adultery": Connaughton, *Omai: The Prince Who Never Was*, 136.

52 "is rather tall and slender": Alexander, *Omai: Noble Savage*, 100.

52 "How many moons": Ibid., 133.

53 "as much at home upon the waves": Colman, *Random Records*, 165.

53 "as smoothly as Arion": Ibid., 166.

8 Fresh Discoveries

53 "Our equipment is in every way adequate": Clerke, quoted in Beaglehole, ed., *Journals of Captain James Cook*, vol. 3, 3.

54 "stout as a publican's wife": Hough, *Murder of Captain James Cook*, 14.

54 "not one fault to allege against her": Hough, *Captain James Cook*, 196.

54 "very dull sailing vessel": Gascoigne, *Captain Cook: Voyager Between Worlds*, 56.

55 The platters kept coming: The full menu of the celebratory dinner is listed in Beaglehole, *Life of Captain James Cook*, 504.

55 "There is nothing perhaps more adverse": Gibbon, quoted in Damrosch, *The Club*, 331.

56 "The expectation of a rupture": Smith, quoted in O'Shaughnessy, *Men Who Lost America*, 4.

56 "the object of which": Cook and King, *Voyage to the Pacific Ocean*, vol. 1, 9.

56 "neither natural, nor acquired abilities": Cook, quoted in Barnett and Nicandri, *Arctic Ambitions*, 233.

57 "The public...must not expect": Cook's comment about his literary shortcomings is reprinted at the Princeton University website Strait Through: Magellan to Cook & the Pacific, library.princeton.edu/.

57 "It was curious to see Cook": Ryskamp and Pottle, *Boswell: The Ominous Years*, 309.

57 "Being in a ship": See "Quotes on Soldiers and Sailors," The Samuel Johnson Sound Bite Page, samueljohnson.com/.

57 "Who will read them through?": Alexander, *Omai: Noble Savage*, 109.

9 The Secret Instructions

58 "I cannot leave England": Beaglehole, *Life of Captain James Cook*, 507.

58 "fully sensible of the good treatment": Beaglehole, ed., *Journals of Captain James Cook*, vol. 3, 5.

58 "Omiah to take leave": Connaughton, *Omai: The Prince Who Never Was*, 174.

59 "came from Ireland": Ibid., 171.

60 "convinced that the English Nation": Barrington, quoted in Williams, *Voyages of Delusion*, 298.

60 "not to touch upon": Beaglehole, ed., *Journals of Captain James Cook*, vol. 3, ccxxi.

60 "His Majesty's ships": Ibid., 7.

60 "injuries and usurpations": These Declaration of Independence quotes are taken from Hibbert, *George III,* 153.

63 "Curse the scientists": Obeyesekere, *Apotheosis of Captain Cook,* 14.

64 "to decamp without beat of drum": Cowley and Deacon, *In the Wake of Captain Cook,* 121.

64 "There's a fatality attends": Hough, *Murder of Captain James Cook,* 37.

64 "in high spirits": Alexander, *Omai: Noble Savage,* 147.

64 "When he talked about England": Ibid., 146.

65 to make Mai "the instrument": Connaughton, *Omai: The Prince Who Never Was,* 175.

65 "virtually drew up his own instructions": Williams, *Voyages of Delusion,* 288.

65 "Upon your arrival in Tahiti": Cook's secret instructions from the Admiralty are reprinted in full in Dale, ed., *Seventy North to Fifty South,* 10–15.

66 "The singularity of the circumstance": Thomas, *Cook: The Extraordinary Voyages,* 285.

Book Two: The Weight of My Resentment

10   Isla Del Infierno

69 "exceedingly leaky in all her upper works": Beaglehole, ed., *Journals of Captain James Cook*, vol. 3, 14.

70 "He was particularly cleanly": Zimmermann, *Third Voyage of Captain Cook,* 107.

70 "He was very strict": Ibid., 106.

70 "small and bony": Beaglehole, ed., *Journals of Captain James Cook*, vol. 3, 10.

71 "impregnated lemon": Anderson, in Beaglehole, ed., *Journals of Captain James Cook*, vol. 3, 733.

71 "The road was very bad": Ibid.

71 "expressed his surprise that English physicians": Ibid.

72 "I shall get hold of him": Beaglehole, ed., *Journals of Captain James Cook,* vol. 3, 509.

73 "For the space of ten minutes": Beaglehole, ed., *Journals of Captain James Cook,* vol. 3, 736.

73 "our situation…was very alarming": Ibid., 12.

73 "To bring a ship": Beaglehole, ed., *Journals of Captain James Cook,* vol. 3, 736.

74 "proceeded from too accurate a knowledge": Ibid.

74 "dreadful tempest": Rickman, *Journal of Captain Cook's Last Voyage,* 12.

74 "frittered in a thousand pieces": Ibid.

74 "discharging the water": Ibid.

74 "When he was cut up": Ibid., 13.

75 "their numberless windings and shiftings": Ibid., 16.

75 "Whatever may be the design": Ibid.

75 nature has "given them the power": Ibid.

75 "nothing could be more tedious": Ibid., 13.

75 "A passage through the tropical latitudes": Ibid., 16.

75 "He was never again seen to rise": Ibid., 14.

75 "young, sober, and of good character": Ibid.

75 "It is more than probable": Ibid.

76 "in a ship built of ginger bread": Gore, quoted in Beaglehole, *Life of Captain James Cook,* 512.

76 "Omai first showed us the way": Beaglehole, ed., *Journals of Captain James Cook,* vol. 3, 14.

77 "droll animal": Samwell, quoted in McCormick, *Omai: Pacific Envoy,* 188.

77 "he is very expert": Samwell letter, quoted in Beaglehole, ed., *Journals of Captain James Cook,* vol. 3, 1514.

77 "God going to England": Ibid., 1515.

77 "Like all ignorant people": Ibid.

78 "We had the vile practice of ducking": Beaglehole, *Life of Captain James Cook,* 509.

78 an "old ridiculous ceremony": Bea-

glehole, ed., *Journals of Captain James Cook*, vol. 3, 743.

78 "We have a man tired": Ibid., cliv.

78 a "tired ship, commanded by a tired man": Gascoigne, *Captain Cook: Voyager Between Worlds*, 40.

11 Tavern of the Seas

81 "though not very dexterous": Beaglehole, ed., *Journals of Captain James Cook*, vol. 3, 755.

81 "is as famous here and more noted": Samwell, quoted in Beaglehole, *Life of Captain James Cook*, 509.

82 "We have reason to conclude": Beaglehole, ed., *Journals of Captain James Cook*, vol. 3, 21.

82 "The Cape is very plentiful": Samwell, quoted in Aughton, *Fatal Voyage*, 34.

82 "delightful gardens": Gilbert, *Captain Cook's Final Voyage*, 20.

82 "The Dutch...strictly adhered to the maxim": Cook, quoted in Aughton, *Fatal Voyage*, 34.

82 "some of the meanest and lowest scoundrels": Cook, quoted in Dale, ed., *Seventy North to Fifty South*, 31.

83 "The people here are surprised": Beaglehole, *Life of Captain James Cook*, 511.

84 "brought a pox with him": Anderson, quoted in Alexander, *Omai: Noble Savage*, 151.

84 "consented with raptures": Beaglehole, ed., *Journals of Captain James Cook*, vol. 3, 511.

84 "exceedingly picturesque": Rickman, *Journal of Captain Cook's Last Voyage*, 19.

84 "somehow majestically great by nature": Ledyard, *Last Voyage of Captain Cook*, 3.

84 "the land near the town": Ibid.

85 "the air here...has an uncommon serenity": Beaglehole, ed., *Journals of Captain James Cook*, vol. 3, 757.

85 "This gentleman...entertained us": Ibid.

86 "They tell us...that the policing": Ibid., 19.

86 "Thus did we resemble the ark": Ledyard, *Last Voyage of Captain Cook*, 4.

87 "Here I am...hard and fast moored": Clerke, quoted in McLynn, *Captain Cook: Master of the Seas*, 287.

87 "as to make our bark plunge exceedingly": Ibid.

87 "our intended attack upon the North Pole": Ibid.

87 "We are now ready to proceed": Cook letter to Banks, quoted in Beaglehole, *Life of Captain James Cook*, 511.

12 The Isle of Desolation

88 "very high sea which made the ship roll": Beaglehole, ed., *Journals of Captain James Cook*, vol. 3, 24.

88 "we began now most sensibly to feel": Ibid.

89 "The sea frequently broke over the ship": Ibid.

89 "nasty, raw, wet, disagreeable weather": Ibid., 26.

89 "a large louse": Ibid., 24.

89 "a kind of prawn or shrimp": Ibid.

89 "the great hazard in sailing": Ibid.

89 "most importunate": Ibid., 26.

89 "tedious and dangerous": Ibid.

90 "In these situations": Ibid.

90 "We who are not acquainted": Ibid.

91 "an adventurer whom on close scrutiny": Beaglehole, *Life of Captain James Cook*, 514.

91 "a prodigious sea": Beaglehole, ed., *Journals of Captain James Cook*, vol. 3, 27.

91 "entangled amongst the islands": Ibid.

92 "without the least sign of fertility": Ibid., 41.

92 "a rotten kind of turf": Ibid., 43.

92 "Not a stick of wood": Ibid., 35.

92 "Every gully afforded a large stream": Ibid., 36.

92 "Perhaps no place hitherto discovered": Ibid., 40.

92 "so insensible of fear": Ibid., 36.

92 "not the most delicate" fare: Rickman, *Journal of Captain Cook's Last Voyage*, 36.

93 "melancholy croaking": Hough, *Murder of Captain James Cook*, 51.

93 "In all enjoyments": Zimmer-mann, quoted in Barrow, *Captain Cook in Hawaii*, 15.

93 "Past dangers were forgotten": Rickman, *Journal of Captain Cook's Last Voyage*, 36.

94 "perhaps fitter to excite laughter": McCormick, *Omai: Pacific Envoy*, 198.

94 "too barren for any human being": Gilbert, *Captain Cook's Final Voyage*, 22.

13   Lunawanna-alonnah

96 "in the dark": Dale, ed., *Seventy North to Fifty South*, 47.

96 "shortness of our time": Beagle-hole, ed., *Journals of Captain James Cook*, vol. 3, 49.

97 "a shark of uncommon size": Ibid., 782.

98 "a bottom of ooze and sand": Ibid., 50.

98 "very indifferent eating": Gilbert, *Captain Cook's Final Voyage*, 23.

99 "growing to astonishing height": Rickman, *Journal of Captain Cook's Last Voyage*, 41.

99 "troublesome vexatious insects": Burney, quoted in Barnett, ed., *Captain Cook's Final Voyage*, 37.

99 "large black ant": Beaglehole, ed., *Journals of Captain James Cook*, vol. 3, 794.

99 "What the ancients tell us": Ibid., 786.

99 "They did not express that sur-prise": Ibid., 784.

100 "They approached us from the woods": Dale, ed., *Seventy North to Fifty South*, 49.

101 their "harmless cheerfulness": Beaglehole, ed., *Journals of Captain James Cook*, vol. 3, 54.

101 "lived like the beasts of the forest": Rickman, *Journal of Captain Cook's Last Voyage*, 41.

101 "Few people may more truly be said": Burney, quoted in Barnett, ed., *Captain Cook's Final Voyage*, 36.

101 "They have few wants": Beagle-hole, ed., *Journals of Captain James Cook*, vol. 3, 55.

102 "they seized them by the ears": Ibid., 53.

102 "incapable of entering into my views": Dale, ed., *Seventy North to Fifty South*, 50.

102 "I have no doubt [what] will be their fate": Ibid.

103 "The report astonished them all": Beaglehole, ed., *Journals of Captain James Cook*, vol. 3, 992.

103 "would prevent our having further intercourse": Ibid.

103 "fond of the thickest cover": Ibid., 53.

103 "They were convinced": Dale, ed., *Seventy North to Fifty South*, 50.

104 "canoe or any vessel": Beagle-hole, ed., *Journals of Captain James Cook*, vol. 3, 54.

104 "With all our dumb oratory": Ibid., 993.

105 "The language here": Dale, ed., *Seventy North to Fifty South*, 51.

105 "much deformed": Beaglehole, ed., *Journals of Captain James Cook*, vol. 3, 54.

105 "drollery of his gestures": Dale, ed., *Seventy North to Fifty South*, 51.

105 "We could easily see that this little Aesop": Beaglehole, ed., *Journals of Captain James Cook*, vol. 3, 993.

105 "appeared something like friars": Ibid., 994.

105 "were rejected with great disdain": Dale, ed., *Seventy North to Fifty South*, 52.

105 "ordered all the women to retire": Ibid.

106 "live in a tranquility": Cook, quoted in Nicandri, *Captain Cook Rediscovered*, 385.

106 "so vast that the human mind can scarcely grasp it": Thompson, *Sea People*, 22.

14   A Shocking Scene of Carnage

107 "He was very reserved": Zimmer-mann, quoted in Barrow, *Captain Cook in Hawaii*, 14.

108 "Captain Cook has not the least hopes": Salmond, *Trial of the Cannibal Dog*, 226.

109 "a narrow escape": Ibid., 227.

109 a "great uneasiness": Burney, "Mr.

Burney's Report of Massacre at Grass Cove," 1.

109   "stove in among the rocks": Ibid.

110   "All the way down the hill": Ibid., 8.

111   "began to scramble away": Ibid., 9.

111   "the heads, hearts, and lungs": Ibid.

112   "destroying the *mana*": Salmond, *Trial of the Cannibal Dog*, 4.

112   "We could hear the Indians in the woods": Burney, "Mr. Burney's Report of Massacre at Grass Cove," 10.

112   "I had not the least suspicion": Ibid., 2.

112   "our very best seaman": Ibid., 12.

113   "I shall make no reflections": Salmond, *Trial of the Cannibal Dog*, 2.

113   "I have always found them": Ibid.

15   The Land of the Long White Cloud

114   this spectacular country: My portrait of New Zealand's geology and natural history and the arrival of the Polynesian voyagers who became the Māori people is largely drawn from *The Penguin History of New Zealand*, by Michael King; *Sea People*, by Christina Thompson; *The Fatal Impact*, by Alan Moorehead; *James Cook and New Zealand*, by A. Charles Begg and Neil C. Begg; *A Travel Guide to Captain James Cook's New Zealand*, by Graeme Lay; and *The Trial of the Cannibal Dog*, by Anne Salmond.

117   "Neither professions of friendship": Beaglehole, ed., *Journals of Captain James Cook*, vol. 3, 59.

117   "They must be well assured": Ibid.

117   "Nothing can be a greater proof": Gilbert, *Captain Cook's Final Voyage*, 24.

118   a "perpetual and universal chirping": Hough, *Murder of Captain James Cook*, 67.

118   "nails, broken glass, beads [and] other European trumpery": Rickman, *Journal of Captain Cook's Last Voyage*, 49.

118   "they very soon laid it aside": Beaglehole, ed., *Journals of Captain James Cook*, vol. 3, 60.

118   "They all keep the exactest time": Ibid., 814.

119   "admirably calculated to strike terror": Ibid., 996.

119   "Among all the savage sons of war": Ledyard, *Last Voyage of Captain Cook*, 7.

119   "They fell desperately in love": Ibid., 8.

119   "It is not easy to say": Rickman, *Journal of Captain Cook's Last Voyage*, 57.

120   "They ate the very dregs": Beaglehole, ed., *Journals of Captain James Cook*, vol. 3, 66.

120   "after the sacrifice": Ibid., 60.

120   "the most dismal cries": Ibid., 999.

120   "the most melodious notes": Gilbert, *Captain Cook's Final Voyage*, 25.

120   "Their masterpiece seems to be carving": Beaglehole, ed., *Journals of Captain James Cook*, vol. 3, 813.

121   "Their substitute for a knife is a shell": Ibid.

121   "to ornament his person": Ledyard, *Last Voyage of Captain Cook*, 9.

121   a "wholesome beverage": Rickman, *Journal of Captain Cook's Last Voyage*, 57.

121   "little inferior": Beaglehole, ed., *Journals of Captain James Cook*, vol. 3, 803.

121   "He seemed to be a man more feared": Ibid., 62.

122   "middle aged, very strong, and of fierce countenance": Ibid., 998.

122   "turbulent and mischievous": Ibid., 818.

122   "I believe they were not a little surprised": Ibid., 62.

122   "If I had followed the advice": Ibid.

122   "From my own observations": Ibid., 71.

16   Return to Grass Cove

123   "I thought they showed manifest signs": Beaglehole, ed., *Journals of Captain James Cook*, vol. 3, 64.

123   "like people who are under no apprehension": Ibid., 63.

124   "prejudices of a naval education": Davies, "Cook: The 'Adventure' and Misadventure in Queen Charlotte Sound."

124   "If these thefts": Beaglehole, ed., *Journals of Captain James Cook*, vol. 3, 64.

124   "This custom of eating their ene-

mies": Salmond, *Trial of the Cannibal Dog,*
224.

125 "Some said she was pulled to
pieces": Beaglehole, ed., *Journals of Captain James Cook,* vol. 3, 68.

125 "The stories these people choose to
tell": Ibid., 69.

125 "They are much clearer in their
demands": Barnett, ed., *Captain Cook's
Final Voyage,* 42.

125 "Traffic was greatly altered":
Ibid., 39.

125 "confident of their own power":
Beaglehole, ed., *Journals of Captain James
Cook,* vol. 3, 66.

125 "Perhaps...our not resenting":
Ibid.

125 "It seemed evident that": Ibid.

126 "As an instance how much they
trusted": Barnett, ed., *Captain Cook's Final
Voyage,* 39.

126 "without showing the last mark":
Cook, quoted in Beaglehole, ed., *Journals
of Captain James Cook,* vol. 3, 68.

126 "There is Kahura, *kill him!*": Ibid.

126 "Mai's arguments, though reasonable enough": Ibid.

127 "looked like one caught in a trap":
Ibid.

127 "The remainder of his account":
Ibid.

127 "could answer no purpose":
Ibid., 69.

127 "As to what was past": Ibid.

128 "For the authoritarian persona":
Obeyesekere, *Apotheosis of Captain Cook,* 27.

128 "If ever they made a second
attempt": Beaglehole, ed., *Journals of
Captain James Cook,* vol. 3, 69.

128 "I must confess": Ibid.

129 "for we were all so confoundedly
hungry": Salmond, *Trial of the Cannibal
Dog,* 1.

130 "You're all a set of damned cannibals": Ibid.

130 "Poor Neddy munched up his dog":
Ibid.

131 "We debauch their morals": Beaglehole, ed., *Journals of Captain James Cook,*
vol. 2, 175.

131 "serve[d] only to disturb that ...
tranquillity": Ibid.

132 "I was apprehensive Mai had
deceived": Beaglehole, ed., *Journals of
Captain James Cook,* vol. 3, 70.

132 "with far less indifference": Ibid.

132 "She and Te Weherua parted": Ibid.

133 "wept both in public and in private": Ibid., 76.

133 "They cried most piteously": Ibid.,
1001.

Book Three: Faraway Heaven

17   Aphrodite's Island

137 "As we approached his island":
Alexander, *Omai: Noble Savage,* 173.

138 "You may well suppose the satisfaction": Ibid., 174.

138 "tall, stout, black-haired, pock-
marked": McCririck, *Stories of Wales,*
book 3, 31.

138 "sat all day on the forecastle":
Beaglehole, ed., *Journals of Captain James
Cook,* vol. 3, 1051.

139 "He would never listen to any
plan": Ibid., 173.

139 a "farce of flattery and vanity":
McCormick, *Omai: Pacific Envoy,* 224.

140 "It was evident to every one":
Beaglehole, ed., *Journals of Captain James
Cook,* vol. 3, 186.

140 "His heart was so full": Alexander,
Omai: Noble Savage, 174.

140 "The women are thought to be
more friendly": Beaglehole, ed., *Journals
of Captain James Cook,* vol. 3, 187.

140 "Not more feathers": Ibid.

141 "disappointment and vexation":
Alexander, *Omai: Noble Savage,* 178.

142 "had imbued a good deal": McCormick, *Omai: Pacific Envoy,* 230.

142 "when he saw the great abundance": Ibid.

143 "There was a damned lit-
tle...state": Cowley and Deacon, *In the
Wake of Captain Cook,* 147.

143 "He never mentioned religion":
Barrow, *Captain Cook in Hawaii,* 14.

144 "Mai, assisted by some of his

friends": Beaglehole, ed., *Journals of Captain James Cook*, vol. 3, 189.

144   "gave them a better idea": Howarth, *Tahiti: A Paradise Lost*, 138.

144   "It is impossible to describe": Alexander, *Omai: Noble Savage*, 181.

145   "like St. George going to kill": McCormick, *Omai: Pacific Envoy*, 228.

18   This Barbarous Custom

146   "Moderation was one of his chief virtues": Barrow, *Captain Cook in Hawaii*, 15.

146   "It remained not under a moment's consideration": Beaglehole, ed., *Journals of Captain James Cook*, vol. 3, 189.

147   "The readiness with which they consented": Ibid.

147   "a very rich and agreeable liquor": Ibid., 1057.

147   "drink to their female friends": Beaglehole, ed., *Journals of Captain James Cook*, vol. 3, 189.

148   "conducted himself with a great deal of respect": Ibid., 192.

148   Mai "did not fail to magnify": Alexander, *Omai: Noble Savage*, 184.

149   "flocked to us": Beaglehole, ed., *Journals of Captain James Cook*, vol. 3, 1060.

149   "They are...angels": Hough, *Murder of Captain James Cook*, 99.

150   "almost frantic with joy to see us": Ledyard, *Last Voyage of Captain Cook*, 30.

151   "dance that rather bespoke of an excess of joy": Beaglehole, ed., *Journals of Captain James Cook*, vol. 3, 978.

151   "The ships were little in a condition": Ibid., 1059.

152   "this extraordinary and barbarous custom": Ibid., 199.

153   "an intolerable stench": Ibid., 980.

153   "the most worthless, unconnected rascal": Cowley and Deacon, *In the Wake of Captain Cook*, 147.

153   "were never apprised of their fate": Beaglehole, ed., *Journals of Captain James Cook*, vol. 3, 204.

153   "seemed often to expostulate with the dead": Ibid., 979.

153   "feed only on the soul": Ibid., 984.

154   "It is the god!": Howarth, *Tahiti: A Paradise Lost*, 137.

154   "horrid...the grossest ignorance": Beaglehole, ed., *Journals of Captain James Cook*, vol. 3, 983.

154   "ocular proof": Ibid., 978.

154   "We of course condemned it": Ibid., 205.

154   "Mai...put the chief out of all manner": Ibid., 206.

154   "we left him with as great a contempt": Ibid.

19   Duped by Every Designing Knave

155   "a good opportunity to get some insight": Aughton, *Fatal Voyage*, 87.

155   "After we were out in the bay": Ibid.

155   "flourished their weapons": Beaglehole, ed., *Journals of Captain James Cook*, vol. 3, 212.

156   "The troops on our stage": Ibid.

156   "This method of fighting": Ibid., 213.

156   "Everyone had a full view of him": Ibid.

156   "vain and gullible fool": Connaughton, *Omai: The Prince Who Never Was*, 231.

156   the "property he was master of": Beaglehole, ed., *Journals of Captain James Cook*, vol. 3, 186.

157   "If I had not interfered": Ibid., 193.

157   "It was my wish to fix him with Tu": Ibid.

157   "He rejected my advice": Ibid.

157   Mai's "vanity and extravagance": Aughton, *Fatal Voyage*, 82.

157   "He chose rather to associate with the black guards": Alexander, *Omai: Noble Savage*, 186.

158   "a sore on a healthy body": Howarth, *Tahiti: A Paradise Lost*, 140.

158   "envied for undeserved riches": Ledyard, *Last Voyage of Captain Cook*, 38.

158   "Men sprung from the dregs": Connaughton, *Omai: The Prince Who Never Was*, 214.

159   "Seamen in these matters are

so infernal": Alexander, *Omai: Noble Savage*, 52.

160 "Many persons would have rejoiced": McLynn, *Captain Cook: Master of the Seas*, 323.

161 "delectable...as pleasant and happy": Alexander, *Omai: Noble Savage*, 56.

161 "They told me...they were come to cure me": Beaglehole, ed., *Journals of Captain James Cook*, vol. 3, 214.

161 "I submitted myself to their direction": Ibid.

162 "I found the pains entirely removed": Ibid., 215.

162 "sometimes performed by the men": Ibid.

163 "Now I found myself lightened": Beaglehole, *Life of Captain James Cook*, 551.

163 "The satisfaction I felt": Ibid.

164 "a finer beast than he was": Aughton, *Fatal Voyage*, 81.

164 "The act...is primarily symbolic": Obeyesekere, *Apotheosis of Captain Cook*, 12.

20   A Kingdom for a Goat

167 "not inferior...to any harbor": Beaglehole, *Life of Captain James Cook*, 557.

168 "truly romantic": Ellis, *Authentic Narrative of a Voyage*, 146.

168 slabs of basalt "that rise in a variety of forms": Ibid.

168 "It is scarcely possible": Connaughton, *Omai: The Prince Who Never Was*, 240.

168 "The ruins of war": Beaglehole, ed., *Journals of Captain James Cook*, vol. 3, 228.

168 "pestered" and "haunted": Ibid., 226.

169 "we were certain that we got quit": Ibid., 1382.

170 "We could not but admire": Ibid., 1069.

170 "all which he says are the consequences": Ellis, *Authentic Narrative of a Voyage*, 144.

170 "a mark of disgrace with them": Beaglehole, ed., *Journals of Captain James Cook*, vol. 3, 227.

171 "He has a son who he intends to succeed him": Ellis, *Authentic Narrative of a Voyage*, 144.

171 "a plan had been laid": Dale, ed., *Seventy North to Fifty South*, 151.

172 "fixed in my resolution": Ibid.

172 "I was now very sorry": Ibid., 152.

172 "Without hesitation": Ibid.

172 "This bloody advice": Beaglehole, *Life of Captain James Cook*, 559.

173 "I doubt not...but Captain Cook had good reasons": McCormick, *Omai: Pacific Envoy*, 247.

174 "The Captain...ordered the canoes": Rickman, *Journal of Captain Cook's Last Voyage*, 161.

174 "The damage which the inhabitants...sustained": Zimmermann, *Third Voyage of Captain Cook*, 66.

175 "Although I am told": Alexander, *Omai: Noble Savage*, 193.

175 "We thought it rather extraordinary": Zimmermann, *Third Voyage of Captain Cook*, 66.

175 "Cook and Mai were in a close": Obeyesekere, *Apotheosis of Captain Cook*, 39.

176 "these good people, whose ridiculous conduct": Beaglehole, *Life of Captain James Cook*, 559.

176 "Captain Cook's precipitate proceeding": Beaglehole, ed., *Journals of Captain James Cook*, vol. 3, 1383.

177 an "odd unintelligible phenomenon": Beaglehole, *Life of Captain James Cook*, 557.

177 "passing madness": Hough, *Murder of Captain James Cook*, 111.

177 a "decay of his splendid intellect": Ibid., 250.

177 "This troublesome, and rather unfortunate affair": Beaglehole, ed., *Journals of Captain James Cook*, vol. 3, 232.

21   The Ardor of Inviolable Friendship

178 "I neither would assist them in such a design": Beaglehole, ed., *Journals of Captain James Cook*, vol. 3, 234.

178 "I wanted to reconcile him": Ibid., 233.

179 "I had always met with more troublesome people": Ibid., 237.

179 because the islands "lay con-

tiguous to one another": Horwitz, *Blue Latitudes*, 79.

180   "A very mean looking boy he is": Beaglehole, ed., *Journals of Captain James Cook*, vol. 3, 234.

180   "there might be no inducement": Ibid., 239.

181   "The number of cockroaches": Ibid., 236.

181   "They eat and destroy everything": Ibid., 238.

182   "The principal performer": Ibid., 1070.

183   Although he was "hasty tempered": Barrow, *Captain Cook in Hawaii*, 15.

184   "deprived of his ears": Beaglehole, ed., *Journals of Captain James Cook*, vol. 3, 236.

184   "The extraordinary impudence": Ibid.

184   to make a "severe example of him": Ibid.

184   a "hardened scoundrel": Ibid.

184   until ... "particles of his skin came away": Zimmermann, *Third Voyage of Captain Cook*, 68.

184   "blown our poor friend Mai's fortunes": Hough, *Murder of Captain James Cook*, 115.

186   "I was always of [the] opinion": Beaglehole, ed., *Journals of Captain James Cook*, vol. 3, 239.

187   much "mirth and jollity": Beaglehole, ed., *Journals of Captain James Cook*, vol. 3, 237.

187   "The curiosity of the people": Gilbert, *Captain Cook's Final Voyage*, 48.

187   "a goodnatured sensible young fellow": Beaglehole, ed., *Journals of Captain James Cook*, vol. 3, 1073.

187   "more than overbalanced by his great good nature": Beaglehole, *Life of Captain James Cook*, 563.

187   "I cannot avoid expressing it as my real opinion": Connaughton, *Mai: The Prince Who Never Was*, 261.

187   "Such is the strange nature of human affairs": McCormick, *Omai: Pacific Envoy*, 264.

188   "It is here as in many other coun-

tries": Beaglehole, ed., *Journals of Captain James Cook*, vol. 3, 235.

188   "This ... will certainly have some effect":

188   "real and unaffected sorrow": Barnett, ed., *Captain Cook's Final Voyage*, 84.

188   "Mai sustained himself": Beaglehole, ed., *Journals of Captain James Cook*, vol. 3, 240.

188   Mai's "eyes were never dry": Rickman, *Journal of Captain Cook's Last Voyage*, 177.

22   Faraway Heaven

189   My account of Mai's final years and what became of his property on Huahine is largely drawn from McCormick, *Omai: Pacific Envoy*; Alexander, *Omai: Noble Savage*; Connaughton, *Omai: The Prince Who Never Was*; and Clark, *Omai: First Polynesian Ambassador to England*.

190   "The house ... was torn to pieces": Alexander, *Omai: Noble Savage*, 205.

190   The missionary noted that after several generations: Ibid., 207.

23   Scorched Up by the Heat of the Sun

194   "We left ... with the greatest regret": Beaglehole, ed., *Journals of Captain James Cook*, vol. 3, 256.

195   "dreadful" breakers: Ibid., 257.

195   "had the appearance of being scorched": Ellis, *Authentic Narrative of a Voyage*, 163.

195   "so tame ... as to be taken off the bushes": Ibid., 165.

196   "On every side of us swam sharks": Beaglehole, ed., *Journals of Captain James Cook*, vol. 3, 258.

196   "We tried in many places": Ellis, *Authentic Narrative of a Voyage*, 166.

196   "a noble supply": Ledyard, *Last Voyage of Captain Cook*, 43.

196   "and then the sport began": Beaglehole, ed., *Journals of Captain James Cook*, vol. 3, 258.

197   "I have seen one, larger than common": Ibid.

197   "instead of quenching their thirst":
Ibid., 1080.

197   "speechless through fatigue": Rickman, *Journal of Captain Cook's Last Voyage,*
189.

197   "Considering what a strange set of
beings": Beaglehole, *Life of Captain James
Cook,* 572.

198   "to amuse themselves": Rickman,
Journal of Captain Cook's Last Voyage, 188.

198   "prosperous gale": Ibid., 209.

24   A New Race of People

199   "excited our curiosity much":
Beaglehole, ed., *Journals of Captain James
Cook,* vol. 3, 1081.

199   "We were charmed with its appearance": Rickman, *Journal of Captain Cook's
Last Voyage,* 215.

201   "None of them would come near
enough": Ledyard, *Last Voyage of Captain
Cook,* 44.

201   "They shook their spears at us":
Ibid.

202   "How…shall we account for this
nation": Beaglehole, ed., *Journals of Captain James Cook,* vol. 3, 279.

202   "It can scarce be imagined": Rickman, *Journal of Captain Cook's Last Voyage,*
223.

203   "It required but very little address":
Beaglehole, ed., *Journals of Captain James
Cook,* vol. 3, 264.

204   "I never saw Indians so much
astonished": Ibid., 265.

204   They "ran up to us": Ledyard, *Last
Voyage of Captain Cook,* 44.

204   "called to those in the canoes":
Ibid.

204   "breathed fire from their mouths":
Joesting, *Kauai: The Separate Kingdom,* 38.

204   "the volcano family": Westervelt,
Hawaiian Historical Legends, 64.

204   "This is the fruit of a sorceress":
Ibid.

205   "Another mischief-making sorceress": Ibid.

205   "When we showed them beads":
Beaglehole, ed., *Journals of Captain James
Cook,* vol. 3, 265.

205   "I am only going to put it into my
boat": Ibid.

205   "My guests…were exceedingly
curious": Ibid., 265.

206   "the most expert swimmers": Ibid.,
281.

206   handled their boats "with great
dexterity": Ibid., 1321.

206   "They get astride with the[ir]
legs": Ibid.

206   They were "exceedingly beautiful": Ibid., 1083.

206   "Every precaution was taken":
Ibid., 266.

206   "created a general murmur": Rickman, *Journal of Captain Cook's Last Voyage,*
217.

207   "much chagrined on being
refused": Beaglehole, ed., *Journals of Captain James Cook,* vol. 3, 1084.

207   "injured with the venereal disorder": Ibid., 266.

207   "They must be nursing babies":
Barrow, *Captain Cook in Hawaii,* xii.

207   a "tall handsome man about forty
years": Beaglehole, ed., *Journals of Captain James Cook,* vol. 3, 1348.

207   "with the greatest reluctance":
Ibid.

208   they called it a "water squirter":
Joesting, *Kauai: The Separate Kingdom,* 38.

208   "a cowardly, dastardly action":
Beaglehole, ed., *Journals of Captain James
Cook,* vol. 3, 267.

208   "It does not appear": Ibid.

208   "the good effects of at once showing our superiority": Obeyesekere, *Apotheosis of Captain Cook,* 41.

208   "These barbarians must be
quelled": Ibid.

209   "The very instant I leaped ashore":
Beaglehole, ed., *Journals of Captain James
Cook,* vol. 3, 269.

210   "until the body grease dripped":
Joesting, *Kauai: The Separate Kingdom,* 26.

210   "I ratified these marks of friendship": Beaglehole, ed., *Journals of Captain
James Cook,* vol. 3, 269.

210   "an open, candid, active people":
Ibid., 281.

25 In the Land of the Menehune

212 "By the weird glare of the lightning": Twain, *Roughing It*, 374.

212 "Every one whom we met fell on their faces": Beaglehole, ed., *Journals of Captain James Cook*, vol. 3, 269.

213 "They have a very great variety": Ibid., 283.

214 "pleasing and tender": Ibid.

215 "They were determined...to see whether our people were men": Beaglehole, ed., *Journals of Captain James Cook*, vol. 3, 1349.

215 "The women used all their arts": Ibid., 266.

215 "rotatory movement": Danielsson, *Love in the South Seas*, 78.

215 "A young female was taught": Diamond, "Sexual Behavior in Pre Contact Hawai'i: A Sexological Ethnography," *Revista Española del Pacifico* 16 (2004): 37–58.

216 among "the last generation of Hawaiians": Fornander, *Account of the Polynesian Race*, 162.

217 "Never...was there a breath of suspicion": Barrow, *Captain Cook in Hawaii*, 15.

217 Cook "never had any connection": Gascoigne, *Captain Cook: Voyager Between Worlds*, 187.

218 "It has by no means the appearance": Beaglehole, ed., *Journals of Captain James Cook*, vol. 3, 285.

219 "These people...have nearly the same notions": Ibid., 271.

220 "his people would not let him stir": Ibid., 281.

220 "I said all I could": Ibid.

220 "They gently took away my hand": Ibid.

Book Four: New Albion

26 Foul Weather

225 "a great number of little sparks": Beaglehole, ed., *Journals of Captain James Cook*, vol. 3, 289.

225 "It was the first time I had been so near": Ledyard, *Last Voyage of Captain Cook*, 47.

226 "happen to fall into your hands": Benjamin Franklin, "To All Captains and Commanders of American Armed Ships," March 10, 1779, available at National Archives website, founders.archives.gov/.

226 "treat the said Captain Cook": Ibid.

227 "We are all shaking with cold": Beaglehole, ed., *Journals of Captain James Cook*, vol. 3, 288.

230 "high and craggy": Ibid., 1087.

231 "the faint barking of sea lions": Lopez, *Horizon*, 60.

231 "Ashore, perhaps a few Alsean hunters": Ibid., 128.

231 "it's highly probable all [would have] perished": Beaglehole, ed., *Journals of Captain James Cook*, vol. 3, 292.

023100 "the ruggedest weather": Ledyard, *Last Voyage of Captain Cook*, 45.

231 "Our ships complained": Ibid.

232 "Looking ahead...we saw a large reef": Rickman, *Journal of Captain Cook's Last Voyage*, 288.

232 He merely called the weather "unsettled": Beaglehole, ed., *Journals of Captain James Cook*, vol. 3, 292.

232 "unprofitably tossed about": Lopez, *Horizon*, 55.

232 "It is really a rather lamentable business": Beaglehole, ed., *Journals of Captain James Cook*, vol. 3, 292.

233 to "recruit your wood and water": Barnett, *Captain Cook in Alaska*, 13.

27 Soft Gold

234 "We were now so far advanced": Rickman, *Journal of Captain Cook's Last Voyage*, 233.

234 "mild and inoffensive": Beaglehole, ed., *Journals of Captain James Cook*, vol. 3, 296.

235 "floating houses": Thomas, *Cook: The Extraordinary Voyages of Captain James Cook*, 363.

235 "These people, they must have been fish:" King, *First Peoples, First Contacts: Native People of North America*, 123.

238 "Nothing would go down with them": Beaglehole, ed., *Journals of Captain James Cook*, vol. 3, 302.

238 "greedily purchased": Rickman, *Journal of Captain Cook's Last Voyage*, 236.

238 "I have heard it remarked that human flesh": Ledyard, *Last Voyage of Captain Cook*, 48.

239 "in order to render themselves agreeable": Beaglehole, ed., *Journals of Captain James Cook*, vol. 3, 1095.

239 "found means at last to disburden our young gentry": Ibid.

240 "I have nowhere met with Indians": Ibid., 306.

240 "The moment our people began to cut": Ibid.

240 "I very soon emptied my pockets": Ibid.

240 "pointing the way for him": Ledyard, *Last Voyage of Captain Cook*, 48.

241 "We judged from every appearance": Beaglehole, ed., *Journals of Captain James Cook*, vol. 3, 1093.

241 "Their number was alarming": Rickman, *Journal of Captain Cook's Last Voyage*, 235.

241 "As we did not know": Beaglehole, ed., *Journals of Captain James Cook*, vol. 3, 1093.

241 "engagement of tongues": Ibid.

241 "sputtering his words": Ibid.

241 "the same violent actions and gestures": Ibid.

242 "The strangers were not allowed to have any trade": Ibid., 299.

242 "We saw plainly": Ibid., 1398.

243 "very good caviar": Ibid., 319.

243 "filthy as hog sties": Ibid., 318.

243 "Their houses have a most disagreeable effluvia": Ibid., 1328.

244 "would sometimes relax": Ibid., 303.

244 "he became again the despot": Ibid.

245 "is supposed to be superior to any": Gilbert, *Captain Cook's Final Voyage*, 72.

245 "To us who were bound for the North Pole": Beaglehole, ed., *Journals of Captain James Cook*, vol. 3, 1089.

245 "made him happy as a prince": Ibid., 307.

246 "By way of encouragement": Ibid.

28 In Bering's Wake

246 a "perfect hurricane": Beaglehole, ed., *Journals of Captain James Cook*, vol. 3, 334.

246 "Our danger...was equal to any": Rickman, *Journal of Captain Cook's Last Voyage*, 240.

246 "I judged it highly dangerous": Beaglehole, ed., *Journals of Captain James Cook*, vol. 3, 334.

246 "not a little": Ibid.

247 "cool and intrepid among dangers": Barnett, *Captain Cook in Alaska*, 225.

247 "When no one else had a suspicion": Barrow, *Captain Cook in Hawaii*, 15.

248 "with very little intermission": Ledyard, *Last Voyage of Captain Cook*, 51.

248 "On the unknown coast of America": Barrow, *Captain Cook in Hawaii*, 15.

249 "where geographers have placed the pretended Strait": Beaglehole, ed., *Journals of Captain James Cook*, vol. 3, 335.

250 "Instead of the looming haystack": Williams, *Voyages of Delusion*, 288.

250 "We are forwarding our business": Beaglehole, ed., *Journals of Captain James Cook*, vol. 3, 338.

250 "We continue to have most extraordinary fine weather": Ibid., 340.

251 "All hands were employed": Rickman, *Journal of Captain Cook's Last Voyage*, 247.

252 "The account of that voyage": Barnett, *Captain Cook in Alaska*, 91.

253 "A vast promontory": Rickman, *Journal of Captain Cook's Last Voyage*, 246.

254 "I believe that he who learns" Collingridge, *Captain Cook*, 332.

254 "Our hopes of a passage": Beaglehole, ed., *Journals of Captain James Cook*, vol. 3, 1106.

254 "On the 12th of May": Gilbert, *Captain Cook's Final Voyage*, 76.

255 "not without hopes of the dear passage": Ledyard, *Last Voyage of Captain Cook*, 53.

29 Deep Water and Bold Shores

255 "our endeavors to delineate matters": Beaglehole, ed., *Journals of Captain James Cook*, vol. 3, 345.

256 "An incredible number of whales and seals": Ellis, *Authentic Narrative of a Voyage*, 246.

256 "It now becomes almost tautology": Beaglehole, ed., *Journals of Captain James Cook*, vol. 3, 355.

256 a "little Mediterranean sea": Barnett, ed., *Captain Cook's Final Voyage*, 138.

258 "thickset, good-looking people": Beaglehole, ed., *Journals of Captain James Cook*, vol. 3, 351.

258 "fat and jolly": Ellis, *Authentic Narrative of a Voyage*, 236.

259 "are indeed much better": Beaglehole, ed., *Journals of Captain James Cook*, vol. 3, 349.

259 "not the same nation": Nicandri, *Captain Cook Rediscovered*, 230.

259 "descendants from some Chinese": Beaglehole, ed., *Journals of Captain James Cook*, vol. 3, 1111.

259 "some affinity to…the Greenlander": Nicandri, *Captain Cook Rediscovered*, 230.

259 "The inhabitants bear a very striking resemblance": Ledyard, *Last Voyage of Captain Cook*, 53.

260 "We thought we understood from them": Beaglehole, ed., *Journals of Captain James Cook*, vol. 3, 353.

260 "Tis ten to one": Ibid.

260 "The land seemed to close": Ibid., 352.

261 "for some time in a bad state": Anderson's will is reproduced by John Robson at his website.

261 "His decline was too rapid": Beaglehole, ed., *Journals of Captain James Cook*, vol. 3, 1430.

261 "communicated with the one we last came from": Nicandri, *Captain Cook Rediscovered*, 231.

261 "deep water and bold shores": Williams, *Voyages of Delusion*, 315.

262 "I resolved to spend no more time": Nicandri, *Captain Cook Rediscovered*, 231.

262 "We had the good fortune": Barnett, *Captain Cook in Alaska*, 99.

30 Possessed

262 "a vast river, having a strong southerly current": Ledyard, *Last Voyage of Captain Cook*, 54.

263 "If I had not examined this place": Beaglehole, ed., *Journals of Captain James Cook*, vol. 3, 368.

263 "The season…was advancing": Ibid.

263 "a fine spacious opening": Ibid., 359.

263 "burning mountains": Rickman, *Journal of Captain Cook's Last Voyage*, 257.

263 "was like a giant bird": Pete, *Shem Pete's Alaska*, 347.

264 "All the people were very frightened": Ibid.

264 "a discovery I was sorry to make": Hough, *Murder of Captain James Cook*, 146.

265 "I was fully persuaded": Beaglehole, ed., *Journals of Captain James Cook*, vol. 3, 361.

265 "low shores, very thick and muddy water": Ibid.

265 "as favorable for settlement": Ibid., 368.

265 "After all our pains": Nicandri, *Captain Cook Rediscovered*, 241.

265 "As we had proceeded so far": Beaglehole, ed., *Journals of Captain James Cook*, vol. 3, 364.

266 "All hope of a passage": Ibid., 366.

267 "late pretended discoveries": Ibid., 368.

267 "If the discovery of this river": Ibid.

268 "The people of the village saw Cook's men": Pete, *Shem Pete's Alaska*, 347.

269 "to prevent any evil intentions": Beaglehole, ed., *Journals of Captain James Cook*, vol. 3, 369.

269 "not in a conspicuous place": Barnett, *Captain Cook in Alaska*, 116.

269 "behaved very friendly": Gilbert, *Captain Cook's Final Voyage*, 81.

31 Risen in a New World

271 "to publish so erroneous a map": Barnett, *Captain Cook in Alaska*, 169.

272 "a sensible young man": Beaglehole, ed., *Journals of Captain James Cook*, vol. 3, 406.

272   a "much esteemed member of our little society": Ibid.

272   "If we except our commander": Ibid., 1430.

272   "The enlivening rays of the sun": Ibid., 410.

274   "The sight of the ships": Ibid.

274   "perhaps...as an offering to their gods": Ibid., 1132.

275   "in constant readiness": Ibid., 411.

276   "Their chief demand with our people": Ibid., 412.

276   "long visaged, stout-made men": Ibid.

32   Big with Every Danger

277   "It was as if they had threaded": Hough, *Murder of Captain James Cook*, 155.

277   "We are in high spirits": Ibid.

278   a sudden "sharpness of the air": Ibid., 416.

278   "Some time before noon ... we perceived a brightness": Ibid.

278   "compact as a wall": Ibid., 417.

279   "quite impenetrable": Ibid.

279   "Our situation was now more and more critical": Ibid., 418.

279   "This was what I ... most feared": Ibid.

280   "The frost set in so hard": Rickman, *Journal of Captain Cook's Last Voyage*, 238.

281   "boldness of daring and skill": Nicandri, *Captain Cook Rediscovered*, 259.

281   "so active and vigorous in their operations": Ibid., 370.

281   "closet studying philosophers": Nicandri, *Captain Cook Rediscovered*, 264.

282   "whose opinion respecting the formation of ice": Ibid., 259.

282   "large, unwieldy sluggish animals": Ledyard, *Last Voyage of Captain Cook*, 57.

282   "in herds of many hundred": Beaglehole, ed., *Journals of Captain James Cook*, vol. 3, 420.

282   the guardians would "wake those next to them": Ibid.

282   "defend the young one to the very last": Ibid.

283   "sweet as marmalade": Ibid., 419.

283   "I think them pleasant and good eating": Barnett, *Captain Cook in Alaska*, 151.

283   "an ill reward": Ledyard, *Last Voyage of Captain Cook*, 58.

283   the "disgustful" meat: Gilbert, *Captain Cook's Final Voyage*, 92.

283   "It was a matter of doubt whether a ship": Nicandri, *Captain Cook Rediscovered*, 261.

283   did not think it "consistent with prudence": Barnett, *Captain Cook in Alaska*, 156.

284   "The Captain informed the ship's company": Ibid., 156.

284   "It was high time to think of leaving": Nicandri, *Captain Cook Rediscovered*, 278.

285   the "great dislike I had to lay inactive": Barnett, *Captain Cook in Alaska*, 160.

285   "If he could no longer pursue his first great object": Nicandri, *Captain Cook Rediscovered*, 267.

285   "Upon the coast of America": Ledyard, *Last Voyage of Captain Cook*, 67.

286   "We were well convinced already": Ibid., 59.

Book Five: Apotheosis

33   Pathway of the Gods

289   "a little curve like the last kink": Twain, *Roughing It*, 370.

290   "I have nowhere in this sea": Beaglehole, ed., *Journals of Captain James Cook*, vol. 3, 490.

291   "The shouts of joy and admiration": Ledyard, *Last Voyage of Captain Cook*, 69.

291   sounded like the song of the 'ō'ō: Subin, *Accidental Gods*, 360.

292   "expressed the greatest joy": Beaglehole, ed., *Journals of Captain James Cook*, vol. 3, 503.

292   a succession of "beautiful cascades": Ibid., 495.

293   "Captain Cook had observed that in a harbor": Ibid., 503.

293   a "maritime market": Ibid., 1154.

294   These men were in "great distress": Beaglehole, ed., *Journals of Captain James Cook*, vol. 3, 498.

294 "to a set of poor harmless and innocent people": Ibid., 474.

295 "all the climates from the torrid to the frigid": Ibid., 478.

295 "It was not possible to keep [them]": Ibid., 486.

295 "she immediately jumps overboard": Ibid., 1154.

296 "dreadful surf": Ibid., 485.

296 "I have nowhere within the tropics": McLynn, *Captain Cook: Master of the Seas*, 368.

296 "Being... advertised of his danger": Barnett, ed., *Captain Cook's Final Voyage*, 201.

296 a whale "playing so near to the ship": Beaglehole, ed., *Journals of Captain James Cook*, vol. 3, 1153.

297 "This conduct of the commander": Ledyard, *Last Voyage of Captain Cook*, 68.

34   Approaching Adoration

298 *"Good-looking gods they were!":* Subin, *Accidental Gods*, 360.

299 "the very abject and slavish manner": Beaglehole, ed., *Journals of Captain James Cook*, vol. 3, 507.

299 "If Cook happened to turn his head": Ledyard, *Last Voyage of Captain Cook*, 70.

299 "well sprinkled with pagan temples": Twain, *Roughing It*, 374.

300 Cook "was quite passive": Beaglehole, ed., *Journals of Captain James Cook*, vol. 3, 506.

300 a "long and rather tiresome ceremony": Ibid.

302 "When Captain Cook appeared": Kirch, *Shark Going Inland Is My Chief*, 255.

302 "Captain Cook... generally went by this name": Cook and King, *Voyage to the Pacific Ocean*, vol. 3, 5.

303 his "direct encouragement of idolatry": Williams, *Death of Captain Cook*, 150.

304 "Koa took me by the hand": Beaglehole, ed., *Journals of Captain James Cook*, vol. 3, 491.

35   Golden Days

305 "Every article that wanted either to be reviewed": Rickman, *Journal of Captain Cook's Last Voyage*, 309.

305 "The water of the pond was so strong": Beaglehole, ed., *Journals of Captain James Cook*, vol. 3, 548.

306 "like a kind of nectar to us": Ledyard, *Last Voyage of Captain Cook*, 81.

306 "They observed that the color of our skins": Ibid., 76.

306 "It is very clear that they regard us": Beaglehole, ed., *Journals of Captain James Cook*, vol. 3, 525.

306 "took great pleasure in admiring herself": Ibid., 1158.

306 "a married man here would as soon let you": Ibid., 1182.

307 "These people are so eager after our iron": Ibid., 1164.

307 "No women will on any account come": Ibid., 1161.

308 "with the rising of the first sky-rocket": Rickman, *Journal of Captain Cook's Last Voyage*, 319.

308 "some of a very sweet note": Beaglehole, ed., *Journals of Captain James Cook*, vol. 3, 1167.

309 "of stupendous height": Rickman, *Journal of Captain Cook's Last Voyage*, 316.

309 "impeded by such impenetrable thickets": Ledyard, *Last Voyage of Captain Cook*, 82.

309 "They provide themselves with a thin board": Beaglehole, ed., *Journals of Captain James Cook*, vol. 3, 1164.

36   A Welcome Overstayed

311 The king's own vessel... was "most superb": Rickman, *Journal of Captain Cook's Last Voyage*, 313.

311 "an old man and very feeble": Ledyard, *Last Voyage of Captain Cook*, 75.

311 "tall and thin" and "seemingly much emaciated": Beaglehole, ed., *Journals of Captain James Cook*, vol. 3, 1168.

311 "a countenance very expressive of conscious dignity": Ledyard, *Last Voyage of Captain Cook*, 75.

311 "He gave us to understand": Rickman, *Journal of Captain Cook's Last Voyage*, 315.

312 "A more rich or elegant dress than this": Beaglehole, ed., *Journals of Captain James Cook*, vol. 3, 1179.

313 "stout, comely, and bold-looking": Ledyard, *Last Voyage of Captain Cook*, 75.

313 "The cohabitation is between the chiefs": Ibid., 89.

314 "They had heard what terrible things": Ibid., 75.

314 had "so much to do with the sun": Ibid., 76.

314 "It was supposed...that we had drained": Beaglehole, ed., *Journals of Captain James Cook*, vol. 3, 527.

315 "good and benevolent disposition": Ibid., 517.

316 "I had proposals by our friends to elope": Beaglehole, ed., *Journals of Captain James Cook*, vol. 3, 518.

316 "no better motive than what actuates children": Ibid., 519.

316 "The Captain, to avoid giving a refusal": Ibid.

317 "I must confess": Cook and King, *Voyage to the Pacific Ocean*, vol. 3, 25.

317 a "considerable concourse of the natives": Ledyard, *Last Voyage of Captain Cook*, 93.

318 "insensible of the daily decline": Ibid., 92.

318 "ritually purifying the ground": Kirch, *Shark Going Inland Is My Chief*, 261.

319 "All hands chagrined": Beaglehole, ed., *Journals of Captain James Cook*, vol. 3, 527.

37 **The Water's Edge**

320 "Our return to this bay was as disagreeable": Ledyard, *Last Voyage of Captain Cook*, 95.

320 "He was very inquisitive": Barnett, ed., *Captain Cook's Final Voyage*, 223.

326 "With many tears and entreaties": Beaglehole, ed., *Journals of Captain James Cook*, vol. 3, 535.

326 "dejected and frightened": Ibid.

326 "It was at this period...we first began to suspect": Ibid.

326 "an artful rascal": Ibid.

327 "We can never think of compelling him": Ibid.

327 "had no other effect": Ibid.

328 *"Take to the boats!"*: Ibid., 536.

328 "far exceeding all the noise": Ibid.

328 "Had Captain Cook come down to the boats": Ibid., 537.

329 "By an infatuation that is altogether unaccountable": Ibid.

330 "a most miserable scene of confusion": Ibid., 536.

330 "They never gave the soldiers time": Ibid.

330 almost "sent me to the bottom": Ibid.

331 "All of my people...were totally vanquished": Ibid.

331 "thought of shooting him on the spot": Kennedy, *Death of Captain Cook*, 83.

331 "If he be a god, he will not make a noise": Gascoigne, *Captain Cook: Voyager Between Worlds*, 217.

331 "the multitude immediately shouted": Ibid.

332 "a fellow gave him a blow": Beaglehole, ed., *Journals of Captain James Cook*, vol. 3, 1198.

332 "As soon as one had struck him": Ibid.

38 **The Bones of Captain Cook**

333 "Our father—we have lost our father": Hough, *Murder of Captain James Cook*, 228.

333 "Grief was visible in every countenance": Gilbert, *Captain Cook's Final Voyage*, 108.

334 "remained a mere spectator": Zimmermann, *Third Voyage of Captain Cook*, 101.

334 "To have come away at such a time": Beaglehole, ed., *Journals of Captain James Cook*, vol. 3, 1200.

334 "The whole affair": Kennedy, *Death of Captain Cook*, 81.

334 a "confounded fray": Beaglehole, ed., *Journals of Captain James Cook*, vol. 3, 534.

334 "this most unhappy disaster": Ibid.

334 "Upon the whole": Ibid., 538.

335 "I cannot help lamenting": Ibid., 540.

336 "The safest and best method we could take": Ibid., 539.

337 "Women were heard howling and crying": Ibid., 1209.

337 "By the light of the fire": Ibid., 555.

337 "It smelled strong": Ibid., 1209.

337 "This…he strongly denied": Ibid.

338 the "impudent rascal": Ibid., 544.

338 "making many flourishes and antic gestures": Burney, *Captain Cook's Final Voyage*, 228.

339 "even danced around us": Zimmermann, *Third Voyage of Captain Cook*, 103.

339 "too gross an insult to bear": Beaglehole, ed., *Journals of Captain James Cook*, vol. 3, 544.

339 "the circumstance of the hat": Ibid., 1210.

339 the captain's "plan of operations": Ibid., 561.

339 "It is difficult to guess what could induce": Ibid., 1210.

340 "as trophies of their vile victory": Ibid., 563.

340 "Our people in this day's transactions": Ibid., 562.

340 "If this had not been done": Ibid., 563.

341 "We found in it the following bones": Beaglehole, ed., *Journals of Captain James Cook*, vol. 3, 1216.

341 "Such was the condition": Ibid.

342 "universal gloom": Ibid., 568.

342 "a place become too remarkably famous": Ibid., 567.

342 "I had been so used to look[ing] up to him": Hough, *Murder of Captain James Cook*, 243.

342 "In every situation, he stood unrivaled": Barnett, *Captain Cook in Alaska*, 225.

39 The Long Concealed Arrangements of the Almighty

344 "The disorder I was attacked with": Hough, *Murder of Captain James Cook*, 241.

345 "the melancholy account of the celebrated Captain Cook": Barnett, *Captain Cook in Alaska*, 222.

345 Cook's voyages "have enlarged natural philosophy": Ibid., 224.

345 "Had we been born on an island": Williams, *Death of Captain Cook*, 85.

346 "the memory of the ablest and most renowned navigator": Cook and King, *Voyage to the Pacific Ocean*, vol. 1, lxxxvii.

348 "She kept her faculties to the end": Hough, *Captain James Cook*, 369.

349 "justifiable homicide": Twain, *Roughing It*, 371.

349 "monumental stump": Ibid., 372.

349 "hung up in a native hut": Ibid., 371.

349 "one of these children grew to be a very old man": Ibid.

349 "always expected Lono's return": Ibid., 375.

Epilogue: Lono's Tears

353 This short passage is primarily drawn from Westervelt, *Hawaiian Historical Legends*; Fornander, *An Account of the Polynesian Race*; Malo, *Hawaiian Antiquities*; Kirch, *A Shark Going Inland Is My Chief*; Kamakau, *Ruling Chiefs of Hawaii*; Sahlins, *How "Natives" Think*; Ellis, *Polynesian Researches: Hawaii*; Barrow, *Captain Cook in Hawaii*; Twain, *Roughing It*; Beckwith, *Hawaiian Mythology*; and Subin, *Accidental Gods*.

Selected Bibliography

Museums and Galleries
Anchorage Museum, Anchorage, Alaska, United States
Bishop Museum, Honolulu, Hawai'i, United States
The Box, Plymouth, United Kingdom
British Museum, London, United Kingdom
Captain Cook Birthplace Museum, Marton, Middlesbrough, United Kingdom
Captain Cook Memorial Museum, Whitby, Yorkshire, United Kingdom
Fare Pote'e Museum, Huahine, French Polynesia
Maritime Museum of Tasmania, Hobart, Tasmania, Australia
Maritime Museum of the Atlantic, Halifax, Nova Scotia, Canada
Museum of Anthropology, University of British Columbia, Vancouver, Canada
Museum of Archaeology and Anthropology, Cambridge, United Kingdom
Museum of Tahiti and the Islands, Tahiti, French Polynesia
National Gallery, London, United Kingdom
National Maritime Museum, Greenwich, United Kingdom
National Museum of the Royal Navy, Portsmouth, United Kingdom
National Portrait Gallery, London, United Kingdom
Natural History Museum, London, United Kingdom
Royal British Columbia Museum, Victoria, British Columbia, Canada
Royal Observatory Greenwich, London, United Kingdom
Staithes Story Museum, Staithes, United Kingdom
Te Papa, Museum of New Zealand, Wellington, New Zealand
Vancouver Maritime Museum, Vancouver, Canada

Parks, Monuments, and Historic Sites
Cape Flattery, Olympic Coast National Marine Sanctuary, Washington, United States
Captain Cook Memorial, Whitby, Yorkshire, United Kingdom
Captain Cook Monument, Resolution Park, Anchorage, Alaska, United States
Captain Cook State Recreation Area, Kenai Peninsula, Alaska, United States
Cook/Furneaux Memorial at Adventure Bay, Bruny Island, Tasmania, Australia
Cook Memorial at Meretoto/Ship Cove, Queen Charlotte Sound, New Zealand
Fortress of Louisbourg National Historic Site, Nova Scotia, Canada
Hawai'i Volcanoes National Park, Hawai'i, United States
Hinchingbrooke House, Huntingdon, Cambridgeshire, United Kingdom
Kealakekua Bay State Historical Park, Hawai'i, United States

Kenai Fjords National Park, Alaska, United States
Marae Taputapuatea, Taputapuatea Commune, Raiatea, French Polynesia
Nootka Heritage Lighthouse, Nootka Sound, British Columbia, Canada
Otter Crest State Scenic Viewpoint, Oregon, United States
Puʻuhonua o Hōnaunau National Historical Park, Hawaiʻi, United States

Archives
Archives New Zealand, Wellington, New Zealand
Archives, Royal Museums Greenwich, London, United Kingdom
Beinecke Rare Book and Manuscript Library, Yale University, New Haven,
     Connecticut, United States
British Library, London, United Kingdom
National Archives, Kew, London, United Kingdom
National Archives, Washington, D.C., United States
Victoria University of Wellington, Wellington, New Zealand

Accounts from Participants of Cook's Third Voyage
Barnett, James K., ed. *Captain Cook's Final Voyage: The Untold Story from the Journals of James
     Burney and Henry Roberts.* Pullman: Washington State University Press, 2017.
Beaglehole, J. C., ed. *The Journals of Captain James Cook on His Voyages of Discovery.* Vol. 3,
     The Voyage of the Resolution and Discovery 1776-1780. Cambridge, U.K.: Cambridge
     University Press for the Hakluyt Society, 1967. Beaglehole's densely annotated
     work, which runs more than a thousand pages in length, includes not only the
     journals of Captains Cook and Clerke, but copious passages from the journals of
     many other participants, including Anderson, Bayly, Burney, Edgar, Gore, King,
     Samwell, Trevenen, and Williamson.
Burney, James. "Mr. Burney's Report of Massacre at Grass Cove, December 17, 1773."
     Special collections, Archives New Zealand, Wellington.
Cook, James, and James King. *A Voyage to the Pacific Ocean, Undertaken by Command of His
     Majesty, for Making Discoveries in the Northern Hemisphere.* 6 vols. 2nd ed. London: G.
     Nicol, 1785.
Ellis, W. *An Authentic Narrative of a Voyage Performed by Captain Cook and Captain Clerke.*
     London: G. Robinson, 1783.
Gilbert, George. *Captain Cook's Final Voyage: The Journal of Midshipman George Gilbert.*
     Edited by Christine Holmes. Honolulu: University Press of Hawaiʻi, 1982.
Ledyard, John. *The Last Voyage of Captain Cook: The Collected Writings of John Ledyard.*
     Edited by James Zug. Washington, D.C.: National Geographic, 2005.
Rickman, John. *Journal of Captain Cook's Last Voyage to the Pacific Ocean, on Discovery.* Lon-
     don: E. Newbery, 1781.
Samwell, David. *The Death of Captain Cook and Other Writings by David Samwell.* Edited by
     Martin Fitzpatrick, Nicholas Thomas, and Jennifer Newell. Cardiff: University
     of Wales Press, 2007.
————. *A Narrative of the Death of Captain James Cook.* London: G.C.J. and J. Robinson,
     1786.
Zimmermann, Heinrich. *The Third Voyage of Captain Cook.* Fairfield, Wash.: Ye Galleon
     Press, 1988.

Books and Articles
Ackroyd, Peter. *London: The Biography.* New York: Nan A. Talese, 2001.
————. *Thames: The Biography.* New York: Anchor, 2009.
Adams, Mark. *Tip of the Iceberg: My 3,000-Mile Journey Around Wild Alaska, the Last Great
     American Frontier.* New York: Dutton, 2018.

Alexander, Caroline. *The Bounty: The True Story of the Mutiny on the Bounty.* New York: Viking, 2003.

Alexander, Michael. *Omai: Noble Savage.* London: Collins & Harvill, 1977.

Anderson, Bern. *The Life and Voyages of Captain George Vancouver: Surveyor of the Sea.* Seattle: University of Washington Press, 1960.

Andrewes, William J. H. *The Quest for Longitude: The Proceedings of the Longitude Symposium.* Cambridge, Mass.: Collection of Historical Scientific Instruments, Harvard University, 1996.

Aslet, Clive. *The Story of Greenwich.* Cambridge, Mass.: Harvard University Press, 1999.

Aughton, Peter. *The Fatal Voyage: Captain Cook's Last Great Journey.* London: Tauris Parke Paperbacks, 2007.

———. *Resolution: Captain Cook's Second Voyage of Discovery.* London: Weidenfeld & Nicolson, 2004.

Barnett, James K. *Captain Cook in Alaska and the North Pacific.* Anchorage: Todd Communications, 2008.

———. *Captain George Vancouver in Alaska and the North Pacific.* Anchorage: Todd Communications, 2017.

Barnett, James K., and David L. Nicandri, eds. *Arctic Ambitions: Captain Cook and the Northwest Passage.* Seattle: University of Washington Press, 2015.

Barrie, David. *Sextant: A Young Man's Daring Sea Voyage and the Men Who Mapped the World's Oceans.* New York: William Morrow, 2015.

Barrington, Daines. *The Possibility of Approaching the North Pole Asserted.* London: British Library Historical Print Editions, 1818.

Barrow, Terence. *Captain Cook in Hawaii.* Honolulu: Island Heritage, 1978.

Beaglehole, J. C. *The Life of Captain James Cook.* Stanford, Calif.: Stanford University Press, 1974.

Beaglehole, J. C., ed. *The Journals of Captain James Cook on His Voyages of Discovery.* Vol. 1, *The Voyage of the Endeavour, 1768–1771.* Cambridge, U.K.: Cambridge University Press for the Hakluyt Society, 1967.

———. *The Journals of Captain James Cook on His Voyages of Discovery.* Vol. 2, *The Voyage of the Resolution and Adventure 1772–1775.* Cambridge, U.K.: Cambridge University Press for the Hakluyt Society, 1967.

Beckwith, Martha. *Hawaiian Mythology.* Honolulu: University of Hawai'i Press, 1970.

Begg, A. C., and N. C. Begg. *James Cook and New Zealand.* Wellington: A. R. Shearer, Government Printer, 1970.

Black, Jeremy. *George III: America's Last King.* New Haven: Yale University Press, 2006.

Bligh, William. *A Voyage to the South Seas.* London: George Nicol, 1792.

Boswell, James. *The Life of Samuel Johnson.* London: Penguin Classics, 1986.

Bown, Stephen R. *Scurvy: How a Surgeon, a Mariner, and a Gentleman Solved the Greatest Medical Mystery of the Age of Sail.* New York: Thomas Dunne, 2003.

Burney, Frances. *Journals and Letters.* New York: Penguin Classics, 2001.

Cameron, Roderick. *The Golden Haze: With Captain Cook in the South Pacific.* Cleveland: World Publishing Co., 1964.

Carroll, Rick. *Huahine: Island of the Lost Canoe.* Honolulu: Bishop Museum Press, 2005.

Chang, David A. *The World and All the Things Upon It: Native Hawaiian Geographies of Exploration.* Minneapolis: University of Minnesota Press, 2016.

Chisholm, Kate. *Fanny Burney: Her Life.* London: Chatto & Windus, 1998.

Clark, Thomas Blake. *Omai: First Polynesian Ambassador to England.* San Francisco: Colt Press, 1969.

Cline, Nancee Pace. *Queen Emma's Church in Kealakekua: Crossroads of Culture.* Self-published, 2010.

Collingridge, Vanessa. *Captain Cook: A Legacy Under Fire*. Guilford, Conn.: Lyons Press, 2002.

———. *Captain Cook: The Life, Death and Legacy of History's Greatest Explorer*. London: Ebury Press, 2003.

Colman, George. *Random Records*. Vol. 1. London: Henry Colburn and Richard Bentley, 1830.

Connaughton, Richard. *Omai: The Prince Who Never Was*. London: Timewell Press, 2005.

Cook, James. *The Journals*. London: Penguin Books, 1999.

Cook, Robin. *Whitby in the Time of Cook*. Whitby, U.K.: Captain Cook Memorial Museum, 2018.

Corn, Charles. *The Scents of Eden: A History of the Spice Trade*. New York: Kodansha International, 1999.

Cowley, Gordon, and Les Deacon. *In the Wake of Captain Cook: The Life and Times of Captain Charles Clerke, R.N. 1741–79*. Boston, U.K.: Richard Kay Publications, 1997.

Dale, Paul W., ed. *Seventy North to Fifty South: The Story of Captain Cook's Last Voyage*. Englewood Cliffs, N.J.: Prentice Hall, 1969.

Damrosch, Leo. *The Club: Johnson, Boswell, and the Friends Who Shaped an Age*. New Haven: Yale University Press, 2019.

Dana, Richard Henry. *Two Years Before the Mast*. New York: Signet Classics, 2009.

Danielsson, Bengt. *Love in the South Seas*. London: George Allen & Unwin, 1956.

Davies, John. "Cook: The 'Adventure' and Misadventure in Queen Charlotte Sound, 1773-1777." *Journal of the Nelson and Marlborough Historical Societies*, vol. 2, no. 1, 1987.

Daws, Gavan. *Shoal of Time: A History of the Hawaiian Islands*. Honolulu: University of Hawai'i Press, 1974.

Dening, Greg. *Mr. Bligh's Bad Language: Passion, Power and Theatre on the Bounty*. Cambridge, U.K.: Cambridge University Press, 1994.

Doughty, Andrew. *Hawaii, The Big Island Revealed*. Lihu'e, Hawai'i: Wizard Publications, 2021.

———. *The Ultimate Kauai Guidebook*. Lihu'e, Hawai'i: Wizard Publications, 2022.

Dugard, Martin. *Farther than Any Man: The Rise and Fall of Captain James Cook*. New York: Washington Square Press, 2002.

Ellis, William. *Journal of William Ellis: A Narrative of a Tour Through Hawaii in 1823*. Honolulu: Hawaiian Gazette Co., 1917.

———. *Polynesian Researches: Hawaii*. Rutland, Vt.: Charles E. Tuttle Co., 1974.

———. *Polynesian Researches: Society Islands, Tuhuai Islands, and New Zealand*. Rutland, Vt.: Charles E. Tuttle Co., 1969.

Fairchild, Hoxie Neale. *The Noble Savage: A Study in Romantic Naturalism*. New York: Russell & Russell, 1961.

Fish and Ships!: Food on the Voyages of Captain Cook. Whitby, U.K.: Captain Cook Memorial Museum, 2011.

Flavell, Julie. *When London Was the Capital of America*. New Haven: Yale University Press. 2011.

Forbes, David W. *Encounters with Paradise: Views of Hawaii and Its People, 1778–1941*. Honolulu: Honolulu Academy of Arts, 1992.

Fornander, Abraham. *An Account of the Polynesian Race: Its Origins and Migrations and the Ancient History of the Hawaiian People to the Times of Kamehameha I*. Vol. 2. London: Forgotten Books, 2015.

———. *Fornander's Ancient History of the Hawaiian People*. Honolulu: Mutual, 1999.

Frame, William, with Laura Walker. *James Cook: The Voyages*. Montreal: McGill–Queen's University Press, 2018.

Fullagar, Kate. *The Warrior, the Voyager, and the Artist: Three Lives in an Age of Empire*. New Haven: Yale University Press, 2020.

Gascoigne, John. *Captain Cook: Voyager Between Worlds.* London: Hambledon Continuum, 2008.

———. *Joseph Banks and the English Enlightenment: Useful Knowledge and Polite Culture.* Cambridge, U.K.: Cambridge University Press, 1994.

Gifford, Bill. *Ledyard: In Search of the First American Explorer.* Orlando, Fla.: Harcourt, 2007.

Gill, Crispin. *Plymouth: An Illustrated History.* Wellington, U.K.: Halsgrove, 1993.

Goodhue, Cornelia. *Journey into the Fog: The Story of Vitus Bering and the Bering Sea.* Garden City, N.Y.: Doubleday, Doran, 1944.

Gough, Barry. *Juan de Fuca's Strait: Voyages in the Waterway of Forgotten Dreams.* Madeira Park, B.C.: Harbour, 2012.

Gray, Edward G. *The Making of John Ledyard: Empire and Ambition in the Life of an Early American Traveler.* New Haven: Yale University Press, 2007.

Hadlow, Janice. *A Royal Experiment: Love and Duty, Madness and Betrayal—The Private Lives of King George III and Queen Charlotte.* New York: Picador, 2015.

Haley, James L. *Captive Paradise: A History of Hawaii.* New York: St. Martin's Press, 2014.

Hanbury-Tenison, Robin, ed. *The Seventy Great Journeys in History.* London: Thames & Hudson, 2006.

Harman, Claire. *Fanny Burney: A Biography.* New York: Knopf, 2001.

Harrison, Christina. *The Botanical Adventures of Joseph Banks.* London: Royal Botanic Gardens, Kew, 2020.

Hetherington, Michelle. *Cook & Omai: The Cult of the South Seas.* Canberra: National Library of Australia, 2001.

Hibbert, Christopher. *George III.* New York: Basic Books, 1998.

Horwitz, Tony. *Blue Latitudes: Boldly Going Where Captain Cook Has Gone Before.* New York: Picador, 2002.

Hough, Richard. *Captain James Cook: A Biography.* New York: W. W. Norton, 1995.

———. *The Murder of Captain James Cook.* London: Macmillan, 1979.

Howarth, David. *Tahiti: A Paradise Lost.* New York: Penguin Books, 1983.

James, Van. *Ancient Sites of Kauai: A Guide to Hawaiian Archaeological and Cultural Places.* Honolulu: Mutual, 2015.

Jenkins, Simon. *The City on the Thames: The Creation of a World Capital.* New York: Pegasus Books, 2020.

Jewitt, John R. *The Adventures and Sufferings of John R. Jewitt, Captive of Chief Maquinna.* Vancouver: Douglas & McIntyre, 1987.

Joesting, Edward. *Kauai: The Separate Kingdom.* Honolulu: University of Hawai'i Press, 1987.

Johnson, Terry. *The Bering Sea and Aleutian Islands: Region of Wonders.* Fairbanks: Alaska Sea Grant College Program at the University of Alaska, 2003.

Johnston, A. J. B. *Endgame 1758: The Promise, the Glory, and the Despair of Louisbourg's Last Decade.* Sydney, Nova Scotia: Cape Breton University Press, 2015.

Jonaitis, Aldona. *The Yuquot Whalers' Shrine.* Seattle: University of Washington Press.

Kamakau, Samuel Mānaiakalani. *Ruling Chiefs of Hawaii.* Honolulu: Kamehameha Press, 1961.

Kāne, Herb Kawainui. *Voyage: The Discovery of Hawaii.* Honolulu: Island Heritage, 1976.

Kennedy, Gavin. *The Death of Captain Cook.* London, Gerald Duckworth, 1978.

King, J. C. H. *First Peoples, First Contacts: Native Peoples of North America.* Cambridge, Mass.: Harvard University Press, 1999.

King, Michael. *The Penguin History of New Zealand.* Auckland: Penguin Books, 2003.

Kippis, Andrew. *The Life of Captain Cook.* London: G. Nicol, 1788.

Kirch, Patrick Vinton. *A Shark Going Inland Is My Chief.* Berkeley: University of California Press, 2012.

————. *On the Road of the Winds: An Archaeological History of the Pacific Islands Before European Contact*. Berkeley: University of California Press, 2000.

Kitson, Arthur. *The Life of Captain James Cook*. Alpha Editions, 2018.

Kuykendall, Ralph S., and A. Grove Day. *Hawaii: A History*. Englewood Cliffs, N.J.: Prentice Hall, 1948.

Langdon, Robert. *Tahiti: Island of Love*. Sydney: Pacific Publications, 1979.

Lauridsden, Peter. *Vitus Bering: The Discoverer of the Bering Strait*. Chicago: S. C. Griggs, 1889.

Lay, Graeme. *A Travel Guide to Captain James Cook's New Zealand*. Auckland: New Holland Publishers, 2017.

Layland, Michael. *A Perfect Eden: Encounters by Early Explorers of Vancouver Island*. Victoria, B.C.: TouchWood Editions, 2016.

Lincoln, Margarette, ed. *Science and Exploration in the Pacific: European Voyages to the Southern Oceans in the 18th Century*. Woodbridge, U.K.: Boydell Press, 1998.

Littlepage, Dean. *Steller's Island: Adventures of a Pioneer Naturalist in Alaska*. Seattle: Mountaineers Books, 2006

Lopez, Barry. *Horizon*. New York: Knopf, 2019.

Lucas, Lois. *Plants of Old Hawaii*. Honolulu: Bess Press, 1982.

Mackaness, George. *The Life of Vice-Admiral William Bligh*. New York: Farrar & Rinehart, 1932.

Mackesy, Piers. *The War for America, 1775–1783*. Lincoln: University of Nebraska Press, 1993.

MacLean, Alistair. *Captain Cook: Explorer, Navigator, Hero*. London: HarperCollins, 2020.

Malo, David. *Hawaiian Antiquities*. Honolulu: Hawaiian Gazette Co., 1898.

Maschmeyer, Gloria J., and John Wedin. *Paradise of the North: Alaska's Prince William Sound*. Anchorage: Greatland Graphics, 1995.

McCann, Joy. *Wild Sea: A History of the Southern Ocean*. Chicago: University of Chicago Press, 2019.

McCormick, E. H. *Omai: Pacific Envoy*. Auckland: Auckland University Press, 1977.

McCririck, Mary. *Stories of Wales*. Book 3. Denbigh: Gee and Sons. 1963.

McLane, Gretel Blickhahn. *Hawaii: Big Island*. Singapore: Press Pacifica, 1981.

McLynn, Frank. *Captain Cook: Master of the Seas*. New Haven: Yale University Press, 2011.

Melville, Herman. *Omoo*. New York: Penguin Books, 2007.

Michener, James A. *Hawaii*. Greenwich, Conn.: Fawcett Publications, 1973.

Miller, Debby S. *A Wild Promise: Prince William Sound*. Seattle: Braided River, 2018.

Moore, Peter. *Endeavour: The Ship That Changed the World*. New York: Farrar, Straus and Giroux, 2018.

Moorehead, Alan. *The Fatal Impact: The Invasion of the South Pacific, 1767-1840*. Sydney: Mead & Beckett, 1987.

Murphy, Robert. *The Haunted Journey: The Heroic Story of Vitus Bering's Discovery of Alaska*. Garden City, N.Y.: Doubleday, 1961.

Murray-Oliver, Anthony. *Captain Cook's Hawaii: As Seen by His Artists*. Wellington: Millwood Press, 1975.

Musgrave, Toby. *The Multifarious Mr. Banks: From Botany Bay to Kew, the Natural Historian Who Shaped the World*. New Haven: Yale University Press, 2020.

Newell, Jennifer. *Trading Nature: Tahitians, Europeans, and Ecological Exchange*. Honolulu: University of Hawai'i Press, 2010.

Nicandri, David L. *Captain Cook Rediscovered: Voyaging to the Icy Latitudes*. Vancouver: UBC Press, 2020.

Obeyesekere, Gananath. *The Apotheosis of Captain Cook: European Mythmaking in the Pacific*. Princeton, N.J.: Princeton University Press, 1997.

————. *Cannibal Talk: The Man-Eating Myth and Human Sacrifice in the South Seas*. Berkeley: University of California Press, 2005.

O'Brian, Patrick. *Joseph Banks: A Life*. Chicago: University of Chicago Press, 1993.
———. *Master and Commander*. New York: W. W. Norton, 1990.
Oliver, Douglas L. *The Pacific Islands*. Honolulu: University of Hawai'i Press, 1979.
Orchiston, Wayne. *Nautical Astronomy in New Zealand: The Voyages of James Cook*. Levin, New Zealand: Carter Observatory, 1998.
O'Shaughnessy, Andrew Jackson. *The Men Who Lost America: British Leadership, the American Revolution, and the Fate of the Empire*. New Haven: Yale University Press, 2013.
Parkinson, Sydney. *Journal of a Voyage to the South Seas in HMS Endeavour*. London: Caliban Books, 1984.
Pete, Shem. *Shem Pete's Alaska: The Territory of the Upper Cook Inlet Dena'ina*. Edited by James Kari and James A. Fall. Fairbanks: University of Alaska Press, 2016.
Pitzer, Andrea. *Icebound: Shipwrecked at the Edge of the World*. New York: Scribner, 2021.
Raban, Jonathan. *Passage to Juneau: A Sea and Its Meanings*. New York: Vintage Departures, 2000.
Ragnall, Steve. *Better Conceiv'd Than Describ'd: The Life and Times of Captain James King (1750–84), Captain Cook's Friend and Colleague*. Kibworth Beauchamp, U.K.: Matador, 2013.
Rauzon, Mark J. *Isles of Amnesia: The History, Geography, and Restoration of America's Forgotten Pacific Islands*. Honolulu: University of Hawai'i Press, 2016.
Richardson, Jeff, and Kenneth F. Wilson. *The Aleutian Islands of Alaska: Living on the Edge*. Fairbanks: University of Alaska Press, 2008.
Rigby, Nigel, and Pieter Van Der Merwe. *Captain Cook in the Pacific*. Greenwich, U.K.: National Maritime Museum, 2002.
Rigby, Nigel, Pieter Van Der Merwe, and Glyn Williams. *Pioneers of the Pacific: Voyages of Exploration, 1787–1810*. Greenwich, U.K.: National Maritime Museum, 2005.
Roberts, Kenneth. *Northwest Passage*. Garden City, N.Y.: Doubleday, Doran, 1937.
Robinson, Chris. *Plymouth: Bronze Age to Today*. Plymouth: Pen & Ink, 2019.
Robson, John. *The Captain Cook Encyclopædia*. Mechanicsburg, Pa.: Stackpole Books, 2004.
———. *Captain Cook's War and Peace: The Royal Navy Years, 1755–1768*. Annapolis: Naval Institute Press, 2009.
———. *Captain Cook's World: Maps of the Life and Voyages of James Cook R.N.* Sydney: Random House, 2000.
Rodger, N. A. M. *The Insatiable Earl: A Life of John Montagu, Fourth Earl of Sandwich 1718–1792*. New York: W. W. Norton, 1994.
———. *The Wooden World: An Anatomy of the Georgian Navy*. New York: W. W. Norton, 1996.
Rogers, Captain Richard W. *Shipwrecks of Hawaii: A Maritime History of the Big Island*. Haleiwa, Hawaii: Pilialoha, 1975.
Ryskamp, Charles, and Frederick A. Pottle. *Boswell: The Ominous Years, 1774–1776*. London: William Heinemann Ltd., 1963.
Sahlins, Marshall. *How "Natives" Think: About Captain Cook, for Example*. Chicago: University of Chicago Press, 1996.
Salmond, Anne. *Aphrodite's Island: The European Discovery of Tahiti*. Berkeley: University of California Press, 2009.
———. *The Trial of the Cannibal Dog: Captain Cook in the South Seas*. Auckland: Penguin Books, 2004.
Salute, Jean-Louis. *The Tahiti Handbook*. Singapore: Editions Avant et Apres, 2007.
Seiden, Allan. *Kamehameha: Destiny Fulfilled*. Honolulu: Mutual, 2019.
Shearar, Cheryl. *Understanding Northwest Coast Art: A Guide to Crests, Beings and Symbols*. Madeira Park, B.C.: Douglas and McIntyre, 2000.
Smith, Bernard. *European Vision and the South Pacific*. Melbourne: Oxford University Press, 1989.

Smith, Vanessa. *Intimate Strangers: Friendship, Exchange and Pacific Encounters.* Cambridge, U.K.: Cambridge University Press, 2010.

Smyth, Admiral W. H. *The Sailor's Word-Book.* London: Conway Maritime Press, 2005.

Subin, Anna Della. *Accidental Gods: On Men Unwittingly Turned Divine.* New York: Metropolitan, 2021.

Sullivan, Robert. *Captain Cook in the Underworld.* Auckland: University of Auckland Press, 2014.

Taylor, James. *Picturing the Pacific: Joseph Banks and the Shipboard Artists of Cook and Flinders.* London: Adlard Coles, 2018.

Taylor, Stephen. *Sons of the Waves: The Common Seaman in the Heroic Age of Sail.* New Haven: Yale University Press, 2020.

Theroux, Paul. *The Happy Isles of Oceania: Paddling the Pacific.* New York: Houghton Mifflin, 2006.

Thomas, Nicholas. *Cook: The Extraordinary Voyages of Captain James Cook.* New York: Walker & Co., 2003.

———. *Discoveries: The Voyages of Captain Cook.* London: Penguin Books, 2018.

———. *Islanders: The Pacific in the Age of Empire.* New Haven: Yale University Press, 2010.

———. *Voyagers: The Settlement of the Pacific.* New York: Basic Books, 2021.

Thomas, Nicholas, ed. *The Voyages of Captain James Cook.* Minneapolis: Voyageur Press, 2016.

Thompson, Christina. *Come on Shore and We Will Kill and Eat You All: A New Zealand Story.* New York: Bloomsbury, 2008.

———. *Sea People: The Puzzle of Polynesia.* New York: HarperCollins, 2019.

Thornton, Cliff. *Captain Cook in Cleveland.* Stroud, U.K.: Tempus, 2006.

Thrum, Thos. G. *Hawaiian Folk Tales.* Honolulu: Mutual, 1998.

Trask, Haunani-Kay. *From a Native Daughter: Colonialism and Sovereignty in Hawaii.* Honolulu: University of Hawai'i Press, 1999.

Twain, Mark. *Roughing It.* Layton, Utah: Gibbs Smith, 2017.

Vaillant, John. *The Golden Spruce: A True Story of Myth, Madness and Greed.* Toronto: Vintage Canada. 2006.

Westervelt, William Drake. *Hawaiian Historical Legends.* London: Forgotten Books, 2008.

Wichman, Frederick B. *Kauai: Ancient Place-Names and Their Stories.* Honolulu: University of Hawai'i Press, 1998.

———. *Nā Pua Ali'i O Kaua'i: Ruling Chiefs of Kaua'i.* Honolulu: University of Hawai'i Press, 2003.

Williams, Glyn. *The Death of Captain Cook: A Hero Made and Unmade.* London: Profile Books, 2008.

———. *Naturalists at Sea: Scientific Travelers from Dampier to Darwin.* New Haven: Yale University Press, 2015.

———. *The Prize of All the Oceans: The Triumph and Tragedy of Anson's Voyage Round the World.* London: HarperCollins, 1999.

———. *Voyages of Delusion: The Quest for the Northwest Passage.* New Haven: Yale University Press, 2002.

Williams, Glyndwr, ed. *Captain Cook: Explorations and Reassessments.* Woodbridge, U.K.: Boydell Press, 2004.

Index

Illustration Credits

First Insert

Captain James Cook: Painting by William Hodges, circa 1776. National Maritime
   Museum, Greenwich, London

Greenwich Hospital, Royal Observatory, and the Thames: Painting by Canaletto, circa
   1752. Tate Britain, London

Lord Sandwich: National Maritime Museum, Greenwich, London

Mai: Painting by Joshua Reynolds, 1776. Wikimedia Commons

Joseph Banks: Painting by Joshua Reynolds, circa 1773. National Portrait Gallery,
   London

King George III: Painting by Allan Ramsay, circa 1765. Art Gallery of South
   Australia

Captain Clerke: Painting by Nathaniel Dance-Holland, 1776. Government House,
   Wellington, New Zealand

William Bligh: Painting by John Webber, 1776. National Portrait Gallery, Canberra

David Samwell: Sketch by Gilles-Louis Chrétien, 1798. National Library of Wales

John Ledyard: Sketch by unknown artist. Dartmouth College Library

John Webber: Swiss National Museum

Tasmanian woman and child: Engraving, after Webber's sketch, published in 1784 in *A
   Voyage to the Pacific Ocean*. Author's collection

Tahiti scene: Painting by William Hodges, circa 1776. National Maritime Museum,
   Greenwich, London

Tahiti, human sacrifice: Engraving, after Webber's sketch, published in 1784 in *A Voyage to the Pacific Ocean*. Author's collection.

Huahine: Engraving, after Webber's sketch, published in 1784 in *A Voyage to the Pacific
   Ocean*. Author's collection

Second Insert

Prince William Sound: Engraving, after Webber's sketch, published in 1784 in *A Voyage
   to the Pacific Ocean*. Author's collection

Shooting walrus off Alaska: Painting by John Webber, 1784. National Maritime
   Museum, Greenwich, London

Herb Kāne painting: Painting by Herb Kawainu Kāne. © Herbert K. Kāne, LLC

Priest's canoe off Kealakekua Bay: Engraving, after Webber's sketch, published in 1784
   in *A Voyage to the Pacific Ocean*. Author's collection

Woman of Kealakekua: Engraving, after Webber's sketch, published in 1784 in *A Voyage
   to the Pacific Ocean*. Author's collection

Man of Kealakekua: Engraving, after Webber's sketch, published in 1784 in *A Voyage to the Pacific Ocean*. Author's collection

Cook death scene: Painting by Johan Zoffany, circa 1795. National Maritime Museum, Greenwich, London

Formal Captain Cook portrait: Nathaniel Dance-Holland, circa 1775, National Maritime Museum, Greenwich, London

"You Are On Native Land" photo: Hampton Sides